Thirty Years Among the Dead
Obsessions And "Curses" Removed Through The Work Of The Medium Mrs. Wickland

by Dr. Carl A. Wickland, M.D.

With an Introduction by Timothy Green Beckley

Inner Light

Thirty Years Among the Dead

Obsessions And "Curses" Removed Through The Work Of The Medium Mrs. Wickland

by Dr. Carl A. Wickland, M.D.

© 2014 Timothy G. Beckley / Inner Light / Global Communications

All rights reserved. No part of these manuscripts may be copied or reproduced by any mechanical or digital methods and no exerpts or quotes may be used in any other book or manuscript without permission in writing by the Publisher, Timothy G. Beckley dba Inner Light / Global Communications, except by a reviewer who may quote brief passages in a review.

Complete and Unabridged Edition

Published in the United States of America By
Timothy G. Beckley dba Inner Light / Global Communications
Box 753 · New Brunswick, NJ 08903

Staff Members
Timothy G. Beckley, Publisher
Carol Ann Rodriguez, Assistant to the Publisher
Sean Casteel, General Associate Editor
Tim R. Swartz, Graphics and Editorial Consultant
William Kern, Editorial and Art Consultant

Sign Up On The Web For Our Free Weekly Newsletter
and Mail Order Version of Conspiracy Journal
and Bizarre Bazaar
www.ConspiracyJournal.com

Order Hot Line: 1-732-602-3407
PayPal: MrUFO8@hotmail.com

Thirty Years Among the Dead

Obsessions And "Curses" Removed Through The Work Of The Medium Mrs. Wickland

by Dr. Carl A. Wickland, M.D.

Originally published in 1924

Table of Contents

Introduction	v
Inter-Relationship of the Two Worlds	1
Psychical Research	11
Subconscious Mind and Auto-Suggestion Hypotheses Untenable	17
Earth Sphere Conditions and the Magnetic Aura	53
Tormenting Spirits & Marriage Disturbances	79
Spirits and Crime	101
Spirits and Suicide	115
Spirits and Narcotics, Inebriety, Amnesia	137
Psychic Invalidism	169
Orphans	191
Materialism and Indifference	209
Selfishness	237
Orthodoxy	271
Christian Science	307
Theosophy	331
Philosophy	355
Conclusion	383

Little Girl Lost

A FASCINATING LOOK AT PSYCHIC RESEARCH AND ABNORMAL PSYCHIATRY
OBSESSIONS CURED AND "CURSES" REMOVED BY A MEDICAL DOCTOR AND PSYCHIATRIST WORKING IN CONJUCTION WITH A SPIRITUALIST MEDIUM

By Timothy Green Beckley

Dr. Carl A. Wickland
Born: February 14, 1861
Passed Over: November 13, 1945

Not long ago on a Saturday night I was listening, as usual, to my friend Joshua P. Warren, who hosts the show Speaking of Strange. The program can be heard on the Internet and is also broadcast live over station WWNC in Ashville, NC. Josh is a master of the art of storytelling and keeps his sizable audience mesmerized for three hours on a weekly basis. Sometimes he is funny, sometimes he can be dead serious, but he is always relevant, regardless of whether he is talking about the paranormal world news or giving a summation of an important historical event.

Somehow, on this particular Saturday, the conversation took on an ominous tone as Josh talked about serial killers and the masses of deranged individuals in general. He spoke of how sometimes madmen roam the Earth, showing a side of evil that goes way beyond the pale.

One such "mastermind of the macabre" that Josh pointed to as being so atrocious as to not even be considered a human being was Stalin's henchman. Secret Police Chief Laurenti Beria was responsible for the murder of thousands of Polish citizens, Jews, gays and minorities. Many of the victims were experimented upon while still living. Others were shot in the head execution style or stabbed with the point of a walking stick that had been dipped into some deadly toxic substance.

Compounding this ungodly slaughter of those who had committed no crime was the fact that, after the corpses were dragged into a field and left to rot, Beria and his murderous minions would sit around and drink vodka while they spoke of their crimes against humanity as if they were trivial or of some admirable merit.

As I listened to Josh's commentary, I began to wonder what would compel even the most depraved of individuals to behave in such a twisted manner.

I thought about it and recalled a book that I had seen advertised years ago in one of Ray Palmer's magazines. I don't recall if it was Fate, Search or Hidden World, but the nature of the volume in question came back to haunt me. The work on abnormal psychology was written by a physician and psychiatrist named Dr. Carl A. Wickland, whose wife was an accredited medium. Together for thirty years they conversed with spirits of the dead who had led less than exemplary lives while inhabiting a human body. They had been the worst lowlifes – criminals, alcoholics, drug users, wife-beaters, and the all around depraved.

The Wicklands theorized – No! They claimed to have absolute evidence – that these demented spirits of the dead liked to hang around the living so that they could continue their vulturine activities. In essence, they would leech onto those who were prone to similar fits of debauchery or were well on their way to a life of unabated revelry and eventual damnation.

Dr. Wickland's concept was that, if you hang around that sports bar or strip club, you eventually are going to be possessed by more than the likes of Derek Jeter or Blaze Starr.

Together the doctor and his wife tried to cure as many obsessed persons as they could, persuading discarnate spirits to give up their hold on their victims and thus restore their patients to normal, happy lives. As Wickland saw it, those that came to him for treatment were suffering from a variety of mental illnesses. He believed that destructive entities had attached or fastened on to them and were affecting their behavior in a devastatingly injurious way.

Many had abandoned all hope of a normal, sane life. The accepted methods of treating and possibly curing such aberrant behavior through neurological and conventional medical means did not hold much weight with the doctor and his mediumistic spouse.

Instead, his wife would converse with the clinging spirits in combination with low voltage electric shocks to dislodge the spirits of the dead from their patients. Dr. Wickland would touch the patients with a Wimhurst generator wand along the neck and spine in order to dislodge the dead spirit that had become fastened to the patient. In the next room, Anna Wickland sat in a trance, ready to serve as a communicating medium. She would converse with the detached spirits, try to calm them down as much as possible, and instruct them to be on their way.

Although their form of therapy is radically different than any used today, they did seem to have some positive results and certainly garnered a world of supporters who believed what they were doing was a positive way to confront the disincarnated souls who would attempt to make our lives miserable.

"I often see the spirits who cause insanity," said Dr. E.N. Webster, of the Mental Section of the American Medical Association. "At times I even hear their voices. Insane persons who are spoken of as hopelessly insane are frequently lost under the overwhelming control of a spirit or crowd of spirits. We frequently find by postmortem examination that no physical disorder exists in the brain or nervous system of such persons."

Another contemporary, James H. Hyslop Ph.D, professor of ethics and logic at Columbia University, stated openly that he believed there was evidence that "obsession lies at the basis of much insanity and can be cured. The medical world will have to wake up and give attention to this problem or materia medica (pharmacology) will lose control of the subject."

Hyslop further stated: "The existence of evil spirits affecting the living is as clearly taught in the New Testament, and implied in the Old Testament, as any doctrine there expounded . . . The term obsession is employed by psychic researchers to denote the abnormal influences of spirits on the living . . . The cures effected have required much time and patience, the use of psychotherapeutics of an unusual kind, and the employment of psychics to get into contact with the obsessing agents and thus to release the hold which such agents have or to educate them to voluntary abandonment of their persecutions."

Here is the eerie paranormal "truth," at least as far as Dr. Wickland saw it, about:

Spirits and Crime – Spirits and Suicide – Spirits and Narcotics, Insobriety and Amnesia – As well as Tormenting Spirits and Marriage Disturbances.

In retrospect, we might say that this form of treatment served as a form of rehab during a time when the subject of abnormal psychology was still in its infancy.

Thirty Years Among The Dead has been a classic for decades (it was originally published in 1924). It has long been sought after and in recent times has only been available through used book dealers and usually in a greatly abridged form. As far as is known, this is the only printed edition that is full and complete.

As the late, great, Dr. Hereward Carrington once noted: "It is evidence that spiritual obsession is at least a possibility which modern science can no longer disregard, while there are many striking facts in its support. This being so, its study becomes imperative-not only from the academic viewpoint, but also because of the fact that hundreds and possibly thousands of individuals are, at the present moment, suffering in this manner, and their relief demands some immediate investigation and cure."

Perhaps with all the madness we see in the world and all those who suffer in silence and walk the streets with mental illness – hearing voices that tell them to kill – suffocating their lives and affecting us all in a very negative manner – we should take another look at Dr. Wickland's controversial theories – for it is he who for thirty years walked among the dead!

Above: Dr. Wickland and medium, wife, Anna Wickland.

Above Right: Dr. and Mrs Wickland with the Static Generator.

Right: James Hyslop, staunch supporter of the Wickland's methods of curing obsessed patients.

x

THIRTY YEARS AMONG THE DEAD

Chapter I

Inter-Relationship of the Two Worlds

The reality of an invisible world surrounding the physical world is for many difficult to comprehend, since the mind sphere is often limited to the visible and tangible; however, it requires but little thought to realize the constant change of matter as it occurs in three forms, solid, liquid and gaseous, in its range back and forth between the visible and invisible.

Visible nature is but the invisible, the Real, made manifest through a combination of its elements; science informs us that fully ninety-five per cent of vegetation is derived out of the air, or atmosphere. Is not mankind living at the bottom of an invisible ocean, the atmosphere, which is even more important to physical existence than any of the visible physical substances, since life can continue but a few moments out of it?

Nitrogen gas, constituting the greater bulk of the atmosphere, enters vitally into vegetable and animal growth and existence. Hydrogen and oxygen gases are constantly changing from a state of invisible vapor to visible and solid form. Carbon offers another example of similar transformation. Sounds, odors, the thermic law of heat and cold, and multitudes of other phenomena, ranging from the infinitesimal electron to the energy which moves the planets and suns, are all intangible, invisible factors.

All activities, whether chemical, vital or mental, operate invisibly, as observed in chemical affinity, in energy, in plant life, in animal life, in intelligence and mentalization. So in every department of our manifest physical nature it is evident that all elements have their root and permanence in the invisible. The invisible is the source of the visible.

Thus when we realize that the objective is only a combination of invisible substances and forces, the existence of an unseen world is readily comprehensible. Considering the wonderful advancement of science into the field of nature's finer forces, it is inconceivable that any thinking mind can fail to recognize the rationale of the independent existence of the human spirit apart from the physical body. No subject has been better authenticated through the ages and in all literature than that of spirit existence and a future life.

Fiske, the historian, says: "Among all races of men, as far as can now be determined, ancestor worship" (contact with the spirits of the departed) "was the earliest form of worship . . . prevailing in Africa, Asia, China, Japan, among the Aryans of Europe and the American Indian tribes."

Allen, in his "History of Civilization" writes: "Rude tribes the world over are found to have ideas of a human soul, a spirit world, and generally a belief in immortality. Savages consider the next life simply a continuation of this; they also recognize an other self which has mysterious powers. Death is the abandoning of the body by this mysterious other self, which is conceived of as still existing in the near neighborhood. The loves and hates of this world are transferred to the spirit world."

Confucius said: "Bemoan not the departed with excessive grief. The dead are devoted and faithful friends; they are ever associated with us."

The writers of classic times – Socrates, Herodotus, Sophocles, Euripides, Plato, Aristotle, Horace, Virgil, Plutarch, Josephus, Maximus of Tyre -repeatedly refer to spirit existence as a well known fact. Cicero wrote: "Is not almost all heaven filled with the human? Those very gods themselves had their original here below, and ascended from hence into heaven."

That early Christianity recognized spirits is too well authenticated in the writings of St. Anthony, Tertullian, Origen and their contemporaries to require emphasis. The Bible is replete with references to spirit existence. "We also are compassed about with so great a cloud of witnesses." Heb. 12:1. "Beloved, believe not every spirit, but try the spirits, whether they are of God." 1 John 4:1. "The spirits of just men made perfect." Heb. 12:23. "There is a natural body and there is a spiritual body . . . First that which is natural, and afterward that which is spiritual." 1 Cor. 15:44, 46. Many other similar biblical citations might be given.

Swedenborg contributed volumes on this subject. Dr. Samuel Johnson said: "I do not believe in spirits -I have seen too many of them." John Wesley wrote in "The Invisible World": "It is true that the English in general indeed most of the men of learning in Europe -have given up all accounts of witches and apparitions as mere old wives' fables. I am sorry for it, and I willingly take this opportunity to offer my solemn protest against this violent compliment which so many that believe in the Bible pay to those who do not believe it. Such belief is in direct opposition, not only to the Bible, but to the suffrage of the wisest and best of men in all ages and nations. They well know that the giving up of witchcraft is in effect giving up the Bible."

That psychic phenomena occurred at the house of Mr. Samuel Wesley, father of Rev. John Wesley, at Epworth, and continued with noises and disturbances of various kinds for many months, is well known.

Shakespeare, Milton, Wordsworth, Tennyson, Longfellow, and many other poets wrote with profound understanding of the continued existence of man.

We are all familiar with the convincing results of the psychical research work of modern scientists, philosophers, ministers, physicians, psychologists and other investigators -Prof. Crookes, Alfred Wallace, Sir Oliver Lodge, Sir Arthur Conan Doyle, Rev. R. J. Campbell, Archdeacon Colley, Rev. Newton, Rev. Savage, W. T. Stead, Camille Flammarion, Dr. Baraduc, Dr. Janet, Prof.Richet, Cesare Lombroso, Dr. Hodgson, Dr. I. K. Funk, Prof. James, Prof. Hyslop, Dr. Carrington and many others. Dr. Thomas J. Hudson, author of "The Law of Psychic Phenomena," wrote: "The man who denies the phenomena of spiritualism today is not entitled to be called a skeptic, he is simply ignorant."

The Rev. Dr. George M. Searle, Rector of the Catholic Church of St. Paul the Apostle, New York City, said: "The reality of the existence of spirits in modern spiritism is no longer an open question, even among scientific men who have examined the subject. Any one who considers the manifestation of them as mere humbug, trickery or delusion, is simply not up to date."

"In our times no one denies the real existence of spiritualistic facts, except a few who live with their feet on the earth and their brains in the moon," wrote G. G. Franco, S. J., in "Civilta Cattolica." "Spiritistic phenomena are external facts which fall within the range of the senses and can easily be observed by all, and when such facts are attested by so many well informed and credible witnesses, it is useless, as well as foolish and ridiculous, to fight against proved evidence. The facts remain assured, even for reasonable men."

The spiritual world and the physical world are constantly intermingling; the spiritual plane is not a vague intangibility but is real and natural, a vast zone of refined substance, of activity and progress, and life there is a continuation of life in the physical world. On the physical plane of expression the soul obtains knowledge through experience and contact with objective things, and intelligence finds itself by manifesting through physical organs; in the spiritual plane progression of the individual continues, the mind unfolding along lines of reason, through spontaneity of service, the attainment and appreciation of high ideals and an ever broadening conception of life's purpose.

The change called "death," -the word is a misnomer -universally regarded with gloomy fear, occurs so naturally and simply that the greater number, after passing out of the physical are not aware that the transition has been made, and having no knowledge of a spiritual life they are totally unconscious of having passed into another state of being.

Deprived of their physical sense organs, they are shut out from the physical light, and lacking, a mental perception of the high purpose of existence, these individuals are spiritually blind and find themselves in a twilight condition -the "outer darkness" mentioned in the Bible -and linger in the realm known as the Earth Sphere. Death does not make a saint of a sinner, nor a sage of a fool. The mentality is the same as before and individuals carry with them their old desires, habits, dogmas, faulty teachings, indifference or disbelief in a future life. "As a man thinketh in his heart, so is he." Prov. 23:7.

Assuming spirit forms which are the result of their thought life on earth, millions remain for a time in the earth sphere, and often in the environment of their earth lives, still held by their habits or interests. "Where your treasure is there will your heart be also." Matt. 6:21.

Those who have progressed to the higher spirit world ever endeavor to enlighten these earthbound spirits, but the latter, due to preconceptions concerning the hereafter, labor under the delusion that the departed are "dead," or are "ghosts," and often refuse to recognize their friends or to realize their own condition.

Many are in a state of heavy sleep, others are lost or confused; troubled minds may be haunted by fear of the strange darkness, those conscience stricken suffer in anguish or remorse for their, earth conduct; some, impelled by selfish or evil inclinations, seek an outlet for their tendencies, remaining in this condition until these destructive desires are outgrown, when the soul cries out for understanding and light, and progressed spirits are able to reach them and aid them.

Lacking physical bodies through which to carry out earthly propensities many discarnate intelligences are attracted to the magnetic light which emanates from mortals, and, consciously or unconsciously, attach themselves to these magnetic auras, finding an avenue of expression through influencing, obsessing or possessing human beings. Such obtruding spirits influence susceptible sensitives with their thoughts, impart their own emotions to them, weaken their will power and often control their actions, producing great distress, mental confusion and suffering.

These earthbound spirits are the supposed "devils" of all ages; "devils" of human origin, by-products of human selfishness, false teachings and ignorance, thrust blindly into a spirit existence and held there in a bondage of ignorance.

The influence of these discarnate entities is the cause of many of the inexplicable and obscure events of earth life and of a large part of the world's misery. Purity of life and motive, or high intellectuality, do not necessarily offer protection from obsession; recognition and knowledge of these problems are the only safeguards.

The physical conditions permitting this impingement are varied; such encroachment is often due to a natural and predisposed susceptibility, a depleted nervous system, or sudden shock. Physical derangements are conducive to obsession, for when the vital forces are lowered less resistance is offered and intruding spirits are allowed easy access, although often neither mortal nor spirit is conscious of the presence of the other.

This encroachment alters the characteristics of the sensitive, resulting in a seemingly changed personality, sometimes simulating multiple or dissociated personalities, and frequently causes apparent insanity, varying in degree from a simple mental aberration to, and including, all types of dementia, hysteria, epilepsy, melancholia, shell shock, kleptomania, idiocy, religious and suicidal mania, as well as amnesia, psychic invalidism, dipsomania, immorality, functional bestiality, atrocities, and other forms of criminality.

Humanity is surrounded by the thought influence of millions of discarnate beings, who have not yet arrived at a full realization of life's higher purposes. A recognition of this fact accounts for a great portion of unbidden thoughts, emotions, strange forebodings, gloomy moods, irritabilities, unreasonable impulses, irrational outbursts of temper, uncontrollable infatuations and countless other mental vagaries.

The records of spirit obsession and possession extend from remotest antiquity to modern times. Dr. Tyler, the noted English Anthropologist, in his "Primitive Culture," says: "It is not too much to assert that the doctrine of demoniacal possession is kept up, substantially the same theory to account for substantially the same facts, by half the human race, who thus stand as consistent representatives of their forefathers back in the primitive antiquity."

In Muller's "Urreligionen" we find: "The general belief of the barbaric world today is that such attacks as epilepsy, hysteria, delirium, idiocy and madness are caused by some demon gaining control of the body."

Homer referred repeatedly to demons and said: "A sick man pining away is one upon whom an evil spirit has gazed." Plato held that demons obsessed mortals. Socrates speaks directly of demons influencing the possessed (insane). Plutarch wrote: "Certain tyrannical demons require for their enjoyment some soul still incarnate; being unable to satisfy their passions in any other way, incite to sedition, lust, wars of conquest, and thus get what they lust for." Josephus says: "Demons are the spirits of wicked men."

Obsessing or possessing spirits are frequently mentioned both in the Old and New Testaments. In I Samuel 16:23, we read: "David took an harp, and played with his hand: so Saul was refreshed, and was well, and the evil spirit departed from him."

So common was the belief in spirits and spirit obsession in the time of the apostles that the ability to cast out evil spirits was considered one of the most important signs of genuine discipleship, and it must be admitted that a considerable portion of the work accredited to Jesus was the casting out of demons.

A few quotations from the New Testament will suffice. "Jesus gave his twelve disciples power against unclean spirits, to cast them out." Matt. 10:1. "'Jesus preached . . . and cast out devils." Mark 1:39. "A certain mad which had devils long time . . . Jesus had commanded the unclean spirit to come out of the man . . . He that was possessed of the devils was healed." Luke 8:27, 29,

36. "Vexed with unclean spirits." Luke 6:18.

"The evil spirits went out of them." Acts 19:12.

"Master, I have brought unto thee my son, which hath a dumb spirit ... And he asked his father: How long is it ago since this came unto him? And he said, Of a child ... Jesus rebuked the foul spirit, saying unto him, Thou deaf and dumb spirit, I charge thee, come out of him, and enter no more into him. And the spirit cried, and rent him sore, and came out of him: and he was as one dead; insomuch that many said, He is dead. But Jesus took him by the hand, and lifted him up; and he arose." Mark 9:17, 21, 25-27.

(Similar occurrences are not at all uncommon in psycho-pathological research.)

Among the writers of early Christianity we find that St. Anthony says: "We walk in the midst of demons, who give us evil thoughts; and also in the midst of good angels. When these latter are especially present, there is no disturbance, no contention, no clamor; but something so calm and gentle it fills the soul with gladness. The Lord is my witness that after many tears and fastings I have been surrounded by a band of angels, and joyfully joined in singing with them." Tertullian with authority challenged the heathery to a trial of superiority in the matter of casting out demons. Minucius Felix, a Roman advocate and apologist, wrote in "Octavius": "There are some insincere and vagrant spirits, degraded from their heavenly vigor . . . who cease not, now that they are ruined themselves, to ruin others."

Dr. Godfrey Raupert, of London, who several years ago was especially delegated by Pope Pius X to lecture to Catholic audiences in America on Spiritualism, said in substance: "It is no longer possible to put the subject of psychic phenomena aside. The scientific men all over the world have recognized spiritism as a definite and real power, and to shelve it is a dangerous policy. Consequently the Pope has asked me to tell Catholics the attitude to take toward the subject ... The Church admits the reality of these spiritistic phenomena and their external intelligences, in fact, it has always admitted their reality. The problem at present is to discover the nature of the intelligence. We are now on the borderland of new discoveries which may revolutionize the world. It is not the time yet for an explanation of all the phenomena. We must suspend our judgment until the subject is better known. The study of spiritism is a new one and therefore dangerous . . . A partial knowledge of the subject may cause grave dangers."

(Resulting in obsession or possession.)

"There is no doubt about the fact of diabolical obsessions in the olden time. That the Church (Catholic) recognizes the possibilities is evidenced by the rules prepared for exorcising," is the quoted statement of Monsignor Lavelle, Rector of St. Patrick's Cathedral, New York.

Julian Hawthorne wrote, in one of the leading newspapers: "Thousands of evil-minded and evil-acting men and women die every day. What becomes of their souls, or spirits?

They want to get back here . . . the increasing boldness and frequency with which they take advantage of their opportunities is illustrated in many ways. . . Two acts of defense are open to us. We may stop the source of supply of these undesirable visitors and we may close the doors."

Dr. Axel Gustafson', who publicly acclaimed his views regarding the fact of spirit obsession, in quoting cases which had come to his attention, said: "The spirits of the revengeful have power after death to enter into and possess the living under certain conditions."

Prof. Herbert L. Stetson, of Kalamazoo College, Michigan, stated, in a lecture at the University of Chicago: "Demon obsession is no myth; illness is often due to demoniacal possession. . . .

THIRTY YEARS AMONG THE DEAD

Belief in demons is widespread."

"I often see the spirits who cause insanity," is the statement of Dr. E. N. Webster, of the mental section of the American Medical Association. "At times I even hear their voices. Insane persons who are spoken of as hopelessly insane are frequently lost under the overwhelming control of a spirit or crowd of spirits. We frequently find by postmortem examination that no physical disorder exists in the brain or nervous system of such persons."

Prof. William James wrote in "Proceedings S. P. R.": "That the demon-theory will have its innings again is to my mind absolutely certain. One has to be 'scientific' indeed, to be blind and ignorant enough to suspect no such possibility."

Prof. James H. Hyslop, while editor of the Journal of the American Society for Psychical Research, wrote: "There is growing evidence of the fact of obsession which lies at the basis of much insanity and can be cured. The medical world will have to wake up and give attention to this problem or materia medica will lose control of the subject."

In one of Prof. Hyslop's latest books, "Contact with the Other World," we find the following:

"The existence of evil spirits affecting the living is as clearly taught in the New Testament, and implied in the Old Testament, as any doctrine there expounded.... The term obsession is employed by psychic researchers to denote the abnormal influence of spirits on the living.... The cures effected have required much time and patience, the use of psychotherapeutics of an unusual kind, and the employment of psychics to get into contact with the obsessing agents and thus to release the hold which such agents have, or to educate them to voluntary abandonment of their persecutions.... Every single case of dissociation and paranoia to which I have applied cross-reference has yielded to the method and proved the existence of foreign agencies complicated with the symptoms of mental or physical deterioration. It is high time to prosecute experiments on a large scale in a field that promises to have as much practical value as any application of the scalpel and the microscope."

In "Modern Psychical Phenomena," Dr. Hereward Carrington states: "It is evident . . . that spiritual 'obsession' is at least a possibility which modern science can no longer disregard, while there are many striking facts in its support. This being so, its study becomes imperative-not only from the academic viewpoint but also because of the fact that hundreds and perhaps thousands of individuals are at the present moment suffering in this manner, and their relief demands some immediate investigation and cure. Once grant the theoretical possibility of actual obsession, and a whole vast field of research and investigations is opened up before us which demands all the care, skill and patience which modern enlightenment and psychological understanding can furnish."

Never before in the history of medical science has there been such widespread interest, by the public at large, as well as by medical men and public officials, in the subject of the cause, treatment and cure of nervous and mental diseases. Statistics show that insanity is increasing with alarming rapidity everywhere, yet medical experts differ widely as to the causes of mental deterioration, and science is not yet in possession of knowledge of the exact etiology of functional insanity. "The whole world will go mad before long," declared Dr. Winslow of England.

The greater number of neurologists and alienists entertain the belief that the active and underlying cause of insanity has its origin within the deranged nervous system, but very little as yet is actually known of the true cause.

Dr. W. M. L. Coplin, Director of the Bureau of Health and Charities, Philadelphia, Pennsylvania, said "Insanity, in most cases, is unaccompanied by any perceptible change in the brain structure. The brain of the patient, when examined under a microscope, shows absolutely nothing which differs in any way from the appearance of the brain of the perfectly sane person. It is therefore evident that the insanity might be due to toxemia, the effect of some subtle organism in the nature of bacilla.... Something causes insanity but what it is, we do not yet know."

Dr. Britton D. Evans, Superintendent of the Morris Plains, New Jersey, Insane Asylum, stated: "Brain tumor or brain fever may not affect the mind.... A man may have trouble of the brain and still have a normal mind."

Dr. Th. Ziehen, a noted German alienist, and an authority on hysteria, wrote: "For many functional neuroses there is as yet no accurate limitation and definition. As pathological anatomy does not aid us, no uniform and exclusive cause for hysteria can be demonstrated."

Dr. William Hanna Thomson, physician to the Roosevelt Hospital and Professor of the Practice of Medicine and Diseases of the Nervous System, New York University Medical College, in referring to Tuke's Dictionary of Psychological Medicine, asserted that: "The contributors to this great encyclopedia are from the most eminent professors, experts, and superintendents of insane asylums in Great Britain, the United States, France, Germany, Hungary, Belgium, Denmark, Switzerland and Russia. In the articles by the writers on kleptomania, dipsomania, chronic mania, etc., there is not a word about the pathological anatomy, (because none can be found). Just so it is in the article on melancholia, puerperal insanity, katatonia, circular insanity, homicidal insanity or epileptic insanity; in none of these is there a word about pathological anatomy, for the sufficient reason that not one of these forms of insanity shows any pathological or diseased condition in the brain different from the sound brain of a healthy man killed in an accident."

He also said: "It is high time that we now look in the direction of toxemia (or blood poisoning) for the explanation of the insanities which produce no changes whatever in the brain."

Recent announcement was made that a large percentage of cures reported by the New Jersey State Hospital for the Insane at Trenton were effected by the removal of diseased teeth, tonsils or affected organs. In a resume of the Trenton method, Dr. R. S. Copeland wrote: "The hypothesis upon which this treatment is founded is that insanity is a toxemia or poisoning due to germ infection in some part of the body. If this is true it follows that removal of the infected tissue, when the case has not gone too far, will be followed by disappearance of the mental disturbance."

When statistics compiled by the United States Government, as well as by others, show that the increase in the number of the insane is proportionately greater than the increase of the general population, it seems incongruous to credit decayed teeth and diseased tonsils as being primary causes of mental unbalance at this time when dental and surgical attention is so general, whereas, the facts are that when dentistry was little known and practised, and people went about with all conditions of decayed teeth, insanity was less prevalent than now.

Without attempting to discredit the Trenton reports, it may be stated that our experience has shown that in many cases of mental derangement, although the patient bad badly decayed teeth, mental balance was fully restored by dislodging the obsessing spirit before any attention was given to the teeth.1

Since it has been found that obsessing spirits are sensitive to pain, I am constrained to suggest that such cures as announced by the Trenton Hospital may, at least in part, be due to the fact that intruding spirits were dislodged, by dental or surgical interference.

THIRTY YEARS AMONG THE DEAD

To the investigator in Abnormal Psychology on the spiritistic hypothesis much of the symptomatology of the "War Neurosis" or shell shock, -excepting cases of malingering as recorded by Dr. F. E. Williams, Acting Medical Director, National Committee for Mental Hygiene, New York City, suggests obsession or possession by spirits of dead soldiers, unconscious of their transition, as the exciting cause. This is indicated by "delirium, hallucinations, anxiety states, functional heart disorders, paralysis, tremors, gait disturbances, convulsive movements, pain, anesthesia, hyperesthesia, blindness, disorders of speech, etc."

The spirit hypothesis regarding War Neurosis is further evidenced by the rapid recovery of patients under severe electrical treatment -(driving out obsessing entities?) "as instituted by Dr. Vincent who, Dr. Williams stated, would cure in a few hours patients that had been in the care of other psychiatrists for months, and would have them walking about and climbing ladders."

The above theory is also favored by Dr. Williams' further statements that: "This neurosis is rare among prisoners who have been exposed to mechanical shock . . . as well as among wounded exposed to mechanical shock.... Severe injury to the central nervous system and brain is not accompanied by symptoms found in shell shock.... Success attends the therapeutic measures employed for the psychological rather than the mechanical side. . . . Diagnosis should be made and treatment begun at once before the shell shock" -(obsession) -"becomes a fixed psycho-neurosis."

Newspapers recently reported the case of a young man, Frank James, a boy thug of New York City, who, after a fall from a motorcycle when ten years old, changed from a cheerful, affectionate and obedient child into a surly, insolent boy, developing into a confirmed robber and criminal. After several terms in the reformatory and five years in Sing Sing prison he was declared hopelessly insane, and sent to the State Insane Asylum.

Frank James, however, escaped, and when pursuers attempted his capture, was hit on the head with a club, and falling unconscious, was taken to a hospital. The next morning the boy awoke, extraordinarily changed; he was gentle and deferential, showing no further indications of an unbalanced mind, and from that time exhibited not the slightest impulse to commit crime of any kind. The article concludes: "Just what happened to the mechanism of the boy's brain is not entirely understood by medical men."

How explain such a case on the toxemia theory? Could a blow on the head eradicate the supposed toxemia and restore mental balance? The simple explanation from our viewpoint would be that, following the shock of the boy's fall, an obsessing spirit criminal had taken control of the boy, and that the blow from the club on the man's head, with its accompanying pain, caused the obsessing entity to become dislodged.

The success credited to hydrotherapy as practiced in institutions for the insane, especially when a strong stream of water, or a continuous bath, is used, can also be accounted for by the dislodgment of obsessing entities, who object to the discomforts incident to such treatment.

Dr. Prince, in the Journal of Abnormal Psychology, wrote: "If we are to establish sound principles underlying the mechanism of the mind we must correlate the findings of all methods of research, experimental as well as clinical, and give due consideration to the results obtained by all competent investigators."

After careful elimination of all superstitious notions and absurdities adherent to the subject of Normal and Abnormal Psychology, excluding also febrile and idiopathic psychoses or idiosyncrasies, as well as all neuro-pathogenic psychoses, there still remains a residuum of abnormality in a majority of cases of mental aberrations.

That alienists of renown and the foremost authorities widely disagree as to the cause of insanity is sufficient reason for thinking men to investigate any theory which promises to lead to results, regardless of personal or popular prejudice. The situation which confronts us is a serious one, and nothing but the broadest toleration and liberality can cope with it. Since insanity is chiefly a manifestation of mental or psychological disturbance -a Psychic neurosis-the symptomatology therefore should offer a guidance in ascertaining the etiology, and assist as well in arriving at a solution of the mental pathology.

This proposition, however, necessitates not only research and study of Normal and Abnormal Psychology but, in order to have a complete premise, also implies the recognition of the duality of man, matter and spirit, physical and spiritual. Insanity is not a stigma; the public attitude toward this affliction should be one, not of aversion but of understanding, and a realization of the close inter-relationship of the visible and invisible worlds.

Spirit obsession is a fact -a perversion of a natural law -and is amply demonstrable. This has been proven hundreds of times by causing the supposed insanity or aberration to be temporarily transferred from the victim to a psychic sensitive who is trained for the purpose, and by this method ascertain the cause of the psychosis to be an ignorant or mischievous spirit, whose identity may frequently be verified.

By this method, and without detriment to the psychic, it has also proven possible to relieve the victim, as well as release the entity from its condition of spiritual darkness through an explanation of the laws governing the spirit world, which the experiences to follow will demonstrate.

Inter-communication between the visible and invisible worlds is a natural privilege and is established through a person of a certain psychic constitution, capable of acting as an intermediary, through whom discarnate intelligences can readily come en rapport with the physical plane. Of the various phases of contact the most valuable for research purposes is that of unconscious trance, whereby direct communication may be established with the invisible world and the mental condition of discarnate intelligences, either advanced or ignorant, may be ascertained.

Ignorant psychic experimentation may prove injurious when dabbled in by those who neglect the necessary precautions and lack understanding of the laws which govern the subject, just as ignorance and disregard of the laws governing everyday life may prove dangerous. The misuse of a thing is no argument against its use.

Psychical Research belongs especially to the domain of science; common sense and discrimination are essentials in all such experimental work, as well as a thorough mastery of the laws involved. Under these conditions scientific research becomes an invaluable factor in the investigation of Spiritual Science.

Sister's Spirit

THIRTY YEARS AMONG THE DEAD

Chapter II

Psychical Research

Psychical research contains elements of the greatest importance to humanity, and has already become a vital factor in the social life of the world at large. It is undoubtedly true, however, that the various branches of research are endeavoring to classify their findings on purely psycho-physiological bases.

The Psycho-Analyst advances the theory that many of the psychoses have their seat or origin in some psychic lesion, or trauma, either concealed or forgotten. The Analytical-Pychologist, by mental measurements and intelligence tests, is making the segregation and classification of mental defectives possible. So also the Neurologist and Psychiatrist are diligently seeking to isolate the etiological factors in the various neuroses,, mental aberrations and insanities, and to ascertain the best methods of prevention and treatment.

While these branches of research are loath to accept the hypothesis of discarnate intelligences as contributing, exciting factors in many of the psychoses and aberrations, they are nevertheless rendering important service in uncovering and bringing to light the unstable qualities in the neurotic, the susceptible and those predisposed to mental unbalance.

Psychical Research presents two general phases for investigation: the Normal and the Abnormal.

The Normal phase, from the standpoint of the physician, as well as the minister, deals, among other issues, with the question: What becomes of the Dead? This problem is of vital interest to the patient who lingers on the borderland of transition, doubtful of the future, or perhaps trembling in fear of his probable condition after the tomorrow of death. Should it not be the noblest part of the physician's calling, in such situations, to be in a position to assure his patient from actual knowledge, that there is no death, but a birth into new fields of activity and opportunities in the higher mental spheres?

In the Abnormal phase of Psychical Research there is demand for broadest Possible knowledge on the part of the physician pertaining to the mysterious functioning of minds, discarnate as well as incarnate. Research in Abnormal, as well as Normal psychology, indubitably indicates, not only the existence of spirits, but also unquestionably demonstrates that such entities play an important role in the various psychoneuroses and insanities.

The physician, undoubtedly, comes in more intimate touch with the consequences of promiscuous dabbling in Psychical Research, so frequently resulting in mental aberrations, than any other person, for he is usually the first one to be called into consultation, and upon his decision depends largely the disposal of such an unfortunate victim. For this reason, if no other, it should surely be not only the privilege, but also the urgent duty of the physician to become thoroughly acquainted with the various phases of Psychical Research, particularly its dangers in the hands of thoughtless investigators, especially the predisposed psycho-neurotic.

The alarming results often occurring in connection with Psychical Research prompted me to follow up a line of investigation to ascertain the underlying causes thereof, for these also concern the physician. The serious problem of alienation and mental derangement attending ignorant psychic experiments was first brought to my attention by the cases of several persons whose seemingly harmless experiences with automatic writing and the Ouija Board resulted in such wild insanity that commitment to asylums was necessitated.

The first of these cases was that of Mrs. Bl., whose attempts at automatic writing led to mental derangement and altered personality. Normally she was amiable, pious, quiet and refined but became boisterous and noisy, romped about and danced, used vile language, and, claiming she was an actress, insisted upon dressing for the stage, saying that she had to be at the theatre at a certain time or lose her position. Finally she became so irresponsible that she was placed in an asylum.

Another case was Mrs. Bn., who, through the practice of automatic writing, changed from an artist and a lady of refinement to an altogether different and violent personality. Screaming at the top of her voice she continually rubbed her temples and exclaimed, "God save me! God save me!" Rushing into the street she knelt in the mud, praying, and refused food, declaring that if she should eat before six o'clock P.M. she would go to hell.

Mrs. Sr., who bad followed the same practices, also became mentally deranged and violent, necessitating police interference. Rising in the night she posed in the window of her millinery shop as Napoleon, whom she presumed herself to be, and after committing many other irresponsible acts, requiring restraint, was sent to the Detention Hospital.

In like manner, Mrs. Wr. became obsessed with hallucinations that God was constantly talking to her and condemning her for wrong acts of which he accused her; after attempting suicide at the request of this so-called God she was taken to the asylum.

Many other disastrous results which followed the use of the supposedly innocent Ouija Board came to my notice and my observations led me into research in psychic phenomena for a possible explanation of these strange occurrences.

My wife proved to be an excellent psychic intermediary and was easily controlled by discarnate intelligences. In answer to her doubts concerning the right of "disturbing the dead" these intelligences asserted that a grievously wrong conception existed among mortals regarding the conditions prevailing after death.

They stated that there is in reality no death, but a natural transition from the visible to the invisible world, and that advanced spirits are ever striving to communicate with mortals to enlighten them concerning the higher possibilities which await the progressive spirit. But death— the freeing of the spirit from the body—is so simple and natural that a great majority do not, for a longer or shorter period, realize the change, and owing to a lack of education concerning the spiritual side of their natures, they continue to remain in their earthly haunts.

They maintained that many such spirits were attracted to the magnetic aura of mortals although the spirit, as well as the mortal, might be unconscious of the intrusion -and thus, by obsessing or possessing their victims, they ignorantly or maliciously became the cause of untold mischief, often producing invalidism, immorality, crime and seeming insanity.

The risk of interference from this source constituted, they said, the gravest danger to the unwary novice in psychic research, but to be in ignorance of these facts was an even greater risk, especially in the case of the susceptible neurotic.

These intelligences also stated that by a system of transfer, that is, by attracting such obsessing entities from the victim to a psychic intermediary, the correctness of the hypothesis could be demonstrated and conditions could be shown as they actually exist. After this transference of psychoses the victims would be relieved, and the obsessing spirits could then be reached by the advanced spirits, who would care for them and instruct them regarding the higher laws of life.

They claimed they had found my wife to be a suitable instrument for such experimentation and proposed that, if I would cooperate with them by caring for and instructing these ignorant spirits, as they allowed them to take temporary but complete possession of my wife's body, without any injury to her, they would prove their assertions were correct.

Desirous of learning the truth or falsity of such important claims, which, if true, would have a great bearing on the cause of much that is otherwise baffling in criminology, as well as in psychopathology, we accepted what seemed a hazardous undertaking. In order to carry out their purpose the Guiding Intelligences allowed many manifestations to take place, often very unexpectedly, and some of these occurred while I was pursuing my early medical studies.

One day I left home without any intention of immediately beginning my first dissecting work, therefore my wife's subconscious mind could not possibly have taken any part in what transpired later.

The students were required to dissect a lateral half of a body; the first subject was a man about sixty years of age and that afternoon I began dissecting on a lower limb. I returned home at about five o'clock and had scarcely entered the door when my wife was apparently taken with a sudden illness, and complaining of feeling strange, staggered as though about to fall. As I placed my hand on her shoulder she drew herself up and became entranced by a foreign intelligence who said, with threatening gesture: "What do you mean by cutting me?"

I answered that I was not aware of cutting any one, but the spirit angrily replied: "Of course you are! You are cutting on my leg!"

Realizing that the spirit owner of the body on which I had been operating had followed me home, I began to parley with him, first placing my wife in a chair. To this the spirit vigorously objected, saying that I had no business to touch him. To my answer that I had a right to touch my own wife the entity retorted: "Your wife! What are you talking about! I am no woman -I'm a man." I explained that he had passed out of his physical body and was controlling the body of my wife, and that his spirit was here and his body at the college. When he finally seemed to realize this I said: "Suppose I were now cutting on your body at the college that could not kill you, since you yourself are here."

The spirit admitted that this seemed reasonable, and said: "I guess I must be what they call 'dead,' so I won't have any more use for my old body. If you can learn anything by cutting on it, go ahead and cut away."

Then he added suddenly: "Say, Mister, give me a chew of tobacco."

I told him that I had none, and then he begged for a pipe, saying: "I'm dying for a smoke."

THIRTY YEARS AMONG THE DEAD

This request was, of course, also refused. (The fact that Mrs. Wickland has always abhorred the sight of any one chewing tobacco precludes the possibility of her subconscious mind playing any role in this episode.)

After a more detailed explanation of the fact that he was actually so-called "dead," the spirit realized his true condition and left. Subsequent examination of the teeth of the cadaver indicated that the man had been an inveterate tobacco user in life.

Upon another occasion, when I had been appointed assistant demonstrator for a class of students in dissecting, the body of a colored man had been selected as a subject but the body had not yet been disturbed when, one evening, Mrs. Wickland became entranced and a strange spirit, speaking through her, exclaimed:

"You ain't goin' to cut on dis colored man, Boss!"

I told him that the world called him dead; that he was not in his old body, but was now controlling a woman's body. He would not believe this and when I showed him my wife's hands, saying they were not colored but white, he replied: "I'se got whitewash on dem; whitewashin' is my business."

This spirit proved to be very obstinate, offering a variety of excuses and explanations rather than accept the truth, but he was finally convinced and departed.

Another incident will still further demonstrate to what a seemingly unbelievable degree spirits may cling to their earthly bodies through ignorance of their transition, or so-called death.

In the dissecting room was the body of a woman, about forty years of age, who had died at the Cook County Hospital, Chicago, the previous June. In January, seven months after her death, a number of students, myself included, were assigned this subject for dissection. I could not be present the first evening but the others began their work.

Nothing was ever said to me of what occurred during those few hours, but for some reason, unknown to me, the other students never touched that subject again. The next day there was no school in the afternoon so I began to dissect alone, working on the arm and neck. The dissecting room was in the rear of a long basement and very quiet, but once I distinctly heard a voice say: "Don't murder me!"

The voice sounded faintly, as from a distance, but since I am not in the least superstitious and not at all inclined to credit small incidents to the actions of spirits, I concluded that it probably came from children in the street, although I had not heard any playing nearby.

The following afternoon I was again working alone when I was rather startled by a rustling sound coming from a crumpled newspaper lying on the floor, a sound something like that produced when a newspaper is crushed, but I paid no particular attention to it and did not mention these occurrences to my wife.

The episodes had quite passed out of my mind until a few days later. We were holding a psychic circle in our home and our invisible co-workers had already departed when I noticed that my wife still remained in a semi-comatose condition. I stepped up to her to ascertain the reason when the controlling spirit rose suddenly, struck at me angrily and said: "I have some bones to pick with you!"

After a period of struggle with the stranger I asked what the trouble was.

"Why do you want to kill me?" the entity demanded.

THIRTY YEARS AMONG THE DEAD

"I am not killing any one," I answered.

"Yes, you are -you are cutting on my arm and neck! I shouted at you not to murder me, and I struck that paper on the floor to frighten you, but you wouldn't pay any attention."

Then, laughing boisterously, the spirit added with great hilarity: "But I scared the other fellows!"

It was necessary to explain at great length the actual situation of the spirit, who said her name was Minnie Morgan, but finally she understood and left, promising to seek a higher life.

The ease with which spirits assume control of the psychic intermediary, Mrs. Wickland, is so perfect that the majority of them at first fail to comprehend the fact that they are so-called dead and are temporarily occupying the body of another.

Those intelligences whose reasoning faculties are alert can generally be made to realize that their situation is unusual when attention is called to the dissimilarity between their own former bodily features, hands and feet, as well as clothes, and those of the psychic. This is especially so when the spirit is a man, for the difference will then be more readily noticed. Following the statement that the body which is being controlled belongs to my wife, spirits usually retort: "I am not your wife," and a great deal of explanation is required before they can be brought to a recognition of the fact that they are in temporary possession of another's body.

On the other hand, there are spirits, fixed and rooted in obstinate skepticism, who stubbornly refuse to understand that they have made the transition out of the physical. These will not listen to reason and fail to be convinced of their changed condition, even when a mirror is held before them, declaring that they have been hypnotized, and prove so obdurate that they must be forced to leave, and are taken in charge by the invisible coworkers.

The transference of the mental aberration or psychosis from a patient to the psychic intermediary, Mrs. Wickland, is facilitated by the use of static electricity, which is applied to the patient, frequently in the presence of the psychic. Although this electricity is harmless to the patient it is exceedingly effective, for the obsessing spirit cannot long resist such electrical treatment and is dislodged.

Induced by our invisible helpers the spirit may then entrance the psychic, when it becomes possible to come into direct contact with the entity, and an endeavor is made to bring him to a realization of his true condition and of his higher possibilities. He is then removed and cared for by the advanced spirits and Mrs. Wickland again returns to her normal self.

In many cases remarkable evidence that discarnate entities were the offending cause of aberration has been obtained by a system of experimental concentration in a psychic circle. Obsessing spirits have been dislodged from victims frequently residing at a distance, conveyed to the circle by the co-operating intelligences and allowed to control the psychic. Such spirits often complain of having been driven away, yet are ignorant of being spirits, or of having controlled or influenced anyone.

But the similarity between the actions of the controlling spirit and the symptoms of the patient, as well as the relief obtained by the latter through this removal, indubitably prove the spirit to have been the cause of the disturbance. In many cases the identity of the spirit has been unquestionably authenticated. After this transfer and permanent dislodgment of the obsessing spirit, the patient gradually recovers, although there may be a number of spirits requiring removal from the same patient.

THIRTY YEARS AMONG THE DEAD

It may be asked why advanced intelligences do not take charge of earthbound spirits and convert them without having them first control a psychic intermediary. Many of these ignorant spirits cannot be reached by the intelligent spirits until they come in contact with physical conditions, when they are compelled to realize their own situation and are then started on the road to progression.

While the control of the Psychic by an ignorant spirit in a circle generally brings the spirit to an understanding and is of interest to the investigator, at the same time groups of other spirits in darkness are brought to profit by the lesson conveyed through the actions of the controlling spirit.

Many controlling spirits act as if demented and are difficult to reason with, this condition being due to false doctrines, fixed ideas and various notions imbibed in physical life. They are often unruly and boisterous, when it is necessary to control them by holding the hands of the psychic to keep them in restraint.

Upon realizing their true condition many spirits experience a sensation of dying, which signifies that they are losing control of the psychic. Other spirits, again, are in a sleepy stupor, wishing to be left alone, and severe language is at times required to arouse them, as will be observed in the records following.

In these records reference is often made to a "dungeon" in which refractory spirits may be placed, and controlling spirits sometimes complain of having been kept in a dungeon. Due to a certain psychic law, intelligent spirits have the faculty of placing about an ignorant spirit a condition simulating a prison, an impenetrable, cell-like room from which there is no escape. Herein stubborn spirits must stay seeing nothing but the reflection of their own personalities, their past actions appearing before the mind's eye until they become repentant and show a willingness to adapt themselves to the new condition and to conform to the spiritual laws of progression.

The nature of Mrs. Wickland's psychism is that of unconscious trance; her eyes are closed and her own mentality is held in abeyance in a sleep state for the time being. She herself has no recollection of anything that transpires during this period. Mrs. Wickland is not subject to any negativism between these experiences; she is at all times her rational self, clear minded and positive, and after thirty-five years of psychic work has not suffered impairment or detriment of any kind.

She is constantly protected from the invisible side by the supervision of a group of strong intelligences known as "The Mercy Band," which is guiding this work, endeavoring to bring humanity to a realization of the simplicity of the transition called death, and the importance of a rational understanding of what becomes of the spirits. The purpose of our work has been to obtain reliable and incontestable evidence at first hand regarding "after death" conditions, and detailed reports of hundreds of experiences have been stenographically made in order to record the exact situation of the communicating intelligences.

THIRTY YEARS AMONG THE DEAD

Chapter III

Subconscious Mind and Auto-Suggestion Hypotheses Untenable

During thirty years of indefatigable research among the "dead" such startling conditions have been revealed that it seems incredible intelligent reasoners along other lines of thought could have so long ignored the simple facts, which can so readily be verified. There is utter impossibility of fraud in these experiences; foreign languages, totally unknown to Mrs. Wickland, are spoken, expressions never heard by her are used, while the identity of the controlling spirits has again and again been verified and corroborations innumerable have been made.

On one occasion I conversed with twenty-one different spirits, who spoke through my wife, the majority giving me satisfactory evidence of being certain friends and relatives known to me while they were incarnated. In all, they spoke six different languages, while my wife speaks only Swedish and English.

From one patient, Mrs. A., who was brought to us from Chicago, thirteen different spirits were dislodged and allowed to control Mrs. Wickland,3 and of these, seven were recognized by the patient's mother, Mrs. H. W., as relatives or friends well known to her during their earth lives.

One was a minister, formerly pastor of the Methodist church of which Mrs. H. W. was a member, who had been killed in a railroad accident nine years previous, but was still unconscious of the fact; another was her sister-in-law; there were also three elderly women, family friends for years, a neighbor boy and the mother-in-law of the patient -all entirely unknown to Mrs. Wickland.

Mrs. H. W. conversed at length with each one, as they spoke through Mrs. Wickland, verifying innumerable statements made by the spirits and assisted in bringing them to a realization of their changed condition, and of the fact that they had been obsessing her daughter. This patient is today entirely well and actively occupied with social, musical and family affairs.

Another case will show clearly the transfer of psychosis from patient to intermediary, and the impossibility of either "subconscious mind" or "multiple personalities" playing any role as far as the psychic is concerned.

One summer evening we were called to the home of Mrs. M., a lady of culture and refinement; she was a musician of high rank and when the social demands made upon her proved too great she suffered a nervous breakdown. She had become intractable and for six weeks had been in such a raving condition that her physicians had been unable to relieve her, and day and night nurses were in constant attendance.

We found the patient sitting up in her bed, crying one minute like a forlorn child, and again screaming in fear: "Matilla! Matilla!" Then suddenly fighting and struggling, she would talk a wild gibberish of English and Spanish, (the latter a language of which she had no knowledge).

Mrs. Wickland immediately gave her psychic diagnosis, saying the case was unquestionably one of obsession, and this was unexpectedly confirmed when Mrs. Wickland, who was standing at the foot of the bed, with wraps on ready to leave, was found to be suddenly entranced. We placed her on a davenport in the music room, where for two hours I talked in turn with several spirits who had just been attracted from the patient.

There were three spirits: a girl named Mary, her suitor, an American, and his Mexican rival, Matilla. Both of the men had vehemently loved the girl and as fiercely hated each other. In a jealous rage one had killed the girl, and then in a desperate fight the two rivals had killed each other.

All were unaware of being "dead," although Mary said, weeping wretchedly: "I thought they were going to kill each other, but here they are, still fighting."

This tragedy of love, hatred and jealousy had not ended with physical death; the group had unconsciously been drawn into the psychic atmosphere of the patient, and the violent fighting had continued within her aura. Since her nervous resistance was exceedingly low at this time, one after the other had usurped her physical body, with a resulting disturbance that was unexplainable by her attendants.

With great difficulty the three spirits were convinced that they had lost their physical bodies, but at last they recognized the truth and were taken away by our invisible coworkers.

Meanwhile the patient had arisen, and speaking rationally to the astonished nurse, walked quietly about her room. Presently she said: "I am going to sleep well tonight," and returning to bed, fell asleep without the usual sedatives, and rested quietly throughout the night.

The following day, attended by a nurse, she was brought to our home; we dismissed the nurse, discarded her medicines, and after an electrical treatment, the patient had her dinner in the general dining room with the other patients, and that evening attended a function given in our social hall.

Another spirit was removed from her the next day; this was a little girl who had been killed in the San Francisco earthquake, and who cried constantly, saying she was lost in the dark. It is needless to add that she was comforted and promptly cared for by spirit friends, who had been unable to reach her while she was enmeshed in the aura of a psychic sensitive.

After some months of treatment, rest and recuperation, the patient returned to her home and resumed her normal life again.

One of our early experiences in Chicago occurred on the 15th of November, 1906. During one of our psychic circles, Mrs. Wickland, entranced by a strange entity, fell prostrate to the floor, and remained in a comatose condition for some time. The spirit was at last brought to the front, and acted as though in great pain, repeatedly saying: "Why didn't I take more carbolic acid? I want to die; I'm so tired of living."

In a weak voice the spirit complained of the dense darkness all about, and was unable to see an electric light shining directly into her face. She whispered faintly: "My poor son!" and when pressed for information said that her name was Mary Rose, and that she lived at 202 South Green Street, a street entirely unknown to us at that time.

At first she could not remember any date, but when asked: "Is it November 15th, 1906?" she replied: "No, that is next week." Life had been a bitter disappointment to her; she had suffered constantly from chronic abdominal ailments, and finally, resolving to end her miserable existence, she had taken poison. She could not at first realize that she had succeeded in destroying her physical body, for, like most suicides, she was in total ignorance of the indestructibility of life and the reality of the hereafter. When the real purpose of life, experience and suffering had been made clearer to her she was overcome with repentance and offered a sincere prayer for forgiveness.

Then her spiritual sight opened slightly and she saw dimly the spirit figure of her grandmother, who had come to take her to the spirit world. Subsequent inquiry at the address given by the spirit proved her statements to be true; a woman by the name given had lived at this house, she still had a son living there, and we were told that Mrs. Rose had been taken to the Cook County Hospital and had died there the week before.

Upon investigation at the hospital we found further verification of the facts and were given a copy of the record of the case:

Cook County Hospital, Chicago, Ills.

Mary Rose.

Admitted November 7th, 1906.

Died November 8th, 1906.

Carbolic Acid poisoning.

No. 341106.

Another case will show that identification of a spirit is often possible.

Mrs. Fl., a patient who had been declared incurably insane by several physicians, was a refined lady of gentle disposition, who had become very wild and unmanageable, swearing constantly, and fighting with such violence that several persons were required to restrain her.

She was also subject to coma states, again to fainting spells, would refuse food, announce that she "had been married above by celestial powers," and used extraordinarily vile language; these various phases alternated constantly, but no full proof of obsession was evidenced until one day when Mrs. Fl. lost all power of speech, and, mumbling idiotically, simulated perfectly a deaf and dumb person.

At this time a gentleman from an adjoining state came to the house to visit a patient and, shortly after his arrival, the nurse who attended Mrs. Fl. reported that the patient had again changed and was talking like a little child. So striking was this alteration that the gentleman was asked to step into the room to observe the patient. He was a total stranger to her but as he entered the room she pointed to him and said, in a high childish voice:

"I know that man! He used to put bows on my shoulders. And he pulled my toofies! He took me to a gypsy camp too! He lived right across the street from me, and he used to call me Rosebud. I'm four years old."

The astonished gentleman corroborated every statement, saying that he had known such a child in his home town in Iowa, but that she had died the year before. He explained that he was very fond of children and had on several occasions taken the child to a gypsy camp, and that whenever he bought taffy-on a stick for the little girl, he would tug at the stick while she was eating the candy and playfully threaten to pull her teeth.

It was evident that affection had attracted the spirit child to her friend, and that she found in Mrs. Fl. a vehicle through which she could make her presence known to the gentleman. The patient was relieved of this spirit and gradually of other obsessing influences, and several months later was pronounced entirely competent to sign legal papers, being declared normal and sane by a judge and jury.

Another case in point was that of Mrs. O., who was a cook in a restaurant. She had observed a waitress acting queerly, laboring under delusions and hallucinations, and brought her to my office. After an electrical treatment the patient declared she felt greatly relieved and returned to her home.

But that night Mrs. O. herself became disturbed by an unaccountable condition which prevented her from sleeping, and her restlessness continued until ten o'clock the following morning, when, in the midst of her preparations for dinner, she suddenly became wild, tore her hair, and threatened to harm herself.

I was sent for and arriving, found Mrs. O. raving in a demented condition, complaining of being chased here and there and being unable to find a resting place. Suspecting the presence of an invisible entity, I placed Mrs. O. in a chair, pinioned her arms to prevent a struggle, and after several remarks the entity declared it was a man, but denied being dead, or obsessing a woman.

The spirit said his name was Jack, that he was an uncle of the troubled waitress, and that he had been a vagabond in life. After reasoning with the intelligence he began to realize his situation, and, promising to cause no further annoyance, left. Mrs. O. then immediately became her normal self and returned to her work without any further disturbance.

It was later ascertained from the waitress that she had had an uncle named Jack, who had been a vagabond, and that he was dead. In this experience Mrs. O. had acted as the psychic intermediary to whom the spirit obsessing the waitress had been transferred. A number of years ago Dr. Lydston wrote in the Chicago papers of a patient who, although having no knowledge of French or music sang well the "Marseillaise" in French when placed under the influence of an anesthetic. Dr. Lydston, denying the continued existence of the ego, explained this phenomenon as one of subliminal consciousness, or unconscious memory, comparing it with the case of the uneducated domestic, who, in delirium, recited classic Latin as perfectly as her former employer, a Professor of Latin, had done during his life.

I replied, in a newspaper article, that such phenomena were frequently met with in psychic research, and stated that, despite the classification of materialistic scientists, these cases clearly proved the posthumous existence of spirits and their ability to communicate through mortals. I added that if the truth were known about these two cases, we would find that the man who sang French was a psychic sensitive and had at the time been controlled by some outside intelligence, while in all probability the domestic who recited Latin was obsessed by the spirit of the former professor.

Shortly after this the gentleman alluded to by Dr. Lydston called on me, having read my article, and said: "I don't know anything about French, but I do know that I am bothered to death by spirits."

In the study of cases of "Multiple Personalities," "Dissociated Personalities," or "Disintegrated States of Consciousness," modern psychologists disclaim the possibility of foreign intelligences on the ground that these personalities give neither evidence of supernormal knowledge, nor of being of spiritistic origin.

Our experience, to the contrary, has proven that the majority of these intelligences are oblivious of their transition and hence it does not enter their minds that they are spirits, and they are loath to recognize the fact.

In the case of Miss Beauchamp, as recorded by Dr. Morton Prince, in "The Dissociation of a Personality," reporting four alternating personalities, no claim was made that any outside intelligences were responsible for the various personalities, and yet "Sally" (personality 3) insisted that she herself was not the same as Miss Beauchamp (Christine), that her own consciousness was distinct from that of Miss Beauchamp, and told of Miss Beauchamp's learning to walk and talk. "When she was a very little girl just learning to walk ... I remember her thoughts distinctly as separate from mine."

Similarly in the case of Bernice Redick of Ohio, the young school girl who constantly changed from her normal self to the personality of "Polly," an unruly child, every indication is given of the influence of a discarnate spirit, probably ignorant of being dead, controlling Miss Redick.

That such "personalities" are independent entities could easily be proven, under proper conditions, by transference of the same to a psychic intermediary, as similar experiments have so abundantly demonstrated.

Any attempt to explain our experiences on the theory of the Subconscious Mind and Auto-Suggestion, or Multiple Personalities, would be untenable, since it is manifestly impossible that Mrs. Wickland should have a thousand personalities, and since it is so readily possible to cause transference of psychosis from a supposedly insane person to Mrs. Wickland, relieving the victim, and in this way discovering that the disturbance was due to a discarnate entity, whose identity can often be verified.

Individuals who are clairaudient suffer greatly from the constant annoyance of hearing the voices of obsessing entities (the "auditory hallucinations" frequently observed by alienists), and when such a person is present in a psychic circle where the spirits are dislodged and transferred to the psychic intermediary, interesting developments occur.

An illustration is the case of Mrs. Burton, a clairaudient patient who was constantly combating obsessing spirits, and who, while attending our circle, was relieved of her unwelcome companions. In the following records the conversation of the spirits through the psychic, Mrs. Wickland, will elucidate the characteristics of the several entities.

Spirit: CARRIE HUNTINGTON Patient: MRS. BURTON.

Doctor Tell us who you are.

Spirit I do not wish you to hold my hands.

Dr. You must sit still.

Sp. Why do you treat me like this?

Dr. Who are you?

Sp. Why do you want to know?

Dr. You have come here as a stranger, and we would like to know who you are.

THIRTY YEARS AMONG THE DEAD

Sp. What are you so interested for?

Dr. We should like to know with whom we are associating. If a stranger came to your home, would you not like to know his name?

Sp. I do not want to be here and I do not know any of you. Somebody pushed me in here, and I do not think it is right to force me in like that. And when I came in and sat down on the chair you grabbed my hands as if I were a prisoner. Why was I pushed in here? (Brought in control of psychic by guiding intelligences.)

Dr. You were probably in the dark.

Sp. It seems somebody took me by force.

Dr. Was there any reason for it?

Sp. I do not know of any reason, and I do not see why I should be bothered like that.

Dr. Was no reason given for handling you in this manner?

Sp. It has been a terrible time for me for quite a while. I have been tormented to death. I have been driven here, there and everywhere. I am getting so provoked about it that I feel like giving everything a good shaking.

Dr. What have they done to you?

Sp. It seems so terrible. If I walk around I am so very miserable. I do not know what it is. Sometimes it seems as if my senses were being knocked out of me. Something comes on me like thunder and lightning. (Static treatment of patient.) It makes such a noise. This terrible noise -it is awful! I cannot stand it any more, and I will not either!

Dr. We shall be glad if you will not stand it any more.

Sp. Am I not welcome? And if I am not, I do not care!

Dr. You are not very particular.

Sp. I have had so much hardship.

Dr. How long have you been dead?

Sp. Why do you speak that way? I am not dead. I am as alive as I can be, and I feel as if I were young again.

Dr. Have you, not felt, at times, as if you were somebody else ?

Sp. At times I feel very strange, especially when it knocks me senseless. I feel very bad. I do not feel that I should have this suffering. I do not know why I should have such things.

Dr. Probably it is necessary.

Sp. I feel I should be free to go where I please, but it seems I have no will of my own any more. I try, but it seems somebody else takes possession of me and gets me into some place where they knock me nearly senseless. If I knew it, I never would go there, but there is a person who seems to have the right to take me everywhere, but I feel I should have the right to take her. (Referring to patient.)

THIRTY YEARS AMONG THE DEAD

Dr. What business have you with her? Can't you live your own life?

Sp. I live my own life, but she interferes with me. I talk to her. She wants to chase me out. I feel like chasing her out, and that is a real struggle. I cannot see why I should not have the right just as well as she has.

Dr. Probably you are interfering with her.

Sp. She wants to get rid of me. I am not bothering her. I only talk to her sometimes.

Dr. Does she know you talk to her?

Sp. Sometimes she does, and then she chases me right out She acts all right, but she gets so provoked. Then, when she gets into that place, I am knocked senseless and I feel terrible. I have no power to take her away. She makes me get out.

Dr. You should not stay around her.

Sp. It is my body, it is not hers. She has no right there. I do not see why she interferes with me.

Dr. She interferes with your selfishness.

Sp. I feel I have some right in life -I think so.

Dr. You passed out of your body without understanding the fact, and have been bothering a lady. You should go to the spirit world and not hover around here.

Sp. You say I am hovering around. I am not hovering around, and I am not one to interfere, but I want a little to say about things.

Dr. That was why you had the "thunder" and "the knocks."

Sp. That was all right for a while, but lately it is terrible. I must have understanding.

Dr. You will have it now.

Sp. I will do anything to stop that terrible knocking.

Mrs. B. (Recognizing the spirit as one who had been troubling her.) I am mighty tired of you. Who are you, anyway?

Sp. I am a stranger.

Mrs. B. What is your name?

Sp. My name?

Mrs. B. Have you one?

Sp. My name is Carrie.

Mrs. B. Carrie what?

Sp. Carrie Huntington.

Mrs. B. Where do you live?

Sp. San Antonio, Texas.

THIRTY YEARS AMONG THE DEAD

Mrs. B. You have been with me a long time, haven't you? (It had been a number of years since Mrs. B. had been in San Antonio.)

Sp. You have been with me a long time. I should like to find out why you interfere with me. I recognize you now.

Mrs. B. What street did you live on?

Sp. I lived in many different places there.

Dr. Do you realize the fact that you have lost your own mortal body? Can you remember having been sick?

Sp. The last I remember I was in El Paso. I do not remember anything after that. I went there and I do not seem to remember when I left. It seems that I should be there now. I got very sick one day there.

Dr. Probably you lost your body then.

Sp. After El Paso I do not know where I went. I went some distance. I traveled on the railroad and it was just like I was nobody. Nobody asked me anything and I had to follow that lady (Mrs. B.) as if I were her servant, and I feel very annoyed about it.

Mrs. B. You worried me to death because you sang all the time.

Sp. I had to do something to attract your attention, because you would not listen to me any other way. You traveled on the train and it took me away from my home and folks, and I feel very much hurt about it. Do you understand?

Mrs. B. I understand you far better than you do me.

Dr. Can't you realize what has been the matter with you?

Sp. I want to tell you that I do not want those knockings any more. I will stay away.

Dr. Understand your condition; understand that you are an ignorant, obsessing spirit, and that you have no physical body. You died, probably at the time you were sick.

Sp. Could you talk to a ghost?

Dr. Such things certainly do happen.

Sp. I am not a ghost, because ghosts cannot talk. When you are dead, you lie there.

Dr. When the body dies, it lies there. But the spirit does not.

Sp. That goes to God who gave it.

Dr. Where is He? Where is that God?

Sp. In Heaven.

Dr. Where is that?

Sp. It is where you go to find Jesus.

Dr. The Bible says: "God is Love; and he that dwelleth in Love dwelleth in God." Where will you find that God?

Sp. I suppose in Heaven. I cannot tell you anything about it. But I know I have been in the worst hell you could give me with those knockings. I do not see that they have done me any good. I do not like them at all.

Dr. Then you must stay away from that lady.

Sp. I see her well now, and I can have a real conversation with her.

Dr. Yes, but this will be the last time.

Sp. How do you know it will?

Dr. When you leave here you will understand that you have been talking through another person's body. That person is my wife.

Sp. What nonsense! I thought you looked wiser than to talk such nonsense.

Dr. It may seem foolish, but look at your hands. Do you recognize them?

Sp. They do not look like mine, but so much has taken place lately, that I do not know what I shall do. That lady over there, (Mrs. B.) has been acting like a madman, and I have taken it as it came, so I shall have to find out what she thinks of doing, and why she does those things to me.

Dr. She will be very happy to be rid of you.

Mrs. B. Carrie, how old are you?

Sp. You know that a lady never wants to tell her age.

Dr. Especially if she happens to be a spinster.

Sp. Please excuse me, you will have to take it as it is. I will not tell my age to any one.

Dr. Have you ever been married?

Sp. Yes, I was married to a fellow, but I did not care for him.

Dr. What was his name?

Sp. That is a secret with me. I would not have his name mentioned for anything, and I do not want to carry his name, either. My name is Carrie Huntington, because it was my name, and I do not want to carry his name.

Dr. Do you want to go to the spirit world?

Sp. What foolish questions you put to me.

Dr. It may seem foolish to you, but, nevertheless, there is a spirit world. Spiritual things often seem foolish to the mortal mind. You have lost your body.

Sp. I have not lost my body. I have been with this lady, but she does one thing I do not like very well. She eats too much. She eats too much and gets too strong, then I have no power over her body, not as much as I want to. (To Mrs. B.) I want you to eat less. I try very much to dictate to you not to eat that and that, but you have no sense. You do not even listen to me.

Mrs. B. This is the place I told you to go to, but you would not go by yourself.

Sp. I know it. But you have no business to take me where I get those knockings. I do not want to stay with you if you take those awful knockings.

Dr. They are in the next room. Do you want some?

Sp. No, thank you. Not for me any more.

Dr. Listen to what is told you, then you will not need any more. You are an ignorant spirit. I mean you are ignorant of your condition. You lost your body, evidently without knowing it.

Sp. How do you know?

Dr. You are now controlling my wife's body.

Sp. I never saw you before, so how in the world can you think I should be called your wife? No, never!

Dr. I do not want you to be.

Sp. I don't want you either!

Dr. I don't want you to control my wife's body much longer. You must realize that you have lost your physical body. Do you recognize these hands? (Mrs. Wickland's hands.)

Sp. I have changed so much lately that all those changes make me crazy. It makes me tired.

Dr. Now, Carrie, be sensible.

Sp. I am sensible, and don't you tell me differently, else you will have some one to tell you something you never heard before.

Dr. Now Carrie!

Sp. I am Mrs. Carrie Huntington!

Mrs. B. You listen to what the Doctor has to say to you.

Sp. I will not listen to any one, I tell you once for all. I have been from one to another

and I do not care what becomes of me.

Dr. Do you know you are talking through my wife's body?

Sp. Such nonsense. I think that's the craziest thing I ever heard in my life.

Dr. Now you will have to be sensible.

Sp. Sensible? I am sensible. Are you a perfect man?

Dr. No, I am not, but I tell you that you are an ignorant, selfish spirit. You have been bothering that lady for some time, and we have chased you out by the use of those "knocks." Whether you understand it or not, you are an ignorant spirit. You will have to behave yourself, or else I will take you into the office and give you some more of those "knocks."

Sp. I don't want those knocks.

Dr. Then change your disposition. Realize that there is no death; when people lose their bodies they merely become invisible to mortals. You are invisible to us.

Sp. I will have nothing to do with you!

Dr. We want to help you and make you understand your condition.

Sp. I don't need help.

THIRTY YEARS AMONG THE DEAD

Dr. If you don't behave you will be taken away by intelligent spirits and placed in a dungeon.

Sp. You think you can scare me! You will find out what will happen to you.

Dr. You must overcome your selfish disposition. Look around; you may see some one who will make you care. You may see some one who will make you cry.

Sp. I don't want to cry. I like to sing, instead of cry.

Dr. Where is your mother?

Sp. I haven't seen her for a long time. My mother? My mother! She is in Heaven. She was a good woman, and is with God and the Holy Ghost, and all of them.

Dr. Look around and see if your mother is not here.

Sp. This place is not Heaven, -far from it. If this is heaven then it is worse than hell.

Dr. Look for your mother; she will put you to shame.

Sp. I have done nothing to be ashamed of. What business have you to give me those knocks and have me put in a dungeon? That lady and I made a bargain.

Dr. She made a bargain to come here and get rid of you. You have been fired out by electricity. You have lost your company.

Sp. Yes, for a while they all left me. I can't find them. (Other obsessing spirits.) Why did you chase that tall fellow away?

Dr. This lady wants her body to herself; she does not want to be tormented by earthbound spirits. Would you like them around you?

Sp. I don't know what you mean.

Dr. Can't you realize that you bothered that lady and made her life a perfect hell?

Sp. (To Mrs. B.) I have not bothered you.

Mrs. B. You woke me up at three o'clock this morning.

Sp. Well, you have no business to sleep.

Dr. You must live your own life.

Sp. I will.

Dr. That will be in a dark dungeon if you do not behave yourself.

Sp. How do you know?

Dr. You cannot stay here. You had better be humble and ask for help -that is what you need. My wife and I have been following this work for many years, and she allows all sorts of spirits to use her body, so they may be helped.

Sp. (Sarcastically) She is very good!

Dr. You ought to be ashamed of yourself. Do you see your mother?

Sp. I don't want to see her. I don't want to call her away from Heaven.

Dr. Since Heaven is a condition of happiness she could not be in any "Heaven" with a daughter like you, -she could not be happy. Suppose you were in Heaven, and had a daughter, would you like her to act as you do?

Sp. I do not act contrary. What is the situation? Tell me that!

Dr. I have already told you the situation. You are controlling my wife's body.

Sp. How do I do that?

Dr. Because of higher laws, and because you are a spirit. Spirit and mind are invisible. You are so selfish that you do, not care to understand.

Sp. This is not Heaven.

Dr. This is Los Angeles, California.

Sp. For God's sake, no (An expression never used by Mrs. Wickland.) How did I come here?

Dr. By staying around that lady. That is how. She had to take those "knocks" to get you out.

Sp. She's a fool to do it.

Dr. She wants to get rid of you and she will get rid of you.

Sp. I will not have those knocks any more.

Dr. Higher spirits will show you something you do not like, if you do not behave yourself.

Sp. (Shrinking from some vision.) I don't want that!

Dr. It is not what you want; it is what you get.

Sp. Is that so!

As nothing could be done to bring the spirit to an understanding, she was taken away by intelligent spirits.

Upon a later occasion, when the patient, Mrs. Burton, was in the circle, another spirit was removed from her and, controlling Mrs. Wickland, spoke in a very individualistic manner.

Spirit: JIMMIE HUNTINGTON Patient: MRS. BURTON

The spirit kicked off both shoes, and seemed greatly disturbed.

Dr. What seems to be the trouble? Have you been in an accident of some kind? (Holding psychic's hands firmly.) You have no shoes on.

Sp. I took them off.

Dr. Tell us who you are.

Sp. I don't know whether I want to.

Dr. Tell us where you came from.

Sp. I don't know that I have to do that.

Dr. We would like to know who you are. What seems to be the trouble? You don't seem to be comfortable.

THIRTY YEARS AMONG THE DEAD

Sp. I am not.

Dr. What have you been doing lately?

Sp. I haven't been doing anything. I have just been walking around.

Dr. And what else?

Sp. Why, nothing in particular. It seems that I have been shut up somewhere. (In patient's aura.)

Dr. In what way?

Sp. I don't know how it is, but I couldn't get out.

Dr. How would you explain that?

Sp. I can't explain it in any way.

Dr. Did you hear any talking?

Sp. Yes, many people talked.

Dr. What did they say?

Sp. One said one thing, one another. They all think they are so smart.

Dr. Did you ever have any chance to say anything?

Sp. Yes, but I got so mad, because there was always a woman there; she knew all I wanted to say. I felt that some, times I should have a chance. Whenever they talked, that woman talked. A man has no chance to say anything when a woman begins to talk.

Dr. You must have been a married man.

Sp. Why yes, I am married.

Dr. Was it a success, or a failure?

Sp. I don't know what it was -an excuse anyway. I was not so very happy. Women always talk too much. They can't leave a fellow alone a minute at a time.

Dr. What did they talk about?

Sp. It's that woman, she talks and talks and talks. (Patient, Mrs. Burton, who talked constantly.) She never can keep still very long at a time. I felt sometimes like shaking her good. We just had some new company come in. They talk and talk. It makes me sick; they make me get out. They are the worst I ever saw.

Dr. Did anything happen at all?

Sp. Lightning played around my head, until I didn't know where I was. (Electrical treatment given patient.) I thought it was far distant, but, my God and Stars in Heaven, how it hit me!

Dr. What did you want to do at such times?

Sp. I wanted to get hold of that lightning and try to stop it hitting my head, but the lightning strikes every time -it never misses. Lightning used to be different; it didn't always strike, but now it never misses. I never saw anything like it. There are stars before your eyes, and it feels terrible, but even while the lightning strikes that woman keeps right on talking. (Patient talked throughout treatment.)

Dr. What does she talk about?

Sp. Nothing. She wants to be boss, and I want to be boss; so there we are.

Dr. What does she say?

Sp. You know how it is with women -they talk and talk, but there is never anything to it.

Dr. Does the lady address you?

Sp. She torments me all the time. I feel like shaking her, but I don't seem to have any power any more. Then there is another woman, and she goes right at it too. It makes me sick. What can you do with a woman to make her stop talking? If you can get any woman to stop talking, you'll have a pretty hard time to do it.

Dr. What is your name?

Sp. It's a long time since I heard it.

Dr. Where did you come from? Are you in California?

Sp. No; I'm in Texas.

Dr. What did your mother call you when you were a boy?

Sp. James was my name, but they always called me Jimmie. Gosh! I don't know what is the matter with me. That lightning gets on my knees and feet, then from my head to my feet, but what I can't understand is, it never misses its aim.

Dr. How old are you?

Sp. I will say that I am a man about fifty years of age, but I want to say that during all my life, I never saw such lightning before, and what I can't understand is that nothing ever catches fire from it. Gosh! Yesterday I got into a regular nest; it was the worst I ever saw in my whole life. I think every one was a devil. (Obsessing spirits.) There's another one standing over there, and that came yesterday.

Dr. How long have you been dead, Jimmie?

Sp. What do you mean?

Dr. I mean, how long is it since you lost your body?

Sp. I haven't lost it yet.

Dr. Don't you realize that you are in a strange condition?

Sp. I have been that for a long time.

Dr. Did you ever work in the oil business in Texas?

Sp. I don't know where I have been working; things are very queer.

Dr. Where did you work?

Sp. In a blacksmith shop.

Dr. Do you know what year it is?

THIRTY YEARS AMONG THE DEAD

Sp. No, I don't.

Dr. How are you going to vote this Fall? For whom will you vote for President?

Sp. I don't know yet.

Dr. How do you like the present President?

Sp. I like him; he is pretty good.

Dr. Do you know anything in particular about him?

Sp. He's all right; there's no flies on Roosevelt.

Dr. Is he President?

Sp. Of course he is. He just got in. McKinley was also a good man, but you know, Mark Hanna had an awful influence over him. It is a long time since I bothered with politics. I have been shut up a long time, but, my God and Stars in Heaven, I'm nearly crazy from that woman talking all the time.

Dr. What woman is it that talks so much?

Sp. Can't you see her?

Dr. She might not be here.

Sp. Oh, yes, she is, it's that woman. (Indicating patient.)

Dr. What does she talk about?

Sp. Nothing but nonsense. She makes me sick.

Dr. What does she say in particular?

Sp. Nothing; she has not sense enough. She mocks me every once in a while. I'm going to get her some day! Stars in Heaven, she's terrible!

Dr. Now, friend, I want you to understand your condition. You have lost your physical body, and are now a spirit.

Sp. I have a body. If only that woman would keep still.

Dr. This is not your body.

Sp. Stars in Heaven, whose body is it?

Dr. My wife's.

Sp. Stars in Heaven and the Heat from the Sun! I'm not your wife. How could I be your wife when I'm a man? That's funny!

Dr. You are an invisible spirit.

Sp. Spirit? Do you mean a ghost? For Heaven's sake, talk United States.

Dr. Ghosts and spirits are the same thing.

Sp. I know ghosts and I know spirits.

Dr. They both mean the same thing. (Taking hand of psychic.)

Sp. Say, it's not nice for a man to hold another man's hand. If you want to hold hands, get hold of some lady's hand and hold that. Men don't hold each other's hands, -that's cold joy.

Dr. Tell us what that woman says.

Sp. She just talks and says nothing.

Dr. Is she young or old?

Sp. She's not so very young. I get so mad at her.

Dr. I am telling you the fact when I say you are a spirit.

Sp. When did I die then?

Dr. It must have been some time ago. Roosevelt has not been President for many years. He is a spirit like yourself.

Sp. Just like I am? Why, he's dead then.

Dr. So are you.

Sp. When I am here and listening to you, I can't be dead.

Dr. You have lost your body.

Sp. Say, don't hold my hand. It's such cold joy.

Dr. I am holding my wife's hand.

Sp. Well, you can hold her hand, but let mine alone.

Dr. Do you recognize this hand as yours?

Sp. That isn't my hand.

Dr. It is the hand of my wife.

Sp. But I'm not your wife.

Dr. You are using my wife's body only temporarily. You lost your own body a long time ago.

Sp. How did that happen?

Dr. I don't know. Do you know you are in Los Angeles, California?

Sp. God, and Stars in Heaven, how did I come to California? I had no money. You know, there are two women here. One doesn't talk so much. She looks to me like she was sick. (Another spirit obsessing patient.) She doesn't say much, but I suppose she is so annoyed because that other woman talks so awful. Please don't hold my hand; I like 'to feel free. If I were alone with a lady, and I could hold her hand, that would be a different story. Aren't you satisfied to hold just one hand?

Dr. I have to hold both because you will not be quiet. Now, let us not lose any more time.

Sp. I wish sometimes I didn't have so much time on my hands.

Dr. We will give you something to do.

Sp. You will? That's good. If you can give me some work of some kind, I shall be very glad.

THIRTY YEARS AMONG THE DEAD

Do you want me to fix horses, shoes? I used to shoe horses.

Dr. In what state?

Sp. Texas. That's a big state.

Dr. Did you roam around a good deal?

Sp. Yes, quite a little. I was in Galveston, Dallas, San Antonio, and many other places. I traveled everywhere I wanted to go. I went to Houston and other cities.

Dr. You are a spirit and have been allowed to control my wife's body for a short time. We do not see you.

Sp. Say, just look at those devils there, limping around like a bunch of little imps. (Obsessing spirits.) They are all around that woman. (Mrs. B.)

Dr. You take them all with you when you leave.

Sp. Not much I won't. (Touching necklace.) What in the world is this?

Dr. That is my wife's neck ornament.

Sp. Your wife?

Dr. You have been brought here for enlightenment. You were fired out from that other lady.

Sp. Yes, with lightning. For the life of me, I never saw anything like it. There used to be thunder and lightning storms in Texas, and in Arkansas, but lightning did not strike every time as it did on me.

Dr. You will not have that thunder and lightning any more.

Sp. I will not? That's good.

Dr. Was your mother living in Texas?

Sp. Certainly, but she is dead. I should know, because I was at her funeral.

Dr. You were at the funeral of her body, not her spirit, soul or mind.

Sp. I suppose she went to Heaven.

Dr. Look around and see if you can see her.

Sp. Where?

Dr. She might be here.

Sp. What place is this anyhow? If I am your wife I have never seen you before.

Dr. You are not my wife.

Sp. You called me your wife.

Dr. I did not say you are my wife. You are temporarily using her body.

Sp. For God's sake in Heaven and hell, how can I get out of your wife?

Dr. Be sensible. What do those imps say?

Sp. They say they are going to stay, but I say, and say it strong, that they are all going to go.

Dr. Do you want them to go with you?

Sp. I should say I do.

Dr. You can help them a great deal by reforming them and making them understand their condition. They need help. You are all ignorant spirits and have been bothering that lady. I am the one who gave you "lightning" and chased you out. You can all 90 to the spirit world and learn how to progress.

Sp. Is that woman going too? There is a whole lot, a gang, but I haven't seen any of them until lately.

Dr. Can you see anybody you know? Just sit quietly for a moment and look around.

Sp. (Excitedly) Why, here comes Nora! (A spirit.)

Dr. Who is Nora?

Sp. Nora Huntington; she's my sister.

Dr. Ask her if your name is Jimmie Huntington.

Sp. She says it is, and that she hasn't seen me for such a long time. (Suddenly puzzled.) But she's dead.

Dr. Let her explain the situation.

Sp. She says: "Jimmie, you come home with me." Where shall I come?

Dr. What does she say?

Sp. She says: "To the spirit world," -but I don't believe her.

Dr. Was your sister in the habit of lying to you?

Sp. No.

Dr. If she were honest before, would she lie now?

Sp. She says she has been hunting for me for years and she didn't know where I was.

Dr. Where has she been?

Sp. Why, she's dead. I was at her funeral, and I know well that she was not buried alive.

Dr. You went to the funeral of her body, not her spirit.

Sp. This is her ghost then?

Dr. She is probably an intelligent spirit. We do not need to argue about that any more. Let her explain.

Sp. She says: "Let us go, Jimmie, and take the 'gang' with us." She says she is a missionary and helps everybody she can; she says she helps unfortunates. I have been unfortunate too.

Dr. Tell this lady, this other spirit you have been talking about, to go with you.

Sp. She says if she leaves she has no body.

Dr. Tell her she has a spirit body. She doesn't need a physical body. Tell her that they will teach her how to progress. You take the imps along too.

Sp. I can't carry them all with me. How do you know they all want to go with us?

Dr. They will go if you can show them anything better than they have now. Probably they never had any chance in life.

Sp. I never thought of that.

Dr. We cannot blame them altogether. Show them the better way and they will follow.

Sp. Where am I now?

Dr. In California.

Sp. Where in California?

Dr. Los Angeles.

Sp. If you are in California, it doesn't mean that I am there too.

Dr. How could you be anywhere else, since you are here?

Sp. Of course, that is reasonable. The last I remember, I was in Dallas, Texas, and the first thing I knew I was struck on the back of my head. I was shoeing a horse when I was struck. Did he kill me?

Dr. He evidently chased you out of your body. Nobody ever dies. If you don't go soon, your sister will become tired of waiting for you.

Sp. I'll go with her, if you'll let me, but I'll have to walk.

Dr. How are you going to walk? With my wife's body? You will have to learn a new lesson. Just think yourself with your sister and you will be there instantly. You will have to travel by thought.

Sp. Stars in Heaven, that's a new wrinkle!

Dr. Now, friend, you can't stay any longer.

Sp. That's a nice way to talk to me!

Dr. I don't want you to use my wife's body any longer.

Sp. What body will I get hold of when I get out from here?

Dr. When you leave this body you will have your spirit body. That is invisible to us.

Sp. Can I jump from this body into a spirit body?

Dr. Your sister will explain. Just think yourself with your sister. You do not need any physical body for that purpose.

Sp. I am commencing to get sleepy.

Dr. Go with your sister and follow her instructions; you will learn many new lessons in the spirit life. Take all the gang and the little imps with you.

Sp. (To spirits) Now you come along with me, all of you, the whole lot of you.

Dr. Will they all go with you?

Sp. Now we are going. Come on, the whole gang of you.

Goodbye.

On a subsequent date a spirit "Harry" was brought to the circle for enlightenment, and, controlling Mrs. Wickland, maintained an interesting conversation regarding another spirit that had been troubling Mrs. Burton.

Spirit: HARRY

Dr. Where have you come from?

Sp. I don't know where I am, and I don't know what is the matter with me.

Dr. Would you care to know what is the matter?

Sp. I don't know what is the matter.

Dr. Did something happen to you?

Sp. That is what I should like to find out.

Dr. What have you been doing lately?

Sp. I don't know.

Dr. Tell us who you are. Do you know?

Sp. Well, I should say -well, I think I do.

Dr. Where do you think you are?

Sp. I don't know.

Dr. Yes, you do.

Sp. No, I don't know. Everything is so queer, and it just seems to me I don't know what's the matter.

Dr. Can't you look back and see whether something happened to you?

Sp. I can't look back, I have no eyes in my back.

Dr. I mean, think back.

Sp. Think of my back?

Dr. No, think of your past. Just use your thinking faculties.

Sp. I don't know anything.

Dr. You must not be so mentally lazy.

Sp. What can a man do?

Dr. This is a woman sitting here. Are you a man or a woman?

Sp. I am a man, that fellow is a man, and the others are women. I have always been a man. I was never a woman, and never will be. You know I am a man.

THIRTY YEARS AMONG THE DEAD

Dr. Look at your hands; where did you get them?

Sp. Those are not my hands.

Dr. Look at your feet.

Sp. They are not mine, either. I never was a woman, and I don't want women's hands and feet, and I don't want to borrow any one's body now.

Dr. Are you old?

Sp. Well, I'm not a young kid.

Dr. You are probably old in years but not in knowledge.

Sp. No, I don't know that I have so much knowledge.

Dr. If you had knowledge you would not be in your present position.

Sp. That has nothing to do with knowledge.

Dr. Knowledge is just what you lack. Tell us what your name is. Is it Mary?

Sp. Have you ever heard of a man being named Mary? That's ridiculous.

Dr. Then tell us what your name is. I can only guess.

Sp. For goodness sake alive, man, it is a man's name, not a woman's.

Dr. Introduce yourself.

Sp. What in the devil do you need my name for?

Dr. You are well versed in English. Did you have white hair as you have now? (Referring to hair of psychic.)

Sp. I had gray hair.

Dr. Did you wear curls as you are doing now?

Sp. No, I don't like them.

Dr. Did you wear a comb?

Sp. Did you ever know of a man wearing a comb?

Dr. Where did you get that wedding ring?

Sp. I didn't steal anything. I don't want a woman's hand.

Dr. John, where did you come from?

Sp. I'm not named John.

Dr. What did your wife call you? What did your mother call you?

Sp. She called me Harry. I was not married.

Dr. What is your other name?

Sp. I do not need to tell my name to a lot of women.

Dr. There are some gentlemen present.

Sp. How in the world did I get into this crowd of women? I hate women.

Dr. You must have been disappointed in love. What was the trouble?

Sp. I'd be a big fool to tell my secrets to a lot of women.

Dr. Why did she marry the other man?

Sp. Who?

Dr. The girl who jilted you.

Sp. She never in my life -no!

Dr. Weren't you disappointed in love?

Sp. No.

Dr. Then why do you hate women?

Sp. I must not tell you any of my secrets before this bunch of women, so they can sit here and laugh at me. I should like to know why all these women are staring at me. What's the matter with that man over there? (Spirit.) I mean the one behind that lady (Mrs. Burton seated in circle).

Mrs. B. I'm a man hater; he can keep away from me.

Sp. Why is that man around her? Is he her husband? Lady, what does he hang around you for? What's the matter with You? Do you like him so well that you want him to stick to you like glue?

Dr. Ask him how long he has been dead.

Sp. He sure is an ugly thing. I'm afraid of him. He looks like he wants to fight.

Dr. Ask him how long he has been dead.

Sp. Dead? He sticks so she can't move without him. Whenever she moves, he moves. He seems to me like a monkey.

Mrs. B. Say, take him away with you, will you?

Sp. Why should I take him for? For God's sake, I don't know the fellow! Do you like him, lady?

Mrs. B. No, I don't. I'm tired of him.

Sp. What's the matter with him? Is he your husband?

Mrs. B. No, he is not, and I don't understand it myself.

Sp. Do you like him?

Mrs. B. No, I want him to get away from me.

Sp. Where am I, anyhow?

Dr. You are in Los Angeles, California.

Sp. There's also a woman around her, and she sticks like glue.

THIRTY YEARS AMONG THE DEAD

Mrs. B. Are you here to help us? Can't you take those things away from me?

Sp. Do you like that man who is with you?

Mrs. B. No, I am wild to get rid of him. The door is wide open; he can surely go.

Sp. For God's sake, shut the door! I don't want such a man following me. Why don't you tell the police? Can't the police take him away from you, if you don't want him?

Dr. They are all spirits.

Sp. Spirits?

Dr. Yes, like yourself.

Sp. Oh, you tell me that man is a ghost, the one standing behind that woman there?

Dr. Can you see him?

Sp. He's no spirit, he's a man. He stands there. He's afraid she will get away from him and he can't follow. He says he is sick of her.

Dr. He is a spirit but does not understand it. She does not see him and neither do we. He is invisible to us.

Sp. What kind of a place is this I came to?

Dr. We cannot see you either.

Sp. You can't? Don't you hear me?

Dr. We hear you, but we can't see you.

Sp. Is this a crowd of blind people? I can see them all and lots more. The whole room is full of people.

Dr. We can hear you, but we can only hear you talk through a woman's body.

Sp. Now, you're kidding me. You think that I -I would ever talk through a woman? Not much! I would not go across the street to talk through a woman. You know, I can't understand what this thing is. I don't know why I should be here. I don't know what's the matter; all of you are sitting around looking at me. Why are there people standing around each one here? There are others, standing around looking at me too. Could they have conversation with a fellow?

Dr. If I explain to you, will you try to understand? In the first place, you are dead, as people would say.

Sp. If I'm a dead one, that's a good thing!

Dr. You yourself are not dead.

Sp. But you said I was dead.

Dr. You are dead to your own people and friends. We know you are not dead in reality; you only lost your physical body. But you also have a spirit body when you pass out of your mortal body. You find yourself alive, and you have a spirit body, but you cannot explain it.

Sp. I know I have been walking a very great deal, and it seems to me I never get anywhere. I saw a lot of people here. I came here with the crowd, and before I knew it, everything was light, and I saw you all sitting around in a circle, singing. I thought it was a prayer meeting, so I stopped, and before I knew anything, I could talk. Before then I thought I must be deaf and dumb and blind, because I could not see anything, and I am so tired.

Dr. Most of those you see here are spirits like yourself.

Sp. Why are we here?

Dr. Many have been brought to obtain understanding. You yourself are controlling my wife's body. You are not my wife, but you are using my wife's body. It does not make any difference how strange it seems to you, it is a fact. You are invisible to us, and you are speaking through my wife's organism. That man you speak of is a spirit too. Take him with you when you go. He is invisible to us.

Sp. I should like to fight him.

Dr. Did you ever read the Bible?

Sp. Yes, a long time ago. I have not seen one for a long time.

Dr. You remember reading in the Bible about obsessing spirits that Jesus cast out? He is one of that kind.

Sp. They are all around that woman (Mrs. B.).

Mrs. B. I have the door closed now.

Sp. If you keep the door closed, I'll take them along with me. I want to fight with that fellow anyhow. What's your name?

Dr. What does he say?

Sp. He says his name is Jim McDonald. Don't you know him, lady? If he is a spirit, for goodness sake, why does be hang on to that woman when she doesn't want him?

Dr. Perhaps he found himself there, as you find yourself here. You say you saw a crowd, a light, and here you are.

Sp. That man says he was walking in the dark and saw that lady. Say, will I always have to stay here too?

Ques. What are the names of those around me? (This was asked by another patient.)

Sp. There are two. They fight once, in a while. I see them fighting.

Ques. I fight them too.

Dr. Do not fight them physically; that gives them strength and magnetism. When you fight them in that way, you give them much more strength. You hold them by fighting them as you do. Fight them mentally. Why don't you try to close up?

Sp. I will take them along too, if I can. Don't fist fight them any more. I don't know what's the matter with me. I feel strange.

Dr. Where was your home?

Sp. It was in Detroit, Michigan.

Dr. What year can you recall?

THIRTY YEARS AMONG THE DEAD

Sp. I can't recall any.

Dr. Who is President?

Sp. I don't know for sure, but I think Cleveland.

Dr. He was President a long time ago.

Sp. I have been walking so long that I feel tired. Is there any rest for a weary person? Have you a bed so that I can lie down and rest?

Dr. If you look around you will see intelligent spirits.

Sp. Why, I see some beautiful girls. No, girls, I will not come with you. Don't try to fool me. I'm not going with you, not much!

Dr. They are different from the girls you have known. They are not mortal girls, they are spirits.

Sp. They have a smile like others to give to a man.

Dr. They are different altogether. They help spirits who need help.

Sp. Those girls seem to be honest, but you know, I hate women.

Dr. You should not condemn them all because one was false.

Sp. You see, I want to take all those folks with me. If I can, I will take them with me. I think I will follow those girls, anyhow. (Surprised.) Why, there's my mother! She's been dead and gone a long time.

Dr. She's not dead.

Sp. Don't you think she's in Heaven?

Dr. Ask her. She can speak for herself.

Sp. She says she is in a beautiful place called the spirit world.

Dr. The spirit world surrounds the physical. "Heaven" is a condition within you; when you have found that, you will be contented and happy. That is what Jesus taught also.

Sp. I should like to go with my mother. She's a good old lady. I want to take McDonald along too. Come here, McDonald. I don't want to stay around here any longer, and I want you to come along. He acts as if he is trying hard to wake up. Say, come on, McDonald, let us be good fellows and go with those girls, for they might be honest and sincere. Mother, you come along too. I will go now. Goodby. Come on, you fellows. Say, what do you stick to that woman for, anyhow? I should be ashamed of myself, hanging around her. I'm going. Goodbye.

Mrs. B. Be sure and take them along with you.

Dr. What is your name?

Sp. Harry. That is all I can remember. I have not heard my name for many years.

Dr. Make the others understand the folly of staying.

Sp. I'm going to take those fellows along. Now, you look here! You're going to come along with me. I'll fight every damned one of you that won't come. You ought to be ashamed to stick around a woman like you do. Now, come along with me! You see, they come. I'll look after them all right. Goodbye.

During another circle "Frank," one of the spirits interfering with Mrs. Burton, left her, and controlled the intermediary, exhibiting little trace of memory in any form.

Spirit: FRANK Patient: MRS. BURTON

Dr. Where did you come from?

Sp. I don't know.

Dr. Do you know any one here?

Sp. I don't see anybody I know.

Dr. Don't you know where you came from?

Sp. I don't know myself. How can I answer questions when I don't know?

Dr. How long have you been dead?

Sp. Dead! The idea! Say, what's the matter with me? I think it looks very funny to see you all sitting around here. Are you having a meeting, or what is it called anyhow?

Dr. Yes, it's a meeting. Try to tell us who you are.

Sp. I don't know why I should tell you that.

Dr. You are a stranger to us.

Sp. I don't know whether I shall stay here or not. I am always peculiar among strangers, you know.

Dr. Tell us where you came from.

Sp. For my dear life, I don't know myself, so how can I tell you? Say, why do you hold my arm? I'm a strong man, and can sit still by myself.

Dr. I thought you were a woman.

Sp. God above! Why do you think I'm a woman? You'll have to look again, because I am a man, sure enough, and I've always been a man. But things are funny, and I don't know; it has been so peculiar with me for some time. You know, I was walking along and then I heard some singing, so I thought I would peek in, and before I knew it I was feeling fine. You know I have not been feeling well for some time; everything has seemed unusual. (After becoming enmeshed in aura of sensitive.) I don't know what is the matter with me anyhow. Somebody said to me that if I came in where the singing was, I would find out what is the matter with me. I have asked everybody I saw, but everybody passed by; they were so stuck up they wouldn't talk to a fellow any more. The people all looked like wax to me. Dear life! I've been talking and talking, and walking and walking, and, for dear life, I could never get any one to answer me, or take any notice of me before. (As a spirit he was invisible to mortals and therefore unnoticed by them.) You are the first one to answer any question. I have some little peculiar kind of thing in my throat once in a while, and I can't talk, and then I seem to get well again. But I feel queer, so queer.

Dr. Can you remember anything happening to you at some time?

Sp. Something happens every day. One time I remember one thing and another time something else, but I don't remember anything clearly. I cannot, for dear life, know where I am at. It is the most peculiar thing I ever saw.

Dr. How old are you?

Sp. I cannot tell you that. I haven't known my age for some time. Nobody ever asks me about that and the natural circumstance is that I forgot. (Hearing a passing train.) Why, there's a train coming! It's a long time since I heard that. It seems I live again for a short time. I don't know what it is.

Dr. Where did you live formerly? Where do you think you are now?

Sp. I don't know where I lived before, but right now I am in this room with a lot of people.

Dr. Do you know you are in Los Angeles, California?

Sp. For dear life, no!

Dr. Where do you think you ought to be?

Sp. I cannot seem to recall things. There are times that I can tell you that I am a woman, and then I get some kind of funny thing I do not like. (Static treatment of patient.)

Dr. What do you get?

Sp. When I am a woman, I have long hair, and when the hair is hanging down this funny thing begins. (Mrs. Burton was in the habit of taking her hair down during a treatment.)

Dr. What do you mean?

Sp. It seems like a million needles strike me, and, for Gods sake, it is the worst thing I ever had in my whole life! I don't want to be a woman. I only get that funny thing when I am a woman. (Seeing Mrs. B. in circle.) She's the one with the long hair! (To Mrs. B.) I'm going to get you!

Dr. Do you know that lady?

Sp. Yes, she gets so mad at me at times and wants to chase me away.

Dr. She probably doesn't want you around. Possibly you bother her.

Sp. She bothers me too.

Dr. Try to understand your condition. Cannot you realize that you are so-called dead? At this time you are a woman. Look at your clothes. You say you are a man and yet you are wearing the clothes of a woman.

Sp. For God's sake, I don't want to be a woman any more! I'm a man and I want to be a man. I used to be a man all the time, but I cannot, for dear life, know how I can get out of this condition. That woman says to go, and I try to get out, but I cannot. (Suddenly recognizing Dr. W.) You are the one that gave me that fire! Praise the Lord! I want to get rid of you. I don't like you with all those fires you give me. I don't want to have anything to do with you.

Mrs. B. How long have you been with me?

Sp. With you? You always chase me out. What did you do with that woman that was with me? (Another spirit obsessing the patient, dislodged previously.) She sang for me. We have lost her. I have been hunting and hunting for her. Can you tell me where she is?

Dr. She left that lady and controlled this same body as you are doing now. After that she went to the spirit world. That is where you are going when you leave here.

Sp. That woman (Mrs. B.) has no business to scold me like she does. I haven't done her any harm.

Dr. Suppose you were a lady and some spirit bothered you would you like it?

Sp. Certainly I would not like it very well.

Dr. You bothered her. You are a spirit and she is a mortal. She wants to get rid of you.

Sp. She bothers me with all those needles. They hit her on the head and it seems like the needles are hitting my head.

Dr. She is in her mortal body, but you are a spirit, invisible to us.

Sp. What do you mean?

Dr. Just exactly what I say. Your mind is invisible to us. You are temporarily controlling my wife's body.

Sp. Why, I never saw your wife, and I do not want to. I Will tell you one thing, I am a man, and will never be anything else, and I don't want to be married to you.

Dr. You may be a man, as you claim, but I want you to recognize the fact that you are invisible to us. This is my wife's body.

Sp. For God's sake, sure I am a woman! (Noticing clothes of psychic.) For the land's sake alive, when did these clothes come on me?

Dr. They have been on you quite a while. How did you get here?

Sp. Somebody said: "You go in there and you will get understanding, because you do not need to wander as you are doing." And now I am a woman!

Dr. Only temporarily. Try to understand what I am telling you. You lost your body, perhaps a long time ago.

Sp. That woman (Mrs. B.) is the fault of it.

Dr. You have been bothering that lady, probably for many years, and you may have been troubling others. What is your name?

Sp. I can't think.

Dr. You lost your own body and have been wandering around in that outer darkness which is described in the Bible. Were you a religious man?

Sp. I don't want to have anything to do with the churches. I am sick and tired of them all. They all say, if you do not do so and so you will go straight to hell, where you will burn forever. They teach and preach damnation, you know. I was quite a young man when a minister told me I would go to that terrible hell, and they did not want me in the church any more because I did not do as they said I should. I did not believe any of it. I was not such a very bad man.

After I left that church I thought I would try another. For dear life, I got into the same hell and damnation, and I was tired of it all. They talked of God and holy things. They said I should give my money to God. They said I should give my tobacco to God. I could not see why God should need my tobacco, and what little money I had. I could not see things that way, so I left that church. I went to another church, and they talked and talked to me. After awhile they said that the devil was after me, because I would not give my money to the church.

One time I had been out with the boys for a while. I never drank too much, but I drank enough that time to be lively. I thought, now I will go right straight up to the front and sit down, so I did. They tried to save my soul for God, so they told me. The minister said that the devil was right after me, and I got pretty seared. He said: "And he is going to get you!" I thought I would look behind and probably I might see him, but I didn't. He said: "Come up, come up, and we will save your soul from hell; come and be saved. Come to the front and be converted. You will be born again."

I was a little contrary for a while, and then I, got up, and went right up to the front, as I wanted to see what they would do. The minister said: "Now you kneel down there." So I knelt down. He put his hands on my head and they all sang and sang, and they prayed and prayed for me. They said: "Be converted now." I thought it was grand, all the girls putting their hands on me and singing and praying for me. Then the minister came again, and he said: "You will have to pray, or the devil will get after you." I could not be a hypocrite, so I told him, if I was a sinner I would have to stay one. "I don't believe the devil is a person, anyhow," so I told him, and he was angry. He thought I was a bad pill. They tried all they could to convert me, but it was no good, so I finally went away. After I left there, some men came after me, so I ran as hard as I could, then somebody struck me on the head and I had great pain. I fell down, but I got up again. I wanted to give that man a push down the hill, but he pushed me and I rolled and rolled down that hill. There were lots of people around me after I stopped rolling, and all at once I felt all right again.

Dr. That was probably the time you lost your physical body. You died.

Sp. I did not die.

Dr. What place was it, where you rolled down the hill?

Sp. It was down in Texas. I walked and ran and tried to talk to people, but they would not answer me; they seemed like sticks. I felt so queer in my head. I asked them if they could tell me where my home was. I felt that pain. Once in a while I could get away. I then came to a lady, and she said: "Come along," and before I knew it we had a crowd around us, and she used to sing. (Evidently, the spirit, Carrie Huntington. The Patient, Mrs. B., had often been annoyed by the singing of spirits.) I talked to her once in a while, and then, all at once, she disappeared, and after that I got the needles. (Came more fully into control of patient, and felt electrical treatments more keen.) I felt them pretty bad.

Dr. You are a spirit and are now using my wife's body.

Sp. How in the world did I get into your wife's body? Do You like your wife to be all kinds of tramps?

Dr. Yes, long enough to give the spirits an understanding regarding the invisible side.

Sp. Are these your wife's clothes? Did I borrow them for a while? Did your wife dress me? I am sorry to show myself like a woman and not like a man. What will these people think -that I'm crazy? (Laughter.) It isn't funny.

Dr. You are an ignorant spirit, in outer darkness. Intelligent spirits have brought you here to control this body temporarily, so that you can understand your condition. Also, they took you away from that lady. (Mrs. B.)

Sp. Will she get those awful needles again?

Dr. Are there any more persons where you came from? Or are you the last one?

Sp. The woman and the other man. went; then you gave me the needles. I kicked like a steer to get out, but I could not. How could you expect me to do any better? I thought of the minister that talked about hell.

Dr. That hell was not like this. There are spirits here who will teach you how to progress in the spirit world; they will help you. Is your father living?

Sp. I don't know. I haven't seen my father for about twenty-five or thirty years. Mother is dead, but I don't know whether father is or not. I don't know any of my relatives.

Mrs. B. Did I meet you last November?

Sp. Yes, I have been ill ever since that time. I was not the one that was with you close; that was the young lady. My head is hurting me terribly.

Dr. What year do you think it should be?

Sp. I should think about 1888 or 1891.

Dr. It is 1920 now.

Sp. I think there must be something the matter with me.

Dr. You have been in outer darkness for some time.

Sp. I have been walking and walking, and I got with that lady over there. (Mrs. B.) I wanted to go. I kicked and she kicked, and we had regular kickings. Oh, look there! See! My Mother! Oh, Mother! Can you forgive me? I was not as you wanted me to be. Mother, will you take me? I am so tired; I need your care and help. Will you take me? Oh, my Mother!

Dr. What does she say?

Sp. She calls me. She says: "Yes, Frank, you will come with me. I have been looking for you a long time." I am getting weak; I feel so tired. Mother says: "Frank, we had not the understanding of the real life, because we were not taught what we should have been taught, so that we did not learn to know God's wonderful universe. Religion is a long way from the real life. The ministers all teach that we should just believe and then we are saved. No, no; belief is only a setback. Get knowledge of God. We do not do that."

"Frank, we will help you to learn what a beautiful world there is on the other side when we have understanding. You have to make your own efforts to learn to understand the Golden Rule of God's beautiful teaching of life, and be of help and service to your fellowman."

"Now, Frank," she says, "you have been very mischievous in your life. I know you were a good boy, but you always were too lively. You were ignorant of the real life and went away from home when I died. The home was broken up; you went one way and the rest went another. I did not know, Frank, what things were, but I wish the truth could be taught."

She says: "Now come with me to the spirit world, where we have understanding. There we have love, harmony, peace and bliss, but we have to live for one another. You have to go to school and learn. You must not bother any one any more, as you have done. Come, Frank, and we will go to a beautiful home in the spirit world."

THIRTY YEARS AMONG THE DEAD

Thank you, and Goodbye!

Several weeks later the last intruder left Mrs. Burton, and, through Mrs. Wickland, inquired for the companions who had preceded her, resenting having been held captive.

Spirit: MAGGIE WILKINSON Patient: MRS. BURTON.

Dr. Good Evening, friend; who are you? (Taking psychic's hand.)

Sp. Don't hold my hand! Don't touch me!

Dr. What is your name?

Sp. My name is Maggie.

Dr. Maggie what?

Sp. Maggie Wilkinson.

Dr. Do you know that you are in Los Angeles? Where did You come from?

Sp. I came from Dallas, Texas.

Dr. How did you reach Los Angeles?

Sp. I am not in Los Angeles, I am in Texas. I have been kicking and kicking all the time.

Dr. Why did you do that?

Sp. I have been kicking because I have been in a prison. (Victim's aura.) There were several of us, but they have all disappeared. (Other obsessing spirits, previously dislodged from patient.) They have all gone but me, and I don't like it.

Dr. Would you like to go where your friends have gone?

Sp. I don't care. I really don't care for the others, anyway. They always wanted to have everything, and I was always behind.

Dr. Don't you realize that you are in a strange condition? Tell us how long you have been dead.

Sp. Dead! Why is that woman with me all the time? (Patient.) She always gets fire. She gets the worst kind of things. She gets up on something, puts something over her head, and then fire comes! (When Mrs. Burton seated herself upon a platform beside the static machine, she covered her head with a woolen blanket to make the electricity more effective.)

Dr. Do you feel that you are in the right place?

Sp. Where shall I go?

Dr. To the spirit world.

Sp. What is that?

Dr. That is where people go, after passing out of their bodies, when they have understanding. Don't you realize that something strange has happened to you?

Sp. If you could get that blanket from being put on my head, and that fire, I should be all right. It seems that I was knocked to pieces. How in the world can anyone stand being shot at like that?

THIRTY YEARS AMONG THE DEAD

Dr. That was done to chase you out. Do you not feel free now? What have you been doing since you last had those shots"?

Sp. I am glad I was chased out, for I feel better now than I have for some time.

Dr. Do you realize that you are controlling my wife's body?

Sp. Thank God, I am not.

Dr. This body, which you are using, belongs to my wife.

Sp. Your wife, nothing!

Dr. Do you recognize the clothes you are wearing?

Sp. That's nothing to me.

Dr. Where did you get them?

Sp. I'm no thief! I am going to have you arrested for calling me a thief. The first police station I find, I shall swear out a warrant against you.

Dr. Maggie, what is the color of your hair?

Sp. Brown-dark brown.

Dr. (Touching psychic's hair.) This hair is not brown. These clothes belong to my wife.

Sp. I don't care whether they are my clothes or not; I never asked for them.

Dr. Tell us how long you have been dead.

Sp. I'm not dead. One time you say one thing, and another time you say another.

Dr. I mean, when did you lose your body?

Sp. I haven't lost my body; it's not in the grave.

Dr. Were you ever sick, and did you suddenly become better?

Sp. I was very sick, and when I got better, I was in a prison. I was moving around and some woman bothered me. There were lots of us, but they all got so scared of the fire that they left.

Dr. When did you come to Los Angeles?

Sp. I'm not in Los Angeles; I'm in Dallas, Texas. If I am in Los Angeles, how did I get here?

Dr. You must have come with a lady who has red hair. (Mrs. B., seated nearby.)

Sp. She had no right to bring me here.

Dr. She also came from Texas.

Sp. What became of the others?

Dr. They were brought to an understanding and went to the spirit world. That is where you should be. Why should you hover around that woman?

Sp. Hover around -nothing! I have been in a prison, but I could not help it. I did what I could to get out. Those people I saw said they would help me out, but they didn't. I made quite a disturbance, and they went away from me.

Dr. Probably they brought you here.

Sp. All I see is people sitting around.

Mrs. B. Did you come out here with me? What do you want to bother me for?

Sp. I have nothing to do with you. Oh! you're the one that kept me in the prison!

Mrs. B. What was the name of that girl friend of yours You used to be with? (Referring to another spirit that had been troubling Mrs. B)

Sp. Where? In Texas?

Mrs. B. Yes.

Sp. Her name was Mary, and there was another one, Carrie.

Mrs. B. Did Carrie come with you?

Sp. Yes, of course. Say, what did you keep me closed up for? Why didn't you let me out?

Mrs. B. I kept telling you to get out.

Sp. I know you did, but you didn't open the door so I could go.

Dr. All you had to do was to think yourself free from that lady.

Sp. I can't think myself free.

Dr. Intelligent spirits can think themselves anywhere; it is only ignorant spirits who cannot.

Sp. (To Mrs. B.) Say, what did you keep me around you for?

Dr. You were an uninvited guest.

Mrs. B. I'm glad to get rid of you.

Sp. I'm glad too. I'm mighty glad to get out of that prison. Why didn't you let me out? I knocked and knocked, but you kept me there. (To Dr. W.) You gave me those fire things, then I got out, and I'm glad of it.

Dr. Did you get out after the last treatment?

Sp. You call that a "treatment"?

Dr. If you got out of that lady, I should call it a good treatment.

Sp. You don't know how I suffered from that fire, especially the shooting. You are the one that gave me that fire, and I don't like you!

Dr. I had to give the lady those treatments to get you out.

Sp. You think that devil-machine is a little god. You want me to go -where?

Dr. To the spirit world.

Sp. Where is that?

Dr. A place where the discarnated spirits go to get understanding. You have lost your physical body but do not understand it, and you have been bothering that lady. (Mrs. B.)

Mrs. B. When once I get you and the others out, I shall keep the door closed, and closed so tight that none of you can get in.

Dr. Think yourself free and you will not be in a prison. Mortals cannot travel by thought, but spirits can. You are invisible to us. You are temporarily using the body of another; this body, belongs to my wife.

Sp. You have told me that before.

Dr. Can't you see you are in a strange condition?

Mrs. B. Do you know Maggie Mackin? (Another spirit whose presence Mrs. B. had clairaudiently been aware of.)

Sp. Yes, and I know Mary too.

Dr. How old were you when you passed out of your body? Can you recall something of your past?

Sp. I remember being out riding and the horses ran away, then everything became dark, and since then I do not seem to remember much.

Dr. Do you know what year it is?

Sp. I don't have to answer you. Are you a lawyer or a judge? Who are you?

Dr. I'm a "fireman." Can you realize that it is 1920?

Sp. It doesn't bother me that much. (Snapping fingers.) I don't care.

Dr. I thought you were anxious to get out of your trouble.

Sp. I wanted to get out of that prison, and now I feel better than I have for years.

Mrs. B. You ought to thank Doctor for getting you out.

Sp. That man ought to be arrested for giving those shots. It made you feel like your

head was going to the dickens.

Dr. Can you see any of your friends here?

Sp. There are two Indians, one is a big fellow, and one is a girl, and there is a lady with curly hair and light blue eyes. (Spirits.)

Dr. Does the Indian girl answer to the name of "Silver Star"? (One of Mrs. Wickland's guides.)

Sp. Yes.

Dr. These spirits will help you to progress in the spirit life.

Sp. There's one thing sure, I'm going to Heaven, and not to the other place. I went to church and was a good woman.

Dr. Those persons whom you see are spirits like yourself. We do not see them.

Sp. They are there, just the same. They say if I will go along with them, they will show me a nice home. That would be nice, for I haven't had a home for a long time. Am I going to have that fire any more? I won't go to that woman with the red hair any more, either, and I thank God for that.

Dr. Now think yourself free and go with these friends.

Sp. All right, I will go. Goodbye!

When Mrs. Burton first came to us she could not follow any occupation, but after the obsessing spirits were removed she was able to take a clerical position in a large commercial house.

Awaiting Spirit Contact

THIRTY YEARS AMONG THE DEAD

Chapter IV

Earth Sphere Conditions and the Magnetic Aura

Unenlightened spirits often wander aimlessly for many years in the earth sphere, their lack of knowledge of a higher spirit world, which is attained only through understanding, keeping them in a dreary condition of confusion, monotony and suffering; many remain in the scenes of their earth lives, continuing their former activities, while others fall into a state of heavy sleep from which they are with difficulty aroused.

A spirit who was still following his old occupation without any knowledge of his transition controlled Mrs. Wickland at one of our circles in Chicago.

"Why are you sitting in the dark?" he asked. (We were at that time experimenting with dark circles.)

"I am Hesselroth, from the drug store," he said.

Mr. Hesselroth, the Swedish proprietor of a Chicago drug store, had died the year before in a hospital, but we knew nothing of this man, his death, or his circumstances; however, on this evening one of his friends, Mr. Eckholm, was in our circle.

The spirit was not aware of his death, claiming that he was still attending to his drug store. His friend in the circle said he had been informed that the drug store had been sold to the clerk, and so stated to the spirit, but this the latter emphatically denied, saying: "Abrahamson only manages it for me."

The spirit told of a robbery which had occurred in his house recently, and described the three burglars. He said he had been frightened when they entered, but gaining courage, had gone for his revolver only to find that he was not able to pick it up. He had then struck at one of the burglars, but his hand had gone "right through the fellow," and he could not understand why he could do nothing at all.

After his condition was explained to him he saw many spirit friends appear, who welcomed him to his new home in the spirit world. Later investigation verified the statement made by the spirit that the drug store had not been sold and also the fact that the house had been burglarized.

It could not be held that the subconscious mind of the psychic played any part in this case, nor could the theory of auto-suggestion be maintained, for Mr. Hesselroth was entirely unknown to every one in the room with the exception of his friend, Mr. Eckholm, and this friend held the opposite idea regarding the sale of the store.

Many years later this spirit returned to us in California, speaking again through Mrs.

THIRTY YEARS AMONG THE DEAD

Wickland.

EXPERIENCE, SEPTEMBER 29, 1920

Spirit: MR. HESSELROTH

Spirit: I have come in to say just a few words, for I have been helped out of darkness, and have become a helper in the Band of Mercy.

Doctor Who are you, friend?

Sp. I am one of the helpers here. I come around sometimes, and I came tonight to say a few words to you. I was once in a very dark condition, but now I am one of your Band. I thought you might like to know. If it had not been for you, I would probably still be in the dark. Many years have passed. I have quite an understanding of life now, through you, and through this little circle of the Band of Mercy. It was not here, it was in Chicago that I was helped.

I am very much pleased to be here with you tonight. I should like to give you my name, but I seem to have forgotten it, because I have not heard it for so long. It will come to me, and then I will give it.

Do you remember an old gentleman you used to know -Mr. Eckholm? He was not so very old either. He was a very dear friend of mine, and through him I came to see you.

Dr. At some meeting in Chicago?

Sp. Yes. I had a drug store in Chicago. My name is Hesselroth! I could not think of my name for a moment. I am one of your helpers here. Mr. Eckholm is with me, and he also does all he can. He is very happy to help with your work here. He was heart and soul with it during his earth life. I also feel that I have to do all I can to help, because if you had not helped me, I should have been in that drug store yet, selling medicine.

For a whole year after I passed out, I attended to the business as I did when on earth, only I did not feel that I was sick any more. I took sick in the store, and was sent to the hospital, and I passed out in the hospital. They took my body to the undertakers, not to my home.

You know, it says in the Bible: "Where your treasure is there will your heart be also." When I woke up from the sleep of death, I thought of my store, and there I found myself. I saw that everything was going on all right, but it seemed so strange that I could not talk to any of my customers. I thought that during my sickness I had lost my faculty of speech, so I did not think much about it.

I attended to business, and I impressed my clerk to do things I wanted done. I was running the store and the clerk was managing it for me. I did not realize that I was dead until I came to this gentleman (Dr. W.) in his little circle.

When burglars got into my home I thought of the revolver that I always kept in a drawer. I went there, and tried and tried to get it, but my hand went through everything. Then I thought there must be something the matter with me.

I commenced to see things. I saw my spirit father and mother. Then I thought I must be a little out of my head. So I thought I had better go up to see my friend, Eckholm. I always thought he was just a little off, because he believed in Spiritualism. I wanted to see Eckholm to ask him if ghosts could come back -and there I was a ghost myself!

THIRTY YEARS AMONG THE DEAD

Then I came to this circle and I found I could talk, and after a while the door opened, opened to that beautiful land beyond. I wish you could see the reception I had. My relatives and friends all opened their arms to me, and said: "Welcome to our home in spirit! Welcome to that everlasting life!

Welcome to an understanding of God!"

Such a reception cannot be described until you see it for yourselves and are with us. That is happiness; it is "Heaven."

I will not take any more of your time, but I am glad that I could come and talk tonight. It was about fifteen years ago that I first came here. Eckholm says he feels proud of this work, and he sends love to all of you here.

Now, Good Night!

Pathos and tragedy are often the grim accompaniment of the sufferings of earthbound spirits. The spirit of the following narrative was taken from a patient who was subject to doleful spells of crying and afflicted with intense head pains, all of which ceased after the spirit was removed.

EXPERIENCE, JANUARY 15, 1918

Spirit: MINNIE DAY Patient: MRS. L. W

Psychic: MRS. WICKLAND

Spirit (Crying piteously) Oh, my head hurts so badly! I don't like those needles (electrical treatments given patient), they hurt me so. My head hurts! I am lost, I don't know where I am at. There were thousands and thousands of needles; I had to cry.

Doctor Where do you live?

Sp. I don't know,

Dr. Where did your parents live?

Sp. I don't know.

Dr. Aren't you a little child?

Sp. I am only little, I am Minnie Day.

Dr. Where did you live? How old are you?

Sp. I don't know. Ask Ma.

Dr. Don't you know what city you lived in?

Sp. In St. Louis. Oh! my father is coming! He hit me on the head! And there's Willie.

Dr. Who is Willie?

Sp. He's my brother. Here's my father, and I'm afraid! He says to come with him. Oh, Ma, my head hurts! My Ma says for me to go with her 'cause she has a new home for me and Willie.

Dr. You will go to her home in the spirit world.

Sp. What is the spirit world? What does that mean?

Dr. That is the invisible world around the earth. Do you know that you are dead?

THIRTY YEARS AMONG THE DEAD

Sp. What do you mean?

Dr. I mean that you have lost your physical body. What have you been doing recently?

Sp. I have been running all over trying to find somebody. Mama died a long time ago when I was a little girl. After Ma died Papa was so mean to me and Willie, and he hit me so many times. I feel so bad, and my head hurts. I have been to so many places and my Ma is dead, and I don't know where to go.

Dr. You were in such mental distress that you did not realize your condition. You have lost your physical body and your friends would call you dead.

Sp. Did I die? Sometimes I feel as if I were in a box. We were a big crowd (spirits obsessing the patient) and they Pushed and pushed, and there was one big man and he was so mean to us. He chased us one way, then another, but one day we lost him. (This tormenting spirit had been attracted from the patient two days before.5) I felt so glad he was lost and I thought I could be quiet, but I got all those needles.

Dr. You were influencing a lady and making her cry.

Sp. What do you mean?

Dr. You are a spirit, and were in the aura of that lady. When she had an electrical treatment you felt it and left her. You are using my wife's body now. Look at your hands; do they belong to you?

Sp. Oh, look! I have a ring! But that is not mine, and I have not stolen it. (Excitedly) Take it away! I didn't steal that ring!

Dr. This is not your body, and that is not your ring. It is very likely that you died when your head was hurt. The spirit lives after the body dies.

Sp. But I have been alive.

Dr. You were living, but without a physical body, and came in touch with a sensitive, a lady, who is now in the other house. She acts just as you do, and complains of her head hurting in the same place yours hurts you. She has been acting like an insane person, but it is all due to spirit influence.

Sp. The man was so mean that we had with us, but now he is lost, and we are so glad. We were all seared of him, but we could not run away from him. He was awful mean; he bit and scratched and would fight.

Dr. He was very obstinate. He was controlling this body a short time ago, just as you are now. We have circles like this where spirits may come for help.

Sp. Spirits? I don't know anything about them. My head hurts me.

Dr. The body you are using belongs to my wife, and she has no pain in her head.

Sp. Those needles hurt me so much.

Dr. When the lady had a treatment today you evidently were able to get away and are now allowed to control this body So that we can help you. A short time ago you said that your father and mother were here; are they here now?

Sp. Don't you see Mama? She's standing right there.

THIRTY YEARS AMONG THE DEAD

Dr. Wouldn't you like to go with your mother?

Sp. But she's dead.

Dr. You are "dead" also. There is no "death" really. We only lose our physical bodies. Spirit is invisible.

Sp. Oh, take me away! Take me away! My father is coming, and I'm afraid! He'll strike me again! Take me away!

Dr. Your father probably comes for forgiveness. You understand, he cannot progress in the spirit world until you forgive him. Ask him what he has to say to you.

Sp. He doesn't say anything; he's crying. He comes up to Mama now.

Dr. Doesn't he look sorry?

Sp. He says he is so sorry for what he did. The child spirit was removed and the distressed father took control of the psychic. Crying in anguish he fell on his knees, with his arms outstretched.

Spirit: William Day.

Spirit Forgive me! Forgive me! I didn't know what I was doing. I didn't mean to kill you, Minnie. I was very nervous and the children made such a noise. I was so sad because my wife had died. Give me a chance! Just give me one more chance! I, too, have suffered. If I had only lived! I have been in the dark so long and cannot be helped, and I cannot come near my child, she is so afraid of me. I have tried to reach her to ask for forgiveness, but she is so scared when I come near her that I cannot reach her.

Don't any of you ever strike a child, else you will suffer for years and years. I did not mean to hurt her; I loved her, but I killed her. If there is a God, lift this trouble and sorrow away from me! Give me some light and comfort, in my suffering! I cannot rest I have no peace. I can only see my work that I did in anger. Try to control yourself if you get angry, else you, will suffer as I have. God help me! Oh, God! Give me one more chance -just one!

Dr. Do you realize that you are dead?

Sp. No; I ran away when I killed my child. Somebody got after me and ran very hard, then something hit me in the neck, and I fell down. (Evidently killed.) I got right up and ran, and I have been running so long it seems years. Many times I have seen my wife, accusing me for killing my child. I did kill her, God help me! I have tried to find just a little comfort and light.

Dr. You cannot find light until you have understanding.

Sp. God give me light and understanding! All I see is that poor child's head, split open where I struck her. I tried to ask Minnie for forgiveness, but she shrank from me and I could not get near her, and there was my wife, always accusing me for what I had done.

Dr. She will not accuse you any more.

Sp. Will she forgive me?

Dr. Yes. What is your name?

Sp. William Day.

THIRTY YEARS AMONG THE DEAD

Dr. Can you recall what year it is?

Sp. My brain is in such a turmoil. I have been running and running for so long, trying to get away from that crowd of people that were after me. Everybody I saw, I ran from, knowing that they too would accuse me for killing Minnie. At nights my wife has stood by me accusing me, and then there was the child, with her head all split open, and the blood pouring out. I have had hell. It could not be worse. Is there no help for me? I prayed and prayed, but it did no good.

Dr. Do you know that you are in California?

Sp. California? When did I get here? Did I run all the way from St. Louis to California?

Dr. Do you understand that you are a spirit controlling the body of a mortal?

Sp. Do you mean that I am dead?

Dr. You have lost your physical body.

Sp. Won't I have to stay in the grave until the dead rise?

Dr. You are here now; how did you get out of the grave?

Sp. I have had no rest for I don't know how long.

Dr. There is no such thing as "death." When you pass out of your physical body you lose your five physical sense organs, and unless you have understanding of the spirit life, you are in the dark, and can only see when coming in touch with some mortal.

Sp. The people are hounding me until I am tired out.

Dr. Now you must try to become reconciled with your wife and child.

Sp. Do you think they will ever forgive me? Please, forgive me, wife! I was not worthy of you. You were an angel and I was such a brute. Will you please forgive me? If you will only give me just one chance, I will try so hard. I have suffered so much. Carrie, Carrie! Is it really true that you will forgive me? Is it true? You were such a patient woman and tried so hard to help me, but I was no good. I loved my children, but I had such a bad temper. I really killed my wife by letting her sew just to keep the family together. I made good money, but there were always men around, telling me to come with them, and I did not know anything until my wages were all gone, and I went home feeling like a devil.

Dr. Perhaps the trouble was not all yours, for you might have been obsessed. When you leave here with your wife, you will find a wonderful spirit world.

Sp. I am not worthy to go with my wife, but I will try to do good. I don't want you to go away from me any more, Carrie! (Crying) Minnie, can you forgive your Papa? My dear child, I killed you, but I did not mean to. Forgive your Papa. Will I wake up after a while and find myself in darkness again? Am I asleep or dreaming? Minnie, don't go away from Papa! Please, forgive me!

Dr. You are neither asleep nor dreaming, but are beginning to realize your condition.

Sp. Did they kill me when they hit me in my neck and head? They shot me.

Dr. We can't say certainly, but they probably did.

Sp. If I can just have one more chance I will do my level best to keep my family together.

Dr. There is something else you can do, also, after you acquire understanding -it will be your duty to help poor, unfortunate spirits who are obsessing mortals, making devils of some of them. When you had your own body you may have been obsessed by some spirits.

Sp. I did not care for drink; I hated the very sight of it. But when once I got just a smell of it, something took hold of me and made me feel like a devil and I could not resist it. I could not do anything with myself. God help me and give me just a little comfort.

Dr. When you leave here you will be reunited with your family.

Sp. Are you sure about that?

Dr. Positive; but you must do as the advanced spirits instruct you.

Sp. If there is anything I can do to help you, I will do it, because you have reunited me with my family. I came home drunk and you don't know how I felt when I realized that my wife was dying. I was so drunk that I did not fully realize things until the next morning when I woke up, and there was my wife -dead! I could not understand it. What was I to do? What could I do with the children? My wife dead! My wife and Minnie say they will both forgive me, and now I have my wife and two children, and I am going to start all over again. God bless you all for what you have done for me and my family.

The confusion and mental suffering existing on the earth plane is vividly portrayed by the spirits who are brought to our circle for help.

EXPERIENCE, MARCH 9, 1921

Spirit: MR. MALLORY Psychic: MRS. WICKLAND

The controlling spirit came in while we were singing "That Beautiful Shore" and laughed uproariously.

Doctor: Have you found the "Beautiful Shore"? Tell us what you know about it.

Spirit: It's all humbug.

Dr. Is that so?

Sp. Yes. (Laughing hilariously.) It's silly to believe in such a thing.

Dr. You are on the other side of life; tell us something about it. Have you found nothing? If you do not believe in a hereafter, tell us why. Explain yourself. If you are a skeptic, tell us your belief.

Sp. Belief? Gosh! (Laughing.)

Dr. Tell us what you are laughing about.

Sp. You might just as well laugh as cry; one is just the same as the other. You were singing "That Beautiful Shore," and while you are singing that, you know you are lying.

Dr. Do you imply that life does not mean anything at all?

Sp. It most certainly does not. There is nothing in it. It is just a lie. The whole thing is nothing but a pack of lies -both life and religion -the whole humbug, life, religion and everything connected with it.

Dr. Have you tried to understand your own life -the mystery of it?

Sp. My own life? Humbug, nothing but humbug! (Laughing.)

Dr. How do you know it is humbug? You are laughing at your own ignorance.

Sp. I might just as well laugh as cry, one is no worse or better than the other. It is all lies - damned lies. I had my troubles.

Dr. Where? Over there, or here?

Sp. Everywhere! (Laughing.)

Dr. Are you happy?

Sp. Happy? Such nonsense. There is no such thing, there never was, and there never will be.

Dr. Do you really know anything about it? Did you seek for truth when you had your own body?

Sp. I prayed to God and all that nonsense. Gosh!

Dr. And you found it all a humbug. What has that to do with the actual facts of life?

Sp. Once I tried to be some one. Then the thought came to me that everything was humbug, humbug, nothing but humbug. As a man, you know what I mean. You are talking to a man and you know all about it.

Dr. You are invisible to us. Have you ever seen intelligence?

Sp. What kind of talk is that? I don't believe in nonsense any more. You can have faith, and believe that you can walk on water, but you fall through, just the same. I said, "I have faith that I can walk on water," but I fell through.

Dr. Because you left reason out.

Sp. Reason? You can't walk on water with reason.

Dr. It was not intended that we should walk on water. Water is for drinking and bathing.

Sp. Why are you holding my hands?

Dr. I am holding my wife's hands.

Sp. You don't know what you are talking about. Do you believe that?

Dr. I know that I am holding my wife's hands.

Sp. I used to have faith like that.

Dr. How did you happen to lose faith?

Sp. It is all humbug.

Dr. Life is the beginning of knowledge.

Sp. I haven't had any knowledge yet.

Dr. You will have before you leave here.

Sp. I had faith, and I believed, and then what?

Dr. What next?

Sp. Yes -what next? I worked like a slave for a "minister of God." I do not work for him now;

that was some time ago. I went away from there. He cursed me, and I had my cares and troubles. I swore to God that there is no such thing as God if he could be so mean as to call such a man his "minister." And I lost faith.

Dr. What has that to do with the facts of life and the hereafter?

Sp. When you die you are dead.

Dr. Then why didn't you stay dead when you died?

Sp. Stay dead? I haven't died yet.

Dr. You "died" as far as your body is concerned.

Sp. I have been running away from those hypocrites. In the first place, they took all the money I made. If there is a God, then, for God's sake, why does he always want money? They always say you must have faith; have faith and pay your money to the church, and you should work for God. My work was hard. I worked from six o'clock every morning until late every night -all for God. I worked for God, and often I did not get enough so that I could get along.

Dr. Tell us where you came from.

Sp. All I want is my freedom.

Dr. Won't you tell us where you came from?

Sp. Look at all those devils down there? (Invisibles.) Hear how they curse and laugh. They say: "I know you! I know you!" Look at that one sitting over there. Look at them all. Hear them laugh. They say I should tell you that they want you to pray for them, for they are in darkness.

Dr. We want to help them to a better understanding.

Sp. Oh, listen to them cursing!

Dr. You must show them charity. You do not seem to know what charity is.

Sp. God! Look at that man! They say when you give charity they don't like it.

Dr. I do not mean money. Give them a chance to help themselves. Do you know what year it is now?

Sp. I don't care. I don't care if it is a hundred years from now. I've lost faith in God, humanity and everything and everybody. I used to have faith. Then a "servant of God" took my wife and children away from me, and yet I worked for God from six in the morning to twelve at night.

Dr. But you did not add understanding to your faith.

Sp. I had faith in the Holy Ghost and the Spirit.

Dr. Why did you not add understanding to your faith?

Sp. I had faith enough to move mountains. We were taught to just have faith in the Holy Spirit. Just look at them all, (spirits) sitting there. Look at that one! Here you, Calango! He and I have fights, once in a while, but I always get the best of him. I can talk better now than I have done for a long time. Here, you, Calango, sitting there like a fool! They told me to go in there, so I came in. I think you were afraid of me at first, but I came in just the same.

Dr. How did you come in?

Sp. In here? How did I come in? I don't know.

Dr. Where did you get that hand? (Touching Mrs. Wickland's hand.)

Sp. That hand? I suppose it is mine. It doesn't belong to any body else. Here Calango, you sit here. Now I can talk to you fellows.

Dr. Now stop talking.

Sp. Do you think you are the boss here?

Dr. Yes.

Sp. I have no faith in you, nor any one else.

Dr. I want you to understand that you have lost your physical body. You are controlling my wife's body, yet you are invisible to us. You talk about those men sitting there, -we cannot see them. We are in mortal bodies, but you have lost your physical body.

Sp. Can't you see me?

Dr. We cannot see spirits. You are controlling my wife's body. Intelligent spirits have brought you here.

Sp. You asked me to come. All those in darkness came in too. You invited us. (During a concentration for all earthbound spirits.)

Dr. I said you should listen to intelligent spirits around you who would help you. You are all in darkness.

Sp. Yes, but you invited us in and here we are. I want to tell you, if you don't want us, I won't talk.

Dr. You were invited by intelligent spirits to come here and allowed to control my wife's body, so that we could help you understand that you no longer have a mortal body. The church has not the right understanding of God. You found humbug in the church, so you think everything is humbug. You lost your body probably a long time ago. My wife is a psychic sensitive and you are temporarily controlling her body. Look about; perhaps you can see some one you know.

Sp. I can see Calango.

Dr. You must realize that life means something.

Sp. I have had faith, and enough of it too. I sacrificed my money and my wife, and you see where I am.

Dr. What has that to do with the facts of life? Did you ever study the wonders of Nature?

Sp. I do not believe in God, there is no such thing.

Dr. God has nothing to do with humbug. Did you understand the Bible at all? The Bible says: "God is Love." Humbuggery has nothing to do with universal life. We want to help you understand better things.

Sp. No one ever helps me.

Dr. Do you know you are in Los Angeles, California?

Sp. No.

THIRTY YEARS AMONG THE DEAD

Dr. Try to understand what the real life means; it means something you do not know of. Did you ever make a flower? Can you make grass grow, or suspend life? Did you ever study vegetation?

Sp. That's God's Nature.

Dr. Can ignorance produce intelligence? Did you ever study the marvelous things of God? Break an egg, and you do not find life in it. Take another egg, keep it warm for twenty-one days and a chicken comes out of it.

Sp. That's natural.

Dr. What produces the chicken? We must add knowledge to our faith. The Bible says: "God is spirit: and they that worship him must worship him in spirit and in truth." You do not find that in the churches. They only have blind faith.

Sp. I sure had faith.

Dr. The Bible says: "Know the truth and the truth shall make you free." Although the Bible is not a "Holy Book" it contains some wonderful truths.

Sp. I don't believe it. (Laughing.)

Dr. You're laughing at your own ignorance. My wife allows ignorant spirits to control her body so that we can bring them to an understanding of their condition. She wants you to know that life exists on the other side. We do not know where you came from, but we allow you to control my wife's body. Where was your home?

Sp. My home? That was in Canada, near Montreal.

Dr. I was there in 1881. Are you a French-Canadian?

Sp. My great grandfather was.

Dr. Do you remember your name?

Sp. I can't remember things.

Dr. Now we want you to understand things.

Sp. I was a slave.

Dr. That is all in the past.

Sp. I only see the past and it makes me crazy. Instead of crying as many do, I thought I would laugh at everything. Whenever I got so mad I did not know what to do with myself, I started to laugh. I guess I felt a little better for laughing instead of crying. I had my heart sorrows; they took my wife, my home went, my children went. My wife was a very pretty girl. One day I came home from my work, and I had worked very hard. My wife and children were gone.

But after a while that "minister of God" did not want my wife any more; then she commenced to go back on him, but by that time I had gone down. I said, no church for mine; that if one of "God's ministers" can break up my home and take my wife and children, then there is no God. I went clear down to hell for that fellow. I went down and down, but even down there in the gutter you find friendship and love for each other.

If you are down, they, too, are down with you. All the other people look down on you, but, believe me, these others are true friends. They will help you and divide whatever they have with you. No matter how down you are, if you haven't a cent, you will find they will help you.

One day -I will never forget what I saw, never forget! God! -if there is a God -why in the name of the devil does he allow such things? One day I met my wife. Where was she? She had gone down to the gutter. I found her in one of those fine houses you hear about, where that filthy devil had put her when he was through with her. I looked at her, and she looked at me.

"You here!" I said.

And she said: "You here!"

"Why are you here?" I asked.

"What are you here for?" she asked.

I said: "I came here, probably of my own free will."

She said she had been put there by that glorious "minister of God" to hide his own shame. To hide his own dirty work and not have people ask her questions, he put her in a fast house and let her stay there and she did not care for anything. We were both down, all because of that devil.

I have never gone to church since. I cursed that man and all religious cranks. My wife wouldn't have anything to do with me, and I wouldn't have her. She was lying there, full of disease. There is not an animal living that goes so low as a woman when she goes to the dogs. Can any one believe in a God that would let a woman like my wife suffer as she did through no fault of her own? Why should such things exist?

Dr. Why didn't you use the reason God gave you?

Sp. There are hundreds of people living low down, and they don't care where they go.

Dr. Now you are going to care. Let me talk now. You went to church and adopted a blind faith, that you admit.

Sp. I wanted to be a good man.

Dr. Didn't you feel a desire for something higher? You merely had faith and did not add understanding. God gave you sense, he gave you intelligent reasoning faculties, but you adopted a blind faith and clung to it. That was not God's fault. To our faith we must add knowledge and that will make us free. God did not write the Bible.

Sp. It is a Holy Book. That is what they say.

Dr. It was written by man. Did you ever analyze the marvels of the human mind? I am talking of facts now. Did you ever realize how wonderful the human body is, or how the invisible mind is able to control the material body? Did you ever see the wonders of Nature?

Sp. All that has nothing to do with my misery.

Dr. If you had used your own faculties you would understand that love and mind are invisible.

Sp. Didn't that devil love my wife?

Dr. That was not love. You did not use your faculties. You joined the church in blind faith, without using your reason. We do not see you; you are invisible to us and are using my wife's body temporarily. We are interested in the condition of the so-called dead and many of them are brought here to be enlightened. You have been brought here by intelligent spirits so that you can learn to understand your true condition. You have an opportunity to progress in the spirit world, but you must forget your hatred. You lost your physical body. Do you know what year it is? It is 1921, and you are in California.

Sp. How did I get here? I never was in California.

Dr. How does spirit travel? You spoke of other people here, we do not see them. We do not see you. You are using my wife's organism. Can't you see how wonderful life is?

Sp. Why aren't we taught those things?

Dr. Because "the truth is not in the people." You will have to judge for yourself between the facts of life and the creed of the church. Churches are man-made things; God is Spirit, and you must worship him in spirit and in truth -in spirit and in truth. We have aspirations for a higher life, but that does not give us knowledge. God is Spirit, invisible Intelligence. He manifests himself in all the wonders of the Universe.

Sp. All these people here (invisibles) have had disappointments as I have, but all have different stories. We sit and talk to each other from time to time, all telling of the past. All have their troubles.

Dr. God has nothing whatever to do with that. The Universe is God's Temple and our souls are His Manifestations. Think of the marvelous things in the Universe. You speak of your friends being here, yet we cannot see them.

Sp. They want to know if you can help them all from their troubles.

Dr. Yes, we can. Tell them that life means something. Look around and you may see intelligent spirits who will help you.

Sp. There are six of us and we have all had the same trouble and disappointment, but each has a different story.

Dr. Tell them that none of you need be in the condition you are in.

Sp. There's one group called "The Laughing Fools"; there's another called "The Cursing Fools"; there's another called "The Swearing Fools"; there's another called "The Singing Fools." They sing and pray from morning until night. You get sick and tired of hearing them.

Dr. The Bible says: "As a man thinketh in his heart, so is he." Religious fanatics are the worst. They have not added understanding to their blind faith. We all have faculties but do not use them. Is that God's fault?

Sp. I have not worked for a long time. Sometimes none of us have any food. We have done without it so long that now we do not seem to need it.

Dr. The spirit does not need food.

Sp. We are starving, starving.

Dr. Spiritually starving.

Sp. We are all starving for something, but we don't know what it is. We are all anxious to know. We all say that our souls cry out for something, but we don't know what it is. None of us want to pray. For my part I cannot. I had faith and prayed, but here I am, in all this trouble.

Dr. God has given each one of you reasoning faculties.

Sp. Would you help us all? They all say they are hungry for happiness. All we can see is our past, and we all want something higher. All I can see is my wife as I saw her last down, down.

Dr. So far as your wife is concerned, it was only her body that was diseased, not her spirit.

Sp. When we saw each other we both cried.

Dr. After you have understanding, you can all do a great work in helping others. Listen to the invisible friends who are around you. All be quiet a moment, and your eyes will open to undreamed of things.

Sp. Do you think my wife can get help? She was as pure as a lily. I loved her.

Dr. You can love her still. We must all try to find ourselves. As we grow out of our ignorance we see the higher things of existence, both here and in the spirit life. If we were born into a perfect condition, we would not appreciate it. You have seen "hell," and when you progress you will see "heaven' " You will find a beautiful condition and you will appreciate it. You will then be enthusiastic helpers, eager to serve others. You must all open your hearts for higher things.

Sp. I love my wife. (To the invisibles.) No, boys, don't go yet; wait a little while longer.

Dr. The Bible says: "Ask, and it shall be given you; seek, and ye shall find; knock, and it shall be opened unto you."

Sp. (With heartfelt solemnity.) If there is a God, help me! Help my poor wife! We loved each other. Oh, God! Help us all! We are starving for something.

Dr. His messengers will help you. You will see many who will gladly help you all.

Sp. God help us all!

Dr. If you will look around, you will see spirits who will help you.

Sp. There's my boy -my own little boy, Charlie! You are my boy! You died many years ago, but you are my boy Charlie. Have you come to help your old Dad, my boy? Your poor Dad has suffered hell, my boy. Help your mother, boy, help your mother, poor mother! (Suddenly amazed.) Why -that's my little boy, Charlie, but he's a man now! Charlie, my little boy, can you forgive your old Dad? I tried so hard to have faith and I tried to be good.

If there is a God, open my eyes to see! God help me! (Gazing at some vision, then speaking in a hushed voice.) Now we can all see the glory of God, and we will all go with Charlie. (Astonished.) You! Are you here also? Clara! Come to me, oh, Clara! forgive you. I forgive you, Clara. I know it was not your fault. It was that devil; he took you away from me. I love you and always have loved you. Come, Clara, come with us, and let us go with Charlie. He will probably forgive you.

Dr. What does he say?

Sp. He says: "Come with me to my spirit home, where all is lovely, where you will be happy. It was because of sorrow and suffering that you looked at life as you did."

Dr. Don't you realize there is something beautiful ahead of you?

Sp. Is it Heaven? Why, look there! There's my mother and sister Emma. Are you both here too? Can you forgive Clara and me? I thought you were in Heaven, mother, you were so good. You always loved me.

Dr. Do you realize now that there is something higher than your past?

Sp. Yes. Now I know there is a God. I do believe in God now, for I know His glory. I see and feel His glory.

Dr. After you have understanding you must help the others you were talking about.

Sp. They are all coming with me. I want them all to come, for I cannot leave them. You have helped all of us. Now, we will go; come on, boys. We had names for each other, but they were not our own. In our hatred, and because we laughed, we were called "The Laughing Fools." Most of our time was spent in talking over our past. Now we have all found God; we have found Him in His glory, in His happiness, in the spirit world. We do not need to believe, for we know. He will help us all. Mother, father and sister, all are here.

Come on now, boys. We all listened to what this man said, and you see where it brought us. Today I call you our savior, because you have saved us from darkness, and brought us to glory. You saved us all. Not only myself, but the others have opened their eyes to see the glory of God, and not a God of hatred and envy.

Dr. You can thank my wife, who allows her body to be used so that spirits may be helped.

Sp. I will never forget you. You have given me happiness that I have not known for years and years. You say it is 1921. Is that true? I thought it was 1882.

Dr. Can you tell us your name, friend?

Sp. My name? Yes, it's Mallory. They called me a Laughing Fool. We thank you all for your patience. I was full of hatred when I came, but that has all gone now. God bless you all. I have to call you my savior, because you have saved us from that dark condition and brought us to a beautiful place. Clara, you come too, for I love you dearly. You are well now.

Dr. You will now become useful spirits. Find God and forget the past.

Sp. The last time I saw Clara, she was very sick and was taking morphine all the time. Come to me, Clara, I forgive you. See, Charlie is with us. Can't we help Clara? She seems dazed.

Dr. She is probably still under the effects of the opiate. Your love will bring her to you.

Sp. I never could hate her, she was so pure. Clara, wake up! You are not dead. Forget the past, and live in the new life. Thank you all for bringing me happiness, and also for bringing God to me in my heart. I never properly understood Him before. I found Him in the glory of Nature too. Look at all those beautiful flowers! Is this Heaven?

Dr. It is the spirit world.

Sp. Now I'm always going to be with my loved ones in the spirit world. We will go. Goodbye.

A communication of a different type was received from the spirit of a young man, son of one of the members of our circle. The young man had passed over two months before, but having been unbiased and open-minded was readily enlightened by his spirit friends. In his short visit to our circle, he gave an interesting description of conditions as he observed them in both the earth sphere and the spirit world.

THIRTY YEARS AMONG THE DEAD

EXPERIENCE, APRIL 14, 1920

Spirit: W. Y. Psychic: MRS. WICKLAND.

Spirit: Well Dad, I'm here again. The spirit friends gave me the privilege of coming and talking first. Dad, it's queer that I should go so quickly, but my time had come. I am glad the door is not shut for me. I have seen many heartbroken spirits who go to their relatives and friends, and the door is closed in their faces. (Through skepticism and unconsciousness of the presence of spirits.)

It's hard for them. I have much to be thankful for, because Grandpa B. and Uncle C. stood right beside me when I woke up from the sleep of death. It was queer. It was like an electric shock going through my body.

Life is queer. If each one of you could see the experiences gone through by those who go into the sleep of death!

Dad, I had a little knowledge of the next life, not much, but a little, and it helped. could realize that the change of death had taken place. I recognized my relatives and friends.

Uncle F.6 says I should tell you that I was much better off than he was when he passed to the other side, and that now his work is to help the unfortunate ones who do not understand the real life.

Dad, wasn't it queer that I should wake up to the new birth of life on my earthly birthday? Now I have my spiritual birthday on the same day as my earthly birthday.

Dad, it's glorious! Tell E. so, and B. and mother; tell all of them that I am happy in the thought that I can come to them and that the door is not closed to me. Tell my little son that I am not dead; that I am not in the grave but am with him, and I will learn the laws governing so that I can guide him through life. Let him have an understanding that I am there with him and that I have more strength and power to help him than before.

Thank God that I also had understanding so that I did not come too close to my dear wife; otherwise, I would have gotten into her magnetic aura and might have caused trouble. My dear little wife, -I am glad that I did not make trouble for us both.

I have seen much of the work done among those who have passed out and do not realize it. They go home to their relatives and friends, and want to stay there rather than go on.

Dad, I'm so glad you could come here again, and I'm glad, so glad, that there is no wall between us.

Mr. Y. (Father of spirit.) I am glad too, that I had an opportunity of being here again.

Sp. I feel now that there is no parting. It is only that I have gone to another country, but I am with you all. I am with you when you are all together and talk about me. I do not feel that I have gone.

Tell mother and my dear little wife not to mourn for me, but to feel glad that I can be with them. It was very hard that we should have to part when everything looked so bright for us in our little home, but it was my time to go, and when our time comes to go from this earth life, we have to go. We do not go away, as people think we do; we are here with our loved ones, only our bodies are not visible.

THIRTY YEARS AMONG THE DEAD

I wish you could see how Uncle F. works in the dark earth sphere to help and to serve the unfortunate ones there, to prevent them from obsessing any one. He is so anxious to have everybody know the real truth on the other side, and it is a pity that so much dogma and creed are the stumbling blocks. The little time I have been gone I have learned so much.

I thank you, Dad, that you and mother did not force any strong dogma, or religion, or creed, upon my mind. I was free. Thank you for it.

Mr. Y. It's pretty hard, sometimes, to know exactly what to do regarding religion in bringing up children.

Sp. I wish all could have been as free as I was, then there would not be so much sorrow and doubt. Dad, I'm so glad I can come to you again. The other day, Uncle F., Uncle C. and I went to the earth sphere -not to our home, but to the condition that exists on the lower plane. That is more of a hell than anybody can describe. It's worse than an insane asylum, where one is crazy in one way, and another in another way. You can't imagine what a hell it is.

One has one creed, one another, and they are all in the dark. They are all hypnotized in their creeds and beliefs and you can not get any sense whatever into them. You have to put some object lesson before them to attract their attention. At times music will make them realize their condition. If you can attract their attention, you can sometimes reach the real spirit, but dogmas and creeds are so planted in their minds that they cannot see anything.

If you want to realize in part what the condition of the earth sphere is, go to the worst ward in an insane asylum, and you can then have some realization of the condition on the invisible side when they have no knowledge of the next life.

Imagine a spirit of that character coming in contact with a person's magnetic aura and acting through him, as is often the case. They call that person insane and send him to the insane asylum where there are a lot of other lunatics, both of earth and the spirit side of life. It is terrible to know that such a condition exists and that selfish creeds and dogmas are the cause of it all.

I have to thank you and mother again for not forcing any dogma on me; what little knowledge I had was the real truth of life.

Uncle C. took me, at another time, to different conditions. He said, "Come, we will go," and we went to some place in spirit life. We came to a place which I cannot describe. I can't describe my feelings, I can't describe the conditions, because the music was so sublime, so different from anything I have ever heard. I felt so light; I felt I was lifted up. Such people as were there! I cannot describe them.

Imagine, if you can, a place where there is the most beautiful music, where there is a grand orchestra of masters, all playing in one grand unit of music. Can you imagine what it would be?

I enjoyed it, -but oh I could not realize its full import, because I wanted you and my dear little wife to hear it. I could not enjoy it alone. I wanted to open the door to you all at home, so that you could all listen to it -then I should have felt satisfied.

I thought and thought, and an old gentleman came up to me and patted me on the shoulder, and said: "Young man, I receive your thought. Do not worry. Soon the time will come for which we are all working, when an instrument will be invented on earth, through which all who wish can hear the grand masters in the spirit world. Not yet, but in time."

Dad, my work is to learn to help others less fortunate than myself, and also to learn to be a help and not a detriment to my dear wife and little boy and to you all. I am learning my lessons, and after knowing them I will come to you.

Don't think I am not with you all, but think I am there, for I am, and in that way I can be much closer, especially when you have music, because music brings us much closer to those we love.

Goodbye, and tell my dear wife I send her best love.

With exquisite grace and courteous inquiry came the spirit of one, formerly a famous actress, whose friends had tried in vain to waken her from the "sleep of death."

EXPERIENCE, JULY 7, 1922

Spirit: LILLIAN R. Psychic: MRS. WICKLAND

Doctor: Good Evening, friend! Where have you come from?

Spirit: Somebody told me to come here, but I do not know what I should do. My condition is so strange that I cannot understand it. I do not realize where I am.

Dr. You are in Los Angeles, California.

Sp. No! There are many here who wanted me to come, but I cannot understand why. I do not know any of you here.

Dr. You were brought here to be helped.

Sp. I do not know that I need any help. Things look so confusing to me.

Dr. That is because you do not understand your condition. Where do you think you should be?

Sp. Where my home is.

Dr. What state did you live in?

Sp. Of course, most of the time I was in New York, but at times I was in London and other places.

Dr. Cannot you see any one you know, or the one who brought you here?

Sp. Oh! (Disturbed greatly by pain in limb.)

Dr. Were you in some accident? Were you traveling? What is the last thing you remember?

Sp. I was very sick; I had such pain.

Dr. Probably that was your last illness. Did you become well suddenly?

Sp. No, it seems to me that I have been sleeping, and in some way or another, I am just waking up. Everything looks so queer.

Dr. You do not understand your condition. You do not need to have that pain. If you say: "I will not have that pain," it will disappear. Will you do that?

Sp. Yes, but it seems very hard to say. You are a Christian Scientist, are you not? I looked into Christian Science, but I certainly could not say my pains were imagination.

Dr. You are in a different condition now. Do you ever see any of your friends around you?

THIRTY YEARS AMONG THE DEAD

Sp. Yes, I sometimes see many of my particular friends that have gone before, and then I think to myself that I have gone crazy. My friends are around me, and some one says:

"Wake up!" But I cannot see. I do not want to see them.

Dr. That is because you do not want to understand. Were you afraid of them when they were living?

Sp. No, I was not.

Dr. Then why should you be afraid of them when they have lost their mortal bodies?

Sp. I am afraid and very nervous, and I do not want them to come near me. Why don't my lovely friends come?

Dr. To your earthly friends you are dead, but to your spirit friends you are not dead.

Sp. I was sick, but I cannot remember that I died. I went to sleep but I cannot remember that I failed to wake up. Several of my friends just came and called me to go with them.

Dr. Do you know why they told you to wake up? To your spirit friends you are only sleeping.

Sp. Why do they call me?

Dr. To help you and make you understand.

Sp. I do not know you.

Dr. I am Dr. Wickland. Who brought you here?

Sp. Anna H. (an actress well known to the spirit during earth life) told me to come.

Dr. She spoke to us once as you are doing now.7

Sp. She came to me but I knew she was dead and gone.

Dr. She is not dead. We do not see you, we only hear you talk. You do not see me, you only see my body. Mind is invisible; there is no death.

Sp. So many people have come to me and want me to wake up, and start in my work

again.

Dr. If you do not mind telling us, we should like to know who you are.

Sp. Don't you know me? I was an actress. I was known as Lillian R. I am not dead. William Stead came to me, and also the late King Edward. I was his favorite actress. I cannot understand why I came here. They say I was brought here for you to awaken me.

Dr. We are interested in life's problems and in the question, "What becomes of the Dead."

Sp. I studied some, but only understood slightly the phenomena. I studied, but at the same time my life was so busy, so much taken up with others, and I was also trying to live the best I knew how. I am very tired and sleepy.

Dr. What was the nature of your sickness?

Sp. They told me so many different things until at last I do not know what it was. I had such dreadful pains down this way (from the knee down). I was unconscious for a time. I cannot remember things very clearly; in some way I seem to have lost my memory. I cannot recollect anything of the past. I feel different, as if I had nothing to look forward to in the future. I am not unhappy, but at the same time I am not happy.

Dr. We will explain matters to you. You do not need to worry.

Sp. My friends came and I would not have anything to do with them. They said, "Come along," but I said, "No, no, no! I am not ready yet. I do not want to go."

Dr. You had already gone, but did not understand it. Your friends came to help you, but you did not understand it. Do you know where you are now? This is my wife's body you are using. She is sleeping. You are not talking through your own body.

Sp. (Noticing another invisible, formerly a friend.) John J. A.8 is here.

Dr. This lady is a psychic. She is my wife and allows spirits to control her so that we can make them understand their condition. Mr. John J. A., Mr. Stead and Anna H. could not make you understand.

Sp. I was afraid of them.

Dr. This is a "Clearing House" for just such conditions as yours. You are a spirit and are controlling a mortal body. We on the mortal side can talk to you because we are in our mortal bodies. You have lost your physical body, but have a spiritual body. When you passed away you only went to sleep, and you are just now waking up. You awaken and find yourself in this twilight.

Sp. Someone seemed to give me an electric shock and I seemed to come to life, but still I am dazed. There is a room full of faces, people whom I have known in life, but who have passed on. They have been around me trying to talk to me, but I would not listen.

Dr. That was your mistake.

Sp. Does the spirit still live?

Dr. Certainly it does. We are mortals, but these others whom you see are spirits.

Sp. They are just as real as you are.

Dr. They are more real than we are, because they are free, and we are in a dream state.

Sp. I feel that my being well is just a dream and that I will wake up in pain.

Dr. When you leave here you will go with the others.

Sp. Do you mean I can go with them?

Dr. As soon as you cease to resist them.

Sp. Here comes one, then another, and they say they want me.

Dr. Don't you remember that Longfellow said:

"Life is real! Life is earnest!

And the grave is not its goal;

Dust thou art, to dust returnest,

Was not spoken of the soul."

Sp. What beautiful things I see! Are they not beautiful! This is not a dream.

Dr. They are showing you some of the things on the spirit side of life.

Sp. Just look at those beautiful homes on that hillside! Look at those lovely walks, beautiful lakes and hills, lovely flowers that bloom everywhere! Isn't it beautiful! Can I go there?

Dr. There is nothing to hinder you except your own unwillingness and resistance.

Sp. I was an actress in life, still in my heart I believed in a God. You know the church always looks down on actresses. I always liked to give the world the best there was in me. I wanted to show what we can do to help amuse people.

Dr. You can do the same thing now in your new life.

Sp. In a way, many would say that I was not a Christian. In my own way I believed in being good and doing good for others -that was my belief. At times I went to church, but at times I did not feel at home in that atmosphere. I always tried to do my best.

Dr. The reason you did not feel at home in church was because the spirit of truth was not there.

Sp. Look at the lights! Are they not beautiful! they are singing and vibrating into different shades and tunes. The colorings are wonderful. I will try to do there what I could not do here. I should, many times, have liked to give the world more than good and happy thoughts. I knew at times that life must have a greater purpose than is generally realized. I was true to myself, in my own heart. Such beautiful things I can see! Is that Heaven?

Dr. Yes, but not the Christian "Heaven." Not the "Heaven of Salvation," but the spirit world surrounding the earth world. Jesus taught the existence of spirits and a spirit world, and Paul says: "There is a natural body and there is a spiritual body . . . first that which is natural and afterward that which is spiritual."

Sp. Anna H. says she is different now from what she was when I knew her. She says I do not know her now. She is serving and helping the unfortunate ones. She says she wanted to do what she could to wake me up. May I ask what you are doing here?

Dr. This is an Institution for research and the obtaining of knowledge concerning what becomes of the dead. This is also a Spiritual Clearing House. This lady you are controlling is my wife; she is a psychic intermediary and you are allowed to use her body and brain to convince you of your present condition. You are using a body not your own. (Raising Mrs. Wickland's hand.) This is not your hand.

Sp. No, it is not. It is queer.

Dr. The queer part is the human ignorance on these points.

Sp. The church does not teach these things.

Dr. The church limits itself to faith alone, and does not desire to add the required knowledge regarding the natural continuation of the spirit after death. The Bible says that to our faith we must add knowledge and Jesus taught: "Know the truth and the truth shall make you free." If you had understood these truths you would have accepted the spirit friends who came to you when you awakened.

Sp. It is all so beautiful that I should like to go with them. They say that when I am stronger I shall finish my work over there. How will they take care of me? I am very weak.

Dr. You will not be so weak when you leave this body. "As a man thinketh in his heart, so is he." You will be received with love and taken to a beautiful home. You will be so overjoyed with your new condition that you will not have time to be weak.

Sp. Will I not go into a sleep again?

Dr. When you were sick and in great pain you were probably given opiates and they may have had a stupefying effect.

Sp. Thank you. Now they are calling me and I feel that I want to go. I feel such gratitude to you for helping me, and for being the means of my understanding, and also for helping me to reach my friends so that I may know how to go to them, instead of shutting the door against them and leaving myself in the dark.

I thank you all that I had the opportunity of being awakened to such a beautiful condition as I now see. I was only in the darkness of my own consciousness. They call me, and keep on calling me, and they all say they are glad to invite me to their home in the spirit world.

There is one thing they want me to say, but I do not know whether I am strong enough. One gentleman says: "I was King Edward in life, but I am an ordinary person now. wanted to wake you up, because I have been awakened from the life I led. My mother was a Queen, but she is a Queen no longer. She has to serve others more than she did when she was on earth.

"My mother knew of spirit phenomena and she also knew of spirit return, but she did not know what her duty was, and she was waited on all her life. She was never allowed to do anything or have any real responsibility. She serves here and there. Now I have to serve and help until I understand the real life."

This gentleman says that is the message he wished to send. He came to say this because you probably thought he was still a King. He is here only as a man. He wants to help you as the others are doing. He is not of noble or royal blood any more. All my friends have come to shake hands and they all seem to be one family. I want to say Good Night, but how will I go?

Dr. "Thought is the solver of Nature's problems." Think of your friends over there and you will be with them. You will have to fix your mind from here to there. Think, "I am actually there."

Sp. I certainly want to thank you for the opportunity of coming here and for awakening me so that I can be with my friends over there.

The organism of every human being generates a nervous force and magnetism which surrounds him with an atmosphere of vital emanations and psychic light known as the Magnetic Aura. This aura is visible as a light to earthbound spirits in their condition of darkness, and they may become attracted to persons peculiarly susceptible to their encroachment.

Such spirits are often unable to leave this psychic atmosphere and in the resulting state of confusion -("confusional psychosis"?) -although struggling for freedom, they find themselves living the life of the psychic with him, resenting his presence and bewildered by a sense of dual personality.

After a number of spirits had been taken from a patient who was very unmanageable at first, we had the following experience, which clearly shows the suffering that spirits may endure when enmeshed in the aura of a mortal.

THIRTY YEARS AMONG THE DEAD

EXPERIENCE, JANUARY 23, 1918

Spirit: EMILY JULIA STEVE Patient: MRS. L. W

Psychic: MRS. WICKLAND

Doctor: Tell us who you are. We are interested in all spirits who are in darkness. Tell us how long you have been dead.

Spirit I guess something happened to me.

Dr. Do you realize that you have passed out of your own body?

Sp. I don't want my hands held. I am a lady of means (an expression often used by the patient) and want to be shown the courtesies and respect due a lady.

Dr. Did they call you "Mrs." or "Miss"?

Sp. I am a lady of means, and I am not used to this kind of questioning. I just feel like giving you a piece of my mind.

Dr. What seems to be your trouble?

Sp. You, it seems, have such a way of giving me all kinds of strange things in my back, (static treatment of patient) and I cannot see why you should do so. You have also kept me in prison. It must have been you that put me in prison. Who are you, anyway?

Dr. I am a friend, and I want to talk to you.

Sp. In the first place, I don't know you, and in the second place I have nothing to talk to you about. Who are you? Tell me your name.

Dr. I am Dr. Wickland.

Sp. I really didn't mean to ask your name, for I'm not at all interested to know it.

Dr. Wouldn't you like to go to the spirit side of life?

Sp. I do not like to hear about such things. I am no spirit.

Dr. Look at your hands; do they belong to you?

Sp. You are the means of my having been kept in prison so long, and now you are trying to show me things that are not true, and so I will not listen to you.

Dr. How did you happen to come here?

Sp. I do not know myself. It is very curious. I seemed to be in prison and before I knew anything, I was here. I do not see how I came. There were a whole lot of us, and somehow I have been left alone. I have been in prison but I do not know what I have done.

Dr. Where were you, when you had those others with you? Where were you staying? (Referring to obsessing spirits in patient's aura.)

Sp. I was staying where I belonged. There were a lot of us, all bunched together, men and women. We had a home, but we could not get out of it. Sometimes we were in warm quarters. For a time I have been by myself and I have been in a dark place. Before I was in prison we could talk one at a time (control the patient) but now I am all alone. You have no right to put all those burning things on me.

THIRTY YEARS AMONG THE DEAD

Dr. That kind of electrical treatment is very good for earthbound spirits—ignorant ones.

Sp. Ignorant! How dare you talk like that to me? How dare you?

Dr. Don't you know that you have passed out of your mortal body? You have lost your physical body.

Sp. How do you know I have?

Dr. Because the body you are talking through is not your own. It is my wife's body.

Sp. I never saw you before you put those sharp things in me.

Dr. You were not using this body at that time.

Sp. What does it all mean?

Dr. It means that you have been using another person's body.

Sp. Well, that explains many things, in a way. Sometimes I felt that I did not belong where I was, then once in a while I felt I was myself again. There was one big old man, a big fool, but we had to do just as he said. (Another spirit obsessing patient, previously removed.) I did not feel like doing as he said, because I had all the money I wanted, so why should I bother with such a rascal? I felt I had to do what he said, and yet I could not see why I should. I was not in my own home, and yet I had to be there, and I never could understand why I could not get away. He kept several of us with him.

Dr. Did the electricity help you to get away?

Sp. Yes, it did, but it hurt like fury. It seems as if it tore the life out of me.

Dr. The electricity liberated you, just the same.

Sp. We could not get away from that man. We had to do as he said. He ran and ran all the time, (the patient often ran away) and we had to do the same. There was a little girl, and she cried all the time. (Obsessing spirit,10 previously dislodged from same patient.) At times I was free, and at times I was in such misery. Some times I felt I could float from one place to another.

Dr. At such times you were a free spirit.

Sp. Don't say that word. How I do hate it. I do not have any use for anything of that kind.

Dr. You do not recognize the fact that when you pass out of the mortal body, you do not die, but that you live; you then become a spirit.

Sp. You know I am not dead. Cannot you understand that I am talking to you, and that I can move my hands and arms?

Dr. My friend, while you are talking, we cannot see you. We can only see my wife. You are talking through my wife's body. This is Mrs. Wickland sitting here. What is your name?

Sp. I am Mrs. Emily Julia Steve. I was married, but my husband died some years ago.

Dr. Do you know that you are in California?

Sp. I have never been there. I went first to Chicago, and from there to St. Louis. (The patient had also lived in St. Louis and had there first developed her aberration.)

Dr. Where did you live in St. Louis?

THIRTY YEARS AMONG THE DEAD

Sp. I was traveling, I did not live there. I did once live on La Salle Avenue, Chicago, but I was there for a little while only. It was near La Salle and Division. From there I went to St. Louis, and from there -well, I really don't know where I went. I do know that my head was bothering me a great deal. (Patient complained similarly.)

Dr. Do you remember being sick?

Sp. I cannot recall much of anything. (Suddenly greatly excited.) No! No! I think there is something the matter with me. Do you think I am going crazy? Look! Look! There is my husband! No, no! He is a ghost. Just look at him!

Dr. We are talking to a ghost when we talk to you, and we are not afraid.

Sp. There is my child, too! There is my little baby! I am losing my mind. My Lily, my little Lily! Oh, my Lily! Hugo, my husband! I know I am losing my mind. Why, there's my mother! I know my mind is giving way. I am afraid -they are all coming toward me! Hugo, my husband, is it really you? My little Lily, how I do love you! I am so afraid.

Dr. Understand that you have lost your physical body and are now a spirit. Try to realize this.

Sp. Please explain why Hugo, my mother and Lily are around me. Are they not happy in Heaven? Why don't they stay there?

Dr. Do you know anything about Heaven?

Sp. Heaven is above, where Christ and God are.

Dr. Jesus said: "The Kingdom of God is within you." The Bible says: "Ye are the Temple of God and the Spirit of God dwelleth in you." Again: "God is Love, and he that dwelleth in Love dwelleth in God." God is above, God is below, God is everywhere.

Sp. Don't you believe in a personal God?

Dr. God is Spirit. God could not be only in one place.

Sp. I am getting so tired that it is hard for me to understand what you say. If there were only a place where I could rest, I would gladly go. I cannot describe to you what misery I have been in. I have no home anywhere that I can go to, no place to rest my weary head. I went from one place to another, and I could not find home or peace. I have prayed that I might find rest for just a little while, but somebody always comes and disturbs me. There were so many around, each crowding the other, and I probably was mean myself, but I could not help it. I felt as if a wild beast had gotten hold of me, and I fought everybody like a tiger, and when I was through I was weak for days and, days.

I suffered terribly. That horrible man was always after us, and that poor little child was crying all the time, she was so crowded. I wish I had a little home of my own where I could go, and not have that man around me again. He was terrible -you have no idea. He was such a rascal, but he went away and we have not seen him for quite a while.

The little girl who cried so much has also gone. She always had trouble with her head. I did not mean to be a bad woman, but that man tormented us all so much that we did not know what to do.

Dr. Wouldn't you like to go with your husband and mother and little girl, and have them all take care of you, so that you can rest? Try to realize that you have lost your physical body.

Sp. When did I lose my body?

Dr. We cannot tell you that.

Sp. Sometimes I have felt I was a big woman, and I could fight everybody, and then I would seem smaller, and it was very confusing.

Dr. That may have been caused by your influencing different people. You can be free from that condition.

Sp. Then will I have a rest? Will I wake up and find that I have only had a dream, and then have that horrible man and that crying child around me? I do not want to ever see that man again. He used to fight those women as if he were a demon, and he was so angry, and he treated the little girl very badly. She was afraid of him.

Dr. Now try to forget what has happened, and live for the future. Go with your husband and he will explain the beauties of the spirit world to you.

Sp. My husband, Hugo! I love him so dearly, and after he died life was not worth living to me. My dear child went to him just a month afterward. She was a child three years of age. Hugo, my husband, was my life. I did not care what became of me after he left. When my husband lived, we traveled a great deal. We went everywhere. We went to Alaska and there he took cold and had pneumonia, and my little child got very sick. It is hard to live all that over again.

Dr. Why go all over that again, when your people are here to take you away with them?

Sp. I want to go with them but I am afraid, because they are dead. Hugo says he has been looking for me for years and years, but he could not find me, and I cannot tell him where I have been. When Hugo and Lily died, I took very sick, and the doctors said I was a nervous wreck. I grew very much worse, and I remember them taking me to a place called Elgin (probably an asylum). I have just a faint recollection of that. When I grew better (evidently died) I went to St. Louis, because I had a sister there. Since I began to talk I feel different, and now I want to go with all my people. Just look at that beautiful bed. Now I can rest, and with Hugo I shall not have worries any more.

God bless you all and help you. Hugo says to tell you he is so pleased he found me at last and to say we shall be reunited and never part again. God bless you, each and all.

THIRTY YEARS AMONG THE DEAD

Chapter V

Tormenting Spirits & Marriage Disturbances

Obsessing spirits may purposely torment helpless sensitives, sometimes for revenge, but more often with a desire to punish the latter who, they declare, are interfering with them.

These tormenting spirits frequently cause their victims to commit deeds of violence upon themselves and do not seem to suffer from pain which they inflict upon the physical body of the sensitive, yet, contradictory as it may seem, many labor under the delusion that the body of the mortal is their own.

After the death of her husband Mrs. L. W. developed a melancholia which was followed by "hallucinations of hearing," and, constantly tormented by hearing the voices of spirits, she often dashed madly out of the house, screaming and pulling out her hair.

At such times her daughter, who was clairvoyant, saw spirits about her mother, particularly the spirit of a jeering man, and the patient herself often saw this man saying:

"There comes that terrible man again."

The patient was brought from St. Louis to Los Angeles in the belief that a change of scene and climate would be beneficial, but the violent attacks increased; in these seizures she bit her hands and arms, beat her face with a slipper and tore off her clothes. She finally became uncontrollable and was taken to the Psychopathic Ward, declared insane and committed to a sanitarium, where she remained for a year without any improvement. After escaping three times she was placed in our care, and within a few months the tormenting spirits were taken away, the lady became entirely normal, has since remained well, and is assisting her daughter with her household occupations.

A few days after her arrival at our Institute the spirit of the "jeering man", so often seen by the patient's daughter, was removed and allowed to control Mrs. Wickland.

EXPERIENCE, JANUARY 13, 1918

Spirit: JOHN SULLIVAN Patient: MRS. L. W

Psychic: MRS. WICKLAND

The spirit struggled furiously for a time and restraint was required.

Spirit: What in the world are you holding me for? I have nothing whatever to do with you folks. I don't like any of you. I don't see what right you have to hold me. I never did you any harm, and I'll make it pretty hot for you before I get through.

Doctor: You came to us as a stranger and at once started fighting. What else could I do but hold you in restraint?

Sp. I don't want to be held down like this.

Dr. Who are you?

Patient: Mrs. L W.

Sp. Why should I tell you who I am? I don't know any of you, and I don't care who you are. Just leave me alone so that I can go.

Dr. Tell us who you are, friend. You seem to be a pretty strong girl.

Sp. If you take me for a girl you had better look again!

Dr. Tell us where you came from and what you want.

Sp. What do you want to know for?

Dr. Perhaps we can help you out of your present condition.

Sp. Don't hold me so tight, then I will talk.

Dr. Tell us all about yourself.

Sp. In the first place I don't want those needles (referring to electrical treatment given patient) put on me. Then, I have been kept a prisoner for a while. Now I'm out I feel just like fighting. (Freed from aura of patient and the restraint placed upon him by intelligent spirits.) What in the world did you put all those needles on me for? If I can go away from here, I will go back home.

Dr. Where is your home?

Sp. My home is where I came from.

Dr. I am curious to know how you got those "needles" on your back.

Sp. It was just like I was on fire every time I had them. I don't want to sit here and be held down, and I'm going.

Dr. How did you happen to have the benefit of such "needles"? I am very curious to know.

Sp. I don't know myself, but I got them.

Dr. How did you happen to come here?

Sp. I don't know.

Dr. Did you come here with somebody you were attached to?

Sp. I was only attached to myself.

Dr. Where have you been recently?

Sp. I have been in darkness. I got away from my home, then I could not see anything. It seemed as if I was blind.

Dr. Were you not in a strange condition when you were in that place you call home?

Sp. It wasn't my real home, but it was just like it.

Dr. Did you become disgusted sometimes and then act queerly?

Sp. Sometimes I did not know where I was and then I acted up all the time. Once in a while we had a big fight. There were several people around, but I will get them some day.

Dr. Who were they?

Sp. Why, I don't know; all kinds of people.

Dr. Were there any women?

Sp. There were so many you could not rest. Women! Some day I am going to get hold of the rest of them and shake them up.

Dr. I don't see why you should want to harm others.

Sp. One woman would come at me one way, and one another, and it made me mad, but what can a fellow do when he has a whole lot of women around? (Other obsessing spirits in patient's aura.)

Dr. Where do you think you are now?

Sp. Where? I don't care where I am.

Dr. Where have you been living?

Sp. We have been living at different places. We have been from one place to another, until I am plumb disgusted with everything. I feel like running away so nobody can find me.

Dr. You could not get away from yourself.

Sp. I have had nothing but women around me, women, women, until I am sick and tired of women. I got one woman down and I bit and kicked, and still she clung to me. (The patient, Mrs. L. W.) She has no business to hang around me like she does. Some day I shall kill her.

Dr. Do you know what you have been doing?

Sp. I don't care what I have been doing. I took a chunk out of her wrist one day, but she clung to me just the same. Then I pulled her hair out as much as I could, but still she clung. I couldn't get rid of her.

Dr. Friend, wouldn't you like to know what you have been doing?

Sp. I don't care to know, but it makes me so mad, because since I got those needles in me I don't seem to have any power.

Dr. Where is the woman now?

Sp. I haven't seen her for a while.

Dr. What harm did she ever do you?

Sp. She has no business to hang on to me like she does.

Dr. Suppose we reverse matters, and say that it is you who have been hanging on to her.

Sp. She has no business to dress me up in woman's clothes and put woman's hair on my head.

Dr. How long have you been dead?

THIRTY YEARS AMONG THE DEAD

Sp. Dead! I'll show you that I'm not dead, and I will also show you that you are not strong enough to hold me either! Talk about me being dead! (Laughing harshly.)

Dr. Do you not realize that you have been in a strange condition for some time?

Sp. It's the worst I have ever been in. Keep your hands off me, for they are like fire, they are so hot.

Dr. Has it ever occurred to you to ask how that woman could "dress you up"? Don't you think you have been very selfish?

Sp. Selfish? Selfish? She's the selfish one.

Dr. Suppose you were an ignorant spirit hovering around the woman?

Sp. Me, hang around a woman? Not me, no sir!

Dr. Such things happen, just the same. Did you ever read your Bible? Do you remember how they cast out spirits in olden times? You are also a spirit, such as they had to deal with.

Sp. There were devils, and I'll show you I'm no devil!

Dr. You have been tormenting a woman and I chased you out with electricity.

Sp. Well, now I've caught you! (Attempting to fight.) I'll bet you are the one who put me in the dungeon. Now I will get that woman and bite her to pieces! That woman hanged on me all the time and I want to get rid of her.

Dr. You were hanging on to her. She is rid of you now. Try to understand that you are a spirit and come to your senses. I am telling you the absolute truth.

Sp. I wish I could get hold of that woman. I will smash her up good, and I will smash her face again.

Dr. Why should you want to do harm to the woman? She is not bothering you.

Sp. I would like to get after you too!

Dr. If you don't behave yourself you will get more of the electricity.

Sp. I would rather stay here, but you hold me too tight.

Dr. You tell us you are a man, but we can't see you. We can only see a woman.

Sp. Haven't you got any eyes? Don't you know I am a man?

Dr. You have woman's clothes on.

Sp. I tore them off, but she put them on, and I tore them off.

Dr. You have lost the woman that you say has been bothering you and are now controlling another woman.

Sp. What do you mean by that?

Dr. You are an ignorant, earthbound spirit, hovering around the earth plane bothering a woman. You are now using my wife's body.

Sp. I'm not using anybody's body but my own. Why did that woman hang on to me?

Dr. You were doing the "hanging on." Since you have been taken away from her, the woman is getting along nicely.

Sp. Did you put me in that dungeon?

Dr. No, intelligent spirits put you there. You are very selfish -selfish to the last degree. Don't you think you should try to realize your condition? If your record were written, would you care to have everybody read it?

Sp. I don't care. I get so mad to think I should have a woman hanging on to me, and then have her dress me in woman's clothes. I hate women.

Dr. That lady has been brought here because she has been bothered by foolish spirits. We realized that it was obsession, and we drove you away with electrical treatments. We are now trying to bring you to your senses.

Sp. If I could just get hold of that woman I would bite her to pieces. I will bite her arms too!

Dr. Try to be sensible, then you will have understanding and be able to progress and be happy.

Sp. There is no happiness.

Dr. Have you ever tried to understand God, or the real question of life?

Sp. There is no God or there would be no misery.

Dr. If there is no Supreme Being how do you happen to be? How do you exist? Can you explain how it is possible for you to talk to us through my wife's body?

Sp. Is it your wife that is hanging on to me all the time?

Dr. You were bothering a lady who came here for help. I chased you away from her, then intelligent spirits put you in a dungeon. Now you are using my wife's body for a time.

Sp. Why in the world should I be bothering women when I hate them? I will smash every one I can.

Dr. Friend, if you ever expect to be happy, you will have to change your attitude. You have lost your own body and are hovering around the earth plane obsessing people. Selfish spirits always do that. The insane asylums are full of obsessed people. You have tormented this woman for three or four years.

Sp. How in the devil could I get hold of that woman? I hate women, and why in the world should I have a woman hanging on to me all the time? I wouldn't hang on to a woman for love or money, for I hate women. I would like to crush every woman; they are all deceitful creatures. God never made such a thing as a woman. They are the most selfish creatures in the world. If you treat them to all kinds of nice things, they are all right, but when you turn your back, they stab you. They get all the money they can out of you. I swore revenge on all women, and I will have that revenge. I could have had a good home once if it hadn't been for a woman. Revenge is sweet and I will have it.

Dr. Now the time has come when you must stop and consider the question of life more seriously. Don't you think you have made many mistakes yourself? Examine your past life and see whether you have been perfect.

THIRTY YEARS AMONG THE DEAD

Sp. No one is perfect.

Dr. Don't you think that perhaps you had many faults?

Sp. No man is perfect, but I am as good as the average man.

Dr. Try to understand the mystery of life. You have probably been dead many years. Intelligent spirits are here now to help you and they will teach you many wonderful things. You have been allowed to come here and use my wife's brain and body that we might try to help you.

Sp. She's a fool to allow it.

Dr. She allows it because she has charity for such as you. All women are not false.

Sp. My mother was a very good woman. If it was not for her, I would kill every woman I come in contact with. But she has been dead forty or fifty years.

Dr. You are dead, too, as far as the body is concerned. You are a spirit now. Look around and tell us what you see, be honest now.

Sp. I see my mother, but I'm afraid of her.

Dr. We are not afraid of you.

Sp. Well, my mothers a ghost.

Dr. She's a spirit like yourself. What does your mother say to you?

Sp. She says: "John, I have been hunting for you for years." But I am afraid of her.

Dr. Does she appear ghostly?

Sp. No, but I am afraid. Why, here's my father, too! And there's Lizzie! Don't you come near me; I don't want you either. Don't you come near me! I don't want you, Lizzie, you snake!

Dr. Probably she has come to ask you to forgive her for something she did.

Sp. I will never, never forgive her.

Dr. Sometimes mistakes happen. There may have been a misunderstanding. You may have taken for granted things that were not true.

Sp. I hate her, and I don't want her near me!

Dr. Try to put hatred out of your heart and be sensible.

Sp. Lizzie, you go away, or I will kill you! You acted like a snake! I don't want to listen to you. You are as false as they make them. I don't believe what you say. Don't you come here with all kinds of excuses, for I don't believe you? I am mad at you and I will stay mad. You are a big liar!

Dr. What does the spirit say to you? Who is she?

Sp. That's Lizzie, who made all my trouble, and she says all the trouble was caused by jealousy. But I was not jealous!

Dr. Listen to what she has to say.

Sp. (Listening.) That's a fine story! We were going to be married and she was a nice girl. She says I looked at everything the wrong way, and that I was jealous.

THIRTY YEARS AMONG THE DEAD

Dr. You were probably stubborn and hot-headed.

Sp. (To Lizzie.) You're a liar. You went with that other fellow, you know you did. She says that when she went home that evening she happened to meet that fellow on the street car. He only walked a block with her, and I happened to see them walking together. I went home and stabbed myself.

Dr. That was certainly a brave act. I suppose you committed suicide.

Sp. I wish I could have died, but I could not. I would have been far better off, but I'm going to have revenge on women.

Dr. Why don't you try to be sensible and forgive the girl?

Sp. Say, do you believe her story? I suffered a great deal from that stab I gave myself, and I did wish I could die. There's Lizzie walking around and she's crying.

Dr. Listen to your own conscience.

Sp. I loved that girl and what did I get from her?

Dr. I think your mother spoiled you when you were a boy.

Sp. My mother thought the world of me and gave me every thing I wanted, so that I could have a good time. No, Mother, don't come near me! There is no help for me.

Dr. The first lesson you must learn is to crucify self. Jesus said: "Except ye become as little children, ye shall not enter into the kingdom of Heaven." I don't think you understand what that means. All you cared for was self, and your mother spoiled you.

Sp. Mother says she is very sorry now. Here's Lizzie again. I don't believe her, because she did go with that fellow.

Dr. Suppose she did; what of it? You must have had a very jealous disposition.

Sp. She says she did not go with him, and that she has told me what she did.

Dr. Do you know that she is dead?

Sp. She is not. If she is, is she a ghost?

Dr. You say she stands there. Does she look like a ghost?

Sp. No, she doesn't. My mother says: "John, be reasonable and sensible. Your own conscience accuses you." It is hard, when you love a girl, to see her with another fellow. What I suffered on account of Lizzie! After seeing her with the other fellow, I went home and stabbed myself, just a little bit, to try and scare her. I thought if I did that she would come to me.

Dr. You committed suicide but you do not realize that you are a spirit and have been troubling a lady, and obsessing her. She is a patient of ours.

Sp. What do I care for her? I hate women and she won't leave me alone. All I wanted was revenge, and I got it.

Dr. That lady has done all kinds of wild things because you were obsessing her.

Sp. Mother and Lizzie both stand there crying, but nobody cares for me, so what's the use?

Dr. What name did you have beside John?

THIRTY YEARS AMONG THE DEAD

Sp. John Sullivan.

Dr. I should think you would feel ashamed to have bothered that lady.

Sp. I'm not any more ashamed of myself than you are!

Dr. Do you think you loved this girl? Or was it only selfishness on your part? You simply wanted her, that's all.

Sp. She could have been mine, but I made her suffer. My love turned to hate. No, Lizzie, you don't need to cry. I shall never forgive you, if you ask me a hundred times.

Dr. If your mother had given you a few thrashings you would not be in the condition you are now. Try to forgive Lizzie, and by doing so you will be helped yourself.

Sp. I shall never forgive her. The women were all crazy after me. I was considered a good looking man.

Dr. That was your trouble. If you had been homely you would have had some sense. You must try to be sensible now, because you are using my wife's body.

Sp. Well, take your wife! I don't want her. Say, Mother, it's no use you and Lizzie standing there and crying, for I shall never forgive her.

Dr. If you don't forgive when you have this opportunity you will find yourself in a dark dungeon when you leave here, and there you will stay until you repent. Try to understand that the wrong is within yourself.

Sp. I'll not forgive. I loved my mother and I always had plenty of money.

Dr. What city did you live in?

Sp. St. Louis.

Dr. Do you know you are in California?

Sp. I know where I am. I am in St. Louis, and it's winter. It's about nineteen degrees below zero.

Dr. What year do you think it is?

Sp. 1910.

Dr. It is the 13th of January, 1918.

Sp. I do hate to see women cry. Mother, stop crying. To see a woman cry always distresses me.

Dr. Doesn't your conscience trouble you at all?

Sp. What's the use of worrying about things?

Dr. Listen to what your mother says, then she can help you.

Sp. Mother, I'll tell you, -if you had spanked me more when I was a little boy and not given in to me so much, I might have been a different fellow from what I am now. It is too late in life to change, and what's more, one never gets anywhere by changing.

Dr. You still have more misery ahead of you unless you are willing to forgive.

Sp. I don't care to be in that dungeon you speak of. Why do parents give their children all they want? You see, Mother, what nice work you have done. Aren't you proud of your son? You brought me to this. This is your work.

Dr. You pretend to love your mother, but you have no charity or sympathy for anybody.

Sp. I hate the word sympathy. My father says I shall have to change. I am too old to change now. (Frightened and shrinking from something.) Take that away! Take me away! I'm sick!

Dr. You must be serious and honest.

Sp. My mother says she knows that she raised me wrong. Don't let me go in that dungeon! I'll forgive Lizzie -I'll do anything! I am tired of life, and tired of everything.

Dr. When you reach the spirit side of life you must try to be of service to others, instead of a detriment. Try to undo the wrong you have done by obsessing this lady.

Sp. She tormented me and I hate women. I got revenge. I took a slipper and pounded her face. I did it for revenge on women, for I hate them all.

The spirit could not be brought to realize his situation and he was taken away to be placed in a "dungeon" until he could overcome self and his hatred toward humanity.

Several years ago, a friend of ours complained of the peculiar and erratic actions of a business associate, Mr. P., who had suddenly become extremely irritable and despotic to those in his employ, highly unreasonable, impossible to please, and subject to violent attacks of swearing.

As obsession seemed indicated we concentrated for the gentleman in question, and after several weeks an irate spirit spoke through Mrs. Wickland and frankly admitted having tormented this man, wanting revenge for attentions which he claimed the latter had been paying to his wife. (The situation had existed during his life but he did not discover this until after his death.)

The spirit gave the name of a man prominent in local business circles; he had passed out some time before but was not aware of the fact. He said that he had been sick for a long time, but could now go where he pleased without any trouble, for he had become well.

He could not understand why his wife would no longer speak to him, or why his child, who had always been so affectionate, was now so cold toward him. He declared that some of his friends were false to him and had for some time been paying attention to his wife, sending her gifts and flowers, but that he would have revenge on them as soon as he was through with his present victim.

The spirit said that he could not think very clearly, but supposed that was because he had recently taken an anesthetic, which he thought also accounted for the peculiar lightness of his body, and a feeling of having no weight. He was puzzled by the fact that whenever he thought about any persons he immediately found himself with them and involved in their affairs. Recently he had been around Mr. P. but could not get away from him; this had exasperated him exceedingly, he had "done a lot of swearing," kept the man awake, made him go to work "early," and had annoyed him in every way possible.

After many explanations the spirit finally realized that he had "died," although this was at first difficult for him to comprehend, for he "had always thought death ended all, and that was all there was to it."

THIRTY YEARS AMONG THE DEAD

Being assured that activity and progression awaited him in the spirit world, and that matters would there be explained to him to his entire satisfaction, he left. The following day there was such a remarkable improvement in the conduct of Mr. P., and his behavior was so wholly normal that the entire office force noticed the change, although Mr. P. himself never knew of the experimental effort which had been made in his behalf.

A patient, Miss R. F., was intermittently seized by impulses to run away, and at such times became greatly agitated, but shortly after entering our Institute she was relieved of the instigator of these wanderings.

EXPERIENCE SEPTEMBER 15, 1920

Spirit: EDWARD STERLING Patient: Miss R. F.

Psychic: MRS. WICKLAND.

An intelligence took control of the psychic, and, rising, attempted to run away, becoming very indignant when restrained.

Doctor Won't you sit down?

Spirit No!

Dr. Where are you going?

Sp. Home.

Dr. Home? Where is your home?

Sp. I want to go to find it. (Struggling for freedom.)

Dr. What a nice lady you are, to act like this.

Sp. Lady? Lady? I'm no lady, I'm a man!

Dr. Where did you come from?

Sp. That doesn't make any difference. I'm going home.

Dr. Where is your home?

Sp. Wherever I can find it. I know I am not going to sit here any longer. I'm going, I'll tell you that!

Dr. (Recognizing the phraseology of the patient.) Why did you cut off your hair? (The patient, under an irrational impulse, had cut her hair short.)

Sp. Do you think I want to wear long hair like a woman? No, sir, I don't! I'm going, yes, sir! I'm going, I tell you.

Dr. Where will you go? You have no home.

Sp. I won't stay here; I'm going.

Dr. How long have you been dead?

Sp. I'm not dead. I'm going! I don't want those awful things put into me, all over my body. (Referring to static electrical treatment applied to patient.) It's just like sticking sharp things into me, real sharp things.

THIRTY YEARS AMONG THE DEAD

Dr. You felt the electricity I gave to a patient.

Sp. I tried twice to run away, but I was brought back.

Dr. Why did you make that lady cut off her hair?

Sp. I didn't make anybody cut their hair off. It's my body, and I can cut my hair off if I want to. I went to sleep and when I woke up my hair had grown so long that I did not know what to do. I went to sleep and I slept a long time, and after waking up, I found I had long hair, and I wasn't going to have that so I would look like a woman. I could not go to a barber shop, cause I was too ashamed to be seen on the street, so I cut it off myself.

Dr. You did not cut your own hair, you cut off the hair of the lady you were controlling.

Sp. It was my own hair I cut. Why do you keep me here like this? I haven't done anything to you or anybody else.

Dr. You have been disturbing a lady and doing her a great wrong. You say you are a man, and yet you are wearing lady's clothes. How do you account for that?

Sp. I couldn't get any man's clothes.

Dr. Shouldn't that fact open your eyes and show you that there is something the matter with you?

Sp. Can't I sit down?

Dr. Yes. if you will sit quietly. Should you not try to find out what is the matter with you?

Sp. I don't want to stay here; I'm going home.

Dr. If you will sit still and listen, I will explain your situation. You are so-called dead.

Sp. I am not dead, I'll have you know. Stop holding me!

Dr. I am not holding you, I am holding my wife. You must realize that you are in a strange position. You passed out of your mortal body but do not understand your situation.

Sp. Let me go; I want to get out of here. What are you holding my hands for?

Dr. I am not holding your hands; I am holding my wife's hands.

Sp. Your wife's hands! I never saw you before, and I'm not your wife. Do you think a man marries another man? I never heard such talk!

Dr. What I tell you is true, just the same. You are an ignorant spirit and do not understand your condition.

Sp. You let me alone. I want to go home.

Dr. Did you ever stop to think what happens to a person when he dies?

Sp. I am not dead. I just went to sleep.

Dr. That was the sleep of death.

Sp. I slept so long that when I woke up my hair had grown long.

Dr. Not only had your hair grown, but you also had on woman's clothes. How did you get them?

Sp. I'm not dead, just the same.

Dr. You have lost your physical body. When you lose that, you are supposed to be "dead."

Sp. If I was dead I would go to the grave and stay there until the last day. You stay there until Gabriel blows his horn.

Dr. That is only ignorant belief. You were too lazy to understand life's mysteries.

Sp. I was taught that when I died, if I believed in God and Christ, and that Christ died for our sins, I would go to Heaven.

Dr. Why did you not go to "Heaven" when you died? You have "died" so far as the world is concerned. You are here, and yet we cannot see you. I see only my wife's body.

Sp. I have never seen your wife and I don't know her.

Dr. Have you ever heard about mediums?

Sp. Yes, but I don't believe in them.

Dr. You are speaking through a medium now. You claim to be a man and yet you are using a woman's body to speak through.

Sp. Lies, nothing but lies!

Dr. It is true, nevertheless. You have woman's clothes on. You know there is something strange about your condition. You probably do not know that you are in Los

Angeles, California.

Sp. No, I am not.

Dr. Where should you be?

Sp. I have been on the go for some time, traveling.

Dr. Look at your hands; they are not yours.

Sp. I never saw you before you put all that electricity into me, and I feel like giving you a good licking. What do you think of any man doing such a thing to another man? It goes right through you. You don't know how it hurts. I'm not going to stand for any more such nonsense. I stood it for a long time, then I went. When I left, a great big Indian (spirit) got hold of me and put me in prison. I got loose after awhile and came here.

Dr. You have been bothering a woman who was a patient of ours, and electrical treatments given to her dislodged you.

Sp. What is the matter with me? I have felt so crowded.

Dr. Can't you understand that you are in a strange situation? You were probably a big man and you felt crowded because you were occupying a body smaller than your own physical body. Why don't you open your mind and learn the facts?

Sp. There's nothing to learn.

Dr. It has probably been a long time since you lost your body. What year is it?

Sp. I had a good long sleep and I don't know.

THIRTY YEARS AMONG THE DEAD

Dr. Shouldn't your present strange condition cause you to ask questions? We cannot see you, we can only hear you talk.

Sp. What sense is there in talking to a person when you don't see him?

Dr. This lady is a psychic, and you are a spirit talking through her body.

Sp. I don't believe you.

Dr. This is my wife's body. Are you my wife talking to me?

Sp. I'm not your wife! I'm a man!

Dr. I drove you away from the woman you were controlling. You made her act like an insane person. How did you come here?

Sp. You tell me how.

Dr. You are an invisible spirit; you do not understand your situation. The lady you have been bothering happened to be in a nervous condition and susceptible to spirit obsession, and you obsessed her. You made that lady do many insane things. What do you think of such actions?

Sp. I wouldn't say it was anything very grand, but I don't even know any woman.

Dr. You influenced her to cut off her hair and to run away.

Sp. What did I want with long hair? I went to sleep and when I woke up my hair had grown too long, so I cut it off that's all.

Dr. That was the woman's hair you cut.

Sp. It was too long.

Dr. That is her business. Just reverse things. Suppose you had your own body and somebody cut your hair off -would you like it?

Sp. No, I wouldn't, but she couldn't help yourself.

Dr. Don't you think that you were very selfish?

Sp. I don't know. Say, if, as you say, I'm dead, why is it that I'm not in Heaven or hell?

Dr. There are no such places.

Sp. I haven't seen God or Christ or the devil, yet you tell me I am dead.

Dr. You are not "dead."

Sp. Why, just a little while ago you said I was.

Dr. You are dead to the world.

Sp. You said I was dead.

Dr. I said you were so-called dead; you lost your physical body.

Sp. You said I was dead.

Dr. Now listen to reason, or I will have to take you into the office and give you more electricity.

91

Sp. I don't want that; it makes you feel like you were burning up.

Dr. We wanted to get you out, and we succeeded.

Sp. What business is it of yours if I stayed there?

Dr. We wanted that lady to be rid of you.

Sp. You had no right to get me away from her.

Dr. Do you think it was right of you to control her and disturb her life?

Sp. A fellow has got to have some place to live.

Dr. Suppose it had been your mother and a selfish spirit were controlling her and making her act as if insane; do you think that would be right?

Sp. I was not insane, and I did not make her insane either.

Dr. It was an insane act for her to cut off her hair and run away.

Sp. How would you like to have your hair long, if you were a man?

Dr. It was the lady's body and the lady's hair, not yours. Now you have been driven from the lady's body, and you must change your conduct. If you are not careful you will be put into a dungeon. You said a short time ago that an Indian "got hold of you"; you had better be careful or another Indian will get hold of you.

Sp. I will fight him if he does.

Dr. Listen to me. My wife is a psychic and she allows such spirits as you to control her body to bring them to a realization of their condition. You should appreciate the privilege. There are thousands of spirits who would be glad to be in your place at this moment. You know that you are in a strange condition. Perhaps some of your kindred are here. They will take you with them to the spirit world. You must behave yourself and understand and be sensible.

Sp. What shall I do?

Dr. Understand that there is a spirit world, and that you should strive to reach it.

Sp. You mean Heaven?

Dr. The Kingdom of Heaven is within one.

Sp. Don't you believe that Christ died for your sins?

Dr. He did not die for mine. Don't you understand that something is lacking in such a belief? Jesus taught us how to understand, life; he did not die for the sins of any one. Those who believe that Christ died for their sins lack the right understanding of His teachings. It is a sin against God to teach such a doctrine. If it were true, it would mean that God had made a mistake and was forced to provide an intercessor as an offering of atonement for His own mistake. Now friend, you must leave my wife, and you must also leave the other lady alone.

Sp. What are you talking about? I never saw your wife.

Dr. You are temporarily controlling my wife's body. We cannot see you. If you do not come to your senses pretty soon, we shall have to force you out, and then you will be in the "outer darkness" which the Bible speaks about.

Sp. It is not right that God should treat me as he has. I prayed and prayed and prayed. I went to church and paid a whole lot of money to the church, because they said if I did not give money I would go straight to hell when I died and I thought when I paid my money I should get my money's worth.

Dr. What did Jesus say? "God is Spirit and they that worship him must worship him in Spirit and in truth." God is Spirit, not a spirit. The Bible says: "God is Love, and He that dwelleth in Love dwelleth in God." Where will you look to find such a God except within your own self? "Ye are the temple of God, and the spirit of God dwelleth in you." What is Heaven? It is a condition of your own mind, attained when you understand life's purpose.

Sp. Isn't Heaven a place? It says so in the Bible; it says Heaven is paved with golden streets. Isn't that so?

Dr. That, like many other statements in the Bible, is symbolical of great truths of life.

Sp. You said a short time ago that Jesus did not die for your sins. What do you believe?

Dr. I recognize that we are all spiritual beings in mortal bodies while on earth. When we pass out of our mortal bodies with understanding, we will not waken in darkness, but our spiritual eyes will be open, and advanced spirits will help us to progress in the spirit world. Some kind spirit friends of yours may be here now. Do you not realize that some change has taken place with you?

Sp. I can talk more than I could. You said I was talking through your wife. How can I talk through her?

Dr. My wife is a psychic who is so developed that spirits can talk through her, and intelligent spirits have allowed you to control her. However, you will not be able to stay long.

Sp. I think I will stay here. I feel better. I feel pretty good now.

Dr. You will feel still better after you realize the beautiful condition in the spirit world. You will have to become as a little child, then you can "enter the kingdom of Heaven." Do not merely believe, but try to understand. What is your name?

Sp. Edward.

Dr. And your other name?

Sp. I don't know.

Dr. Where did you live? Do you know that you are in Los Angeles, California? Do you know what year it is?

Sp. No, I don't know.

Dr. Why don't you know?

Sp. I have no memory. I can't think. I don't know anything any more. (Such a state of bewilderment suggests that the cause of amnesia conditions found in certain patients is probably possession by confused spirit intelligences.)

Dr. That is because you have been in the outer darkness, and, being a wandering spirit, you drifted into that lady's aura, controlled her and made her act as if insane.

Sp. I wanted to have a good, quiet home.

Dr. Is it right to do the things you have done?

Sp. When you have been walking in darkness for a long time, and you see a light, don't you want to stay?

Dr. That is not the right kind of light. You need the spiritual light of understanding.

Sp. Then do you think I ought to go to church and sing, and pray to God, and read the Bible?

Dr. Did you ever make a thorough study of the history of the Bible to learn who wrote it?

Sp. It was God's inspired book.

Dr. God did not write the Bible; the book is man-made. Could one credit God with having written certain things in the Bible, many of which are unfit to be read in respectable society?

Sp. Who wrote the book?

Dr. It was compiled from many sources, during different periods, mainly for the purpose of keeping people in subjection through fear of an imaginary devil and hell. The Bible is a collection of poetry, history, allegories and philosophy, of contradictions and truths. But humanity believes that every word of the Bible is inspired, and insists upon interpreting it literally, instead of accepting what is reasonable. The Bible states that: "The letter killeth, but the spirit giveth life," and "Spiritual things . . . are spiritually discerned." Hence, religion is a process of mental discernment. The teachings of Christ contain wonderful truths, but the allegories have been taught as historical facts by the church, and dogma, doctrine and creed have obscured their underlying spiritual significance.

Sp. Don't you believe that God made the earth in six days and rested on the seventh?

Dr. No; that is only an allegorical statement. The seven days are symbolical of the seven principles in Nature. "God is at once the Creator and the Creation"; if God should rest, all would be at an end. We should understand life as it is, not merely believe what is told us. Now it is getting late and you cannot stay any longer. See whether some one is here whom you know.

Sp. Oh! There's my mother! It's a long time since I saw her. But she died when I was a kid.

Dr. Listen to her; she can help you.

Sp. Oh, mother, will you take me? Take me, mother, I'm so tired. Oh, mother, take me with you!

Dr. Of course she will take you with her, but you will have to rid yourself of all your foolish beliefs and acquire understanding.

Sp. Let me go! (Rising to walk away.)

Dr. You will have to think yourself with your mother. You can't take this body with you because it belongs to my wife. Just think yourself with your mother, and you will be there instantly.

Sp. I'm so tired and weary -so tired. Let me go with my mother. I see her coming; she went away for a while.

Dr. Now go with your mother. God gave you intelligence to think, and you must be reasonable and let your mother and others teach you.

Sp. Mother says I must ask you to forgive me for being so rude, and she also says I must ask that lady to please forgive me for bothering her.

Dr. Can you tell us where you came from?

Sp. I can't remember.

Dr. What year do you think it is?

Sp. It should be 1901.

Dr. That was nineteen years ago. Who is the President?

Sp. McKinley.

Dr. He was shot on the sixth of September, 1901, and died on the fourteenth. This is 1920 now.

Sp. Where have I been all that time? Sleeping? The winter of 1901 I was awfully sick,

and it seems hard to remember anything else after that. It was around Christmas and I caught cold, and I was very sick.

Dr. Where were you when you were taken sick?

Sp. I was working in the woods. I worked in a lumber town at lumbering. I remember something hitting me on the head, and that's all I remember. My mother says my name is Sterling; yes, that's it!

Dr. Can your mother tell what place you came from before you took up lumbering?

Sp. I was born in Iowa, mother says, but when I got hurt, I was working in the woods in Northern Wisconsin. I used to live in Iowa.

Dr. Can you remember the name of the town?

Sp. No, I can't.

Dr. Well, friend, try to obtain an understanding of life, and be of service to humanity, instead of a detriment. You have been bothering a lady and she is not yet entirely free.

Sp. I was not the only one bothering her; there are two more just as bad as I am.

Dr. When you have understanding you must help this lady to get well, and take the other spirits away from her.

Sp. I will try. Thank you! Goodbye.

Haunted houses are often frequented by spirits who seek revenge for wrongs suffered by them during life.

While Mrs. Wickland and I were in Wisconsin, we held a circle in the home of friends and Mrs. Wickland was controlled by the spirit of a man who said he had been murdered by the owner of a near-by stone quarry, but that he was still alive in his house at the side of the quarry.

He laughed spitefully and said: "He killed me, but I am having my revenge! I haunt him!" Although we explained to the spirit the existence of a higher life, he stated that he was not yet ready to leave his old haunts, and refusing to progress, departed.

Our friends then told us that they had known this man in life; that ten years before, the quarry had been owned by three men, one of whom, desiring to own the quarry himself, had bought the holdings of the second man, but the third man, who lived in the house by the quarry, had refused to sell.

A few days later the third man was found dead, and, although there was no proof as to the identity of the murderer, there was a strong suspicion in the neighborhood that the first partner was the perpetrator of the crime.

As time went on the owner of the stone quarry developed a strange reluctance to work the quarry, and rumor said that he was haunted by his dead partner. It became common report that the house nearby was haunted, and when our friends had driven there a year before to pick berries they had had an unusual experience.

After placing the horse in the empty barn, they noticed some berries in the yard and returned to the barn for a basket, when the horse began to rear wildly and neighed in terror.

Stopping in amazement, our friends heard a coarse laugh and looking about saw a grinning man standing in the doorway of the deserted house. It was the man who had died several years before; they had known him in life and recognized him now. The man laughed and vanished, and our friends rushed to the barn, took the horse out and drove away in great haste.

We had a series of letters from Mrs. G. G., who resided in a village in New York; she was a psychic and clairvoyant whose house was haunted by a band of evil spirits. She wrote that she had been in the best of health when she had moved into this house but had soon become afflicted with a strange ailment of the arms and legs which no doctors could relieve.

Spirits who claimed to be her guides advised her to have a psychic circle every evening and "sit" for half an hour, saying they could help her in this way. They explained that she was being injured by the spirit of the woman who had built the house and that she could free herself by having a certain friend of hers attend the next circle.

This friend came and the spirit said she would leave with this woman. When the latter reached her home she was taken with the same sickness with which Mrs. G. G. had been troubled, while Mrs. G. G. recovered.

But disturbances of various kinds continued in the house; even the orchard was haunted, and spirits were heard to say that Mrs. G. G. could not live if she remained there, for they would kill any one who came into that house.

The G.'s sold the house and moved away without telling the purchasers anything of their mysterious experiences. The new owners took possession of the house and the mother, an elderly lady, went to bed the first night apparently well, but in a short time screamed that two men had come into her room threatening to kill her, and before morning she was dead.

Mrs. G. G., however, continued her circles, but was unable to rid herself of spirit influences and finally wrote to us for aid.

"There is no one I can go to or depend upon. I joined the New Thought Society to be helped; they claimed to send out vibrations but I failed to get in on the wave. No one prays more earnestly for help than I, or tries harder to do right. Tell me, if you can, how to get relief."

We concentrated for the lady, as well as the house, and a number of spirits were brought from both. One of the first declared that he did not know he was obsessing Mrs. G. G. Another spirit was Harry Harris, who had so brutally mistreated his wife that she had shot herself.

How his life had ended we did not learn. He insisted that he was not dead, but was living in an old house with a band of outlaws (spirits) and that they would kill any one who dared to move into their house.

Another evening four spirits were brought from the haunted house; first two women, then "Pete," who had been a dexterous pickpocket in life, and a woman named Kate, who had been killed by Pete and had "hounded" him ever since.

To conceal himself Pete was hiding with others in a house that "belonged" to them, and to no one else. "We kill any one who comes in," he said, speaking through Mrs. Wickland.

He admitted having troubled Mrs. G. G. "I stayed with her to get my grub," he said. While Pete was speaking, Kate took control of another medium who was in the circle, and Pete was terror-stricken, while Kate attempted to escape from him. Each thought the other was a ghost, and neither was aware of controlling a psychic.

It was some time before they realized that both had died. Finally Pete sank on his knees and begged Kate to forgive him; a reconciliation followed and both left, promising to reform.

Later, Mrs. G. G. wrote that she had greatly improved.

In answer to an urgent appeal for help, Mrs. Wickland and I called at the home of Mr. and Mrs. C., in Pasadena, where nightly rappings and noises were keeping the family awake for hours.

Mr. C. had purchased this house from the children of an elderly lady who had died some time before. (A fact not known to us until later.) The house had been moved to Mr. C.'s lot, remodeled there, and the C.'s had then moved into it, only to be disturbed by noises of all kinds. Every night, between twelve and four, the door of a closet between two bedrooms was shaken and rattled loudly, and rappings and "crackings" kept the family awake.

While we were seated in one of the rooms of the C. home, discussing the situation, Mrs. Wickland became unexpectedly entranced by a spirit who complained of intense rheumatism, and stormed at the C.'s for living in "her house."

"This is my house," she declared peremptorily, "and these people have no business in it! I will chase them out!"

The controlling spirit proved to be the former owner of the house and later inquiry bore out the statement that she had suffered severely from rheumatism. She could not realize that she was dead but insisted that she was still living in her own house, although troubled by intruders.

"If I am dead, why am I not in Heaven?" she asked.

Many explanations at last resulted in understanding and a penitent departure, and in a letter written several months later Mr. C. stated that all noises had entirely ceased in the house.

That spirits often play a serious part in domestic disturbances and break up many homes we have had ample evidence.

A patient, Mrs. SI., who was brought to us from a Northern state, was the second wife of a Dakota farmer. After the birth of her first child, she developed a tendency to wander away at random and when brought back and questioned she could only give vague answers, but always insisted that her husband, a steady, reliable farmer, was faithless to her.

When the obsessing spirit was transferred to Mrs. Wickland we found that it was none other than the first wife, who indignantly accused her husband of being faithless to her, and said that she was determined to get rid of her "rival." After passing out of the physical body she had remained on the farm, but she was unaware of her death, and did not realize that her "rival" was her husband's second wife.

The spirit, after due explanation and enlightenment, left, and Mrs. SI., restored to herself, returned to her Dakota home.

We had a similar experience with an acquaintance of ours, a gentleman whose first wife had died, leaving him to care for their small son. Later he married again, but before long we noticed that the family life was becoming unhappy, and the culmination came one Sunday morning when the second wife angrily left the house.

The husband desolately came to our home, followed presently by the little boy, and although they had never visited us before, they remained for some hours. In the evening the boy returned, and while Mrs. Wickland was conversing with him and a group of friends, she became controlled by the spirit of a woman who said she was the boy's mother.

She had no knowledge of her death and craved longingly to caress her small son, saying: "I want my boy! I want my boy!" Then she burst forth into a jealous denunciation of her successor and declared she would drive her out of the house.

"I chased her away this morning!" she exulted.

She, too, was finally made to understand the true situation, and, regretting the suffering she had caused, promised to do everything possible to make amends. The second wife returned home again, and, during the ten years which have elapsed since this episode, no further disturbances have occurred in the family. Miss L. was the young fiancée of a widower who had formerly, with his wife, occupied a flat in the same building in which the Young lady lived, and the two women had been intimate friends.

The wife died very suddenly and some time after her death the gentleman became engaged to the young lady. Soon after this the latter began to show mental abnormalities which continually grew worse.

In her normal condition she esteemed the man highly, but when she came to us she had a violent dislike for him, and asserted that she would rather die, or go to an insane asylum, than marry him. She had made several attempts to end her life but had each time seemed to come to herself at the last moment and called for help.

At the time the patient entered the Institute Mrs. Wickland clairvoyantly saw the spirit of a woman of the brunette type possessing the patient, who was a decided blond. This spirit was so interblended with the patient that it was difficult for Mrs. Wickland to determine, from the transfiguration, whether the patient was light or dark. When Mrs. Wickland described this spirit the patient's mother and fiancé both recognized her as the man's former wife.

The patient proved very obdurate; screaming spells alternated with obstinate, stubborn moods, and she could not be left alone at any time. She declared herself insane and scoffed at being cured, and insisted that she wanted to die, for if she lived she would have to marry "that man." One day, during a treatment, she entered a semi-trance condition and a spirit intelligence expressed itself forcefully.

"He shall never marry her! He shall never have her! I will drive her to an insane asylum, or I will kill her, but he shall never have her!' Immediately following this, the spirit of a child spoke defensively as if protecting a mother. The patient's sister, who was present, recognized in the latter intelligence the deceased thirteen year old son of the dead wife.

The climax came a few days later. The patient had been unusually obstinate and unruly, and very contemptuous to her fiancé when he called. After a strong treatment was administered, the patient became quiet and slept well that night. However, during the night Mrs. Wickland was greatly troubled by the presence of a spirit who annoyed her until four o'clock in the morning, when she became completely entranced by the spirit of the man's former wife.

After considerable effort I induced the spirit to talk, but she was with difficulty convinced of her real situation -that she was a spirit and controlling Mrs. Wickland's body. She strongly censured both her former husband and our patient for their treachery to her, and repeated her threats against the girl.

"I will send her to the asylum! I will kill her!" she declared.

A great deal of argument and persuasion were needed to bring the spirit to repentance, but this was at last accomplished.

Upon being asked if her son was with her she said that she had seen him at times, but that he was dead and she did not want to have anything to do with him. The spirit was urged to leave the young woman whom she was tormenting and go with other spirit intelligences to a higher life, of which she showed herself entirely ignorant. Although repentant, she still longed to remain on the earth plane, but finally consented to leave and to cease troubling the patient; then she suddenly became weak and declared she was dying. (This sensation often occurs when spirits realize their actual situation; sometimes they again experience the physical conditions under which they passed out of their earth bodies.)

Chills and violent attacks of coughing added to the spirit's distress and after a painful pseudo-death struggle she left. These symptoms were recognized by her husband and the patient's mother as corresponding exactly with those manifested by the man's wife at the time of her death from pneumonia.

After this the patient recovered rapidly. She was soon able to leave the Institute, is now well and happily married.

A peculiar case was that of Mr. Mc., a well known man in Chicago, whose family name is one of highest social prominence. This man suddenly began to act strangely; he shunned the members of his family, and told his wife and relatives that he wished to live on a higher plane and wanted nothing more to do with them. Then one day he packed his trunk and left home, going to live in a small room which he had rented in the lowest section of the city.

We had never seen this gentleman, but a relative of his, who knew of our work, asked us to concentrate for him at our next psychic circle; we did so and a spirit was brought who controlled Mrs. Wickland. After some solicitation she gave her full name, confessing that she had been the first wife of Mr. Mc., and she then told her story.

She had met Mr. Mc. in Chicago during the World's Fair and, for a time, they had lived together without the formality of marriage until his relatives discovered the situation and compelled them to marry. The girl was accepted in society but rebelled at the restraints of conventional life, and, being of a vain and restless disposition, could not live happily with her husband.

She finally left him and went to the "west side," where she entered a house of ill-repute. Although at times she regretted the folly of her conduct, she continued her mode of living, became a morphine addict and finally committed suicide.

After her death she had returned to her husband, and when he married again she felt angrily aggrieved, and at last influenced him to leave his wife and child, to go to quarters where she herself felt more at home.

We convinced her of the great wrong she was doing in controlling her former husband in this manner, and after she had obtained an understanding of the progress awaiting her in the spirit world, she promised to leave, wishing to attain a higher condition.

When next we saw the relative of Mr. Mc., who had asked us to concentrate for him, we told her of the story related by the spirit, and in amazement she admitted it was true in every detail; that the name given was correct and that Mr. Mc. had been married before, but that the unfortunate episode had been regarded by the family as a skeleton in the closet and was never mentioned.

She later reported that Mr. Mc. had returned to his home, normal and sane, and was again living happily with his wife and child.

THIRTY YEARS AMONG THE DEAD

Chapter VI

Spirits and Crime

Habits, desires and inclinations are rooted in the mind and remain with the individual after he is freed from his physical body, until they are eliminated by the will.

The spirits of many criminals, murderers, those who were executed or are seeking for revenge, remain indefinitely in the earth sphere and often endeavor to continue their former activities and to carry out their evil designs through controlling the bodies of mortals who are sensitive to their influence. In many cases of revolting murder investigations will show that the crimes were committed by innocent persons under the control of disembodied spirits who had taken complete possession of the murderer.

There is little doubt that the murder of Stanford White by Harry K. Thaw in 1906, at Madison Square Roof Garden, New York, was due to spirit influence. Harry Thaw was a psychic sensitive and had shown evidence of this fact all his life, and whatever personal grievances he may have had when he killed Stanford White, he was unquestionably obsessed by avenging spirits who desired retribution for real or fancied injustice done to themselves or kindred.

Harry Thaw was largely only the psychic subject and the physical instrument through which was enacted a terrible drama by the invisible world, the actors being ignorant, revengeful spirits.

On July 15, 1906, several weeks after the tragedy occurred, a strange spirit controlled Mrs. Wickland during a psychic circle and fell prostrate to the floor. Placing the form of my wife in a chair I began questioning the controlling intelligence.

The stranger strenuously objected to being touched, brusquely demanded to be left alone, and called out:

"Hey there, waiter! Bring me a drink'"

"What kind of drink do you want?"

"Bring me a whiskey and soda, and be quick about it!"

"Who are you?"

"None of your business who I am."

"Where do you think you are?"

"In Madison Square Roof Garden, of course."

THIRTY YEARS AMONG THE DEAD

"What is your name?"

"Stanford White, if you have to know."

Holding one hand on the back of his head, on the right side, and clutching at his chest and abdomen as if in great pain, he cried:

"Have a waiter bring me that whiskey and soda!"

I was about to ask further questions when the spirit's attention was attracted to some invisible, and he began to tremble with fear.

"Are you seeing dead people?" I asked.

He nodded his head violently, then shouted, "They are after me!" and, jumping from the chair, ran to a corner of the room in an effort to escape.

His agitation was so great that he lost control of the psychic and was gone. Immediately another spirit took possession of the psychic and in great excitement began to walk back and forth, exclaiming exultantly: "I killed the dog! I killed the dog!

There he lies!" pointing at the floor toward the spot where White had lost control. "The dog! I have been looking for a chance to kill him for several years, and I got him at last! The dog!"

I forced the spirit to sit down and learned that his name was Johnson.

"I killed Stanford White," he boasted. "He deserved death. He had trifled too long with our daughters."

He was very pronounced in his denunciation of society men.

"They steal our children from us and put fine clothes on them, and the parents do not know what becomes of them."

I asked the spirit whether he was aware of being dead, but he laughed at the idea and said:

"How could a dead person talk? The doctor said I had consumption and would die soon, but I didn't die. I never felt better in my life."

When asked to carefully examine his hands, feet and dress he demanded to know how he, a man, became possessed of a woman's body. Lengthy argument finally convinced the perplexed spirit of the fact of his transition, and he departed, thoroughly penitent. He was followed by a third entity, but this intelligence was aware of being a spirit, temporarily controlling a borrowed body.

"I am Harry Thaw's father. Save my boy! Save my boy! He is not guilty. Harry will not be electrocuted." (Later events proved this to be true.)

"He is sensitive to spirit influence and has been all his life. He was always erratic and so excitable that we were afraid to correct him for fear he would become insane. But I see our mistake now. I did not understand the cause of Harry's queer actions while I was in the physical, but now, from the spirit side of life, I can see that Harry has been a tool in the hands of selfish, earthbound spirits most of his life.

"He was obsessed by revengeful spirits when he killed Stanford White. I have tried to reach the external world by every possible avenue, to tell the people that Harry is not insane, but that he is a psychic sensitive."

"Save my boy! Save my boy!" he begged repeatedly.

"What would you have us do?"

"Please write to my wife, and to my attorney, Mr. Olcott." (We did not then know that Mr. Olcott had been Mr. Thaw's attorney, but verified the fact afterward.) "Tell them your experience and what I have said to you, and urge them to recognize and understand Harry's condition.

We promised to comply with the wish of the spirit and he then departed. The following evening, July 16th, another spirit came; he seemed at first to be looking for some one, then asked:

"Where did the other fellows go?"

This spirit also condemned high society in general, and denounced young girls in particular for their foolishness.

"The rich take our girls to their dens; they put them on the stage and the girls disown their parents. They deserve licking!" he declared, and emphasized his words with suitable gestures.

This spirit was laboring under such great mental excitement that he suddenly lost control before I could ascertain any particulars.

On February 10th, 1907 the spirit of Mr. Thaw returned, and reiterated his statement that Harry was a psychic sensitive who was frequently subject to the influence of mischievous spirits. He also urged upon humanity the great need for inquiry into the subject of spirit influence, saying that a proper understanding would prevent untold misery to both spirits and their unfortunate mortal victims.

That Richard Ivens, hanged for the murder of Mrs. Bessie Hollister in Chicago, 1906, was a victim of foreign influences was so evident that alienists, criminologists and psychologists alike declared their belief that Ivens was innocent, and that he had confessed the crime under the hypnotic suggestion of some unknown person.

Ivens would alternately confess his guilt, saying, with a strange, trance-like stare, that a "big man" had compelled him to commit the deed, and then again wildly deny it. Hugo Munsterburg, M.D., Professor of Psychology, Harvard University, wrote in June, 1906:

"It is an interesting and yet rather clear case of dissociation and auto-suggestion. . . . The witches of the seventeenth century were burned on account of similar confessions, and the popular understanding of mental aberrations has not made much progress since that time."

Professor William James of Harvard wrote: "Whether guilty or not, Ivens must have been in a state of dissociated personality. . . . He was not his natural "self" during those fateful first days, but the victim of one of those rare alterations of personality either suggested or spontaneous, which are now well known to occur in predisposed subjects."

We present a sequel to this tragic story.

EXPERIENCE, MARCH 7, 1907

Spirit: RICHARD IVENS Psychic: MRS. WICKLAND

When the spirit assumed control the psychic fell to the floor apparently lifeless, and only after half an hour of strenuous effort was the intelligence brought to consciousness.

"Leave me alone," he moaned, "do you want to hang me again?"

He complained of having great pain in the neck and begged to be left undisturbed, saying he wanted only to sleep.

"What is the trouble with your neck?"

"It is broken. They hanged me and I am dead. I want to remain dead; if you bring me to life they will hang me again."

"What is your name?"

"Richard Ivens."

"Were you guilty of the murder of Mrs. Hollister?"

"I do not know. Others said I was. If I did it I do not know it."

"Why did you plead guilty at times and then again deny your confession."

"I pleaded guilty because those three fellows (spirits) made me. The big man stood over me with a knife and threatened to kill me if I would not plead guilty. When the big man was not there I told them that I did not know whether I killed the lady or not. I told it to the police; I told it to the jailer and to everybody that questioned me, but they would not believe me when I told them the truth.

"Oh, I have suffered so much! Why did you call me back when I was dead? Why didn't you let me sleep? They will arrest me and hang me again!"

Suddenly the spirit shouted with fright: "Don't you see? There is that big man again! He has his knife and the two short fellows are with him. Oh!"

Clutching his knee he cried: My knee! He has driven the knife through my knee -and through the other leg! My leg! My leg! He is the devil! He has stabbed me!"

The terrified spirit was gradually made to understand that his tormentors were spirits, that he was free from his physical body and beyond the power of bodily harm.

"You are using a body not your own and need now to free yourself from all mental delusions. Do you not see other spirits beside your enemies?"

"Why—yes, there are others now; they seem to be friendly, and there—there's Mrs. Hollister!"

"Ask the man with the knife why he hounds you," I suggested.

"He only grins."

"Ask him why he wanted to kill the lady."

"He says, because he hates women -" he stopped abruptly, and, breathless, seemed to be watching a scene of great disturbance.

"They have taken those devils away ! It was a lively fight, but they got them!"

Calming himself he said: "I feel better now. I am so glad that terrible man is gone."

Asked to recall what he could of the Hollister tragedy, he said: "When I saw the woman that night I also saw the big man. My head began to feel very strange; I was grabbed by the throat and lost consciousness. When I came to myself again the big man said that I had killed the woman.

THIRTY YEARS AMONG THE DEAD

I had known the man for about a month, but I did not know he was a spirit. He has been hounding me ever since.

"Why didn't they give me a chance to live, even if I would have been in prison? Oh, the shame I have brought upon my family! I feel so sorry for my poor mother; if she could only know the truth. If I could only speak to her and tell her that I could not help it—that I did not do it! Nobody had any sympathy for me, and nobody would believe me when I told them about the big fellow standing over me with the knife. He made me plead guilty.

"If I committed the crime I am sorry for it, but I don't know that I have done it. Why did they kill me?"

After I had explained the continuity of life and progression into higher spiritual realms, he eagerly asked:

"If they did not kill me, is the lady still alive also?"

"Certainly; doubtless she has come here to forgive you. Although you destroyed her physical body you were not responsible for the act; you were merely used by wicked spirits who hypnotized you."

With this new understanding the weary spirit was taken in charge by invisible helpers, who told us that the "Big Man" and his accomplices had in earth life belonged to a band of "White Caps" which had operated extensively for some years in England and America, mutilating and killing many women in their criminal mania.

Several months later the spirit of the "Big Man" himself was brought to our circle.

EXPERIENCE, JUNE 6, 1907

Spirit: CHARLES-THE-FIGHTER Psychic: MRS. WICKLAND

The spirit seemed stupefied by drink, and when finally aroused was so pugnacious that the aid of several persons was required to quiet him.

"I'm Charles-The-Fighter, and I'll have you all shot!" he shouted.

Turning to some other invisibles he cursed them for having lured him to this place and commanded them to help him, instead of standing idly by. Subdued at last, Charles-The-Fighter was compelled to listen to an elucidation of his real situation. In an endeavor to convince him that he was controlling the body of another he was asked to examine the hands of the psychic.

Seeing the hand of a woman he shrank back, terror-stricken, and cried: "Take that hand away! Take it away! I don't want to see it any more."

Questioned regarding the story of the hand he declared: "I shall never tell! I would

rather die. Oh! There is her face too! And the hand that I cut off to get the diamond ring! They haunted me all this time."

Looking about in horror he seemed to see a vast gathering of specters.

"See all those faces! Have I killed all those people? Have they come to accuse me? There! There is that boy! He was hanged once, but he seems to be after me too. (Ivens.) I killed the woman, but I made him confess to save my own neck. But just wait, you devil, you! I will fix you when I get out of this. I will cut you all to pieces!"

THIRTY YEARS AMONG THE DEAD

But at last Charles-The-Fighter realized that further resistance was useless and that his days of robbery and murder were over. He told of his hideous career of crime and said that he murdered for revenge, stole to buy whiskey, and drank to drown his conscience and to escape the specters which constantly haunted him.

In early childhood he had been happy under the care of his own mother, but after her death his stepmother had abused him so mercilessly that he often rushed sobbing to his room and, on his knees, prayed to his dead mother for help.

This roused the stepmother to a jealous fury and, regardless of the protests of a weak father, she had beaten him angrily, forbidding him to ever mention the name of his mother again.

Her abuse grew into such a cruel tyranny that the boy had developed an over-powering hatred for her and revengefully vowed that when he was grown he would kill every woman possible.

Consistently he had carried out his ghastly purpose and had given his entire life to plotting and perpetrating atrocities and crimes, generally victimizing women. He had died in 1870, during a wild fight with his companions, but he had not been aware of the loss of his physical body. He boasted that for many years he had continued his crimes, always eluding the police.

"Once, in Boston, I wanted to kill a policeman, but when I sneaked up behind him and hit him on the head with a club, the club went right through him and never hurt him. He didn't even turn around."

The spirit thought himself now in the hands of authorities but declared that he was willing to give himself up to escape the haunting faces of his many victims.

"I would be glad to go to hell to get away from this torment."

While listening to an explanation of the law of cause and effect and the conditions prevailing in the spirit world, Charles saw his own mother standing before him. The sight of her had an overwhelming effect; the hardened criminal cowered in his seat and wept piteously while his mother pleaded with him to come with her and learn to expiate his crimes.

Crushed by guilt and remorse he cried abjectly: "I cannot go with you! Dear mother, don't ask me to go with you! You must go back to Heaven and I must go to hell, where I belong. I must be cut to pieces and burned in the fires of hell."

But maternal love prevailed and the spirit, humble and penitent, followed his mother.

In 1894 Harry Hayward, a handsome reprobate with a weakness for beautiful women and a life of gaiety, hired a villain to murder his sweetheart in Minnesota and was hanged. While he was in prison awaiting execution he maintained his debonair attitude to the last, played cards with his jailer with the utmost nonchalance, and ordered ice cream, his favorite dish, whenever possible.

"When you come to hell, where I am going," he told the jailer, "I am going to treat you to ice cream."

During this time I anonymously sent him a book and several papers relating to the spirit world, but otherwise had no connection with him.

On February 27, 1908, a nurse asked us to concentrate for Mrs. McA.,12 a patient whom she was attending, arid whose case strongly suggested psychic invalidism, chronic illness and lassitude due to spirit obsession. The nurse was a psychic sensitive herself and surmised that many of the uncontrollable notions of her beautiful patient were caused by spirit obsession, and had several times endeavored to order any intruder away.

One day Mrs. McA developed an intense desire for homemade ice cream, although ordinarily she did not care in the least for it. But she insisted that her whim be satisfied at once, putting her maids to a great deal of inconvenience.

When the nurse entered the room with the ice cream she had a sudden feeling that some one had rushed upon her and the next instant was seized by so strong a feeling of choking that she was forced to leave the room. Upon recovery she returned and, convinced of the presence of a spirit, flung a window open and silently ordered any foreign entity present to leave the house.

This nurse and Mrs. McA.'s maid attended our circle that evening, and the controlling spirit at once complained of pain in the neck, readily explaining that his neck had been broken when he was hanged, and said his name was Harry Hayward.

"Can't you give me some ice cream? I have tried and tried to get some and today I could almost taste it, but I couldn't quite get it. I was chased away by a woman -she threw me out of the window! I don't like to be thrown out of a window by a woman!" Hayward realized that he was hovering around the earth as a spirit, and when we inquired how he had learned about spirit life he replied that while he was in jail he had read of it in some literature which had been sent him by an unknown person.

He complained that no matter where he went no one would take any notice of him; when he took a seat in a train some one would come along and sit down on his lap, and he would be powerless to move.

He was very pleased to be able to converse with people again and asked many questions about the various persons concerned with his trial and execution, inquiring particularly about the guard with whom he had spent a great deal of time playing cards.

I was under the impression that this guard had died some time before and informed the spirit so, suggesting that possibly he might be able to see him in the spirit world. He was silent a moment, endeavoring to trace his former friend, then said emphatically: "No, that man is not dead. I see him playing cards at his son's home in Minneapolis."

Hayward was readily enlightened concerning the higher life and left, expressing a willingness to progress in the spirit world. The psychic invalid showed marked changes for the better after this, and subsequent correspondence proved Hayward's statement about the old guard to be true. The latter was living, and on the evening of our experience with Hayward had been playing cards in his son's home.

Ten years later, after the spirit of another murderer, who was hanged, had been in our circle, Hayward returned and told something of his earth life.

EXPERIENCE, SEPTEMBER 21, 1918

Spirit: HARRY HAYWARD Psychic: MRS. WICKLAND

I think I should like to come in and say something, for I feel I have been in the same boat as the fellow who preceded me -I mean, on the same platform. I feel but little better than he. I had a little more understanding than he had, and therefore my punishment was a little harder. I had education and all the money I needed, but I wanted more. I also want to tell you that since I have come to the spirit side of life I have wished I could go on every street corner and shout a message to mothers not to raise their children in the wrong way.

Mothers say they love their children; they worship them, and they let them go astray because they cannot say "No" to them.

Do not raise children without discipline. Train children as you train animals, as you train flowers. If you plant a flower in your garden you don't want it to grow up wild, but you train it so that it will grow successfully, and have graceful flowers. But how little does humanity think of the children's growth and training; children are not trained to become blossoms for humanity.

I tell you, if my mother—I do not condemn her by any means—had trained me properly, so that she could have said "No" to me, instead of worshipping me and letting me have all the money I wanted, and if she had punished me when I did wrong, I would have been different.

No, I would not have been hanged if my mother had taught me the beautiful lesson of living for others, and of loving my fellow man as myself. If mothers would think of their children's welfare and raise them in the beautiful thought of living for others, they would all be better.

I lived a very sporty life. Nobody taught me any other. I had a very good time and I liked the girls pretty well, but there came a time when I spent more money than my father allowed me to have. I was only a young man and I should have been made to work. My misfortune was that my mother and father were rich. Work was a disgrace for me, they thought. It would have been far better if they had put me to work instead of giving me money each time I asked for it. I commenced to gamble. You know when you get into that game it is hard to quit.

Money came too easy for me. I met a young lady whom I liked. Young girls always were sweet to me and I was able to have whoever I wanted. The young lady liked me, and I liked her for what I got from her, so we decided that she would insure herself for $10,000 in my name.

I had a scheme. If somebody killed her, I would not get the blame, but I would get the money. I laid a bold scheme. I hired a man to kill her. At the time the deed was to be committed I took another girl to the theater, because I thought that, whatever happened, blame could not then be attached to me.

I hired a man to take her for a buggy ride out to Lake Calhoun and he was to kill her. When they got to the woods, the man killed her, and came home. Being in the theater, the girl I was with could testify I was not at the scene of the killing, but, you know, I was so crazy to get hold of the insurance money that I never thought how it looked to go to the insurance office so soon after the death, and they became suspicious, and finally caught me.

If I had only waited a week or two they would never have surmised anything about me. I was arrested. My mother loved me so much that she tried to put the blame on my other brother. He was married and had two children. The trial cost my parents a whole lot of money, and lasted months and months before they could make any headway. They could not decide whether it was Eddie or I that should be hanged for the deed.

One day, while I was in jail, there came a little pamphlet for me, and some papers, all about the spirit world. I knew I had to go, for finally I had been sentenced to be hanged. I realized my trouble. The papers interested me very much, and I thought I should like to know what the spirit world was. I believed in it in a way, and in another way, I didn't. The doctrine was better than the church had taught, but for a while I treated it more as a joke.

I talked about it quite a little to the watchman, but when the time came for me to be hanged,

THIRTY YEARS AMONG THE DEAD

I shrank from it. It is a very strange sensation when you think you are going to the gallows and your life will be snapped out—you cannot imagine how it feels.

You cannot imagine the sensation you have when you realize that you have only a few hours to live. Still, the little message which had been sent to me gave me a little courage, and I thought probably only my body would be destroyed and not my spirit. So at the last moment I kept up my courage and felt that I wanted to see what the hereafter was.

I have to thank the one who sent me that pamphlet, because it was a bright, cheerful spot to me at the last of my days. When I realized that I had passed out of my body, my first thought was: "I am not dead." I went to my mother, and I spoke to her, and she felt my presence. I still clung to my body, however, and I felt I could not leave it. I got out of it quickly, but I went back to it again. When my body was cremated I stood by and saw it burned.

After that I walked around, but I could not find the spirit world. I walked and walked, from one place to another. I still had my feeling for nice pretty women, so I traveled. In a way, I realized that I was dead, yet I did not fully realize it.

One time I felt I would like to take a journey and I wanted to travel by train. I went to the ticket office to get a ticket, but I had no money. I thought I would talk to the agent nicely and he would give me a ticket, but he paid no attention to me. So I thought, "All right; I'm going on the train anyway," so on I got.

I sat down on one of the seats, and, before I knew it, a great, big, fat man sat right down on my lap. I got real mad. I tried to push him off, but I could not, and I could not get up either. I had to let that man sit on me until he was ready to get off the train! I had not learned the power of thought, to think myself away; I had only learned to walk. I had not yet learned the little thought lesson to think myself in a place in order to be there.

Before long I came to a beautiful lady (Mrs. McA.), and I commenced to like her. Before I knew it, I was in her magnetic aura and I could not get away. She wanted to be in bed all the time, and there I was!

Once I heard some one say: "You must leave this lady and go away; if there is any spirit around her, it must leave and go away." I was there, however. I was very fond of ice cream, and I wanted some, so I impressed the lady to ask for it. When it was brought in, I wanted it. I seemed to come in contact with the lady who was carrying it, and I felt that if I could only get a good hold of her I would get the cream.

All at once I was a lady myself, and when I tried to get that ice cream I had the same sensation that I had when I was hanged. But the lady, who was carrying the ice cream had such power that, before I knew it, she had thrown me out of the window -bodily, mind you.

I have to thank you for delivering me from all that trouble and also want to thank you from the bottom of my heart for the sermon you gave me at that time, which helped me to an understanding of the beautiful world beyond.

I wish again that I could stand on every street corner and tell the mothers to raise their children to be good men and women, and when necessary, punish them while they are little, and not spare the rod and spoil the child. If mothers raised their children properly, there would not be the selfishness there is in the world.

I have a nice little home in the spirit world now, and I have much to do, for my work is not yet done. I am trying to extend help to all those who wish help. I thank you for enlightening me in the first place. Good Night.

The "Car Barn Murderer," of Chicago, was a criminal of a different type, a victim of his environment, and was brought to our circle some time after his execution, when he followed a girl, formerly a family neighbor, who came to visit Mrs. Wickland. He returned several times after that, to tell his story and to bring earthbound spirits of similar experiences to an understanding.

EXPERIENCE, SEPTEMBER 21, 1918

Spirit: PETE NEIDEMEYER Psychic: MRS. WICKLAND

I want to come here tonight to tell you that I also am one who is very thankful to you, although you probably do not care whether I come again or not. But I do know you helped me to something like happiness which I thought never could be mine.

I was nothing but a wild beast in earth life, but still, when you do not give children proper training, how can you expect to have good men? I had no training at all. My mother was very wild and did not care what became of her children. She thought: "Let them take care of themselves."

So you go out in company with others and get into first one game then another. Sometimes you go to church. I didn't believe in that old story about Christ. I could not believe it, and I thought there was no such thing as what they taught about Christ, and if there was, what did I care?

I walked in the path of evil from the time I was a little boy until I got where I could not live any longer, whether I wanted to or not. I will tell you, if you have children, please give them an understanding when they are little. If they take anything from a person, make them take it back where they got it. Don't let them get the idea that you will take it from them and think it is all right, If they steal once, they will again, if not properly taught.

When I stole, my mother thought I was a smart boy. I kept on going from bad to worse. I belonged to a gang of about a dozen boys. We got so bold and desperate that we did not care what became of us. We got into all kinds of hold-ups and the more we got into, the better we liked it. At last we held up and killed people. The result was, that we were caught and hanged.

I am Neidemeyer, and here I am. Years ago I was brought to this circle through our neighbor girl. I liked that girl very much. One day she went away from home and I thought I would go with her. I did not realize that I had been hanged. I did not realize that I was dead. I had gone home and had stayed there for a long time, but I did not know that I was dead. My mother was a strange woman, but from what I have seen since I came to the spirit side of life, I realize that she was obsessed. Nobody could do anything with my mother. My father and my brother were very good people, but my mother and I were the black ones.

This neighbor girl was good, and she always tried to do the best for me that she could. The day I followed her, she went to this man's house (Dr. W.) and she went into a little room and spoke with the psychic through whom I am talking now, and I saw things that day that I had never seen before. I did not know what they meant. Somebody seemed to keep me there, and I could not get away.

Before I knew much I was sitting in a little meeting; I heard singing and before I realized it I was full of life again. I could talk and my throat did not hurt me any more. began to wonder what had happened to me. You talked to me so kindly that it helped me. You talked to me about the real life on the other side. You helped me to an understanding of life -not what the church and ministers taught, that we should pray to God and believe in the blood of Christ, and that Christ died for our sins, and that if we believe that we will go to Heaven.

I was not the kind that could go on that straight road, because I felt that was too easy, and I couldn't believe that we could get to Heaven without any effort on our part. I knew I was bad, yet I felt in my heart that I should do something to try and be good, and do good for what I had done bad. The thought of that seemed to be more reasonable than that of jumping from my bad condition right into Heaven. I thought I would not be a very good example either.

You commenced to talk to me about the philosophy of God in a way I had never heard before, and it appealed to my sense. I hope somebody will talk in that way to my fellow men who are in the condition I was. It would touch their hearts. There are many of them who are not bad, but nobody cares for them. The majority of them do not believe in the Jesus Christ story. As they are now, they are going to the dogs.

Since I came to this little circle the first time and received help, I have had my struggles. It is years since I made my first appearance here. I want to tell you what I have to do since my mother passed out. I have tried and tried to bring her to an understanding of the truth, but she will not listen. I hope some day to be able to awaken her to a higher condition.

As we progress we go from circle to circle. If I believed that Christ died for my sins, that belief and creed would keep me out of the higher spirit world. When I had passed out of my body, you told me that I should look for spirit friends who would help me, and that my first lesson would be to serve others. I have had a very hard time.

The first thing I had to do was to conquer self, and it is very hard to conquer selfishness when you have never thought of anything else but selfishness. We must conquer that before we can do any work at all in the spirit world.

The best way is to be put in a dark room—we sometimes call it a dungeon—where we see nothing but ourselves and our acts of the past. One after another these acts come crowding in. The good ones are so few that they hardly count for anything. When we do see a good act, it seems as if it belongs to some one else. We have to stay there until our hearts and eyes are opened. When we seek to overcome our bad habits and to live for others then we get out of the selfish state.

My heart was very hardened, but finally I cried out: "Not my will any longer, but thine." The first thing to be done is to help serve the, very lowest we come in contact with. I felt that I did not want to assist with this or that, but I had to. I had to learn patience. When we can serve without grumbling and do it for the love of our fellow man, it does not seem so hard.

So I have gone on and on, from one thing to another, always learning, and through learning I have stepped into a more beautiful condition. In the invisible world we advance by stages, but only through learning. I want to thank you tonight for the help you have given me. I have a beautiful little home in the spirit world by this time, and I am happy, but my work is not done yet.

My work is to keep on helping those who need help, and to try to influence the boys on earth not to do the mischief they are planning, but to try to be good, and do the very best they know how for their fellow men. Goodbye.

THIRTY YEARS AMONG THE DEAD

EXPERIENCE, AUGUST 30, 1922

Spirit: PETE NEIDEMEYER Psychic: MRS. WICKLAND

I should like to come here tonight to say a few words. I want to thank you for helping

me to the higher life. I had gone down, down, and had only hatred and selfish thoughts. I was down as far as I could go. My mother was obsessed. She had a great deal of influence over me. She was down on the world and made me do things to the neighbors that I should never have done. My father and brother were good people and were looked up to.

I am Pete Neidemeyer. I want to thank you for having helped me, and now I want to ask you to send good thoughts to my mother. She has passed out but I cannot reach her. She was obsessed by a very evil spirit; she sent evil thoughts to me, and I was very sensitive to them.

You did a Christian act for me which no one else had ever done. I was shunned by all. When you are in a large city, with all its temptations, and have not learned anything about the higher things, you get in bad company. You get so wrapped up with things that are bad that you think everything belongs to you just as much as it does to the other fellow. Jealousy, selfishness and ignorance are three things that we should all try to conquer.

When they get hold of you, they are the devil in you. You feel jealous of everybody that has more than you. You are selfish. You don't want to give anything away, you just want to keep it all for yourself. You want everything that belongs to others. You feel that if there is a God he should have given you a chance as well as the rest of them. In that atmosphere I was brought up. Mother was selfish and jealous. Nobody in the neighborhood liked her; she did not have one friend. I was her pet and I could have anything.

Father told me not to do bad things, but mother said not to mind what he told me, but to go ahead and do as I pleased. I went out and stayed out nights in bad company. We got a gang together. I did not mean to get into the gang as I did, but I was forced into it by the club.

You understand, they have clubs, secret clubs, those fellows, and when you join you have to do just what they say, because you are in their power. If you try to withdraw you cannot because they will squeal on you. They watch you and somebody follows you all the time. The new beginners are the ones who do the dirty work. The leaders very seldom get caught.

There is a school and the new beginners learn to do bad things. Some of the leaders are in the finest society in big cities, and they get to know where we can find people to rob. You may sometimes wonder how we know where to go to find jewelry and money. Our leaders know all about it. They are in fine society all the time. They have money so it wouldn't do any good to squeal on them.

If I should tell you the names of some of our leaders who are in society in Chicago, you would not believe me. You would say that it is not so. If you would tell on them they would at once squeal on you and say you robbed such a house. What could you do? You just have to keep still. That is what the underworld is doing. The "upper world" uses the underworld when it suits its purpose. What we steal in one city, they send off to another city.

Always you will find our leaders in the finest society, but we do not dare say anything. When you once join their club -what I would call the Devil's Club -you can't say anything. You are in their claws, and our leaders are worse than devils, they are so mean. If we should kill, we are the ones who suffer, but they get the money.

THIRTY YEARS AMONG THE DEAD

I came here tonight to thank you for having helped me. Nobody ever gave me a helping hand before. In that car barn murder I did not kill any one. I was with the gang, but the one who did the work did not get hanged; he got away. We four were hanged, because we were there. I was innocent. My work was to watch, which I did, but I did not murder. I was hanged for it.

If you have any influence at all, do not hang people. Let them have another chance, because sometimes you will find they are innocent. Keep them in the pen; give them another chance. If they are hanged, then where are they? All they have in their hearts is hatred. They go back to earth life and do more mischief. They control people and obsession steps in. I had hatred when I was hanged and said if there is life again I will get even and fight for revenge.

You remember Tillie, who lived next door to me? I told you about her before. She used to come to your circles. I followed her once and through her influence I came into your circle and was converted to the higher life.

Tillie always had a good influence over me and sometimes she wanted to talk to me, but mother was always jealous and didn't want her to talk. Mother was very mean to Tillie's people. She got so mad at the time I was hanged that she tormented all her neighbors. She tore up all the fences and closed up all the stable windows on their side. She tried to shoot every body she could. If my father bad had the gun loaded, mother would have been in great trouble.

Tillie was my guardian angel, and through your circle I got over my hatred. Now I try to help others with the light you gave me. My mission is to help the unfortunate ones, like this fellow who came before me. I try to influence people to be more just. If you have a chance to hang any one, don't do it, but give him another chance. You have no right to kill, Nobody should kill another person. We are all God's children. We all make mistakes, and the strong should help the weak.

When one person murders another, no justice is shown, no mercy. The judge and the jury - what mercy do they show a fellow when he has murdered? Why should they kill him instead of giving him another chance? Why don't they give a good word to the poor ones? Why don't they go to the prisoners and teach them of the higher life, and also have psychic circles and try to help them?

As soon as you stop capital punishment you will not have so much killing. When persons are hanged, they have revenge and hatred in their hearts, and all they want to do is kill, kill, kill. So they influence sensitive mortals and make them commit all kinds of crime.

I want to say again, if you have any influence, stop capital punishment. This is a Christian country and nobody has a right to kill another. As they killed Christ, so they kill boys who have been murderers, instead of teaching them while they are young. Isn't is right that they should be taught to do better, and to live better lives?

The time will come when the world will have to understand that it must overcome selfishness. There will be lots of trouble before that time comes. There will be much destruction, but after that, things will be better. I am now doing my work in the spirit world, and I thank you for bringing me to a realization and waking me up. I have little meetings here and there. I give little thoughts of cheer to those in darkness.

I am up against a very hard condition, and that is, to get my mother to understand. I wish you would all send good, kind thoughts to her, because she only had hatred and selfishness and jealousy in her heart. She was so wrapped up in herself that now she will not listen to any one. Help me to wake her up and realize the true condition of life.

THIRTY YEARS AMONG THE DEAD

Oh, how I thank you for helping me! At heart I was not a murderer, yet I was hanged for murder. I was not with the gang that was doing the work; all I did was to watch. I was there with them and that was enough for the jury -I had the name.

Now I am trying to do my part, but I have much to learn. I was very ignorant of the real life. My father wanted me to go to Sunday School. Mother told me I didn't need to go, but I went, and I didn't find anything there that appealed to me, so I quit going. I know now that God is everywhere and that I am a part of God. I had a hard time getting rid of selfishness, jealousy and ignorance; they are the root of all evil. When they are gone, love, kindness and sympathy take their place. Get an understanding of the higher life and you will be happy. All should be brothers and sisters on earth, as we are in the higher life.

In the spirit world our real eyes are opened. You cannot progress until you have learned the lessons of life. You know, a school boy cannot go to University until after he gets through his school books. He must go to Kindergarten before he can enter the University, and he has to get there step by step.

So it is in the spirit world. It is the world of happiness. We cannot appreciate it until we have it before us. Everybody should know these things before they step over the Borderland. We cannot go to the spirit world until we have an understanding of it. When we are one with God then we have happiness.

I do not know much, and I cannot say much, because I have seen so little of it. I have much work to do before I go on. The spirit world is like going into a garden and seeing one beautiful flower here and another there. The flowers all stand up so straight and look at you and seem to say: "Please take me." This one has a certain odor, and that one another, but all are beautiful and fragrant.

The spirit world is like a flower bed, all is beauty and harmony -I mean there is no selfishness. One shines more than another because he has more understanding. We will all get there, but we have to gain advancement for ourselves. No one needs to get discouraged; all will get there, but it takes time.

Thank you for having helped me to an understanding and a home. But for that, I should have been an earthbound spirit, doing more harm than good, for I had hatred in my heart. I am very happy, but I want you all to send a good thought to my mother, so that I can wake her up, and help her to overcome her selfishness, jealousy and ignorance. Just give me a chance to wake her up.

I thank you all.

THIRTY YEARS AMONG THE DEAD

Chapter VII

Spirits and Suicide

A great number of unaccountable suicides are due to the obsessing or possessing influence of earthbound spirits. Some of these spirits are actuated by a desire to torment their victims; others, who have ended their physical existence as suicides, find themselves still alive, and, having no knowledge of a spirit world, labor under the delusion that their self-destructive attempts have failed and continue their suicidal efforts.

When these intelligences come in contact with mortal sensitives, they mistake the physical bodies for their own, and impress the sensitives with morbid thoughts and instigate them to deeds of self destruction.

The fate of a suicide is invariably one of deepest misery, his rash act holding him in the earth sphere until such time as his physical life would have had a natural ending. One suicide case which we contacted was the spirit of a woman, Mrs. X., who had been my Sunday School teacher when I was a boy in Europe, but of whom Mrs. Wickland had never heard.

This lady had been intelligent and spiritual, an earnest church member, happily married and the mother of several children. Without any warning, while apparently happy and contented, she had suddenly hanged herself, and the horrified husband and children could in no way account for the tragedy.

One winter day ten years later, when Mrs. Wickland and I were alone in our home in Chicago, Mrs. Wickland was unexpectedly controlled by a spirit who gasped for breath and seemed to be strangling. This spirit, like so many others, was unconscious of controlling a body not its own, and upon contacting matter, again experienced its last death struggle.

After much questioning I learned, to my great surprise, that this was the spirit of my former friend, who had ended her physical life by hanging herself. She was still bound to the earth sphere and related the indescribable mental hell she had been in during all those years.

"As soon as I found myself out of my body, I saw at once the cause for my rash act. Evil spirits, who had been attracted to me by the jealous thoughts of other persons, were standing near, grinning with devilish satisfaction at their work.

"They had influenced me to end my life; I had no occasion to even think of such folly. An irresistible impulse had suddenly come over me. I fastened the rope around my neck, and only realized what I had done when it was too late.

"I would have given the world to have been able to regain possession of my body. Oh, what horrors of despair and remorse I have gone through! My home shattered, my husband broken-hearted and discouraged, and my little ones needing my care!

"They do not know that I come to them and try to comfort them, and I have seen nothing but gloom and darkness until now."

Comforted and reassured by an explanation of the true spiritual realms, this spirit was eager to go with the higher intelligences and learn how she might be of service to her loved ones on earth.

Many years later, when we had with us a patient of strong suicidal tendencies, this spirit returned to warn her against carrying out her intentions.

EXPERIENCE, NOVEMBER 17, 1918

Spirit: MRS. X. Psychic: MRS. WICKLAND

It is a long time since I have been here. I should like to say a few words to this young lady who is contemplating suicide. Many years ago I was a happy wife, with two dear children and a very kind husband. We lived together happily, since we were both of a cheerful disposition, and because of this there were many jealous thoughts centered upon us.

I did not know at that time that I was a psychic, because I belonged to the Baptist Church. I did the very best I could around the home, but somebody started to upset us. One day, when my husband went to work, I kissed him goodbye and was very happy, but after he was gone, all in a moment something got hold of me. I did not know what I was doing. I didn't know a thing. I remember feeling very strange, as if somebody had taken complete hold of me, and I did not realize what was taking place.

After awhile everything changed. I saw my husband in terrible mental agony, and he was crying very bitterly. When things became a little clearer to me, I saw my body hanging there! Oh, if you could only realize what a condition I was in! My husband stood there in the shed, looking at my hanging body; he was crying heart-brokenly, but I could do nothing to, help him. There I stood at his side, wishing with all my power that I could have that body again, but I could not. There were my two little children weeping for me, and I could not help them.

I did not know what was the matter until I saw some evil spirits standing near, laughing at us. They had gotten hold of me and made me kill myself, because they wanted to break up our happy home.

My husband could never forget the sight of my body hanging in the shed. My children were small and needed my help, but the responsibility of raising them was thrown on my husband. It should have been my duty to have shared that responsibility. Although I had been influenced to do what I did, for ten long years I could see nothing before me but what I had done. I could see how much the children needed me, but I could do nothing for them, and oh, how I suffered! My poor, poor children!

One day, a very cold day, I felt that I had come to life again; I felt a new warmth. I did not know where I was, but I felt that I had come to life. I found myself talking to Dr. Wickland. He told me what had happened, and explained that I was only temporarily controlling Mrs. Wickland, and that friends would take me to the spirit world.

After this I felt somewhat better, and I thank you for having helped me to the beautiful condition I have now.

THIRTY YEARS AMONG THE DEAD

But oh, how I suffered during those ten, long years! All I could see was my body hanging before me, and the children's need of me. My husband and children! How they needed my care -but I was powerless to help them.

I want to warn anybody who is thinking of trying to get out of the physical body. Do not do it under any circumstances. You do not know, you cannot realize, what a hell you will find yourself in. You cannot step into your body again after you once leave it, and you cannot do your duty to others.

Think of my children always having the thought that their mother committed suicide! Neither my husband nor children can ever really forgive me. Even though I was controlled when I did what I did, I have had to suffer. If you had an understanding of the laws of the spirit side of life, you would not commit suicide, knowing the results. Overcome any thoughts of taking your life. Be happy on this earth plane until the time comes for you to go to the spirit world.

The ten years that I suffered was the time I should have remained on earth before passing to the spirit side of life. After my ten years had expired I should have left my body, for my life would have been lived out, but during that time I could have given help to my husband and children.

I should not have reached the spirit side of life before my allotted time, and my punishment was to constantly see my body hanging before me for ten years. All that time I could realize that my husband and children were in great need of my help. Now I am as happy as I can be until my family is reunited, and I am doing all I can to help my children.

I want you to send my love to my dear husband. He feels that he is all alone. I am with him but I can do nothing to comfort him in his loneliness. Goodbye!

On November 20, 1904, while Mrs. Wickland and I were visiting with friends in Chicago, a circle had been formed for a psychic demonstration when Mrs. Wickland heard some one say: "I am in the dark."

She inquired who had made the remark, but no one in the room had uttered a word; however, the gentleman sitting beside Mrs. Wickland declared that he too had heard the voice.

A moment later Mrs. Wickland became entranced and fell to the floor, the spirit clutching at the throat and crying: "Take the rope away! Take the rope away! I am in the dark. Why did I do it? Oh, why did I do it?" When the excited spirit had been somewhat quieted, she told us that her name was Minnie Harmening, that she was a young girl and had lived on a farm near Palatine. As she was speaking brokenly, between sobs, it was difficult to distinguish her words, and I understood her to say that she came from "Palestine," which seemed rather strange.

The spirit was in great grief because she had hanged herself, and thought the body of the psychic was her own, and that the rope was still about her neck. She said that on October 5th, without any cause or premeditation, she had been overpowered by a desire to take her life, and when alone had gone to the barn and hanged herself.

"A big man with a black beard made me do it." (Spirit.) "He met me in the barnyard and hypnotized me, and made me hang myself to a rafter, but I don't know why I did it.

"My brother John found me and cut me down, and my parents were almost beside themselves. But I am not dead. I am at home all the time and I talk to my mother and father. I try to comfort them and make them know that I am not dead, but they do not notice me and do not answer me. My folks all sit around the table crying, and there is my empty chair, but no one answers me. Why don't they answer me?"

THIRTY YEARS AMONG THE DEAD

We could not at first convince her that she was expressing herself through the body of another, but after a lengthy conversation, she was somewhat enlightened and comforted, and left with spirit friends.

Previous to this incident neither Mrs. Wickland nor I had heard of the Harmening suicide mystery and we did not know that such a girl had ever existed. Several days later, a reporter from one of the Chicago dailies came to interview us regarding our research work, and I related our recent experience with the Harmening girl. In great surprise he said that he himself had been the reporter on the Harmening case and that the girl had lived in Palatine, Cook County, Illinois. The dead body of the girl had been found hanging in her father's barn, but no one knew of any cause for suicide, although the girl had always been peculiar.

There was a suspicion of murder because the clothes about the chest had been torn, and the neck badly scratched, leading the authorities to believe that a crime had been committed and the body hanged up to avert suspicion.

On Thanksgiving Day, November 24th, the spirit of Minnie Harmening came to us again, still grieving because of the suffering of her parents, and the intolerant attitude assumed toward her family by the villagers and church members, who considered the family disgraced.

The girl had been a devout member of a German Lutheran Church, but because she had died a suicide the pastor had refused to allow the funeral service to be held in the church, nor would the congregation permit the body to be buried in the consecrated ground of the churchyard.

Minnie said that the funeral service had been held at the home of her parents, but the minister had considered the viewing of body such a sacrilege that he had stepped outside the house while others paid their last tribute, and this had added still more to the grief of her already distracted parents. (These statements I found corroborated in the papers afterward.)

I asked the spirit why her clothes had been torn, and she answered: "I did that myself. The big man (spirit) with the beard told me to hang myself, but as soon as I had kicked the box away from my feet, I felt the rope tightening around my neck and came to my senses. I clawed at the rope and tried to loosen it, but I only tightened it and scratched myself.

Fourteen years later the spirit of Minnie Harmening spoke to us again.

EXPERIENCE, OCTOBER 20, 1918

Spirit: MINNIE HARMENING. Psychic: MRS. WICKLAND

I want to thank you for all the help you have given me.

When I committed the act which took my life I was only a young girl of sixteen. I had so much suffering afterwards and was very, very miserable. I could see my father and mother sitting at the table, crying, and I could not help them.

When the time came for my body to be buried the minister would not take it into the church, and would not bury it, because, he said, I had committed a sin in taking my own life. He also said that I could not be buried in the graveyard because of my act, and he would not even look at the funeral as it passed by.

I did not do the deed myself. I was obsessed. It was very hard for my father and mother and sisters. The minister would not even come into the room where my body lay, but spoke from another room; he was too holy to be where the body was. This made it much harder for my parents.

Do not think that by taking your own life you can bury yourself in the hereafter. I was obsessed when I took my life and did not know what I was doing, but I am suffering because my father and mother are still mourning for me. Very often I go to see my poor old mother, and she is very old now.

I am the girl who lived at Palatine. You remember me, don't you? The neighbors made it still harder for my folks because they told mother what a disgrace it was for the family. I feel very badly about the matter. I want to thank you for the help I received here. It was through you that I received light and understanding. I am happy in a way, but not real happy, because I feel the grief my father and mother have.

When I lived I did not understand obsession. After I had hanged myself I saw a man beside me, staring at me. Just when the rope was around my neck I came to; I tried my best to get it off my neck, but I had kicked the box from under myself and my whole weight was in the rope and I could do nothing. I scratched my body in an effort to free myself, but it was no use. If one takes his own life he goes through a bitter experience, and suffers greatly -yes, suffers greatly.

I thank you very much for the light and understanding I have received, for it has been a great help to me.

Another experience, illustrating the power exercised over sensitive mortals by malignant, earthbound spirits, occurred in Chicago.

Mrs. Wickland and I were resting on a bench in Lincoln Park, on July 12th, 1906, when an elderly gentleman seated himself beside us. Mrs. Wickland at first saw two men on the bench, but upon looking again, noticed only one.

A conversation ensued which drifted into occultism, and when the stranger, Mr. F., expressed an interest in psychic phenomena, we invited him to call at our home. On the following evening Mr. F. called upon us, and later Mrs. Wickland became entranced by the spirit of a man who was greatly agitated. He called Mr. F. by name, saying he was his friend, Mr. B., of Cleveland, who had been with him in Lincoln Park the previous week, and had had an appointment to meet him there again on that very day.

Mr. F. was greatly startled by this communication, for his friend had committed suicide in his club at Cleveland the preceding Sunday.

Mr. B. had lived in Cleveland and had come to Chicago the week before to close a real estate deal, but before final negotiations were completed, had returned for a week-end visit to Cleveland.

He was in a cheerful frame of mind when he left his home on Sunday morning, but after conversing with a group of friends at his club, he had gone into an adjoining room, placed carbolic acid in his glass of wine and drinking it, had fallen dead.

Mr. B. had been a man of wealth and position, to all appearances singularly fortunate and happy, and there seemed no reason for his suicide. The spirit of Mr. B. was greatly troubled and bewildered, and asked his friend what was the matter with him.

"I go home to my wife and children, but they do not seem. to see me or hear me. I have been with you for several days, but you will not talk to me. What is the matter?" Calming the spirit, we finally made him realize that to the world he was "dead," and after explaining the suicide to him, we asked why he had taken his life. "I did not take my life. I went to the club and was talking to my friends, then I went into another room, but I do not know what happened after that. The next thing that I remember is that I saw my body lying on the floor and a man (spirit) watching me and laughing."

After learning more of his condition the spirit urged his friend to write to his wife and tell her that in reality he was not dead at all. On the evening of the 16th, Mr. F. called again, when the spirit of Mr. B. came a second time, still greatly disturbed, and asked his friend why he had not written to his wife, and urgently begged him to do so.

"I know now that I was influenced to commit suicide by evil spirits who were opposed to my carrying out that real estate deal. Rather than see my purpose accomplished they determined to kill me. Please tell my wife the truth and warn all the world to be wiser."

While the trial of a young man, who was accused of killing a college girl, Marion Lambert, was in progress in Waukegan, Illinois, the spirit of the murdered girl was brought to us, on June 17th, 1916, entrancing Mrs. Wickland. She was weeping uncontrollably and in such distress that she was at first unable to speak, then suddenly cried out: "I did it! I did it! Nobody can help me now. If I only could tell them and make them understand -but they will not listen. I am in the dark and can see only the past and everything foolish I have done. Oh, what a foolish girl I was!"

"What is your name?"

"Marion Lambert."

"Where do you think you are?"

"I do not know. I am not acquainted with any one here. (Crying.) They talk of hell, but that could not be as bad as what I have gone through, just because of my foolishness. I would like very much to get out of all this trouble.

"I took my own life. I didn't mean to kill myself —I only meant to take enough cyanide of potassium to scare him.

"And now they blame him for my death! I would so like to do something to make them understand he is not guilty. Oh, but they will not believe me! I talk to the different people at the court house but they take no notice of me, and will not listen to me. Everything is so strange, I don't know what to do.

"I was such a foolish girl. Oh, my poor father and mother! I'm half crazy with trouble and worry. If I could only go to the court house and show them that I am not dead, but that I am alive"

"Why don't they listen to me? I go to the court house but nobody will speak to me, and I have spoken to so many people. I am in such agony, I don't know what to do.

"If I had had more sense I would never have done what I did, but it's no use saying that now—it is too late. I wish I could be in my body again. I studied a great deal, but I was so foolish it did me no good, and now I am suffering. Everything is so dark and I am in such trouble."

The spirit was so hysterical that it was exceedingly difficult to make her understand that she could best help by keeping away from the court house, go with kindly intelligences to the spirit world and learn the higher purposes of life. I

n July, 1919, the interest of the American public was centered in a "murder" case in Los Angeles, in which Harry New was accused of killing his sweetheart, Freda Lesser. The tragedy had taken place on July 4th in Topanga Canyon, where Harry and Freda had driven late in the day. Near the crest a shot was fired which ended the girl's life, and Harry New was arrested on a charge of murder. The girl had been expecting motherhood, and this fact was used in the trial as a motive for the crime. Harry New was convicted of second degree murder and sentenced to San Quentin for ten years.

During the trial we had an interesting experience which would have thrown new light on the case, could it have been accepted as evidence in court.

EXPERIENCE, JANUARY 7, 1920

Spirit: FREDA LESSER. Psychic: MRS. WICKLAND

The controlling spirit was crying pathetically, and seemed bewildered.

Doctor What is the matter with you?

Spiri:t Oh, I feel so bad!

Dr. What seems to be the trouble?

Sp. Lots of trouble.

Dr. Possibly we may be able to help you.

Sp. That's impossible. Oh, I feel so bad! (Weeping.)

Dr. How long have you been dead?

Sp. I am not dead. I am sick and downhearted.

Dr. Why should you be downhearted?

Sp. Because of my own foolishness.

Dr. What have you been doing?

Sp. Lots of things.

Dr. What in particular? Have you been happy?

Sp. Oh, no! I have not been happy. (Wringing hands in anguish.) I wish, I wish, I wish I had not been so foolish!

Dr. Did something happen to you?

Sp. Yes, everything happened.

Dr. What is your name? Is it John?

Sp. I'm not a man. Oh, all those people! And that big crowd! And they will not listenwhen I tell them about it.

Dr. What is your name?

Sp. I feel so bad I can't think. Oh, Harry, Harry! It was not your fault. What are thosepeople doing with him? He hasn't done anything; it was my foolishness.

Dr. What did you do?

Sp. I fought with him. I got hold of the revolver and was going to fool him. He tried to take the revolver away from me, and we both fought for it. I was only trying to fool him. I go to see him but I don't know what to do.

Dr. Why did you take the revolver?

Sp. I was only trying to scare him.

Dr. Did you fire the revolver?

Sp. He tried to take the revolver away from me and it exploded. I feel so bad, and he will not talk to me, and there are all those people bothering him. He did not do anything. It was all my foolishness. He was a good fellow, but I fooled him. Where am I now?

Dr. You are in Highland Park, Los Angeles.

Sp. Why did I come here?

Dr. Some good friend brought you here.

Sp. Why, I went to Harry.

Dr. Do you refer to Harry New?

Sp. Yes, of course I do.

Dr. Did you care for him?

Sp. I care for him more than ever because I cannot get to him. He did not do it -he did not shoot me. I told him that I would kill myself and I went and got the revolver. He didn't get it. I got it from his auto and I had it. I didn't mean to do anything. I was just going to frighten him. It was just foolishness, foolishness, foolishness!

Dr. What is your name?

Sp. Freda -Freda Lesser.

Dr. Do you realize that you have lost your body?

Sp. I don't know anything, except that I go to mother and Harry, and all over, and no one pays any attention to me. I want to tell them how things happened, but no one will listen to me, not any one. I am so distressed, and I don't know why I cannot be heard when I talk. I am so unhappy.

Dr. The people you refer to do not know that you are there. You are invisible to them.

Sp. Oh, that poor fellow is suffering for my foolishness! You don't know what my condition is. No one will listen to what I say, not one.

Dr. They do not know you are there. You are invisible to us; we cannot see you.

Sp. Why can't you see me? (Crying again and wringing her hands.) Foolish girl, foolish girl!

Dr. You must try to control yourself. You have been brought here by kind spirits and allowed to control my wife's body and brain for a short time. You can only use this body temporarily.

Sp. Why can't you tell those people that it was all my foolishness?

Dr. They would not believe me if I did tell them.

THIRTY YEARS AMONG THE DEAD

Sp. Tell them what?

Dr. That a spirit came and talked to us. Do you not realize that at the time the revolver went off, you lost your body?

Sp. I thought I had only hurt myself. Oh, how I suffered! I do not see how I could be dead, because when you die you never suffer any more, and I have suffered.

Dr. No one actually dies; only the physical body is lost. Your suffering was mental.

Sp. But my head hurts so much.

Dr. That is a mental condition also.

Sp. Why can't Harry talk to me?

Dr. He does not know you are there. He cannot see you.

Sp. I go where he is and try to tell them that the whole thing was caused by my foolishness. Oh, if I could only change things! I took that revolver and said I was going to kill myself, but I thought I would only scare him. When he saw I had the revolver he fought with me to get it away. I didn't mean anything -I was only fooling. I love him and he loves me. He did not know how the revolver came in his hands. He had it in his auto. I picked it up and hid it in my clothes for a while and then I told him I was going to kill myself.

Dr. Had you any idea of marrying him?

Sp. Yes, some idea.

Dr. Did you really care for him enough to marry him?

Sp. Yes. We had no quarrel. I was just going to scare him but you know girls do foolish things sometimes. I wanted to test him, to see if he cared for me. (Crying.)

Dr. Remember you are using my wife's brain and body, and must try to calm yourself. Look around and you will find kind spirit friends who will help you.

Sp. I can never be helped any more, I'm so unhappy.

Dr. When you leave here you will be taken to the spirit world. You have not yet found it, because you have been so disturbed with your trouble. Spirit friends are around you, waiting to help you.

Sp. I want to tell those men bow things happened, but they will not listen to me. They don't seem to hear me, or see me. I go to Harry, and because he feels me around him sometimes, they think that he is crazy.

Dr. You are a free spirit now, and you must listen to the spirit friends who are here.

They will teach you how to obtain understanding and overcome your troubles.

Sp. Will they kill Harry for my foolishness?

Dr. I hardly think so.

Sp. Poor fellow, poor fellow! I feel so sorry for him and his mother. They both cry, and my mother cries. Why did I do such a foolish thing? It was a piece of folly.

Dr. Now, look around and see if you can see friends who will help you.

Sp. There's a young lady standing there (spirit) and she says that she was helped here, and she says she brought me here. She says she was in the same trouble I was, and that she was helped, and is so happy now, and that she can help me. She says she was just as foolish as I was; she took poison to scare her fellow, and killed herself.

Dr. Does she tell you her name?

Sp. She says she has been around me, because she does missionary work, helping to take care of girls in the same trouble as myself.

Dr. Does she look sorrowful?

Sp. No, she looks happy. She says she goes around and finds unfortunate girls who are in the same condition she was in when she went to spirit life. (Crying.)

Dr. Don't allow yourself to become excited. You do not realize what a privilege you have in being allowed to control a mortal body and obtain understanding. Many remain in a bewildered condition for years and years.

Sp. The lady standing there says you helped her when she was in the same trouble I am.

Dr. What was her name?

Sp. She says her name is Marion Lambert. She says she works hard to help unfortunate girls who are in trouble and do foolish things, and that she tries to help them to happiness. She says that is her mission and that is why she brought me here. (Crying.)

Dr. Try to understand that you are using the body of this psychic only temporarily, and must not misuse it by becoming excited. This girl you see, came to us some years ago in the same distressed condition that you are in. Now she tells you that she is happy and doing missionary work.

Sp. Can I ever be happy?

Dr. Of course you can. This is only a temporary trouble you are in. No one ever "dies"; it is only the physical body which is lost. The spirit cannot die.

Sp. But I never understood that. I never heard anything about spirits before.

Dr. If any one had spoken to you about spirits while you were in earth life, you would probably have laughed at the idea.

Sp. The lady says she will take care of me; she wants me to rest. I am so tired. She says that I must go with her, and also that I must thank you for the opportunity of coming here. Will I have any more of that awful crying?

Dr. No. You will be taught the real lesson of life. Physical life is only temporary. Every one has troubles of one kind or another, but through trouble we become wiser.

Sp. (Gazing intently at some spirit, her face brightened; then she shook her head.) No, no, that cannot be! (Crying.)

Dr. What do you see?

Sp. I was expecting a baby, and a girl has come holding a baby, which she says belongs to me. Can I have it?

Dr. Certainly you can.

Sp. But I am not worthy. They will look down on me.

Dr. You are not going to remain on earth.

Sp. I feel much happier than I did when I came. When did the baby come?

Dr. The baby was freed when you lost your body.

Sp. I don't see how that could happen.

Dr. Many things happen with which you are not familiar You do not understand the wonderful mystery of life.

Sp. Did I kill the baby, too, when the revolver went off?

Dr. When your body was killed the spirit of the little one was also liberated. While you are talking through this body we cannot see you. The real things of life are invisible. Did you ever see music?

Sp. I have heard it. I hear beautiful music now.

Dr. You are beginning to realize the real things of life.

Sp. Another beautiful lady with white hair is here, and she says she will be my mother for the present, and she will take care of me. She says she belongs to the Mercy Band.

Dr. The Mercy Band of spirits is trying to bring before the world the fact that there is no death, and for many years we have been cooperating with them, helping spirits who are in trouble and darkness.

Sp. This lady is very beautiful. She is not the one who was here first, nor the one with the baby. This one says her name is Mrs. Case.13

Dr. When she was on earth she was greatly interested in this work.

Sp. The other lady says she will take care of my baby, because that is her work. She says her name is Abbie Judson, and she takes care of the waif children. She says she was a Spiritualist when on earth, and that she wrote. Oh, I feel so sorry for poor Harry! Will he ever forgive me?

Dr. He knows the circumstances and he will forgive you.

Sp. Please, can I go with these people? Will I cry any more? I have been crying so much that my eyes hurt me.

Dr. The spirit friends will enlighten you and will teach you life's lessons, and you will be happy.

A sudden death, undoubtedly attributable to spirit influence, was that of Olive T.,14 well known motion picture actress. The newspapers reported that Olive T. had committed suicide one evening, in the early fall of 1920, in Paris, France, and six days later her chum, Anna D., also ended her life.

Shortly after, the following occurred.

THIRTY YEARS AMONG THE DEAD

EXPERIENCE, SEPTEMBER 22, 1920

Spirit: OLIVE T. Psychic: MRS. WICKLAND

The spirit seemed to be in painful contortions, and was crying wretchedly.

Doctor: Who are you, friend? Come, tell us who you are. Tell us what is troubling you, and why you are crying. You have been brought here to be helped.

Spirit: Oh, look! Look at that!

Dr. What do you see?

Sp. Look there! Oh, look! Isn't that horrible, that face? (Alluding to an invisible entity.)

Dr. Do you know where you are? You are in California.

Sp. Help me! Oh, help me!

Dr. You must be reasonable.

Sp. Give me something to drink -champagne, give me some champagne!

Dr. You are now a spirit and will have no further use for champagne. You have lost your body and are now in California.

Sp. (Writhing, with face distorted, as if in intense pain.) Oh, look! Help me!

Dr. Try to realize that you have lost your own body and are now controlling the body of my wife, who is a psychic sensitive. Intelligent spirits have brought you here that you might be helped. You can only stay a short time.

Sp. Give me something to drink!

Dr. Who are you? What is your name? We have nothing to drink and would not give it to you if we had. Try to realize your situation.

Sp. Take me out of this!

Dr. Out of what? Try to be reasonable and the intelligent spirits can help you and bring you to a better understanding.

Sp. (With intense excitement.) Get some champagne for me!

Dr. You must not act so wildly. Realize that you are now a spirit. My wife is a psychic intermediary, and allows spirits like yourself to control her body that they may be helped. Don't you understand that you are in a strange condition?

Sp. I don't care.

Dr. You will not gain anything by acting in this way. Excitement will only add to your misery.

Sp. (Complaining a great pain.) I want champagne, and I want it quick!

Dr. You won't get any more champagne; that life is past. Your earthly life is over. Come to a realization of your actual situation. Intelligent spirits will help you and bring you to a better condition in the spirit life.

Sp. Give me a cigarette !

THIRTY YEARS AMONG THE DEAD

Dr. You will not get any more cigarettes. Tell us who you are and what your situation is. Your only salvation now is to realize your condition; then you will have understanding and progress in spirit life. Where did you come from? You cannot satisfy your earthly cravings any longer. Tell us your troubles. Do you know that you are in Los Angeles, California?

Sp. (Becoming greatly excited and pointing.) Look at that man standing over there! (Spirit.) He's horrible -horrible! I am so afraid of him! Don't let him come near me! He looks terrible. Don't let him touch me!

Dr. Listen to us; we are your friends. We understand your condition. Tell us who you are.

Sp. I cannot tell just now, I am too afraid. Oh! I'm so afraid of that man! He haunts me; he's with me all the time. What is this place?

Dr. This is a psychic circle where we help spirits that are in darkness and ignorance. If you will calm yourself and try to be quiet, we shall be able to help you. Believe what I tell you, then we can help you.

Sp. The man over there is making such horrible faces at me that it frightens me.

Dr. Try to compose yourself, then our spirit forces can aid you.

Sp. I don't understand you.

Dr. You are a spirit, and the man you see is also a spirit. You have lost your physical body and now have a spirit body.

Sp. I don't understand you, and I'm so afraid.

Dr. You do not need to fear, just listen. Our spirit forces will help you if you will be quiet.

Sp. (Suddenly animated at the sight of some invisible.) Oh, Anna! Anna D.! Where did you come from? She's afraid of that man, too. He is going over to Anna! Don't let him get her!

Dr. Tell us who you are, then we can help you more easily.

Sp. I am Olive T.

Dr. Then you passed out just before Anna D. did. Neither of you realizes that you have lost your physical body. She also needs help.

Sp. She's not dead.

Dr. She does not realize, any more than you do, that she has passed out of her physical body.

Sp. Anna, how did you get here?

Dr. You are both spirits, and can stay here only a short time. Do you not realize that you have passed out of your bodies, -that something strange has taken place? (To Olive T.) You were in Paris, and now you are in California.

Sp. California! Please tell me who that nice looking lady is standing over there. (Spirit.)

Dr. Probably she is some spirit who brought you here for help. Ask her who she is.

Sp. Why, it's Anna H.!

Dr. She is serving those who are in trouble.

Sp. (Crying.) I can't see any more! What's the matter with me? Where am I?

Dr. You are in Los Angeles, California.

Sp. Yes, but I'm not with my own folks. Where are they all?

Dr. According to reports, you were in Paris, and had been out one evening, after which you went to your apartment and committed suicide.

Sp. There's the fellow that made me do that, —that man standing over there, the one who made such horrible faces! (Spirit.)

Dr. He will not be able to bother you any more.

Sp. He says he took me to that place where I was. (Crying.) Why should he do that? I got so that I could not sleep because of that fellow; he bothered me all the time.

Dr. You must have been a psychic.

Sp. Don't let him come near me! I have already suffered so much through him. Nobody knows how I have suffered. No one understood my different moods.

Dr. How could they, when they knew nothing about spirits troubling people? You were obsessed, and very few understand obsession.

Sp. I feel very sick, but please do not let me die. I want to live.

Dr. Nobody ever dies; only the physical body is lost. You have lost your physical body, and from now on you will begin to live in the spirit world.

Sp. Say, Anna D., why are you here?

Dr. Does she know that she has passed away?

Sp. (Agitated, and weeping anew with fright.) That fellow standing over there, he is the cause of her death—he says so!

Dr. You are using my wife's brain and body, and you must try to quiet yourself. Anna H. brought you here for help.

Sp. She doesn't care for me.

Dr. Listen to what she says; be calm and listen. By being quiet you can be helped. You must have some regard for my wife's nervous system. She allows spirits like you to control her body, so you must not misuse it. Listen to what Anna H. says.

Sp. Anna H. says that she is now serving those who are in the dark because of their foolishness, selfishness and the misuse of money. She is striving to do her part. (Crying again.) If I had only understood!

Dr. You would not have listened to anything about spirits when you had your body.

Sp. I don't know what you mean.

Dr. I mean that you have lost your mortal body and are now controlling my wife's body. We are talking to you but we do not see you.

Sp. Where am I?

THIRTY YEARS AMONG THE DEAD

Dr. You are in Highland Park, Los Angeles.

Sp. I can't understand things. Anna, Anna D! How did you come here? Are you in Paris, too?

Dr. What does she say?

Sp. She says she doesn't know anything, she feels so strange.

Dr. She is also a spirit and does not understand her condition.

Sp. Anna H. brought her here, too. She says that by serving others she has progressed.

Dr. She controlled this psychic about two years ago.

Sp. She says that she will take care of us both, and that I can get rest and sleep. I will go with her, and will take Anna D. along with me, because Anna H. brought us two together. She says Anna D. also needs help.

Dr. You will find many intelligent spirits who will be willing to help you.

Sp. That horrible fellow cannot bother me any more, can he? He scared both Anna D. and me. We were together so much.

Dr. The man you speak of is also a spirit. He will not trouble you any more.

Sp. I got so that I could not sleep, and I felt so badly.

Dr. I presume that the spirit you speak of impressed you to do the things you did.

Sp. Yes, that is so.

Dr. Now you must go with Anna H.; she and the others will help you.

Sp. She says I can go to sleep and rest. I see so many people and I don't know who they are. (Spirits.) I am tired and want to rest. I have not had any rest for years, it seems, but it is only a short time, I suppose. Now I will go with Anna H. Goodbye!

Shortly after the death of Virginia R., cinema star who died in San Francisco, the spirit of the girl was brought by Olive T. to our circle to be awakened, and afterward, Olive T. herself spoke through the psychic.

EXPERIENCE, APRIL 19, 1922

Spirit: OLIVE T. Psychic: MRS. WICKLAND

I felt that I must come in and thank you for the glory that has been bestowed upon me since the time I was here last.

During our childhood we should be taught the real lesson of life and made to understand life in its true sense. Let pictures be shown of the real life. If they would put on the screen the pictures of the real life, the real understanding, and teach the people that there is no death, teach them of the beautiful conditions on the other side of life which are waiting for every one entitled to them, after they understand the higher life, the world would be different.

I lived in a life of make-believe, and we tried to amuse humanity. I am sorry for the girls who fall into a life of sport. They think they have a good time, -yes, for a while. But there is always some little voice -conscience -that bothers you, no matter how you try to kill it. Oh, if I could only teach the young girls, -tell them of the folly of such a life!

THIRTY YEARS AMONG THE DEAD

If I could only teach them to look up to the higher life, and show them the truth of that life! We should teach people to live for others, not for self. We should teach the girls the principles of life, not falsehood. One thing that is very detrimental to the world is drink and morphine. As conditions are now they are driving the girls and boys to misery. People condemn without acting, and what do they gain? They drive the young to the depths, because when the law forbids things, they want them, and in some way or another they get them. They enjoy them more because they are forbidden.

There is also something else. You know, whiskey and the other alcoholic drinks have a thousand, yes, a million thoughts that go with them. The cranks concentrate their minds on drink, and condemn it, and when sensitives get it, they become wild. They become crazy with all the thoughts that are sent with it. It drives them down and down.

Man should live and learn of God's wonderful manifestations. God is the Life of All, but man is the devil. I do not mean man alone when I say man, but I mean humanity. God gave us a free will, but we misuse it.

People should be taught the true teachings of Christ. They say: "Did not Christ make wine? And did He not give it to the people?" They do not understand that it was the Wine of Life. Christ spoke about the spiritual. The majority of people think he spoke of the material.

Understand God right. Do not let us fear Him. He is not a man sitting on a throne, but He is the Spirit of All Life. Everything around us is a part of this Divine Life. Evil has its place just as the good has. If we had no evil we could not know the good. It is only from the experiences we pass through that we learn the lessons of life, that we gain wisdom, and I learn of the life everlasting that lies before us.

My salvation came in the spirit world when I found the truth, because I had been through misery. After I had gone through the fire of conscience, I was purified. I was anxious to find the truth, and after I found it there was no doubting. I wanted peace and harmony and I was then ready for it. You find gold after it has gone through the fire of purification. After my soul had gone through the fire of conscience, I found God within myself, not on the outside.

Find God and be content within yourself. Learn to understand yourself first before you judge others, then you will not judge. Let us be friends to all, do good to all, and do good whenever we can. Let us conquer self. Whenever self rises within you to torment you and tries to make you give way to anger, and give way to drinking and all kinds of trouble, say to yourself that you are not angry, and that you will not give way to things. Then, instead of saying anything to others, get up and turn around, and your anger will be gone, because you will not say what you wanted to, and many times, in that way, you will have harmony.

When we are in a state of anger, we say things that afterwards we are sorry for, and sometimes these things can never be forgotten. So let us always think, if we feel anger coming over us, that we will not give way to it; let us turn around and say: "No, I will conquer self, I will look to higher things, not the lower. I will conquer, and you cannot come in and torment."

I was in that state of anger and it was my death. What did I do? I killed myself. I did not mean to kill myself, but I did it in a mood of anger. Conquer self before it is too late. Conquer your anger before it goes too far. I was swept by anger, and what happened? I killed myself. Then when I woke up and saw what I had done, I was in anguish. It was through anger -anger and selfishness. Let us conquer, and when anger comes in let us say: "Get thee behind me Satan!"

Turnaround, and that will shutout any spirit that would take possession of you. If I had turned around I would not have done what I did. If I could only tell people of the life they should live, and have them put pictures on the screen of the true life and teachings of Jesus and the lessons He taught, and how much good we could all do for humanity, it would turn many criminals, and they would become good men and women.

This is Olive T. Good Night.

Mrs. R. was a patient with such strong suicidal inclinations that she was unable to eat or sleep, constantly scratched the hair from her head and had wasted away to a mere shadow. She declared that she had killed five hundred persons and her one thought was to end her own life, and since there seemed no hope of recovery, she was placed in a sanitarium where she was confined in a locked room for three years.

After being placed in our care she made several attempts at self-destruction, but within a few weeks she was freed from a gloomy spirit who had himself committed suicide, and from that time there was no further recurrence of the suicidal impulse.

Mrs. R. remained with us for some time, gaining steadily in weight, strength and health; she became entirely normal and returned to live with her relatives, taking up all her former occupations.

EXPERIENCE, FEBRUARY 22, 1919

Spirit: RALPH STEVENSON. Patient: MRS. R

Psychic: MRS. WICKLAND

Doctor: Where did you come from?

Spirit: I was straggling along and saw a light, so I came in.

Dr. Can you tell us who you are?

Sp. No; I don't know.

Dr. Can't you remember what your name is?

Sp. I can't seem to remember anything. What is the matter with my head? It hurts me so badly.

Dr. What seems to be the matter with your head?

Sp. It is difficult for me to think. What am I here for? Who are you?

Dr. They call me Dr. Wickland.

Sp. What kind of a doctor are you?

Dr. Medical. What is your name?

Sp. My name? It is strange, but I can't remember my name.

Dr. How long have you been dead?

Sp. Dead, you say? Why, I'm not dead; I wish I were.

Dr. Is life so unpleasant for you?

Sp. Yes, it is. If I am dead, then it is very hard to be dead. I have tried and tried to die, but it seems every single time I come to life again. Why is it that I cannot die?

Dr. There is no actual death.

Sp. Of course there is.

Dr. How do you know there is such a thing as death?

Sp. I don't know anything. (In great distress.) I want to die! I want to die! Life is so dark and gloomy. I wish I could die and forget, forget, -just forget! Why can't I die? I think sometimes I am dead, then all at once I am alive again. I want to forget all the trouble and agony that I have. Where shall I go so that I can die? Sometimes I get in places (auras) but I am always pushed out in the dark again, and I go from place to place. I cannot find my home and I cannot die. What is the matter? Oh, let me forget just for a little while! Let me be free from my thoughts and this horrible darkness. Why can't I die?

Dr. You are on the wrong path, friend.

Sp. Then where shall I find the right path?

Dr. Within yourself.

Sp. There was a time when I believed in a God, and there was a time when I believed in Heaven and hell, but not any more. It is dark and gloomy and my conscience accuses me so. Let me forget! I want to forget, oh, how I want to forget!

Dr. Do you know that you have lost your physical body?

Sp. I do not know anything about it.

Dr. Why are you here?

Sp. I see you people; I don't know any of you, but as I look in your faces you appear to be good. Will you take me in and give me a little light and some happiness? I have not seen either for years and years.

Dr. What is causing all your trouble?

Sp. Why is it there is no God? Why does He let me be in this darkness and gloom? I was once a good boy, but I was -oh, I can't say it! I must not say it! No, no I must not! (Greatly agitated.)

Dr. Tell us what is on your mind.

Sp. I have done a great wrong; I can never be forgiven. God would not forgive any one like me, -no, no, no!

Dr. Try to understand your condition; we can help you. You say you are a man.

Sp. I am a man.

Dr. You are using a woman's body.

Sp. I cannot think how I could have become a woman in my sorrows and not know it. (Seeing an invisible and becoming wildly excited.) Don't come here -don't, don't! Go away! Look, look! Look over there! Go away! I can't stand it!

Dr. What have you done?

Sp. If I should tell you I would be arrested. I cannot stay any longer; I must go now. I must run away -I must! (The patient, Mrs. R, had, a number of times, attempted to run away.) They are coming after me, and if I stay they will catch me! Let me go! There they are, my accusers!

Dr. Where do you think you are?

Sp. In New York.

Dr. You are far from New York; you are in Los Angeles, California. What year do you think it is? Do you know it is 1919?

Sp. 1919? That can't be.

Dr. What year do you think it is?

Sp. 1902.

Dr. That was seventeen years ago. Can't you realize that you have lost your physical body? There is no actual death, only transition. Only the physical body is lost. Did you ever study the problems of life and death?

Sp. No, I never studied anything. I only believed. My name is Ralph, but I forget my last name. My father is dead.

Dr. No more than you are.

Sp. Of course I am not dead. I wish I were. Will you please take me away from here and kill me so that I can die? (Mrs. R. had often begged to be killed.) Oh, here they are coming again! I will not confess! If I do, they will put me in prison, and I am in trouble enough.

Dr. You are in darkness owing to your ignorance. Confess, and we will help you.

Sp. I cannot confess. I have tried before, but I could not. My past stands out right before me.

Dr. From what you say, you have evidently been obsessing people, and in your effort to kill yourself, you have probably caused others to commit suicide. Haven't you found yourself in queer circumstances at times?

Sp. I did not try to understand myself. (In alarm.) Oh, Alice! (Spirit.) No, no! I am afraid! I did not mean to do what I did. No, Alice, don't accuse me!

Dr. If you will tell us what your trouble is we can help you.

Sp. We told each other that we would die, but we did not die. Alice, why did you tell me to kill you? Why did you? I killed you first, and then I killed myself, but I could

not die. Oh, Alice, Alice!

Dr. She probably understands conditions better than you do.

Sp. She says: "Ralph, we were foolish." I will tell you, but I know I shall be arrested when I get through. Alice and I were engaged to be married, but her parents did not want us to marry because they thought I was not what I should be. We loved each other very dearly, so we decided that I should kill her, then kill myself. I did it, but I never could kill myself, and I guess, as Alice is here, I did not kill her either. Ever since I tried to kill her, she comes and accuses me.

Alice and I were together, and she said all the time: "Now, kill me! Quick, quick! Kill me! Go ahead! Do it! Do it!" I hesitated because I loved her, but she kept on saying: "Do it quick! Do it!" I still hesitated, but Alice said: "Come, now, do it! Be quick!" could not, so she said since she could not go home again, and we could not marry, why not die together.

But she would not do the deed herself. I could not do it either. She kept urging me to kill her, so at last I shut my eyes and shot her, and then I shot myself before I saw her fall. I saw her lying on the floor and I tried to run away after I got up, and I ran and ran and ran, and I have been running and walking ever since, trying to forget, but I cannot.

Sometimes Alice comes to me, but I always say: "No, I am the cause of your death, so stay away from me." I ran and ran to get away from the police and everybody else. A while ago I felt I was an old woman, and I could not get away from being a woman for a long time. I got away, but after a while I was that old woman again.

Dr. You were obsessing somebody at that time.

Sp. Obsessing? What do you mean by that?

Dr. Did you ever read in the Bible of unclean spirits?

Sp. Yes, I did. But when I was that old woman I wanted to die, and I could not. I could not get rid of that old woman hanging around me either. I could not get her away from me. I don't want to be around that old woman any more. (Excitedly.) Oh, Alice, don't come! When I was with the old woman there were such sharp sparks like lightning on me. I thought they would kill me, and I wanted to die. (The patient had often said that she hoped the electrical treatments would kill her.) They seemed to be like a streak of lightning, and it struck me, but I did not die.

Dr. Those sparks were caused by static electricity, which was given to one of our patients, whom you have evidently been obsessing. She always talked of dying just as you are doing; you have been controlling her and ruining her life. The electricity drove you away from her; she will be well, and you will now be helped.

When you leave here you will go with Alice, who will help you to understand your condition. You do not yet realize that you have lost your physical body and that you are still alive. Alice is a spirit, just as you are. You are an invisible spirit and are controlling my wife's body. Spirit and mind never die.

Sp. Do you think I shall ever find peace? I should like to have just one hour of peace.

Dr. You have all eternity before you.

Sp. Will I be forgiven for what I have done?

Dr. Your own confession and sorrow are sufficient. Be patient and willing to learn and you will be helped.

Sp. There's my mother! (Spirit.) Mother! I am not worthy to be called your son. I loved you very dearly, but I can't have you come to me now. (Weeping.) Oh, Mother, will you forgive me? I love you still. Will you take your wayward son and forgive him? Will you give me happiness for a little while? I have suffered, oh, so much! Please take me with you, if you can forgive me. My own mother!

Dr. Does your mother answer you?

Sp. Mother says: "My son, my son, a mother's love is stronger than anything else. I have tried so much, and so many times to come close to you, but you were always running away."

The first spirit left and the mother then spoke through the psychic.

THIRTY YEARS AMONG THE DEAD

Spirit: MRS. STEVENSON.

I am now united with my dear son. For a long time I have tried to come in close touch with him, but could not. Each time that I thought I was going to reach him, he would run away from me. He has seen me many times, but was afraid, because he was taught the false doctrine that when we die we are dead, and that is why people are afraid of the dead. We do not die; we simply pass on to the spirit side of life, to a beautiful condition if we realize the truth. But we must learn much regarding the next life while we are on earth.

Study your own life and yourself, because, if you do not, you will be like my dear son. He has been running for years, trying to get away from me and his sweetheart, and also from every policeman he has seen while in the earth sphere. He has been obsessing a lady for some time, and he had to stay in her magnetic aura because he did not know how to get away. He has been in hell, not a hell of fire, but a hell of ignorance.

Look into conditions of the next life so that you may be prepared, for death comes when it is not expected. Be prepared, not by belief, but by actual knowledge. Find out what is beyond the veil of death. Then, when the time comes for you to go to the spirit side of life, you will go with open eyes and know where you are going, and you will not be, like my poor son, an earthbound spirit.

My poor boy! He is so tired and worried; he is sick mentally. I will nurse him and teach him of the life everlasting so that he can realize the beautiful condition in the spirit world. Do not merely believe; if you only believe you will stay just where you are. We must all practice the Golden Rule -to live for others and serve others; then we will attain happiness when we pass to the spirit side of life.

Thank you for the help you have given my son. A mother's love is strong, and when you see my boy again he will be better, because all doubt will be gone. Doubt is a wall; it is a wall we build for ourselves between life and death, and that doubt can never bring mother and son together.

He ran away from me whenever he saw me, and neither Alice nor I could come near him. He thought he was alive and that he had not killed himself. Some time ago he came in contact with a sensitive person, a woman, and has been obsessing her, but he thought he was in prison.

I thank you all tonight for the help given my son, and may God bless you for the work you are doing. Goodbye.

A Yong Girl "Possessed" By Spirits

THIRTY YEARS AMONG THE DEAD

Chapter VIII

Spirits and Narcotics, Inebriety, Amnesia

Relentless as is the grip which the drug habit holds on its mortal victims, the power of narcotics extends even more tyrannically beyond the grave. The desire is implanted in the very soul itself and the agony of earthbound spirits, whose cravings for gratification are in vain, is beyond description.

Such spirits frequently obtain partial satisfaction through controlling mortal sensitives, and forcing them to become addicts of some drug. Often spirits suffering from the narcotic evil have come to our circle, and many urgent warnings have been given by discarnate intelligences who were formerly subject to this slavery.

Twenty-five years after the first conversation with Minnie Morgan, which occurred during my dissecting work, this spirit, who had been a morphine fiend, returned and told of earth sphere conditions, as well as of the higher spirit world.

EXPERIENCE, JULY 26, 1922

Spirit: MINNIE MORGAN Psychic: MRS. WICKLAND

I feel that I am one of you; although I do not know you, I was helped by you. I certainly had wonderful help in being brought to understand that there is a real life. In the spirit world we know each other as we should be known, not as you know each other in earth life, with all kinds of hidden thoughts.

You wander like wild cattle on the battle field of selfishness and jealousy. Love is so little understood. You do not know what real love is, because God is Love, and God dwells in Love. The majority of people only believe, and think there is some place in the sky to which they go when they die.

Whenever I gave that subject any thought, I made up my mind that I would have a good time while I could and then, when the time came to die, I would be ready to go, because at the last I could throw my sins on Jesus and be washed as white as snow. I started out in life with that belief. I said: "Why can't I have a good time like others? The future will take care of itself."

With that thought many persons go out to sow their wild oats, thinking that when the proper time comes they will be prayed for, and that then they will step into the glory of Heaven. That is what I thought. I tried to live a life of glory -or what I thought was glory. What does that mean? It means to have a good time, to live, and not care what becomes of one's soul.

I said, "Let us have, a good time while we can!" and I started out in life that way. I had my sorrows and I had my good time, as I called it, but that is not a good time. We cannot for one minute step over the laws of nature except we suffer in some way or other.

If we go too far in anything we suffer for it both mentally and physically. We keep on going and going; sometimes our good time is better, sometimes worse. I lived a very fast life and called it a glorious time, but grief and adversity came. In the way of the world I lived very fast. I went to church once in a while to be sure my soul would be taken care of. I paid money to the church so I would be all right, and then I drowned myself in the glory of the world.

It was all right for a while. Each time I had glory, as I called it, I suffered both physically and mentally. I tried to shake it off and go on a little longer. I fell by the wayside. After a while my physical body wore out and I had misery and sickness. At one time I was considered a very pretty girl. I had my beaux and all that goes with a good time, but I went down and down to the very lowest. I was a physical wreck, but I was still on earth.

Never let any one give you the least bit of morphine. When you start on that road you are lost. Not that a soul is ever lost, but you are lost for a time while you are a slave to the drug. You suffer agony. There is nothing worse than to crave morphine and be unable to get it. It seems like every nerve in your body is creeping. I got wild because I could not get it. I did not care for anything. I would have sold my very soul if I could only have gotten morphine. I lost all decency; I lost everything. All I wanted was morphine.

It was terrible. It burned to my very heart. I felt it in every nerve, and I felt as if I were on fire. If only some one would have gotten morphine for me! Just a little! Just a little bit! A little bit! I felt I couldn't stand it any longer. I wanted just a little; a little bit! Only a little! (The spirit seemed to live again all the agony she had endured when in earth life. It also seemed evident that, in addition to the visible circle of investigators, she was addressing an audience of earthbound spirits.)

I died in that terrible condition. My physical body was gone. I had worn it out, just worn it out. Then I was operated on (post-mortem) but I still lived. I wanted to get to my body. They operated on me, and after a while I felt that something was picking me to small pieces. (Dissection.) I cried and I fought, because I wanted that body so I could satisfy my very soul. I was burning up. They picked at every nerve; they looked at my heart, my shoulder, and down to the leg -pick, pick, pick, all the time!

I got so desperate I fought with all my power, and I scared some away from my body. They never touched it again. There were five or six men, with knives, all wanting to do something with my body, pick, pick, pick!

But there came another; he looked and looked at me, and picked and picked, and he drove me wild. I thought if I could only get hold of him I would fix him. He paid no attention to me. I tried to scare him, as I had scared the others, but I could not budge him. He would not move one inch from that body of mine. I followed him and thought I would haunt him, but all at once I got well (controlled the psychic) and began to fight him with all the strength and power I had for picking me to pieces.

To my great surprise, after this gentleman (Dr. W.) talked to me, I found I was dead. I did not know I had lost my body, for I had not been dead at all. This gentleman told me that the people working on my body were students and that it was necessary for them to work on a dead body before they were able to pass their examinations. I scared five of them and they never touched me again, but I could not scare this one.

(To Dr. W.) Now I come to thank you. You were the one who enlightened me and gave me an understanding of the real life beyond. I found I could not throw my sins on Christ. He was our teacher, but we must live our own lives, as He taught us to live, and not throw our sins and troubles on Him.

That is a false doctrine. He is the Life, the Light and the Way. He said: "I am the Light of the world; he that followeth me shall not walk in darkness."

Many others before Him taught the same lesson of life. I found that in the past there had been many teachers like Christ. Confucius was one. He taught the same as did Christ. In the Old Testament we find the same principles as Christ taught; His sayings are the same in the Old as in the New.

Let us all do what we can to find God within us. Learn to live according to Christ's teachings. "Love the Lord thy God with all thy heart . . . and thy neighbor as thyself." I would not have the home in the spirit world that I have if I had not been disturbed and received an understanding of the real life.

I was very wicked and you know the desire I had for morphine. That desire was with me even after I left my body. The desire for anything belongs to the soul, not to the body. The body is only a cloak or dress for your soul. All the desires of life, all the faculties that belong to the soul, go with you to the grave, and beyond the grave.

What would I have been if I had not been given an understanding of how to overcome my desires? I would have been an earthbound spirit and would have gotten into some sensitive person's magnetism, and made that sensitive a morphine fiend so I could have had my desire fulfilled, and the life of the sensitive would have been ruined. I would have lived in the earth sphere for years and years if I had gotten into that condition. I would have ruined one and then another, and so I would have kept on.

Find out what belongs to the soul and what belongs to the body. If this were done we would not have so much trouble and crime, nor so much sickness. We would have Love, and Heaven on earth, because we would have pity for the unfortunate ones who are living just for their own desires.

It says in the Bible: "Prove all things; hold fast that which is good." That means, do not have any desire for anything. If you use too much of anything in this earth life, such as morphine, whiskey or tobacco, then you are a slave and must stop its use. Many people condemn many things and that thought of condemnation is very hard for a sensitive person. Everything on earth is meant for us to use, but not misuse.

Many people condemn liquor, tobacco, morphine, opium, but it is their misuse which should be condemned. They are all necessary things if they are used rightly. Isn't an opiate a good thing if you must undergo an operation? To be operated upon without an opiate would be wrong; the suffering would be too great. Opiates help pain. Many people use these things because they are forbidden. They say: "Forbidden fruit tastes best." When things are forbidden everybody wants them, and they ruin themselves using them.

I lived in the lower world, the underworld, and I know what I am talking about. I took anything to keep my nerves quiet. Anything used moderately, in a sensible way, is all right. When a man who works very hard, either physically or mentally, sits down to rest he is nervous and fatigued. Give him a good cigar and let him relax. His nervousness goes, and he becomes stronger. It is a thorough relaxation; he smokes and feels better. With this complete relaxation comes quietude; the man sleeps and is rested for his work the next day.

THIRTY YEARS AMONG THE DEAD

If people would have more love for each other and less condemnation they would be more like brothers and sisters. That is the life in the higher realms. We cannot reach that stage until we have gotten rid of all desires, all hatred, all selfishness, all envy. We cannot progress until we have thrown away all these things and said: "God help me to love my enemies and friends better than myself." Then we will be ready to travel the road.

Some people think that after they learn the lesson of truth they will step into the glory of Heaven. But Heaven is a condition. In conquering my desire for morphine, I had to do so little by little, step by step, until I could say: "No more morphine for me."

After I had conquered, my friends and relatives met me and said: "Now you are ready to come with us to the home that has been prepared for you." Before that time I had to live all by myself. I was not in a dark dungeon like some are, but all around me was myself, nothing else. I had to learn and strive to overcome.

It says in the Big Book that Christ went to the lower spheres to give help and teach. We all have to teach and help the fallen ones, and give them strength to overcome their desires. I wish I could take you along with me for a few moments to see the conditions in the lower sphere -what they call the earth sphere. Here is the sphere of whiskey, here the sphere of morphine, here the sphere of the opium fiend, here the sphere of selfishness, and here the sphere of misers.

Of all these conditions that of the miser is the worst. He sacrifices everything for money. He will not eat because he thinks he cannot afford it. He starves his mind because he wants money, money, -and what is the result? In the earth sphere he is in the dark, but he sees his money being spent and he is in hell. He suffers terribly. He sees his relatives get his money; it is divided, some going here, some there. If it were all in one place he could count it over and that would be all right; but his relatives all want their share to spend.

Now imagine; that money has been his treasure. Each cent that is spent is like cutting a piece from his body, because his whole mind and soul were in that money, and to see it scattered and spent is hell for him. Think what that means to him. He cannot be helped until he feels that he no longer wants his money; then his soul or better nature will open up and he will be helped. He will be under the guidance of a teacher and will be taught that money belongs to the earth life, not to the spirit. He then has to do good.

A miser never gets his money in the right way. He may not be a thief, but if he loans money, he charges too high a rate of interest. For every cent he got in the wrong way, he has to do right. He must do some kind act and help poor people in their work. He has to lay down his life and earn everything before he can gain happiness in the spirit world. He has to serve first, and he must help those from whom he took money to get it back. You know a "sin against the Holy Ghost cannot be forgiven." It must be atoned for. That is his life in the spirit world.

We have to look at a murderer differently. There are ten different degrees of murder. There is murder by quick temper; that is not real murder. It is committed under stress of strong quick temper. At heart the man is not a murderer; he simply lost control of his temper. Of course he has to suffer and do good where he did wrong.

Temper is a very hard thing to conquer but it must be conquered, because it kills our better nature and makes us do many wrong and unkind things. Then we have the cunning murderer. He plans and schemes; he wants a man's money. He is nice and sweet, and goes to church. He plans and schemes to get that man's life in some way or another, but he does it slowly. He has evil thoughts. In the spirit world this man has to suffer a great deal, and must atone for his actions from the time he began to plan and scheme to murder.

Then there is the psychic sensitive who does not care for anybody. He doesn't belong to one church or another; he takes things easy. What is not done today can be done tomorrow or the next day. He does not use his will. A cunning spirit gets into this man's magnetic aura and controls him. He commits some crime. The man will hang for his deed, but he never did it. He will probably say he does not know that he did anything.

Or he may say: "I must have been drunk when I did it, for I don't remember anything about it." But it was not liquor that did it. Liquor never does that. When a man is drunk his mind is in a stupor. It is a spirit that does the work. If that spirit has been wronged in life, all he wants is revenge. The law does not really find out whether the man is guilty or not; he is hanged.

The majority of murders and hold-ups are committed by spirits. They scheme and scheme, and use mortals as tools, until they wake up and realize what wrong they have been doing.

Often honesty and modesty have both been killed. When I was a child I was very modest, but when I killed modesty, I was ruined. Then I did not care for anything. Honesty is a virtue we should all cultivate. Judges, lawyers and ministers, in the majority of cases, do not give justice; they look for gain. They kill justice, honesty and truth. Let us do all we can to keep those three to the front. Honesty and truth will convert the world. You cannot convert it by condemnation. People are not taught the truth.

Have wisdom and human kindness and you will see better results. Teach wisdom and let more of the Christ spirit be in every one. Live as He taught; do as He did, then happiness will reign. I am sorry to have taken up so much time, but I did not know I would talk so long. Even now I feel I have more to say, but I must stop.

My name, when I lived in Chicago, was Minnie Morgan, but that name does not belong to me and I do not want it any more. That name has a horror for me. Even when I repeat that name I feel a horror of it. My own name is not to be given tonight. We have to earn our names, and I have no name until I have earned it.

After all these twenty-five years -it was in 1897 that I passed out -I have not advanced sufficiently to have even a name. I am happy and I will earn a name, and then I will be called by it. My name was down in the very lowest place. If any one of you should pass out, you would have a name that is honest and good. Your name will follow you and you will want it. I would not cling to mine, for it has such a horror for me. Can you see the difference?

When you have done the best you could in earth life you have traveled the right road, and when you pass to the spirit side of life your relatives and friends will meet you. I had no one to meet me. No friends came; I had gone too low. My friend was morphine. Isn't that a terrible condition?

You know when I wanted morphine I did not always get it in the right way. During my earth life I sometimes stole money to get morphine. Now I have to do good, step by step. I have been doing work in the slums, helping those as unfortunate as I had been. I lived with those who craved morphine. Now I can help them to overcome their desire for it.

That is my work. It is not pleasant, but I have to do it. Some one has to do it, so why not I? I suffer with them. I can give them sympathy, for I, too, have suffered. Give these unfortunate ones your sympathy and loving thoughts, for it will help them. You have not lived as they have, and you do not know what their condition means. Each one that I help to the right road is Heaven to me. Remember, each one is Heaven to me.

The more I help, the more happiness I find. Some day I shall say goodbye to this condition and progress to the spirit side of life. Do not condemn those who have fallen; remember, they have no will of their own. Send kind thoughts to them, and say a prayer: "God help them to have a will of their own to overcome their desire." Send out thoughts to help them overcome; do not send evil, unkind thoughts.

The next time I come you will know what my name is, because by that time I shall have earned it.

Thank you for helping me to the right road, because I am happy in helping others; but I shall have a hard climb to find bliss.

Good Night, and I again thank you for having helped me.

The day after receiving a request by telephone, from an adjoining city, that we concentrate for a pharmacist who was a drug addict and evidently obsessed, the spirit of a morphine fiend was removed from him and brought to our circle, an entity in torment, convulsed with the drug craving and wildly begging for "just one grain."

EXPERIENCE, MARCH 21, 1923

Spirit: ELIZABETH NOBLE Psychic: MRS. WICKLAND

Spirit: Don't bother me. I want rest.

Doctor: Haven't you rested long enough? Do you want to rest forever?

Sp. I have been running; I have not been resting.

Dr. What have you been running away from? The police?

(The spirit began to cough severely.)

Dr. Forget your old condition; that is all past. Tell us who you are and where you came from.

Sp. I am so sick. (Coughing more violently.)

Dr. Do not bring that condition with you. You lost your body, probably a long time ago. Do you know you are a spirit? What is the matter?

Sp. I don't know. (Another paroxysm of coughing.)

Dr. You ought to know. This is not your body; you are not sick now. You are free from your physical body. Think yourself well and you will be well.

Sp. I am sick; you do not know. Who are you?

Dr. I am a doctor, and if you do as you are told you will become well. This is not your body. You are now an invisible spirit.

Sp. I am sick.

Dr. You only hold that idea in your mind. This body is not your own. You are not sick.

Sp. You don't know.

Dr. You are ignorant of your condition and do not realize that you have lost your body.

Sp. I am sick.

Dr. In your mind only; that is an old habit.

Sp. I am dying. I want to lie down. (Coughing.)

Dr. You are only using this body temporarily. Your coughing body is in the grave. You must stop coughing.

Sp. I have no coughing body. This is my body. I can't help coughing.

Dr. Where did you come from?

Sp. I don't know. Why do you tell me I can't cough?

Dr. There is no need of it.

Sp. You don't know anything about it.

Dr. The body which you are using now is not sick.

Sp. I am sick. You give me some medicine, and give it to me quick! Give me some before I get too sick!

Dr. You like to be sick. Don't you want to be well?

Sp. I am sick and ought to be in bed. Think of a poor, sick woman having to stay here.

(Coughing.)

Dr. Think strongly that you are not sick and you will not be.

Sp. Give me some medicine! I want a little morphine; my heart is bad.

Dr. You have lost your body and are a spirit now.

Sp. Give me some medicine, then I'll feel better. Give me fifteen grains. My cough is so bad! Give me some! Give me some morphine, I said! Just a little! Only a little then just one grain! Give it to me in the arm. I like it in the arm best.

Dr. You must stop this foolish talk.

Sp. (Shrieking wildly.) You must give me something quick! I can't stand it any longer! I said, give me some! One grain, just one grain! I must have it! (With face distorted, hands clawing the air fiercely.)

Dr. I thought you said you were sick.

Sp. I am sick.

Dr. From selfishness. Try to understand your condition.

Sp. You give me some morphine before I die!

Dr. You must be quiet, then we can help you. Where did you come from?

Sp. Oh, my God! Give me some morphine! I want medicine. Won't you please, please, give me just one grain?

Dr. What is your name?

Sp. (Claw-like fingers desperately clutching about.) My God, just give me one grain just one!

Dr. Do you know that you are in California?

Sp. No.

Dr. You are in Los Angeles, California. Where do you think you are?

Sp. I don't care. Just give me one little grain! I must have it!

Dr. Forget that and think of something else. You have lost your physical body.

Sp. I have such a bad cough, and my heart is bad. I'm dying.

Dr. How can you "die" when you have already lost your physical body?

Sp. If I have another body, I'm just the same as I was before.

Dr. Forget your old habits and you will feel better.

Sp. I want morphine. When you want it, you want it badly. (Striking right and left.) I can't stand it any longer! Give me some!

Dr. If you listen to us you can be helped out of your present condition. Intelligent spirits will also help you. If you do not want to listen you will have to go. You must overcome old habits; your physical body is gone.

Sp. Please give me fifteen grains!

Dr. I will give you nothing. You no longer have a physical body which craves morphine. You now have an opportunity to be helped.

Sp. Give me some, oh, give me some! If you will only give me some morphine I'll be all right. (Struggling.)

Dr. If you do not quiet yourself you will have to go.

Sp. That is nice! I am sick. I only ask you for morphine.

Dr. You are very selfish.

Sp. I have been running, trying to get some morphine. Why won't you give me some?

Dr. No more of that. You have lost your mortal body and are now using my wife's body. You can be helped, if you will listen. Understand you are a spirit.

Sp. I have such a bad cough. I need morphine.

Dr. No doubt you have been in the earth plane in darkness for a long time. You no longer have your own body.

Sp. I have my own body.

Dr. The body you are struggling with is not yours. Will you try to understand?

Sp. Yes, but I'm very sick.

Dr. You are not sick; you are very selfish. Why don't you pay attention and try to understand that you are a spirit?

Sp. That's all right; I need morphine just the same.

Dr. Get that idea out of your mind. You only imagine you are sick. Did you not say you had been running?

Sp. Yes. I have been to every drug store in town to get morphine. I get it once in a while (through some sensitive) but it doesn't last long.

Dr. You get it by obsessing some one; you have no physical body now.

Sp. I have a body.

Dr. Not a physical body. You are using my wife's body. Intelligent spirits have brought you here to be helped.

Sp. All the help I want is morphine. When I think I can't get it, it makes me sick.

Dr. That is only because you hold that thought in your mind. Tell us where you came from.

Sp. I don't know.

Dr. You don't seem to care.

Sp. No; I want morphine.

Dr. Do you know what year it is?

Sp. I don't care about that; all I want is morphine. I have been to every store in town.

Dr. Which town?

Sp. I don't know; I can't remember. I never stayed in any place long, because I wanted to see the world.

Dr. What is the last place you remember?

Sp. I can't remember.

Dr. What is your name?

Sp. I haven't heard it for so many years that I don't know what they would call me now.

Dr. Try to recall what year it is.

Sp. I want morphine so bad that I can't think or talk about anything else.

Dr. What was your mother's name?

Sp. My mother's name?

Dr. Was it Mrs. Brown, or Green, or White?

Sp. No color at all. If you would give me just one grain, everything would be fine. If you are a doctor, then give me some. They always do.

Dr. You will not get any this time.

Sp. Then you are not a doctor.

Dr. You are controlling my wife's body; you are a spirit.

Sp. I don't care anything about that.

Dr. If you cannot be sincere you will have to go. Overcome your old habits; we can help you.

Sp. I am a sick woman.

Dr. Were you married?

Sp. Yes.

Dr. What was your husband's name?

Sp. Frank Noble.

Dr. What did Frank call you?

Sp. Elizabeth.

Dr. What did your husband do for a living?

Sp. Anything.

Dr. How old are you?

Sp. I am forty-two years old.

Dr. Who is President?

Sp. I don't know, and I don't care. I never entered politics. My husband was crazy over politics. I was busy keeping my house clean. My husband called me "Betty." He used to say: "Betty, you are a good girl."

Dr. Where is Frank?

Sp. I haven't seen him for ages. He was a pretty good fellow.

Dr. Where is your mother?

Sp. My mother is dead.

Dr. Where did you come from?

Sp. I came from from El Paso, Texas.

Dr. Were you born there?

Sp. Ask my husband. (Moaning.) I am too sick.

Dr. Can't you realize that you have no physical body, but are a spirit?

Sp. Then I can go to Heaven and sing. I used to go to church.

Dr. What church did you go to?

Sp. The Methodist.

Dr. Did your husband go too?

Sp. Frank was such a good fellow. I have not seen him for a long time. He liked me and I liked him. (In a shrill voice.) Frank, I want to see you! Frankie, Frankie, will you help me? Are you here, Frankie?

THIRTY YEARS AMONG THE DEAD

Dr. Don't speak that way.

Sp. Would you give me some morphine? Frankie always gave it to me. Dr. Russell always told me that I should take it for my heart. (Affectedly.) Frankie! Frankie!

Dr. Why do you call Frankie in that way?

Sp. Oh, I always call him in time for dinner. I always used to call him; he is a lovely little fellow.

Dr. Don't be so foolish. Be sincere.

Sp. Oh, I'm sincere when I call Frankie. I'm thinking of Frankie. I love him. But I love morphine too. Oh, Frankie is standing there! (Spirit.) When did you come, Frankie? Give me some morphine!

Dr. Does he answer you?

Sp. He says he will not give me anything. Frankie, you used to go to the drug store for me. Be a good fellow now. Just give me one shot, Frankie, and I won't ask you again. You know I'm awful sick. You love me, don't you, Frankie? Then just give me a little, and we will both be so happy together. The spirit was taken away and her husband controlled the psychic.

Spirit: FRANK NOBLE Psychic: MRS. WICKKLAND

Spirit: I am Frank Noble. I have been trying very hard, for some time, to bring my wife here for help.

Doctor: It must have required a good deal of patience on your part.

Sp. Thank you for bringing her to me.

Dr. We are glad to have been of any help.

Sp. My wife was very sick. Once the doctor gave her morphine to help her pain, and from that time she had spells so severe that we could do nothing but call the doctor to give her morphine. It was an awful habit to get into. Many, many times she played sick, I know, when she wanted morphine. She had played that game so long that it really was very easy for her to play sick to scare us all, and to ask for morphine. What could a fellow do? After she had it, she would be well sometimes for whole weeks, and sometimes for a month. The spells she had were very bad.

Dr. Where did you live?

Sp. We came from El Paso, Texas.

Dr. Do you know when you passed out?

Sp. No, I can't tell you. It has been very strange for me. I had a hard time. Of course, I was not a rich man; I had to earn my living doing what I could.

Dr. That is no disgrace.

Sp. I had no education, so had to do whatever I could. Sometimes I worked at mining, other times I worked in the woods, and sometimes I was a carpenter. I did anything to keep my home together. At one time Elizabeth was a very good girl. One time, when she had a child, she was very sick and in great pain. The doctor gave her pills and after a while she wanted more and more, and at last she went insane over morphine. She was very hard to get along with until she got it and after that she was happy, and she would not have another spell for a while. The habit grew on her. She had bad coughing spells and she died in one of them. She took a pill and in some way or other she choked to death. She went through the death scene here tonight.

Dr. She would have coughed a great deal more if I had not checked her.

Sp. For a long time I tried to find her, but when I came near her, she ran away, and only called for morphine. Once in a while I lost her completely, and I did not know where she was. It is strange. When you think of people, you are right with them. Finally I was always able to find my wife whenever I lost her. Sometimes she got into another person. I found her again but she was so afraid of me. I died before she did.

Dr. Did you have any knowledge of the spirit world before you passed on?

Sp. My mother was a medium and I learned the truth from her. Elizabeth would never believe it because she was a Methodist. She thought I would go to hell because I believed in Spiritualism. Look into the truth and you will be much better off. Do not have creeds, dogmas or doubts.

Thank you for helping us, because when my wife gets out of this stupor she is in, she will be better. They put her to sleep under morphine when she was in the hospital. Now she will not bother others any more, and we shall be together.

Thank you for helping us. Good night!

The spirit of Olive T., who had controlled the psychic upon several occasions, returned one evening and, speaking of the real happiness of service, urged that all those subject to the temptations of society life and the excitement of the movie world be warned against the use of drugs, and asked if she might bring in a spirit who was in trouble and needed to be awakened.

A spirit, who seemed to be in a drowsy state, then controlled the psychic, collapsing weakly, but when spoken to began to struggle desperately, as if in the throes of great pain and agony.

EXPERIENCE, OCTOBER 9, 1923

Spirit: WALLACE R. Psychic: MRS. WICKLAND

Doctor: Tell us who you are. Do you realize that you have lost your, physical body?

(The spirit did not seem to hear, but moaned incessantly, and writhed as if in torture.)

Dr. Can you talk? Understand that you are now a spirit.

(Still no answer; the contortions of the body continued.)

Dr. Try to talk. Who are you?

Sp. (Faintly) Wally.

Dr. Wally who?

Sp. Wally R.

Dr. Make an effort to talk; use your will. Will to be your rational self. Try to understand your condition, then we can help you.

(The spirit continued to struggle and groan.)

Dr. Try to talk; you can. Forget your old condition; forget your old habit. You no longer have your old physical body. You are controlling the body of another. Make an effort to talk; wake up. (No answer.)

Dr. Forget your trouble and start anew. Do you know Olive T.? (Who had preceded this spirit.)

(The intelligence moaned and held out imploring hands.)

Sp. (Weakly) My wife!

Dr. Your wife is not here.

Sp. Where is she?

Dr. She is not here. Friends have brought you here. Try to rouse yourself. Often when persons pass out of the physical under the conditions you did (under the influence of narcotics) they remain in a stupor for some time. But it is time for you to waken now. Can you see Olive T. here?

Sp. (In a whisper.) I am sick.

Dr. You must forget that. Your sickness is over. You passed out of your physical body quite a while ago. Do you realize that? You are what people call "dead." But you are not actually "dead"; you have only lost your physical body. You yourself are still living. You are using another body temporarily. Olive T. and others brought you here to be helped. You have been in a stupefied condition for a long time. You feel much better now, don't you?

(The spirit motioned languidly, as if noticing a group of invisibles.)

Dr. Whom do you see? Endeavor to talk. Understand, you no longer have a physical body; you are here in spirit, controlling this body, which belongs to my wife. You have been brought here for the purpose of being helped. Try to be your own natural self. We always enjoyed your pictures. Wake up, and be yourself. Do not think you are dreaming; you are not. (The spirit again stretched out his hands.)

Dr. Do you see friends?

Sp. I am going to die.

Dr. You have already done that, as much as you ever will. You have only lost your physical body. Do you see friends?

Sp. Yes, but I am going to die.

Dr. You cannot die again.

Sp. I see so many who have died.

Dr. They are not actually dead at all. They are spirits like yourself. You have already passed out of your mortal body. You are a spirit but do not understand the fact. This body which you are using is not yours. You have lost your body and have not wakened to your real condition. Friends have brought you here for help.

(But the spirit could not be roused again and was taken away.)

One of the guiding intelligences then came in and said: "The other spirit was so tired that we could not waken him, but now we will be able to take care of him. He is so weak. He has not overcome his old habit. We brought him here so that we could take him to the spirit world.

"Olive T. and others work to help the ones who are in that particular trouble earthbound spirits who have the craving for morphine. Often people do not have the habit, but they are influenced by spirits who have the craving, and who get into their magnetic auras.

"Many persons are easily influenced because they live such nervous, sensitive lives that they are half in spirit. They then become influenced by earthbound spirits who are so much in earth life that they obsess people.

"We are going to help this young man and sometime he will come again when he is stronger, and tell his experience, but he cannot talk tonight.

"He has gradually been awakening for some time, but he is still bewildered and he could not realize the higher life. He has been in many places, and with his wife much of the time. She helped him in fighting his habit, but he was too weak to properly understand. He had no resistive power left.

"After he passed out, his spirit was in a kind of sleep from morphine. Still he has been wandering, in a twilight state, on earth life, to find his home and family, and trying to realize where he was. He thought he was lost.

"We have tried to reach him from our side of life, but it has been very hard. We will now take care of him."

One week later the spirit of Wallace R. returned, somewhat stronger, and telling of his suffering, made an anguished appeal to others to overcome the drug habit.

EXPERIENCE, OCTOBER 17, 1923

Spirit: WALLACE R. Psychic: MRS. WICKLAND

The spirit seemed very weak and was at first unable to talk.

Doctor: Whom have we here? Rouse yourself and talk. Do not think of any sickness. Just talk as you used to do.

Spirit: (Faintly.) That is easy to say.

Dr. Make the effort; you will find it easy.

Sp. I wanted to come in to get a little more understanding. I could not get much the last time. I am in the dark. I am in the darkness -having to overcome my physical habit, which is attached to the soul.

Dr. Have you been here before?

Sp. Yes, I was here not long ago, and I thank you for helping me, but I need more help. Please give me strength to overcome my physical habit of using drugs. I had little understanding of the life hereafter. I lived from day to day, the life of the world. I did not realize what it would mean to be on the other side of life.

Dr. Very few interest themselves in higher things.

Sp. I also want to thank you for having helped me during the time I was sick. At that time I felt such a strong power trying to help me to overcome, and trying to give me strength. I felt drawn somewhere, but I was too weak to realize the power that was sent out to help me.

Dr. We concentrated for you during the time you were sick, as we thought there might be

THIRTY YEARS AMONG THE DEAD

some obsession there.

Sp. I was too weak to realize.

Dr. Of course you did not understand.

Sp. I had no power and there was no battery at our end to help me. My only hope was to try to conquer. I was in such misery and so helpless that many spirits demonstrated through me, and I had no one who understood how to help me conquer the soul craving. (The spirit kept the hands across the chest and constantly twisted the fingers one over the other.) People think when they take drugs that the habit will end when they pass out of the physical. I tried to conquer, but when my mortal body had gone, and my dear, noble wife could not be with me to help me battle in the hard struggle, I seemed helpless. She is a dear noble soul; she stood by me and helped me, but I had not the power to conquer.

After I had lost all the surroundings of earth, I went into a kind of sleep for awhile, but, oh, how I longed for my wife and children! Also how I longed to conquer, but could not. I suffered (writhing painfully), oh, how I suffered!

I tried to go somewhere to get help, to get help to overcome, but I must thank you; you gave me both strength and power. I wish I could have had more power from your good thoughts. Since last I was here, I have gained much. I am not strong yet, but I am able to see and realize how I can win my battle. From the little I have seen of the spirit world since I was here last, I realize how wonderful things are.

(Earnestly.) I wish I could warn many I knew and tell them not to play with drugs. They think it is fun in the beginning, but how they will have to suffer at the last! Even the soul burns from the craving. They should do everything they can to overcome the habit.

They not only suffer here, but they suffer terribly after they pass out; then the soul is on fire. (With an agonized expression, hands and fingers working nervously.) Many, yes, many, come back and try to get the drug, try to get even a little, and they ruin others against their will. I knew many times that I myself did not want it, but there was such a strong power back of me. (Obsession.) If the world could only know!

My dear, noble wife is trying very hard to warn others so they will not meet the same fate and death I did. It was awful. (After the death of Wallace R., his wife, Mrs. R., played a leading role in a moving picture which vividly portrayed the horrors of the narcotic evil.)

Thanks to you here, I have found relief. I feel better; I will gain now. I have opened my soul's eyes and I find there are great possibilities for me, and in time there will be relief for me.

Oh, if I could only warn and help others! So many are taking that deadly drug. They think they can forget sorrow and gain strength from the drug. They do for a while, but it only lasts a little time, then it is worse. They take it a second time, and it is a little worse; a third time, still worse, and so on.

When people drink whiskey it makes them drunk, but after a good sleep they get over it, and they do not have the terrible craving that they do from drugs. The world will go mad if the narcotic evil is not stopped soon. Shutting out liquor did great harm, because people must have a stimulant of some kind. They work hard, very hard, in the movies, and it is nerve racking work. As I said, they must have something to stimulate their nerves so they can go on.

If they took some wine, or beer, or even some whiskey, to quiet their nerves, it would not be such a detriment as morphine is. Most of them use morphine, and, oh (moaning in anguish), if I could only come back and warn them! If only they would believe me! I would tell them to overcome, and let them know what a terrible thing it is to be a slave to a drug. If they only would realize what is beyond, they would never use drugs.

Dr. The condition of the spirits who have taken drugs during earth life must be terrible on the other side.

Sp. (Shuddering.) I don't want to go there. (The earth sphere.) I saw one glimpse of it. Thank you for concentrating for me; it has been of such help. I was weak, but through your concentration they have been able to help me on this side, and give me strength, and also to put me to sleep so I can gain strength.

I was trying to come back somewhere to get help (at some psychic circle), but I could not do very much. I did not understand then. Since I was here the last time and you talked to me I am stronger, and I have come now to thank you and to say I am on the way to health and happiness I wish I had know about you when I was first taken sick; I could probably have overcome and conquered.

If I could only talk to my dear, noble wife and thank her for helping me and for trying to warn others who are on the same road I was! I will conquer now, and then I want the world to know. I want to warn the grown-ups, to warn children, to warn young men, to warn young women, to never, never start taking that deadly drug. I would rather have pain than take it. For a while it kills pain, then opens the wound worse than ever.

You do not know how terrible the suffering is. I could not tell you. If I were burning in hell it could not be worse than having every nerve in my body burning. It drives one mad. No one can realize it except through experience.

Dr. The spirit friends can help you.

Sp. I have help now and I do thank you. Next time, if I can come again, I may be able to tell of my progression in the other world. I have seen very little, but I will learn. I am in a school, a hospital, where I am learning to overcome. People think that when they die, all troubles will be ended. That is the first time you really live, and all your desires and cravings are with you, because they belong to the soul, not the body. The body is only the dress. Now I am in school to learn the lessons of life from the real standpoint, and I am learning.

Thank you all for helping me, and also for giving me the opportunity of learning the lessons of life. I wish many places had circles like this to help spirits in darkness. Some time, send my love to my dear, noble wife. I will try, when I am stronger, to impress her that I am there with her.

Dr. Be brave and forget all about your trouble. Let the Mercy Band of Spirit Forces help you, then you will gradually overcome.

Sp. Yes, I will, and thank you. Goodbye!

Spirits of former drunkards, no longer able to satisfy their desire for liquor in the usual way, may attach themselves to susceptible mortals and through suggestive influence force the latter to drink for them.

Victims of such obsession have been brought to our observation, the most recent case being that of Mrs. V., a periodic inebriate, who, for some time, had endeavored in vain to overcome the tendency to drink.

Having again failed to conquer this irresistible impulse, she came to us one evening, strongly under the influence of liquor, and asked to be given a treatment. After her departure, we held a concentration circle when the spirit of a drunkard, dislodged from Mrs. V., controlled Mrs. Wickland.

EXPERIENCE, APRIL 4, 1923

Spirit: PAUL HOPKINS Patient: MRS. V

Psychic: MRS. WICKLAND

Doctor: Are you a stranger to us? Where did you come from?

Spirit: (Attempting to fight.) It's too warm! Why did you pull me away when I was just going to have a drink and a good time?

Dr. Aren't you ashamed of yourself? Do you think that controlling a lady and ruining her life is a good time?

Sp. When a fellow feels so blue, what can he do?

Dr. You must overcome your old habit.

Sp. I'm so warm. I'm awfully hot!

Dr. Where did you come from?

Sp. Give me something, quick! I'm so dry.

Dr. You have had all you are going to have.

Sp. I'm burning up!

Dr. You made a lady drink for you. Do you know that you are "dead" and are now a spirit?

Sp. All I know is, I'm hot! It was pouring fire all over me. (Static treatment given patient.)

Dr. That was good for you.

Sp. I ran away when all that hot fire came down on me. It's the first time I ever felt anything like that. It was so hot that I thought I was in an oven. They must have new things these days.

Dr. What do you mean?

Sp. Fire pouring down on my back. I am dry; I'm awful dry! Give me something -just a few drops!

Dr. Can't you understand that you have lost your mortal body and are a spirit? Do you understand what I am talking about?

Sp. No. I don't know you.

Dr. But you understand me, do you not? You are a spirit.

Sp. You give me something to drink! I'm awful dry. Give me something, I tell you! I only got a very few drops when you took me away.

Dr. Why don't you behave yourself?

Sp. I can't any more. Just give me a little, only a few drops!

THIRTY YEARS AMONG THE DEAD

Dr. If you don't behave yourself, you will find yourself in the dark.

Sp. Say, will you tell that druggist that he didn't give it to me strong enough? Tell him, will you?

Dr. You are done with druggists.

Sp. I want something to drink.

Dr. Do you think it is honorable to influence a woman and make her drink to satisfy you?

Sp. I've got to get it some way.

Dr. Should you influence that lady to drink whiskey for you?

Sp. Lady? I drank it myself. No lady got any. I want it all myself. You can't get very much these days, and when you get it, you don't give it away. You want it all yourself.

Dr. Don't you realize that you are getting it through a lady?

Sp. You give me some and give it to me quick!

Dr. I want you to understand your condition.

Sp. I'm always a good fellow.

Dr. Good for nothing.

Sp. No.

Dr. That's it exactly-good for nothing. What have you been doing lately?

Sp. I haven't been working for some time.

Dr. Do you know what year it is?

Sp. I don't care.

Dr. You have been interfering with the life of a woman. This is not your own body; can you understand that? It is a woman's body.

Sp. Woman's?

Dr. Yes. See your skirts.

Sp. I don't wear skirts. But, I've been a woman once in a while.

Dr. And through that woman you got the whiskey. You should be ashamed of yourself. You are not satisfied with abusing yourself, but you must also control a woman.

Sp. Why should I be ashamed? I have done nothing but drink some innocent whiskey.

Dr. You know that you are in a strange condition.

Sp. I know I feel funny once in a while.

Dr. You have been brought here and allowed to temporarily control this body so you may be made to understand that you must leave that lady alone. Her name is Mrs. V.; do you know her?

Sp. That's not my name. I haven't heard my name for a long time. Once in a while I feel kind of queer. I am not so correct about things as I used to be.

THIRTY YEARS AMONG THE DEAD

Dr. Should you not ask the reason? The fact is, you have lost your physical body.

Sp. What's the matter with me?

Dr. You are a spirit, and are invisible to us. We cannot see you.

Sp. Can't you see me?

Dr. No.

Sp. You don't see me? I'm a big fellow. Don't you see me? Why? Probably you have had something to drink too. Say, you give me a drink, will you? We will be pretty good fellows together. I shall be happy, if you will give some whiskey.

Dr. You would be in a fine condition then.

Sp. If you will give me whiskey, I will remember you in my will. You give me something to drink, then we will be pretty good fellows together.

Dr. I will do nothing of the kind.

Sp. Won't you help a poor fellow when he gets so dry?

Dr. We want to help you, but not in that way.

Sp. Why did you give me that hot fire?

Dr. I was giving an electrical treatment to a lady, not to you. The lady asked me to. We drove you away from her, but that does not seem to interest you, does it?

Sp. How would you have liked that?

Dr. You deserved it.

Sp. Say, can't you give me some whiskey?

Dr. You are only wasting time. What we are trying to do is to make you understand your condition. You are an invisible spirit, controlling the body of this woman.

Sp. What's the matter with that other woman? Why do I always have to go with her?

Dr. You have been obsessing her. You are selfish and have been controlling and influencing her. It is not the woman's fault, it is your own fault. Did you ever read the Bible?

Sp. The Bible?

Dr. Do you remember how Jesus cast out unclean spirits? You are such a spirit.

Sp. (Looking at hands.) These rings do not belong to me, and yet, how in the devil could they belong to any one else?

Dr. Do you recognize these hands?

Sp. No. I must have had a little too much. But I don't seem so very tipsy. I guess I have had a little too much, probably. You can hypnotize people in many ways; maybe that's it. Or probably I've had too little, and you had better give me more whiskey so I can see just a few drops. I am blind. Give me something and be a good fellow. Give me just one glass more, then I shall be all right. Will you do it?

Dr. You will have to leave if you are not sensible.

Sp. You can't drive me out, and there are not many fellows who could either. I'm pretty strong, you can see that.

Dr. We cannot see you at all.

Sp. I could fight all of you. I have done it before with people. (Rolling up sleeves.) You'd better look out!

Dr. Why can't you listen to what I am telling you? You are invisible to us.

Sp. Can't you see me?

Dr. No. You have lost your own body. This is not your body.

Sp. It isn't? (Attempting to fight.) Give me something to drink!

Dr. Aren't you ashamed of yourself?

Sp. Why should I be ashamed? All I had was a drink.

Dr. You do not understand your condition.

Sp. Why didn't you tell that woman to wait a minute? (The patient had left after her treatment.) She ran away. What for? Tell her to wait a minute.

Dr. You will be taken care of, and will not disturb any more persons.

Sp. She's a pretty good woman. When I want whiskey, she is always ready with the money and gives it to me.

Dr. That will not happen any more.

Sp. I am not alone; there are many others with me.

Dr. Did they all want to drink?

Sp. Yes.

Dr. You were ruining a woman's life. You drank through that woman. You controlled her and she drank for you.

Sp. Do you mean that big, fat woman? Say, she's good hearted. She's always ready to treat me. We have very good times together, glorious times! (Laughing.)

Dr. You have had your last good time. Do you think you are doing something honorable when you upset a woman's life, and make a drunkard of her?

Sp. I'm no drunkard. I can walk just as straight and fast as any one. I have sense. We both have a good drink together.

Dr. There is no sense of shame in you. Try to realize that you are an invisible spirit and have lost your own body. It is 1923 now. Do you know that you are in Los Angeles,

California? You lost your body probably many years ago, and have been hovering around in the earth sphere ever since.

Sp. I want something to drink right now.

Dr. Is that what you call a glorious time?

Sp. It's a good time for a while.

Dr. You were ruining a lady's life.

Sp. I haven't done that.

Dr. When you wanted whiskey you made that lady drink it for you.

Sp. I did not; I drank it myself.

Dr. Yes, through the lady. Don't act so innocent. You impressed the woman to get whiskey for you.

Sp. Well, she has the money. I don't make any money any more.

Dr. Is it right to influence that woman, just to satisfy yourself? Did your mother teach you such things?

Sp. My mother died long ago.

Dr. Suppose your mother were alive; would you like to see her a slave to an earthbound spirit?

Sp. I am not an earthbound spirit.

Dr. Would you like to see your mother surrounded by a crowd of earthbound spirits, who were making her drink? Would that make you happy?

Sp. She wouldn't do it. This woman is good enough for me. She only buys whiskey.

Dr. Yes, and you drink it through her.

Sp. I drink it myself.

Dr. By controlling the lady, Mrs. V., just as you are now controlling the body of this lady.

Sp. I am not controlling any one. I've only had a drink.

Dr. Try to be sensible. This body is not yours.

Sp. Whose is it then?

Dr. It belongs to my wife. She is a psychic sensitive through whom spirits can talk.

Sp. Will she have a drink with me? Will you?

Dr. No.

Sp. I'll treat the crowd.

Dr. I thought you had no money.

Sp. I always get some money from the lady.

Dr. She is not here.

Sp. You get it, and I'll treat the crowd. Come on with me, everybody! I'll treat you all.

Dr. Does the lady pay the bills with money that you earn?

Sp. She's splendid. There's another man helps her to pay for things.

THIRTY YEARS AMONG THE DEAD

Dr. That is her husband.

Sp. Husband?

Dr. Yes, husband. You are making a slave of the woman, and making a drunkard of her. Suppose it were your mother who was being tormented.

Sp. My mother?

Dr. Yes; think that over carefully. Suppose somebody should make a drunkard of your mother, how would you feel? Or of your sister?

Sp. They know better.

Dr. Is your conduct honorable?

Sp. I'm a good fellow, and I always want to be on the best side of the women. Women are always my best friends. They always have money and are willing to spend it.

Dr. Now listen to me. You have actually lost your physical body, probably many years ago. Who is the President?

Sp. I don't know. I can't recall any one.

Dr. Is Lincoln the President?

Sp. No, that was a long time ago.

Dr. Cleveland?

Sp. No.

Dr. McKinley? Arthur?

Sp. He was President a long time ago.

Dr. Do you remember Wilson?

Sp. Wilson? I don't know that fellow.

Dr. Do you know about the big war in Europe, with twenty three nations fighting?

Sp. I don't care; all I want is a drink. I am getting so thirsty. What do I care for war? If

they want to kill themselves, what do I care? They are better off. If they don't know any better than to kill each other, let them go ahead.

Dr. What did your mother call you?

Sp. She called me Paul.

Dr. What was your surname?

Sp. It is a long time since I heard it.

Dr. What did they call your father?

Sp. They called him John Hopkins.

Dr. Then you must be Paul Hopkins. What state were you born in?

THIRTY YEARS AMONG THE DEAD

Sp. I have forgotten. Oh, yes, I was born in Yuma, Arizona.

Dr. Were you ever in Los Angeles?

Sp. Yes, once in a while. They used to have pretty good saloons on Main Street, and I suppose they are there now.

Dr. No, they are all gone.

Sp. Then I don't know what became of them.

Dr. They have all been done away with.

Sp. They were on Main Street, between Second and Third.

Dr. What would your mother think of your condition?

Sp. My mother is dead.

Dr. Her spirit did not die. She would be sorry to find you in this condition.

Sp. I'm in an all right condition. I feel tip-top! I get a glass of whiskey when I want it, and it makes me feel good and happy.

Dr. Does it make you happy to see a man lying drunk in the gutter?

Sp. I have never seen it. But liquor is good! Oh, ho! Who is that? (Seeing some spirit.)

Dr. Who is it?

Sp. I will have to sit up and take notice. She's a nice lady. (To spirit.) Who are you?

Dr. Perhaps it is your own mother.

Sp. She was an old lady. This lady says she knew my mother. My mother was a good Christian woman. I suppose she is with God in Heaven, sitting near the throne.

Dr. Jesus taught that God is Spirit, and God is Love. You cannot find such a God sitting on a throne.

Sp. Where does He sit?

Dr. God is Spirit, and is not in any particular place. He is the Life of all Nature. You are an expression of God himself. Understand that you are an ignorant spirit and must overcome your old habits and that you will then progress.

Sp. This lady says if I behave myself I can go to bed and rest. I'm awfully tired. I am a pretty tired fellow. Will they let me rest myself?

Dr. Yes, and when you wake you will realize that you are a spirit, and that you must overcome old habits and progress as you should on the spirit side of life.

Sp. That lady is a nurse.

Dr. We cannot see her as you do. We do not see you. You are controlling my wife's body.

Sp. I do not understand that. I want to go to that bed.

Dr. You must learn the purpose of life.

Sp. They say if I lie down in that bed I will not get any more whiskey.

Dr. You will be taught how to progress.

Sp. Can I have any more whiskey?

Dr. No.

Sp. Well, I don't care. I'm tired and I feel happy. What can a fellow do? I have no home and no place to go. You must have a good time sometimes, a jollification time.

Dr. You did not understand your condition.

Sp. This lady says I will have a home with my mother. I will go to my mother. Will she like me?

Dr. Mother love never dies. After you acquire understanding you must help this lady whom you have been tormenting. You have made that poor lady a drunkard.

Sp. Have I? I didn't know that. I wanted something to drink, but I did not know I was doing any harm.

Dr. When she came here tonight she was drunk, and I gave her a treatment.

Sp. I had that.

Dr. You made her drunk; she herself does not want to drink. She tries to resist the impulse. She is a sensitive, and you hypnotized her and made her drink.

Sp. It's pretty hard for a fellow to give it up.

Dr. You will have to do your duty and help her.

Sp. I feel pretty tired. I want to go to that bed.

Dr. Think yourself in that bed and you will be there.

Sp. I will? By thinking?

Dr. Yes, be perfectly quiet and think yourself in that bed.

Sp. Remember me. I am a good fellow, and I like you anyhow, even if you gave me that fire. I mean well.

Dr. The lady whom you see will be your nurse and will look after you.

Sp. My mother is here! Oh, mother, my dear, will you forgive me? I was not a good fellow. I will not drink any more whiskey. Mother says she will help me. God bless you for the work you have done for me.

After the foregoing experience a friend reported a marked change for the better in Mrs. V., saying that no further desire for intoxicants was manifested. Mrs. V. herself acknowledged this change and expressed her gratitude for the relief obtained.

Not at all uncommon are the cases of amnesia, when total lapse of memory occurs, all sense of identity is lost and the victim wanders to strange places, returning to his normal self without any knowledge of his recent actions.

We have abundant demonstration that this state is frequently due to the influence of obsessing spirits. One case was that of a young man, C. B., who, shortly after he had established himself in business with his father, rose early one morning and left his home without the knowledge of his parents. No trace of him could be found and after several weeks of anxiety the parents asked us to concentrate for their missing son.

We did so, emphasizing that the young man should have no rest until he would write to his parents. The following morning he wrote to them, saying he was on board a United States Man-of-War at San Francisco, that he had enlisted in the Navy and would be gone for several years.

The boy's parents were anxious to have him at home with them, and wrote him to that effect, saying they would do all they could to obtain his release. The day before our next concentration circle, C. B. wrote his parents that they should do nothing regarding his discharge, for he was entirely willing to serve his term of enlistment.

The following evening we again concentrated for C. B., and a spirit controlled Mrs. Wickland, as related in the succeeding article, clearly giving indication of having been the cause of the young man's recent actions.

EXPERIENCE, DECEMBER 13, 1923

Spirit: JOHN EDWARDS   Patient: C. B

Psychic: MRS. WICKLAND

While singing "Throw out the Life Line" an amusing episode occurred. As the intelligence assumed control of Mrs. Wickland he seemed to be pulling himself along, hand over hand, as if by a rope, and then made the motions of swimming.

Doctor: Did you hold on to the life line? Have you been drifting about? Where did you come from? You do not need to swim on dry land. What is the matter with you?

Spirit: I want to find out what's the matter with me.

Dr. How long have you been dead?

Sp. (To audience.) He calls me dead! I am not dead -but not so much alive either.

Dr. Where did you come from?

Sp. Lots of people brought me here.

Dr. Who brought you?

Sp. A whole lot of people.

Dr. I don't see them.

Sp. I don't see why they want me. I want to be out at sea.

Dr. Have you been out before?

Sp. Yes.

Dr. Why do you want to go out to sea? Have you been out many times?

Sp. Quite a little.

Dr. Don't you want to be on shore?

THIRTY YEARS AMONG THE DEAD

Sp. I don't want to be a dry crab. I was all ready to go out, but you pulled me to shore. I don't see why they should pull me to shore.

Dr. Were you drowned at sea?

Sp. If I had been, how could I be here?

Dr. Your spirit could be here.

Sp. You mean the soul?

Dr. Yes.

Sp. Then that should be with God.

Dr. Where is God?

Sp. If you don't know that, then you ought to go to Sunday School.

Dr. I did go, but I did not find out there.

Sp. Then you did not go to the right one.

Dr. Which one should I have gone to?

Sp. There are all kinds of denominations; they are not all alike, but they all know about God.

Dr. What church did you go to?

Sp. The church where I go is where I can be all alone. I do not go there very often. I can belong to any denomination. When you are on the water you can't go to church, you go to service.

Dr. Which church did you like best?

Sp. They are all alike. It's just a matter of form. They all belong to one God, and teach a hereafter, a Heaven and a hell, and that Christ died for our sins. So you see I feel like this you can just as well belong to one as another. They all praise God, so it makes no difference.

Dr. You were a liberal man.

Sp. I don't know that I was that either. I don't know what kind of a man I was. I had my own religion in a way. I had to go to church once in a while to show the Captain that I could.

Dr. What ship were you on?

Sp. I was on all kinds.

Dr. Were you an ordinary sailor?

Sp. I was in the Navy.

Dr. Can you tell us what year it is?

Sp. I don't even know what month it is.

Dr. Do you know the year?

Sp. I do not know.

Dr. Is it 1922?

THIRTY YEARS AMONG THE DEAD

Sp. No. That's not the year.

Dr. What should it be?

Sp. 1912.

Dr. Where were you sailing?

Sp. One time I went around on the battleship "Cincinnati."

Dr. Where did you go?

Sp. One time around the Coast.

Dr. Did you ever go through the Panama Canal?

Sp. No. I was near it once, but not through.

Dr. What did you do on ship?

Sp. I just did anything that came along.

Dr. How old were you?

Sp. I can't seem to remember.

Dr. And now you want to go to sea again?

Sp. Yes. I don't want to be on land, because I don't feel I belong there. There is something in life when you are on the ocean -something to it. You have regular meals and no worry, if your work is done all right,

Dr. Is there much work to do?

Sp. Oh, yes, lots of scrubbing; there is always something to do. The Captain does not want his men to be idle. If we were left alone we would have a good time. If there is nothing else to do we have to polish all the time. I know something about it. We have to polish the stairways; the machinery, and the fixings around it, all have to be polished. Every day we polish the knobs, the machinery and the stairs. It is all bright and shining. It's a big ship.

Dr. Were you on a battleship?

Sp. I was on different battleships.

Dr. Were you under fire at any time?

Sp. No; we did not fight. The Cuban War was not much of a war. The Philippines was more.

Dr. Were you there?

Sp. We were outside. We did not get in the Bay, not all of us, only a few. Dewey went in. I was there, but not on his ship. I was outside cruising around. Some had to be on guard and watch. If we had all gone in we would have been trapped. There were others around there.

Dr. What is your name?

Sp. My name? It has been so long since I heard it, I have forgotten it. My name is John.

Dr. John what?

THIRTY YEARS AMONG THE DEAD

Sp. John Edwards.

Dr. Were you ever on the Pacific Coast?

Sp. Yes, we were around there one time. I was more on the Eastern Coast.

Dr. Were you discharged when you left the vessel?

Sp. (Slowly.) Left the vessel?

Dr. Didn't you leave the vessel? Or did you have an accident of some kind?

Sp. I don't know.

Dr. Were you sick?

Sp. I don't know.

Dr. Is Manila Bay the last you remember?

Sp. No; that's a long time ago.

Dr. Where did you go from there?

Sp. I was quite young when we were in Manila Bay.

Dr. That must have been in 1898. How long were you at sea?

Sp. I don't know. The last I remember is 1912.

Dr. What happened to you in 1912? Were you sick?

Sp. I seem confused. It seems to me that we were -I do not remember very well -we were painting the boat. I do not know what place it was; I can't think. In some way we were not in the Navy Yard, it was a little outside. We were on the scaffold on the side of the vessel.

Dr. Did something happen to you?

Sp. My head got so funny. I think I had some kind of a vertigo spell. I felt funny. It seemed like my head was swimming.

Dr. Were you painting the boat?

Sp. We were cleaning and fixing it up.

Dr. Were you in dry dock?

Sp. I cannot remember what it was. Something happened so I got in the water.

Dr. You probably dropped off the scaffold.

Sp. I don't know, but I got well right away.

Dr. It is very likely that you lost your body at that time and became a spirit.

Sp. A spirit? What do you mean?

Dr. I mean you lost your mortal body. You are invisible to us.

Sp. But I was going to sea. I felt as if a part of me was a sailor, but I also felt that I was teaching some sailor. (Through obsessing C. B.) I could smell the salt air around him. Sailors have a kind of atmosphere around them; you can tell them when you see them. I wanted to go back again. You feel funny when you are on land. You feel you do not belong there. The land is so solid; you do not feel right. I feel the ocean is the bosom of a mother; you are rocked to sleep. You feel so fine when the waves rock you to sleep.

Dr. When you fell from the boat, you probably lost your body, and you have been a spirit since then. This is not your body. Look at these hands.

Sp. (Noticing hands of psychic.) That is not my hand! (Laughing.) No, I should say not! I had big, big hands. That hand has not pulled any ropes. That's funny -I have a hand like that! (Laughing with amusement.)

Dr. And you have a dress, and long hair. Are those the feet of a sailor?

Sp. They are not mine. Oh, I see! One time, a long time ago, you know, we used to go to one town, then another. I was not on the battleship all the time. You know my father was a sea Captain, and, of course, we were on water all the time. He sailed from New York to India, and around there.

Dr. On a sailing vessel?

Sp. Yes. He had a sailing vessel first, when I was just a little kid. Then he had a vessel. He went between Calcutta, New York and England.

Dr. With a merchant vessel?

Sp. Yes. He had a lot of stuff. Then he went to Australia one time; he dealt in cotton and wool. When I grew up I felt I wanted to be in the employ of the Government, so I joined the Navy, to my father's disgust. He did not like it, but he said I was a sailor born. I think I was born on the water; I do not know the land. My mother taught me to read and write and that was all the schooling I had. We were always on the water. Mother was a pretty good woman.

Dr. Did your mother die?

Sp. My mother is not living, and my father is dead too. They both died some years ago. But this was not what I was going to talk about.

Dr. You were talking about these hands, and this dress.

Sp. I do not see how I could get a woman's hands and dress. That was what I was going to talk about when I drifted away. I do not know, but I should judge I was about eighteen or nineteen when we were in Calcutta. I like to go around and see everything, and I like to talk. I drifted into a meeting one time. In India, Calcutta is a pretty good town and has a nice climate. I drifted into this meeting and I got a whole lot of books. They called this meeting "Theosophy." They were nice people, but queer. When they talk, before you know it, you believe in reincarnation. Is this skirt reincarnation? You said I am dead, so now how can you explain it in any other way? That must explain it, because I am back as a woman.

Dr. You might call this reincarnation, in a way. When you pass out, you leave your mortal body and become a spirit.

Sp. You know, they go to Devachan, and that is a long way off. Say, Madam Blavatsky was a great speaker. I heard her in Calcutta. Then there was Leadbeater. I was only a kid, but, you know, when you get something in your head when you are a kid, it stays there.

My father said: "John, don't you believe that; you will go crazy."

I said: "It is better than nothing; it tells good things. That salvation scheme is not right."

My heart felt so big when I said that. It swelled up when I got those books. It may be that I am back again as a woman. I didn't think I would be a woman. I wanted to be a sailor again.

Dr. You are using a woman's body only temporarily.

Sp. So I am a woman temporarily! (Laughing.)

Dr. You are a spirit, and probably have been since 1912. It is 1922 now. You have been out of your body ten years.

Sp. How do you know I died then?

Dr. You say that is the last date you remember.

Sp. Do you go by that? Then I have been in Devachan? Maybe sailors, don't stay in Devachan so long; maybe their vibrations are better. I know the vibrations are much more vibrating on a steamboat, especially when there are storms! (Laughing.) Really and truly, have I reincarnated?

Dr. It is likely that you passed out of your body at the time you spoke of, and you have been a spirit but were not aware of your condition.

Sp. So I do not know anything?

Dr. Whatever your condition has been, you have been brought here tonight to acquire understanding. We are investigators of psychic phenomena and spirit obsession. Sometimes spirits take control of mortals and cause them to do strange things. You have been attracted here, and are controlling this body, which belongs to my wife. You are using it temporarily. We do not see you; we only hear you talk.

Sp. Then, in reality, I am in a woman. I am only fooling you then.

Dr. My wife is so constituted that spirits can use her body temporarily. Have you ever heard of mediums?

Sp. Yes, I have been to mediums to have my fortune told. You know they are only controlled by Indians.

Dr. Indians are excellent "gate-keepers." They are good protectors for mediums.

Sp. Why did I come here?

Dr. For understanding. You have evidently been doing mischief unconsciously. You are in Los Angeles, California.

Sp. I know I was in San Francisco once. I have not been there for a long time. It was in 1894.

Dr. You probably made a young man leave his home and parents without any provocation at all, and made him enlist as a sailor in the Navy.

Sp. He had no business to do that.

Dr. He is interested in other work. He seemed to lose himself and enlisted in the Navy. He is San Francisco now. There is evidence in his case that some spirit has been interfering with him, and I surmise that you are the one.

THIRTY YEARS AMONG THE DEAD

Sp. For goodness sake, I wouldn't do that! I woke up one morning and I felt I was on land for some reason or other, and I wanted to be on water.

Dr. You were drifting about and came in contact with this young man, who is sensitive to spirit influence. He had been studying too hard and so made himself sensitive. You got into his magnetic aura, acted through him, and caused him to do things he did not want to do. Did you enlist very recently to go out to sea again?

Sp. It seems I woke up early one morning and wanted to go back to the water. I felt I was lost.

Dr. Didn't you realize that you did not have full control of yourself?

Sp. I felt queer. In a way, I was in a dreamy state. Say, I didn't mean to do anything wrong.

Dr. We understand your position, and know you are a good fellow. We don't blame you.

Sp. Who is that boy?

Dr. His name is C. B.; he is a young boy of seventeen.

Sp. He claimed he was twenty-one, or he could not have joined.

Dr. He is large and looks older than he is. We concentrated for him and I suppose we pulled you to shore.

Sp. I felt some one pull me, and then I felt I was in the water. I recall -we were in New York, or somewhere around there, and it was awfully stormy and icy. I was doing something and fell in the water. There was ice all around me. We had been there for a while, but I do not know any more. How did I get into that boy?

Dr. You drifted into his aura.

Sp. Why, here comes my mother! I haven't seen her for a long time. She died in New York. She says: "Oh, John, I have been hunting for you for so long." I didn't know it. If I am dead, why didn't I go to her?

Dr. Many fall into a sleep and remain in that condition for some time.

Sp. Oh, I was in Devachan! That is where I was sleeping to reincarnate!

Dr. Now you must go with your mother. She will take you to her home.

Sp. I will go to my mother and father -my old father.

Dr. Does he have understanding now?

Sp. Mother says, yes, but she had a time with him. He wanted to see the Savior. I never quite believed in that story. I wanted to find out about it, but never did. I think Theosophy is the best, because they do not have that blood question to deal with. I don't believe in one person being killed for others.

If I did anything wrong, why should I not suffer myself? God is Love, and He never wanted any one killed to save another. Such damned foolish things! The church people are so down on Jews, and yet Jesus was a Jew.

Dr. Now you must go with your father and mother.

Sp. I've been in a nice crowd. This has been a good night. I feel pretty good. It has been a good night -to speak with nice people and spend a couple of hours having a good time. You say you cannot see these others here, but there are quite a few.

Now mother says -my dear little mother -she says I must go. She has not seen her son for a long time. We have lots to talk about together. I told you my mother was good. I must say goodbye to you all. (Trying to rise, but unable to do so.) Why, what's the matter with my legs? I cannot stand on them.

Dr. You are only controlling the upper part of the body.

Sp. Then I'm only half a man! (Laughing heartily.) Worse and worse! Only half woman, half sailor! Now I must go with my dear little mother.

Dr. You must learn to think.

Sp. Think! Have I not been thinking before? (Laughing.) Excuse me, but everything seems a joke.

Dr. That's all right. You will have to travel by thinking.

Sp. Not by my legs? Will I not need my legs any more? I haven't any; you know I'm only half a man.

Dr. Just think yourself with your mother, and you will be there.

Sp. Think myself with my mother, and I will be there? I am going now. But you folks are so jolly that I think I'll come again some day. You don't mind if I come, do you? By the way, will you please tell that boy I feel sorry if I did him mischief?

Dr. Will you try to help him? You can.

Sp. I can? How?

Dr. By impressing him to return home. Your mother will explain to you.

Sp. My mother says I should thank you for finding me. But she found her son in a woman! She did not recognize me in a woman -but we have to take things as they come. Now I will go -Good Night.

The day after this the attitude of C. B. changed entirely. He then wrote to his parents urging them to do everything possible to secure his release, as he wanted to come home and continue his work. He added that he could not understand why he had enlisted, and that he seemed to have been in a daze.

Since the young man had enlisted as being of age, while in reality only seventeen, he was, after many difficulties and delays, released from service, and he returned to his home, once more his normal self.

THIRTY YEARS AMONG THE DEAD

Chapter IX

Psychic Invalidism

Spirits who are ignorant of having lost their physical bodies often hold firmly in mind the thought of their former physical condition and continue to suffer pain. This "error of the mortal mind"18 persists until an understanding of transition and spiritual laws is reached, when freedom from ideas of physical limitations is attained.

When spirits who are under this delusion of suffering and disease come into the auras of mortals their condition is conveyed to the sensitives, and chronic lassitude, pseudo-illness and psychic invalidism result. These sensitives endure all the pain of the spirits' former physical condition, and ordinary methods of treatment fail to cure, for the only permanent relief is found through the dislodgement of the ignorant entities.

While we were in Chicago a friend of ours, Miss F. W., a companion to Mrs. McA., prominent modiste in the city, asked us to concentrate for Mrs. McA., who was a chronic invalid. The latter had been ordered by her physicians to take a rest cure and could not be induced to get up again. She was suffering intense pains in the head and was subject to many changeable moods. Miss F. W. and Mrs. McA.'s masseuse were present during the following occurrence.

EXPERIENCE, APRIL 2, 1908

Spirit: GRACE BRUSTED Patient: MRS. McA

Psychic: MRS. WICKLAND

The spirit at first spoke with great difficulty, complained of being very sick and was unable to sit up. She insisted that she was too sick to be up and wished to go to bed. When asked whether she knew any one in the room she at once recognized Mrs. McA's masseuse and demanded that she take her to bed immediately, wait upon her and draw down the shades, as the light was too strong for a sick person.

She gave her name as Grace Brusted, of Boston, said she was a Universalist, and that the year was 1898.

She had been sick for a long time and felt as if she were two persons, at times herself and at other times another person. She was often called Mrs. McA., but was tired of answering to that name, as she did not like Mrs. McA. Recently she had had to do entirely too much work, having had to give orders to the sewing girls; furthermore, Miss F. W. would have to do things in her way or be discharged.

The spirit repeated again that she was tired of living a double life, that she could not understand it and was more than ready to die. The way of progression was then explained and the spirit's grandmother and mother appeared to her, saying that she had always been a spoiled child, but would now have to learn to serve others.

Miss F. W. and the masseuse said that Mrs. McA. had been acting in the same manner as this spirit, even using the identical language, and they later reported that on the following morning Mrs. McA. was in a very genial mood, remarking that it was, the first time for many months that she had wakened without a headache.

After this she improved rapidly, left her bed and resumed her usual activities. For over a period of six years, a friend of ours, an elderly gentleman, eighty-four years old, was afflicted with unaccountable pains in the back of the neck and a peculiar dizziness and vertigo which came upon him with increasing frequency.

When seized with these attacks he felt that walls and buildings would fall and crush him; an extreme nausea accompanied these sensations, and if seated, he would fall forward with his head below his knees and for some time would be unable to straighten himself without help. Unable to find any physical cause for his distress, the possibility of spirit interference was suggested, and we concentrated for him at our psychic circle.

A spirit then controlled Mrs. Wickland and fell forward with head between the knees. We labored with the entity for some time until he was finally able to tell us that his name was Jack Finch, that he was about sixty-five years old and had been an inmate of an institution near Madison, Wisconsin.

He said that when he was quite small some one, probably his sister, had been carrying him and had dropped him to the floor and that this fall had broken his back and left him helpless. As he grew older he became a great care; his mother neglected him and he was finally placed in an institution. He remembered he had been in a cyclone at one time and that something had struck him on the back of the neck, adding still further to his misery.

He had always been in great pain, and his broken back and injured neck produced dizzy spells which would cause him to double over and remain in a cramped position until aid was given. When this dizziness came upon him he would feel as if he were sliding off a roof, or as if the walls were crushing him; again, he often felt as if the bed would fall on him and as if everything were spinning around.

He said that because of his helpless condition no one had ever cared for him, with the single exception of a nurse by the name of "Anasteena," who had been very kind to him at the institution and had always fed him.

"But everything is changed now. Sometimes I feel like a small man, and sometimes like a woman, or like a big man." (Sensations experienced when influencing different mortals.) When the spirit was brought to a realization that he had lost his mortal body and could no longer have any physical pain, he asked: "If I have lost my body, and if I am dead, then why haven't I seen God? Where is He?"

This led to an explanation of the true nature of God, His manifestation in all things, and the existence of the spirit world. Being told to look about to see whether some one was present whom he had known on earth, he said: "Why, there is my mother! She wants me to go with her to her home; she says she will take care of me now. She says I never knew what real life was on account of my crippled body, but that I will commence to really live from now on."

THIRTY YEARS AMONG THE DEAD

While speaking, he saw in the distance another spirit coming toward him, and he exclaimed with great joy: "It is Anasteena! Can I go with her, too?" Assured that he could go with his mother and friend, that he would be well cared for, and would begin a life of happiness, he said fervently, "God bless you!" and was then taken away.

The next day the friend who had suffered from the vertigo attacks found himself free from the ailment and said he had so much surplus energy that he felt he must be forty-eight, instead of eighty-four. Nor was he ever subject to any recurrence of his former trouble.

Mr. Z., from the neighboring town of Burbank, who had suffered for twenty-five years from sleeplessness and an intense nausea without having been able to obtain relief, was brought to us by a physician, who suspected obsession in the case. During the consultation Mrs. Wickland saw the spirit of a man standing behind the patient, and when she described this spirit, the patient recognized an old friend who had passed out a number of years before.

After an electrical treatment had been given to the patient, this spirit left him, and taking control of Mrs. Wickland, spoke to his friend, recalling incidents of their former acquaintanceship.

Mr. Z. had at one time been engaged to the daughter of this spirit, but for religious reasons the engagement had been broken. The two men had, however, continued friendly relations and when the father found himself in financial straits, Mr. Z. had aided him in a business way. When the father later died of cancer of the stomach, he was attracted to Mr. Z. because of his regard for him; becoming enclosed in his aura, he was unable to free himself and had remained with him for twenty-five years, conveying to his mortal friend the symptoms of the disease from which he had suffered while in earth life.

After receiving an explanation of the laws of the higher life he left repentantly, and Mr. Z. was no longer troubled with the nausea condition.

An unusual type of psychic invalidism, due to spirit influence, was the case of Mrs. G., who had for many years suffered intensely from a peculiar spinal affliction, which baffled all skill of physicians.

After Mrs. G. had been under our care for some time a spirit who had died of a broken back and neck was removed and controlled Mrs. Wickland. The guiding intelligences explained that he had drifted into the aura of the patient when she was a child and had become enmeshed in her nervous system, thus transferring to his victim the physical condition under which he had died, and which he still believed himself to be suffering from.

With the removal of the spirit the patient was promptly relieved and suffered no more pain in the back.

EXPERIENCE, JULY 4, 1923

Spirit: JAMES HOXEN Patient: MRS. G.

Psychic: MRS. WICKLAND

The controlling spirit seemed to be paralyzed, with head hanging toward the shoulder. At first unable to speak, he pointed to the neck, and moaned continually as if in great pain. At these indications, both Mr. and Mrs. G., who were in the circle, became intensely interested.

Doctor: Overcome your old habits, friend; forget your pain. (Manipulating hands and arms.) See, your arms are not stiff now. Straighten up; you are not paralyzed. We are going to help you.

Understand that you have lost your old body. You are a spirit and must not hover around the earth plane causing trouble. Talk, and tell us who you are. Where did you come from?

Spirit: Oh! (Making frantic efforts to reach Mrs. G., stretching forth both hands to her imploringly.)

Mrs. G. No, you cannot come back here. I do not want you.

Sp. Oh! (Beginning to cry, and making another effort to reach Mrs. G.)

Dr. You cannot be selfish any longer. You must listen to intelligent spirits who will help you. You can only find happiness by forgetting your present condition. Intelligent spirits will take you to the spirit world. Moaning and crying will not help you.

Mrs. G. The gentleman who is speaking to you is a doctor and he will help you.

Dr. Try to talk.

Sp. I don't want any more fire! (Electric treatments given patient.)

Dr. You surely will have more, if you stay around here.

Sp. I don't want any more. (Struggling.) Oh, that fire!

Dr. Listen to me. Something must have happened to you a long time ago. Can you remember what occurred?

Mrs. G. Answer the doctor.

Dr. Understand your true condition. You died probably a long time ago.

Sp. Oh! My back, my back!

Dr. What is the matter with your back?

Sp. It's broken.

Dr. What happened to you?

Sp. I fell off a horse.

Dr. Where did you live?

Sp. I can't tell just now. I thought I was dead in a way, but I don't feel like dying now. My back and head and neck are all gone to pieces. My head is going off my spine. (The patient had continually suffered from a sensation of the head being dislocated from the spine.)

Dr. When did the accident happen?

Sp. I don't know. I struck right here. (Left side of neck.)

Dr. Forget that condition; you do not need to have that sensation now. This body, which you are controlling, is all right. Do you know you are invisible to us?

Sp. I don't want any more fire. It strikes my neck too hard.

Dr. That was necessary to get you out. Why did you influence that lady and bother her?

Sp. My neck, my neck, and my head! They ache so I can't stand it any longer.

THIRTY YEARS AMONG THE DEAD

Dr. How long have you been troubled this way?

Sp. Many years -a long, long time.

Mrs. G. Were you grown up, or little, when you fell off the horse? Are you a boy or a girl?

Sp. I am a boy. I broke my neck a long time ago, but it hurts yet.

Mrs. G. Where did this happen? Was it in California?

Sp. No; far, far away. I don't know where.

Dr. Think back and your memory will return.

Mr. G. Was it Illinois, or Iowa?

Sp. I have been asleep and you'll have to wait a minute. My head aches so, and my neck. My neck is broken. My head has gone from my spine.

Mr. G. You no longer have a physical head.

Sp. But the fire gets on top of it!

Mrs. G. That is good for you; it will help you.

Sp. It's fire -fire!

Mrs. G. Your neck does not hurt you at all now.

Sp. Yes, it does.

Dr. No, it does not.

Sp. I got paralyzed. My spine! I can't move, and, oh, my neck! I can't move! My neck is broken.

Dr. Can't you understand that your broken neck went to the grave? Your physical body is gone. This body is all right, but you will use it for only a little while.

Sp. You don't know how everything hurts.

Dr. Because you hold that idea in your mind. How could your body hurt you now when it is in the grave?

Sp. How do you know it is?

Dr. This is not your body.

Sp. How do you know my body is in the grave?

Dr. Because you yourself are here. This body you are talking through is not yours.

Sp. How do you know?

Dr. You do not want to understand. You are a selfish spirit. You know that is true.

Sp. I have been to church and I know about Jesus Christ.

Mrs. G. To what church did you go?

Sp. To the Mennonite Church. (Mrs. G. had grown up among the Mennonites.)

173

Mrs. G. Where was that?

Sp. In Kansas, a long time ago. (Mrs. G. had lived in Kansas for some years.)

Mr. G. In what town?

Sp. N.

Mr. G. What is your name?

Sp. I lost it. My neck is so bad.

Mr. G. Did you live in town?

Sp. No, on a farm about a mile north of the College.

Mr. G. What is your name?

Sp. I had a name, but it is such a long time since I heard it.

Mr. G. How did you happen to fall from the horse?

Sp. We were going up the hill and my horse got scared of some rabbits. Then he went off quick. I did not get hold of the reins quick enough.

Mr. G. You were not a good rider.

Sp. I had no saddle. How could I stick on?

Mr. G. Evidently it was not a gentleman's saddle horse.

Sp. I was only a hired man.

Mr. G. How old were you?

Sp. I was about sixteen or seventeen, I think.

Mr. G. What did your mother call you?

Sp. I don't know.

Dr. Did she call you Mabel?

Sp. They never call a boy that. My shoulder and back are broken. My neck has been broken for years and years.

Dr. Will you understand that you have lost your body? What is your name?

Sp. My name is James.

Dr. Was that all they called you? Is this your hand? (Indicating hand of the psychic.)

Sp. No, Jimmie never had a ring.

Dr. You are using this hand temporarily; it does not belong to you. It belongs to my wife.

Sp. I have seen that my hands have been small for a long time. My name is James Hoxen.

Dr. You may have lost your body after that accident.

Sp. My head will drop off!

Dr. Then we will have to pick it up. You are an ignorant spirit, and have been bothering that lady.

Sp. What is a spirit?

Dr. That is what I am talking to.

Sp. This is James.

Dr. I see my wife when I look at this body. Ask any of these people whose body you are speaking through.

Sp. Then I belong to some one else.

Dr. To whom?

Sp. (Stretching his arms toward Mrs. G.) I want to come back to you. I like you.

Mrs. G. You will never come back to me any more. You will have to go to the spirit world.

Sp. Where is that?

Dr. It is the invisible world around the earth plane.

Sp. (Affectedly.) I want to see Jesus Christ.

Dr. Why do you whine?

Sp. That is my way to talk. Will you cure my neck?

Dr. Yes, by making you understand your true condition. As an ignorant spirit you have been bothering a lady. By using the "fire," as you call it, we drove you away. You are temporarily controlling my wife's body. You have lost your physical body, and you must obtain understanding of the invisible side of life, where you are now.

Mr. G. Do you know my name? Did you know any one by the name of G?

Sp. They lived far away.

Mr. G. Did you know anybody by the name of K.? (Mrs. G.'s maiden name.)

Sp. They were in another town.

Mr. G. Were you born in the place where you had the accident?

Sp. I was born far out in the country.

Mrs. G. What year do think it is?

Sp. I don't know.

Dr. Who is the President?

Sp. I never read very much about things. I lived on a farm and did the chores. That was long ago. For a while there has been so much fire.

Dr. I gave you that "fire"; it is electricity.

Sp. I saw fire; it is not electricity. You hold electricity in your hand, and it jerks.

Dr. I caused that fire.

THIRTY YEARS AMONG THE DEAD

Sp. You! Shame on you! Shame on you! You! To do that to an innocent little fellow like me! Shame on you!

Dr. You have been bothering that lady for a long time, and she could not live her own free life. I put the "fire" on you, and you left. Look around and you will see intelligent spirits here who will help you.

Sp. There's a lot of people here. (Suddenly becoming greatly excited and beginning to cry.) Mother! Oh! Oh, Mother!

Dr. She has come to help you.

Sp. Oh, Mother, why did you die? I was only a little boy, and when you died everything was broken up and I had to earn my own living.

Dr. What does your mother say?

Sp. She says: "Oh, Jimmie, where have you been?" She has been looking for me but could not find me.

Dr. That is because you have been with that lady, making a great deal of trouble. Now you can go with your mother.

Sp. It's a long time since I saw my mother.

Dr. It is 1923 now.

Sp. No!

Dr. It is the fourth of July, 1923, and you are in Los Angeles, California.

Sp. No, it must be 1893.

Dr. That was thirty years ago.

Sp. But I was living in 1896; after the accident I was crippled for years. The last I remember it was 1896.

Dr. That was twenty-seven years ago.

Sp. How can all those years be gone? Have I been sleeping?

Dr. Only partially. You have been bothering people.

Sp. I have been kept shut up for years and years. (In aura of patient.) I thought I was going to die once but after I had been shut up for a while, I felt different. I had lady's clothes on and I felt like a woman, but my neck bothered me so, and my head was like it came off my spine.

Dr. You got into that lady's magnetic aura and bothered her. When you lost your body you still had the idea that your neck was broken; but your body went to the grave.

Sp. But I had a neck that always hurt.

Dr. You held the idea in your mind that you still had a broken neck. "As a man thinketh in his heart, so is he." Your mind was on your broken neck, and you did not realize that a change had occurred. This body, which belongs to my wife, has no broken neck.

Sp. Your wife? Where is she?

Dr. Sleeping. Look at your feet; they are not really yours.

Sp. Am I a woman?

Dr. Only temporarily. Now you must go with your mother.

Sp. Mother, will you take me with you?

Dr. What does she say?

Sp. She says, yes, but I must ask that lady to forgive me. But I could not help it. I could not get out. I was shut up such a long time, and I'm tired. Now I will go with my mother. Oh, Mother, come and take me! I will be a good boy.

Dr. Now you will find understanding.

Sp. I feel I am dying. My head is off again.

Dr. That is only a temporary sensation. When you leave, you may feel as if you were dying, but that is only because you are losing control. You could not "die" if you tried, Nobody ever really dies. Spirit never dies.

Sp. Will I have a better body?

Dr. Yes. Now forget your broken neck and your pain.

Sp. I am going with my mother. Please forgive me, lady.

Mrs. G. That's all right, James. Forget the past.

Dr. Intelligent spirits will help you and will teach you wonderful things. Think yourself with your mother and with the Mercy Band of spirits. Goodbye.

Sp. Goodbye.

In the summer of 1923 a gentleman, Mr. I., consulted us about his wife, who for nine months had been confined to her bed suffering from intense pain in the head, diagnosed by others as due to brain tumor, and from a seemingly paralyzed condition of one arm, which was helpless.

We made several calls at the home of the invalid, giving electrical treatments which strengthened the patient, but Mrs. Wickland clairvoyantly saw the spirit of a man with a ghastly head wound and a woman with a crippled arm hovering about the lady.

At our next concentration circle, the spirit of this man controlled Mrs. Wickland, and we learned that in life he had been a house painter who had fallen from a scaffold, and, as he said, "split open" his head.

He did not know that he had died and declared that he was suffering from agonizing pains in the head, but that lately he had a very comfortable bed to rest in. Convinced of his true condition he was taken away, and from that time Mrs. I. had no further pain in the head.

She still remained in bed, however, feeling weak and suffering with the paralyzed arm. After another treatment we returned to our home, inviting Mr. I. to attend our concentration circle that evening.

When he came he said that after our departure his wife felt so much better that she had risen, and for the first time in nine months, spent the day out of bed.

THIRTY YEARS AMONG THE DEAD

The events of the evening, therefore, were of great interest to the gentleman, as the controlling spirit complained of pains corresponding exactly with those endured by his wife.

EXPERIENCE, JULY 17, 1923

Spirit: MRS. Lizzy Davidson Patient: MRS. I.

Psychic: MRS. WICKLAND

The spirit held one arm pressed tightly to the body, moaning incessantly.

Doctor: Good evening. Have we some one here who it sick? Is this one who has passed out with some sickness, and still holds the trouble in his mind? What is the matter?

Spirit: (Groaning.) My arm! Oh, my arm!

Dr. What is the matter with it?

Sp. It hurts me.

Dr. What happened to it?

Sp. Where's my bed? I'm sick.

Dr. Are you sleepy?

Sp. I'm sick in bed. I ought to be in bed.

Dr. Haven't you been in bed long enough?

Sp. I'm awfully sick.

Dr. How many years have you been sick?

Sp. A long, long time.

Dr. How long is it since you died?

Sp. Died? I'm sick, I said. I am not dead. I said "sick." You do not know about me. I am so sick.

Dr. I realize that you are sick in your mind. Otherwise you are not sick.

Sp. Oh! Oh! I'm a very sick woman. Don't touch me! My arm! My arm!

Dr. Was it hurt?

Sp. Why did you take me away when I was so comfortable in bed? Oh, that nice, comfortable bed! (To Mr. I.) He (Dr. W.) took me away just when I was going to lie down and sleep.

Mr. I. I am very glad to see you here.

Sp. He took me along with him, and I wanted to sleep. I am a very sick woman.

Dr. We are going to cure your arm.

Sp. Oh, I want to be in that bed. It's so nice and comfortable. It's such a nice bed, and there is such a nice gentleman to wait on me.

Dr. You will never be in that bed again.

THIRTY YEARS AMONG THE DEAD

Sp. I am a very sick woman. You had better call a doctor.

Mr. G. That gentleman is a doctor.

Dr. How long have you been sick?

Sp. (Recognizing Dr. W.) Why, you are the one who gave me those sparks! Take me away from him!

Mr. G. That was an electrical treatment.

Sp. He told me I should go with him. He said, "Any one who is around this lady, must come with me," so I went with him. Why did you tell me to come with you, and then hold me like this? (To Mr. I.) Can't you do something to protect me?

Mr. I. This is a good place for you.

Sp. You think so! Why did you let this man bring me here?

Mr. G. He did not want you to make an invalid of his wife.

Sp. Can't you tell this man to leave me alone? (To Mr. I)

Mr. I. No, I think you are in good hands.

Sp. No! No! No! I don't want to stay here! (Stamping feet furiously.)

Dr. Do you want to hover around this gentleman's wife, and ruin her life?

Sp. He can take care of us so nicely. I like him and I want to stay there! (Angrily stamping feet.)

Mr. I. They will take good care of you here.

Dr. You are not sick, but you have a bad temper.

Sp. I am sick with my arm.

Dr. Only in your mind.

Sp. Can't I go back to that bed? (To Mr. I.) You are such a nice nurse.

Dr. You have been bothering his wife, hovering around her. That gentleman is taking care of his wife, and incidentally has been taking care of you. You are a spirit. He doesn't want you there any more.

Sp. (Coaxingly to Mr. I.) Don't you want to take care of me again?

Mr. I. No.

Sp. You mean thing, you! (Crying.)

Dr. You must obtain understanding. Are you a cry baby?

Sp. No, I am not a cry baby! (Stamping feet again.)

Dr. Then it is just temper. Now behave, and understand that you have lost your mortal body.

Sp. I have not lost my body.

Dr. You have lost your physical body; that is in the grave.

THIRTY YEARS AMONG THE DEAD

Sp. I am not in the grave!

Dr. But your body is.

Sp. My body is myself. No, I am not in the grave; this is my body.

Dr. Look at your hands; they are not yours.

Sp. Where did I get these rings? I had more stones in mine, didn't I? (To Mr. I.)

Mr. I. My wife had.

Sp. You gave me a nice ring.

Mr. I. No, I did not. I gave it to my wife.

Sp. Yes, you did.

Mr. I. No, I did not.

Dr. You are a selfish, earthbound spirit.

Sp. Spirit! I'm no spirit. I am a good woman, a good, religious woman. I love Jesus.

Dr. Then why are you not with him? You have evidently been dead a long time.

Sp. I say I am not dead! Oh! My arm, my arm.

Mr. G. You forgot that you had a crippled arm. You have been moving it about.

Sp. Yes, I forgot, but I know where my pains are! (Stamping feet.)

Dr. When you have a temper you forget your pains.

Sp. You do not! I have pains just the same. Don't you know that?

Dr. I know you have a temper.

Sp. I am a good Christian lady. I love Jesus with all my heart and all my soul. He is my Savior.

Mr. G. To save you from what?

Sp. From sin.

Dr. Then you cannot be so very good if you have sins.

Sp. Is that so? Say, are we in church? Look at all the people. Did you take me to church?

Dr. This is a place where we release earthbound spirits.

Sp. Earthbound spirits? What are you talking about? Will you pray, and sing "Jesus, Lover of my Soul"?

Dr. No, we will not. Where did you come from?

Sp. I get so mad when I think of that bed. Why did you take me away from that nice bed? I feel so sad. My back and my arm hurt me so much. My arm is paralyzed. I was shot in my arm.

Dr. Who shot you?

Sp. Ask them.

THIRTY YEARS AMONG THE DEAD

Dr. Did they use a hypodermic?

Sp. Yes, that's what I mean. I would like to have one more shot. Will you give me just a little? Oh, please, just a little bit! Give me just a little shot in the arm.

Dr. Were you a drug addict?

Sp. I was sick such a long time, and I couldn't sleep, so they put something in my arm. They put it in so many times that my arm got sore, then it seemed to be paralyzed. They put in too much.

Dr. Well, now we must hurry; it is getting late.

Sp. What's the hurry? Where are you going -out?

Dr. We are going to help you understand your condition. You have lost your mortal body and, are a spirit. This is not your body.

Sp. Is that so? You only think so.

Dr. This is not your body at all; you are only borrowing it temporarily.

Sp. How do you know?

Dr. This is my wife's body.

Sp. I never married you.

Dr. I did not say that.

Sp. You said I was your wife. Yes, you did! I heard it myself.

Dr. I said you were talking through my wife's body.

Sp. Have you ever heard of any one talking through another person's body?

Dr. Tell us who you are.

Sp. Hold my hand, not my arm.

Dr. We will treat your arm, then it will be well. (Manipulating arm.)

Sp. Oh! That electric man!

Dr. Now your arm is not paralyzed at all. Look at your dress. Is it yours? Where did you get it?

Sp. Did you buy this dress?

Dr. My wife did. What is your name?

Sp. Lizzie.

Dr. Lizzie what?

Sp. Mrs. Lizzie Davidson, and I don't want to be called Lizzie! When you speak to me, you must call me Mrs. Davidson.

Dr. Now listen to me. I am telling you a fact when I say you have lost your own body, but you do not realize it. You have been bothering that gentleman's wife (Mrs. I.) for a long time. You have made her an invalid.

Sp. I have not been his wife.

Dr. No, but you have been bothering his wife.

Sp. (Coquettishly, to Mr. I.) You are a nice nurse, and I like you. Don't you like me?

Mr. I. No!

Sp. I don't want your wife to go to sleep, because when she sleeps I can't stay, and I want to sleep in that nice bed, and have you wait on me.

Dr. You have been keeping that lady awake all night.

Sp. Because when she sleeps I have to go.

Dr. That is selfishness.

Sp. I have no home, so I have to make my home with her. She's an awful nice lady.

Dr. Now you will have to find a home of your own in the spirit world.

Sp. Where is that?

Dr. It is the invisible world about the earth plane. Do you believe in Heaven?

Sp. Yes, where God is, and Jesus Christ, and the Holy Ghost. I am going to Heaven.

Dr. Use a little reason. You lost your physical body long ago.

Sp. Where did I lose it?

Dr. We cannot tell that.

Sp. Then how did you find it out?

Dr. You are proving the fact yourself. Do you realize that this is the hand of my wife that I am holding?

Sp. You are holding my hand, and I am not your wife! (Stamping.)

Dr. I am holding my wife's hands, and you are talking through her.

Sp. You are not going to hold me any longer!

Dr. You are talking to us, but we cannot see you. You are invisible to us. Every one here sees that this is my wife's body.

Mr. I. Did you follow Dr. Wickland here this morning?

Sp. He put those awful things in me. (Electricity.) Then he said: "Everybody come along with me!" (To. Dr. W.) Why did you do that and make me get out? And that Indian girl! (Silver Star, one of Mrs. Wickland's guides, who had controlled for a brief time that morning, telling funny stories to attract the spirit's attention.) She made me laugh until I got so weak and sick that before I knew it I was away from that lady. I'm so mad! If I could only get hold of that Indian I would wring her neck all right!

Dr. I thought you said you were a Christian?

THIRTY YEARS AMONG THE DEAD

Sp. Yes, I am. God forgive me for saying that! Let me pray! I made a mistake.

Mr. I. You said the doctor brought you here.

Sp. He did not bring me in this body.

Mr. I. That body has been here all day; you came with the doctor and his wife in their auto this morning.

Sp. What do you mean by auto?

Dr. Don't you know what an automobile is?

Sp. What is it?

Dr. It is a car that runs by itself. There are millions of them in use now. You lost your body evidently a long time ago.

Sp. Are you sure about it? When did I lose it?

Dr. I do not know. We do not know you.

Sp. I told you I am Lizzie Davidson. Let us pray!

Dr. I think you are two-faced.

Sp. I think so, too, sometimes. Sometimes I have dark hair and sometimes light. (The patient had dark hair.)

Dr. How can you explain that?

Sp. I don't know, and I don't care. I only love Jesus.

Dr. Where did you come from? Do you know where you are? You are in Los Angeles, California.

Sp. I am not, I never have been, I never was. I had no money to go there.

Dr. Where did you live?

Sp. In New York.

Mr. I. Was it down on Twenty-seventh Street?

Sp. No, it wasn't.

Dr. It must be a long time since you were on earth, for you have not seen automobiles that run without horses.

Sp. Does the devil run them?

Dr. No, internal combustion.

Sp. Blab! Blab! Internal combustion.

Dr. What year do you think this is? We think it is 1923.

Sp. Then you're off. It is 1883.

Dr. Who is President?

THIRTY YEARS AMONG THE DEAD

Sp Don't you know?

Mr. G. Yes, we know, but we want to see if you know.

Dr. I think it is Harding.

Sp. Wait a little; I have to think. It is Arthur Garfield was shot in 1881, in July.

Dr. Is that the last you remember? Can you recall any President later than that?

Sp. No, just Arthur. He became President after Garfield was shot.

Dr. We have had many Presidents since then: Cleveland, Harrison, Taft and many others.

Sp. I had a brother-in-law named Cleveland.

Dr. Was he the President?

Sp. Not much! He didn't know very much anyway. What kind of people are you?

Dr. We are all investigators. Do you know what becomes of the dead?

Sp. They go to Heaven, and see Christ and the Holy Ghost and the Father, sitting on the throne, and the people sitting at His feet. I love Jesus! I never loved anybody as much as I do Jesus!

Dr. You say it is 1883; that is forty years ago. It is 1923 now. Why are you not in "Heaven" since you have been dead all that time?

Sp. I have not been dead.

Dr. You are dead only to the world; you lost your physical body forty years ago.

Sp. How do you know?

Dr. From your own words. We are now listening to what people call a dead person. You are talking through my wife's body.

Sp. (Seeing a spirit.) Who is that over there?

Dr. Ask them who they are.

Sp. There's Cleveland, my brother-in-law. Hell! What do you want?

Mr. G. Hello, Cleveland! How are you today?

Sp. (Angrily, to Mr. G.) You keep still! You don't know him.

Mr. G. What was his business?

Sp. He was a shoemaker.

Mr. G. He was probably a good one.

Sp. He was not nice to my sister. I don't like you, Cleveland! You always made trouble.

Dr. Listen to what he says.

Sp. (To spirit, Cleveland.) You devil, you!

THIRTY YEARS AMONG THE DEAD

Dr. That is fine talk for a Christian.

Sp. God forgive me! God forgive me!

Dr. Be serious and forgive Cleveland.

Sp. I will never forgive him -never! He went away and took my sister with him. (To spirit.) You devil! You went away with my sister and it broke my heart when you took her. Not now, nor in the world to come, will I ever forgive you -no, not much! Get away there!

Dr. Is that Christian charity? Is that the teaching of Christ?

Sp. People forget themselves sometimes.

Dr. You will have to forgive him, and ask him to forgive you.

Sp. I will ask forgiveness from Christ. From Cleveland I never will.

Dr. Jesus said: "Forgive, and ye shall be forgiven."

Sp. Yes, but nobody practices it. I will pray and that will help.

Dr. No, it will not. Praying won't help you any in this case. You have been in darkness forty years.

Sp. Sometimes I have been a man, and sometimes a lady.

Dr. You have been obsessing people.

Sp. Here, you Cleveland, you have no business to come here and torment me again. What have you done with my sister, you devil, you?

Dr. I thought you belonged to the Holy of Holies.

Sp. Cora! (Spirit.) My sister! Why did you go with that man? I will never forgive him. I suffered so much. I thought you would be with me for the rest of your life. I promised mother I would take care of you all my life then you ran away with that thing! You broke my heart.

Dr. What does she say?

Sp. No, she says she loved him. There is no such thing as loving any man. Say, there's David, too! I suppose you think you are going to make up with me. Not much you aren't! I never will forgive you either.

Dr. Who is David?

Sp. My husband.

Dr. What was the matter with him?

Sp. He was a fool.

Dr. For marrying you?

Sp. The world is coming to an end! People are so full of sin that God does not know what to do with them. He will have to teach them in some way, so let us pray! I want to go to Heaven.

Dr. Do you think you have much chance of getting there?

Sp. I will pray for you. You know, David, you were no good. I have had my troubles.

Dr. Didn't you have any faults?

Sp. No, I prayed to God.

Dr. Doesn't your conscience bother you?

Sp. My conscience?

Dr. Yes. Doesn't it make you feel guilty?

Sp. Cora, you always loved me, and you said you would always be with me for the rest of your life, and then you ran away with that thing.

Dr. What does she say?

Sp. Cora says: "You did not let me go anywhere. It was always church, church, and you wanted me to pray all the time. I got tired of it, and then Cleveland came, and he promised to give me a home. He was very good to me." But I will not forgive him anyhow.

Dr. You were a religious fanatic, and your sister could not stand it.

Sp. She ought to love Jesus.

Dr. You have not found Jesus yourself.

Sp. I haven't found Jesus because I am not dead.

Dr. Will you not believe what your sister says to you? Where did she live?

Sp. She lived in New York, then moved to Chicago.

Dr. Ask her whether she is a spirit.

Sp. She says she's dead. (To sister.) You're dead, and you deserve it, too, because you became a spiritualist at the last, you crazy thing, you! I got mad at you because you ran around to spiritualist meetings all the time. That Cleveland took you because he belonged there and believed in spirits!

Dr. I am sitting here with my wife, and you, an invisible spirit, are talking to us through her.

Dr. Does your sister say anything further?

Sp. She says: "Lizzie, come to your senses!" You don't need to tell me that! Shut up with you! They have crushed me.

Dr. Were you always selfish?

Sp. No. David, he was a good man at times. He always worked and took care of me. I had a good home, but he did not want me to go to church so much. He wouldn't pay his money to the church, so I got mad and called him a stingy fool. I told him if he did not go to church, and pay money to the Lord, he would go to hell. And there he is!

Dr. He is not in hell.

Sp. Yes, he is - but I don't see how he skipped out. David, you died a long time ago and I have prayed for you because I thought you were in hell, and you should have stayed there, because you did not pay any money to the Lord.

Dr. Ask him if he has been in hell.

Sp. He says: "No, there is no such place." You big fool, you are in hell!

Dr. You yourself are in the hell of ignorance. You are bound by selfishness and ignorance.

Sp. Now, David, don't you bother me. You go to hell, because you belong there. You did not go to church.

Dr. Jesus said: "Judge not that ye be not judged!"

Sp. I have been born again in the blood of Jesus. I paid all the money I could to the church.

Dr. And kept yourself in ignorance.

Sp. I have been baptized, immersed, and I am one of the holiest. I was a good church member. I worked hard for my money and have suffered, so I will go to Heaven when I die.

Dr. You never will really die.

Sp. David is dead.

Dr. If he himself were "dead" he could not talk to you.

Sp. Cora died in Chicago.

Dr. If they are "dead" how can they talk to you?

Sp. (Frightened.) Why -they are ghosts! I forgot they are dead.

Dr. Ghosts like yourself. You are a ghost.

Sp. But they are dead.

Dr. Do they look as if they were dead?

Sp. No, they look much prettier than they did before. I suppose they are in Heaven. (To the spirits.) Have you folks seen Christ and God? Have you been in Heaven with Them?

Dr. What do they say?

Sp. They say: "No!" Then you are -I thought so -then you have been in hell. Have you? They say: "No!"

Dr. Ask them if the body you are using is yours.

Sp. (To invisibles.) Well, what are you looking at? Don't you know me? They say, not as I look now. How is that?

Dr. Have I not been telling you that you are invisible to us, and that you are using my wife's body?

Sp. How?

Dr. Spirits can control mortals as you are now doing. Jesus cast out unclean spirits.

Sp. Unclean! I'm not unclean. You insult me again.

Dr. You influenced that gentleman's wife, disturbed her life and made an invalid of her.

Mr. I. Don't you recognize me?

Sp. Yes, you are a very good nurse, and I think I should like to have you nurse me again.

Dr. He was not nursing you, he was nursing his wife.

Sp. We had such a nice bed; I just love it. You tell your wife that she must not get up, because if she does I can't stay.

Dr. You will never go there again.

Mr. I. My wife is up now. She has been up the whole day.

Sp. I want her in bed.

Mr. I. She has been up since the doctor left this morning. She had to remain in bed for nine months.

That Indian girl made me laugh so hard that I could not stay with that nice lady. It makes me so mad! I was listening to what the Indian said, and I laughed so hard at her that I lost control of the lady. (To Mr. I.) What did you come here for?

Dr. He wanted to get rid of you.

Mr. I. I came here to see you tonight.

Sp. (Coyly.) Were you lonesome for me?

Mr. I. (Emphatically.) No!

Sp. I would like to go back with you, can I?

Mr. I. No, you cannot.

Dr. You were very selfish, but you will not acknowledge it.

Sp. Here's my sister Cora and her husband, Cleveland, and my husband, David. No, no! Oh, there's my mother! Did you come from Heaven, Mother? Are you happy in Heaven, Mother, with Jesus and God?

Dr. What does she say?

Sp. She says: "Lizzie, behave yourself." Now, Mother, I was always a good girl to you. Mother says: "You were always selfish, Lizzie."

Dr. That comes from your own mother. Your conscience tells you the same thing. You had a mean disposition -ask your mother.

Sp. Mother, did you come from Heaven? Mother, I'm not dead yet, so I can't go to Heaven. I have to die before I can go there.

Dr. The Bible says: "Ye are the temple of God and the Spirit of God dwelleth in you." Where will you find that God outside of yourself?

Sp. It says in the Bible that God sits on a throne, with Christ on His right hand.

Dr. The Bible says: "God is Love and he that dwelleth in Love dwelleth in God." Where will you find such a God?

Sp. In Heaven.

Dr. Jesus said: "God is Spirit, and they that worship Him must worship Him in Spirit and in truth." Did you do that? No, you simply accepted a dogma, and pretended you were saintly but your conscience condemned you all the time, did it not?

Sp. I was not happy.

Dr. Your conscience tells you that you were a hypocrite.

Sp. How do you know it does?

Dr. Your actions show that. Does your mother say anything more?

Sp. She says: "Lizzie, behave yourself." What does she say that for? She was always after me, because she says I had such a tongue.

Dr. You must change your attitude, or the spirit forces will take you away and place you in a dark dungeon.

Sp. God forgive me! I will pray.

Dr. You are not sincere.

Sp. (To Mr. I.) Will you forgive me?

Dr. If you are sincere in asking, he will.

Sp. David, you were always good to me, but I was not always a good wife to you. I thought you were a devil, and I always talked about you -yes, I did. (Crying.)

Dr. Crying will not help you.

Sp. David, I loved you anyhow. Do you like me, David? I was your dear little wife. He says, "Shame on you!", and that I was nice when I did not have a temper.

Dr. Now you must hurry and go.

Sp. I want to ask that nice man to please forgive me. (To Mr. I.) Will you?

Mr. I. Yes.

Sp. Cleveland, I was mad at you. You were good to my sister, but why did you go away? Why did you go to Chicago and take her away from me? He says his business was there.

(To Mr. I.) Will you forgive me? I mean it, I really mean it this time -will you? If I never meant it in my life before, I do now. Mother, will you forgive me? Will you? I love you. I was very selfish; I know now. I can see it now; I see everything now. My eyes have been opened. Oh, oh! (Crying.)

Dr. Crying does no good. Listen to what your relatives say.

Sp. Can I go with them to Heaven?

Dr. Forget "Heaven," and be sensible. You will never find God as you have imagined. You must be honest with yourself.

Sp. I have never, in all my life, been so humiliated as I have been tonight. You forgive me, David, don't you? And you, Cora, and Cleveland, too?

Dr. Do you know that you are in California?

Sp. How did I get there?

Dr. You evidently have been "dead" some forty years. No one actually dies, but the physical body is lost, and people call that "death."

Sp. Part of the time I have been walking, but for a very long time I have had such a good time in that nice bed.

Dr. Yes, disturbing that gentleman's wife.

Sp. But he has been so good to me; he's so nice.

Dr. Aren't you ashamed to make an invalid of a poor mortal?

Sp. David, will you take me along with you?

Dr. Now you must go.

Sp. I am going. (Rising.)

Dr. You cannot go that way.

Sp. How in the world will I go then? That Indian girl won't take me away, will she?

Dr. She will teach you beautiful truths.

Sp. But she laughed at me.

Dr. Now think yourself with your relatives and you will be there.

Sp. Now I will go. Will I see God?

Dr. Forget that. You do not have the right understanding of God.

Sp. Goodbye!

After this Mrs. I. recovered her strength and was soon walking and driving about.

THIRTY YEARS AMONG THE DEAD

Chapter X

Orphans

Various spirit orphans who have known no family ties during earth life, have been brought to us for aid, and these have usually been eager for knowledge and ready to accept the explanation of a higher life. A lonely orphan came to us one evening, a deserted waif, but observant, analytical and eager for understanding.

EXPERIENCE, MAY 25, 1921

Spirit: MINNIE-ON-THE-STEP   Psychic: MRS. WICKLAND

Doctor: Where did you come from?

Spirit: I don't know.

Dr. What have you been doing?

Sp. I don't know either.

Dr. Should you not find out?

Sp. What?

Dr. Where you are, and where you came from.

Sp. I don't know.

Dr. How long have you been dead?

Sp. Dead? I don't know. I don't know anything.

Dr. Has anybody come to you and told you that you have lost your body?

Sp. No. I have been going around everywhere and talking.

Dr. To whom?

Sp. To every body I could talk to. But some way or another, they don't seem to pay attention to me. I go sometimes in a big crowd and think I will get hold of them all, and sometimes I get right up on the platform and begin to ask them what is the matter with me, but it's just like I was nobody, and I think I am somebody. I think I was good, but nobody wants me.

Dr. What can you remember before that time?

Sp. Before that time? I was somebody. I am probably nobody now.

Dr. Where did you live when you were somebody?

Sp. Always in the same place. Sometimes I get so tired, then I go and lie down and sleep and sleep, and then it seems after I have slept, then I go on again. Sometimes I only go around and around and do not go any further.

Dr. Has nobody ever come to you?

Sp. I see people who think I am nobody. They do not notice me and do not think of me. Sometimes I feel miserable and another time I do not.

Dr. Where is your mother?

Sp. I don't know. Sometimes I go hungry and sometimes I get so hungry I beg of people. Sometimes I get something and sometimes not. If I can get in the kitchen, I get something to eat, and I eat much, then after that I go, and then it seems I am out again.

Dr. Out where?

Sp. Everywhere.

Dr. When you get something to eat, do you feel like somebody else?

Sp. I go hungry, and I have to get something.

Dr. Where do you get something to eat?

Sp. It's the funniest thing. Always somebody else pays the bill, and I have nothing to pay - that's the funniest of all. I never pay for anything. Once in a while I do not get what I like but I have to eat it. Sometimes I feel so bad after eating that I get real sick. I do not like things and I make faces. Sometimes I eat a lot and sometimes a little.

Sometimes I am a man and sometimes a girl. (Obsessing different persons.) I don't know what is the matter with me. Why is everything so funny? I don't know myself. I go and I walk, and I like people to talk to me. I have to talk all the time. I only hear myself talk. Once in a while I get in somewhere where they talk and I can sit down, and sometimes I feel -oh, I don't know! I feel like I was half a person sometimes -somebody else.

Dr. How old are you?

Sp. How old am I? I don't know.

Dr. Don't you know how old you are?

Sp. On my last birthday I was nineteen.

Dr. Have you any father, mother or sister?

Sp. No, I have not.

Dr. Where did your parents live?

Sp. I never saw my father or mother.

Dr. Where did you live?

Sp. I don't know if my father and mother are dead, or where they are. I never knew.

Dr. Did you live in an institution?

THIRTY YEARS AMONG THE DEAD

Sp. I was brought up in a Home, with a lot of children.

Dr. Did you know many of the children?

Sp. There were so many.

Dr. Where was that place?

Sp. I don't exactly know. It is kind of funny. How are things? I feel funny.

Dr. It must be a strange situation.

Sp. This is the first time somebody talked to me. I came here when you were singing about that beautiful shore. I thought I wanted to go on that other shore, and I was just looking to see where it was.

Dr. We will help you reach that shore.

Sp. Before I knew it, I could talk when you talked to me. (Controlled psychic.) This is what I have to say -nobody talked directly to me for a long, long time. If I talked to any one, someone else always answered. I never seemed to have anything to say. No one paid any attention to what I said. That is the funniest thing of all. That is funny. I got out of the home that I was working in because they were awfully mean to me.

Dr. What did they do? Whip you?

Sp. Not exactly. I was working in a family somewhere. I was so hungry, and of course I did not do things as well as they wanted me to. There came a lady and she said she would take me away from the Home. I wished she had not. In the Home it was pretty fair. Of course we had hard times, but it is better than to be scolded all the time. In the Home we had lots of things we did not like, but we had a good time too.

This woman took me, and the first thing she said was that I should have to read the Bible from morning to night. I got sick and tired of the Bible. Then I had to pray. My knees were so sore I could hardly walk on them. I had to be on my knees all the time, reading and praying. She said I should walk with my knees, not my feet.

She tried to save me. She said I had never been a real good girl, and if I did not do as she said, I should go to some very hot place. In the Home we prayed, and the Mother was awful nice. We prayed and believed in God. When that woman took me, I was fourteen. That was my sorry day. I had to work and work and earn something, and she scolded me, as she said I did not do as she wanted me to. It was praying and reading all the time. There was nothing to it. I didn't pray. I had to get down on my knees, but I did not get in my mind what she was saying, because my knees hurt me. She got awful mad when I slipped down, and she pulled my hair. She had a cushion under her knees. She could stay there for hours. She said I was a sinner, because I got tired.

Are you a sinner when you can't stay on your knees a long time? I did not know very much, but I thought many times, really and truly -don't tell anyone, (whispering confidentially) but I thought God would be awfully tired to hear that all the time! I was so tired that I went to sleep. Then she pulled my hair and slapped me. She prayed to God, but she acted so bad. She said if I was not good the devil would get hold of me. I thought sometimes, really and truly, that she was one. If I got on my knees and went to sleep, she came to me and she prayed: "God help me out of this misery! You know, oh, God, how I love you!"

She prayed for herself first, and then for her sister, her mother and her brother and father, and her friends, and at last she prayed for Minnie. They did not know my other name. I do not know who my really and truly father and mother were. I never knew. I never got my history, but they said they found me on the step. They often called me "Minnie-On-The-Step." I got so mad at them. They found me on the step, they said. They gave me the name of Minnie.

Dr. Try to realize that you have lost your own body, and that you are now a spirit.

Sp. What is that? I am a girl.

Dr. You have been wandering around as a spirit.

Sp. What do you mean?

Dr. You, have lost your body.

Sp. Did I die? I really and truly have not been washing dishes for a long time. I have not had any one pull my hair for a long time either. I ran away because the lady was so mean. I was running away from her. Then I had so little to eat. I ran away and I got so hungry. I had no money.

Dr. What happened after that?

Sp. I got far, far off, and I lost my way. I was so hungry that I went to sleep. It came so dark and I was in the woods. I had to run in the woods so that she would not find me. I walked and walked, and I thought I would find some one to give me something to eat.

To the first house I did not go. I went away hungry and I walked a whole day and night, and it seems there was nothing but big trees and forest. Then I went to sleep, and I don't know any more that day. (Passed out.)

Next day I felt better and I walked again and I got to the city. I walked ever and ever so far, and saw lots of people, but they paid no attention to me. I got hungry, so I saw a woman go into a restaurant and we had some dinner. She was eating it all. I got a little. She did not talk to me. Then I went out again, and I kept on walking, and after a while I saw some one else go into a restaurant -some other people. We ate but they paid for it.

Dr. Do you know what you were doing?

Sp. No.

Dr. You were obsessing some one. As a spirit, you were hovering around some mortal and were trying to satisfy your hunger through that person. You probably lost your body in the woods.

Sp. I was so thirsty. The food I did not miss so much, but I thought everything was drying up in my throat. I thought I could drink a barrel of water.

Dr. You carried your last physical sensations in your mind, not realizing that you had lost your body.

Sp. Did I? What time was that? Don't you know me then? How did I get here?

Dr. We cannot see you.

Sp. Can you see my folks?

Dr. No.

Sp. Can you see me?

THIRTY YEARS AMONG THE DEAD

Dr. No.

Sp. What is the matter with me?

Dr. You are invisible.

Sp. Can you hear me talk?

Dr. Yes.

Sp. You can hear me talk, but not see me?

Dr. You are not talking through your own body.

Sp. I am not?

Dr. Look at your hands. Do you recognize them?

Sp. No.

Dr. Do you know that dress?

Sp. I never had one like that in my born days.

Dr. You are using some one else's body.

Sp. Some party probably gave me a dress. I have a ring too.

Dr. The ring is not yours, nor is the hand.

Sp. I commence to be sleepy again.

Dr. You have been allowed to come in and control this body.

Sp. Oh! Look there!

Dr. What do you see?

Sp. I don't know myself. There's a lady, and she's crying. (Spirit)

Dr. Ask her who she is.

Sp. (After listening in amazement.) Oh, my, no!

Dr. What does she say?

Sp. Don't cry so much, lady. I don't like to see crying faces. I want to cry myself when she cries.

Dr. What does she say?

Sp. She says I am her child. She probably is sorry she left me. Is she my really and truly mother? She says: "Oh, my dear child!" She says she has been hunting me for dear life, but she could not get me, and she did not know what to do.

Dr. You are both spirits and you will find intelligent spirits here who will help you.

Sp. She was a good girl, she says, but some man got her in trouble. She says she went to church, and some man wanted to marry her. He went away. He left her after he got her in trouble, she says, and she had nobody. She was so sick. She felt so bad, so she put me on the step of that big Home, she says, and she has never been happy from that time. Then she got sick and died.

Dr. Make her understand that she is a spirit like yourself. You will find intelligent spirits who will help you both.

Sp. My Mother! I want to be with you! I forgive you, Mother. Don't cry. I have never had a mother, and you will be my mother now. She says she has been hunting me for a long time, and somebody said they brought us here to this place so we could meet. She says: "They said I should find my child." Now she found me, didn't she? Can I cry for gladness? I would love to. I feel so glad I have a mother.

Dr. You will both have a home in the spirit world.

Sp. She says my name is Gladys. She says her name is Clara Watsman.

Dr. Where was her home?

Sp. She says St. Louis.

Dr. You will find other spirits here who will take you to the spirit world.

Sp. What is that? Why, here comes an Indian girl! (Spirit.) She's a nice little girl.

Dr. She will teach both of you many wonderful things.

Sp. Oh, I do not want you to look so old, Mother! She was young a little while ago.

Dr. That will all pass away. That is only her condition of sorrow.

Sp. The little Indian girl, Silver Star, put her hand over her, and she said: "Think young, and you will be young."

She is! She is! Thinking young, she will be, she says. Now we go with her. Don't forget -my name is Gladys. That's nicer than "Minnie-On-The-Step." Are we going to Heaven to God?

Dr. You will go to the spirit world, and you will obtain understanding of the higher things of life.

Sp. That woman always said: "God is Spirit; God is Love; God is everywhere." Silver Star says we must thank the doctor. Doctor what?

Dr. Dr. Wickland. You are controlling my wife's body.

Sp. My mother is young and pretty now. Think young and you will be, Silver Star said. Can I come back here sometime?

Dr. Certainly, as far as I am concerned.

Sp. Don't think of me as Minnie-On-The Step, will you? Think of me as Gladys Watsman. Thank you all. I am somebody now. I've got a name. That's worth something to me. Don't you want to be my Grandpa?

Dr. Maybe.

Sp. Thank you all for being patient with me. Goodbye.

Minnie-On-The-Step became an ardent helper of wandering spirit waifs, and has brought a number of them to our circle for understanding, the first one within a few weeks after her own enlightenment.

THIRTY YEARS AMONG THE DEAD

EXPERIENCE, JULY 13, 1921

Spirit: ANNA MARY Psychic: MRS. WICKLAND.

Doctor: Good Evening. Do you know anyone here?

Spirit: Somebody told me if I came in here I would get something to eat.

Dr. You are spiritually hungry.

Sp. Is that something to eat?

Dr. No, it is something for your mind.

Sp. I don't know if I need anything for my mind. I want something for my stomach. I haven't had anything to eat for a long time. Isn't it funny? As soon as you talk to me, I am not hungry. I was awful hungry, but now I'm not.

Dr. What have you been doing?

Sp. Nothing. I get so tired of doing nothing that I don't know what to do. It is tiresome to have nothing whatever to do—no aim in life. You do not know what to do with yourself. I want something to do. You get so nervous when you do nothing. I don't know what to do with myself. I want to go here, there and everywhere, and when I get there, I want to be some place else. I get so tired wanting to know what I should do. The road is always best on the other side.

Dr. What is your name?

Sp. They call me Mary, but my name is Anna Mary. Some call me Mary and some call me Anna.

Dr. Where did your father and mother live?

Sp. I don't know my mother and father.

Dr. How old are you?

Sp. I don't know.

Dr. Were you ever in California?

Sp. No, never in all my life. I never went that far away. I never had so much money to go. We had hot summers and cold winters.

Dr. How did you come in here?

Sp. Sure enough—how did I come?

Dr. Who brought you here?

Sp. Minnie-On-The-Step.

Dr. Is she here now?

Sp. Yes.

Dr. Did you both live in the same place?

Sp. Yes.

Dr. Were you anything like Minnie-On-The-Step?

Sp. She was such a nice little girl. I ran away from that place. I wanted to see the world. I did not want to stay in one place all the time. I was in a Home where there were lots of children, and Minnie-On-The-Step was there too; that was our home. I worked awfully hard and had to scrub and scrub, and carry water, and I got tired of it, so I ran away. They always said I was foolish, but I never thought I was.

Dr. Ask Minnie-On-The-Step if she brought you here.

Sp. She says she did, and that she has been hunting for me, and then brought me here. She says she has a home. (Staring in surprise.) For God's sake in Heaven! If I ever saw such a nice place! Look at that home! It's Minnie-On-The-Step's. It's beautiful! She says it is hers. Well, for Heaven's sake alive!

Dr. Ask her how she got it.

Sp. (To Minnie-On-The-Step.) How did you get it? She say that you, (Dr. W.) and you, and you, and you, (pointing to audience) helped her to get that home. She says her home is going to be for all the children she knew when she was at the Home, and they are all going to that home that she can hunt up. She's so happy. I never knew she cared for me, because she was a little better than I was. For Heaven's sake alive, that's a nice home.

Dr. How did you die?

Sp. I'm not dead. Can't you hear me talking? Why, there's Mary Bloom, and Charlie Hoffman! I don't like Charlie Hoffman! He was stuck up. They teased me. He always got other boys, and they all chased me; they thought I was a horse. They always pulled my hair.

They always hurt me, those boys, and Charlie Hoffman got them together. They used to call me "Tow-Head," but when I got mad they were scared. They ran and I ran after them. Then comes the Matron. She grabbed hold of me and pulled my hair pretty good. She was awful mad when they took me back.

Mary Bloom always scrubbed with me. She says she don't have to scrub any more. Mary Bloom's in Minnie's home. Esther Bloom, Mary's sister, is here too. Minnie says now I must be a good girl and then she will see after me. I will have a nice home and I shall have something to do.

Dr. Do you know who your mother was?

Sp. I was always told my mother was a fine lady. I know she lived in a beautiful house, but she didn't like me because I was foolish.

Dr. Was she ashamed of you?

Sp. She never cared for me. They said she was very beautiful.

Dr. Do you want to go with Minnie-On-The-Step?

Sp. She's a lady now! She doesn't look like she did. She is beautiful.

Dr. What does she say?

Sp. She says that I must understand that I am in the spirit world. Oh, look at that pretty lady!

THIRTY YEARS AMONG THE DEAD

Dr. What does she say?

Sp. She says she has a home where she takes care of little waifs in the spirit world and teaches them the higher philosophy of God. She is beautiful, beautiful! Such pretty white hair! It is as white as silver. When she smiles it is like sunshine. Now she says: "Come, my dear child, with me. You had no happiness in earth life, but you will have it in spirit life with me, because I gather together all such little children as you and teach them the real lesson of life."

Dr. Ask the lady her name.

Sp. She says her name is Abbie Judson. Lady, you won't call me foolish, will you? Will you be my mother? Can I call you mother, lady? I never had a mother. Will you take me in your arms and love me just once, so that I can feel what mother love is? Will you give me a mother's kiss? Will you? I never knew what that is.

She says: "Yes, child I will be your mother. I will watch and guide you. You will have a home with me in the beautiful land beyond." She kisses me! Isn't she lovely! Please love me a little more, lady. Thank God, now I'm happy, for I have found a mother! I shall try to be good to her, then she will be my mother. I have prayed to God many times for a mother, and now I have one.

(To an invisible.) Say, will you forgive me for slapping you once? And I'm sorry that I kicked you, but I got so mad at you. I'm so glad that Minnie-On-The-Step brought me here cause now I have a mother.

Dr. Now you will go to the spirit world, where Happiness is Heaven, and all is harmony. Heaven is a condition of the mind.

Sp. The lady says I must go with her now.

Dr. We know the lady you speak of. She has brought others here for help. She was a teacher in earth life.

Sp. She says she has a beautiful home. Not like a home in earth life, but a home where we shall be taught to praise God in every way.

Dr. Think yourself with the lady and you will become disengaged from this body.

Sp. Glory Hallelujah! Minnie says that when I come with the lady I must not use those words, for they are foolish. But that's the way I always do talk when I'm glad and happy. Mary Bloom and Minnie-On-The-Step say I must thank you for teaching me to go with them. You can call me Anna Mary.

Will my new mother be ashamed of me? I can't read 'cause I never had time to learn. The big Home, where I was, gave me to a lady and she made me work very hard. I got sick and I coughed very hard. But I had to work just the same. I got sick and then I don't remember any more.

Thank you for helping me. Goodbye.

We had been concentrating for some time for a little girl, R. G., who was very sensitive to psychic condition, and troubled constantly by spirits. During the weeks preceding the following experience she had been very disobedient, developed a strong dislike for arithmetic, and had been especially perverse when taken into the city shops.

The mother, knowing that a spirit was influencing the child, had several times given the little girl a cold shower, with excellent result.

THIRTY YEARS AMONG THE DEAD

EXPERIENCE, AUGUST 2, 1922

Spirit: LILY Patient: R. G.

Psychic: MRS. WICKLAND.

The controlling spirit stamped furiously, and spoke angrily in an excited childish voice.

Spirit: No, do not touch me! No, no! I don't want your hands on me. I do not like you! You have so much fire. I am afraid of that fire! (Static treatment given patient.)

Doctor: Tell us who you are.

Sp. I don't know.

Dr. Where did you come from? You must have come from some place. Do you pay for your board?

Sp. I don't pay for it, but I always get something to eat. I have no money.

Dr. Who are you?

Sp. I said I didn't know.

Dr. Did your mother call you Jim?

Sp. I'm no boy! Can't you see? I don't want that fire on my back any more -no, I don't! (Stamping feet)

Dr. Did you always have bad manners?

Sp. Why did you take me away from where I was? I have no place to go. You made me get away with fire, fire, fire! (Stamping.) I want to be with that little girl. (Pointing to R. G.) She belongs to me.

Dr. What right have you to bother that little girl? She does not belong to you. She is no relation of yours.

Sp. (Crying.) I want her!

Dr. Where did you come from? Can't you understand that you are dead?

Sp. I want to be with that little girl. I want her! I want her. (Crying.) You chased me out, you -you -you mean thing! (Stamping.)

Dr. I'm very glad of it. What right have you to be with that little girl?

Sp. I have no home.

Dr. Can't you understand that you are a spirit? You are invisible to us.

Sp. I liked to ride in that automobile. We had such nice times.

Dr. You will not ride in that automobile any more. You are going to the spirit world.

Sp. (To the mother of R. G.) I don't like you! You made me go in the water, you ugly, mean thing! I like to ride in the auto, but I don't like to go into that store. I got mad. I want that little girl! I want her! I got lost in that big store you went to. You had no business to go there!

Dr. You have no business to bother people. You are very selfish.

Sp. I got fire on my back.

Dr. You will get more fire if you do not behave.

Sp. Aren't you ashamed to give a little girl so much fire?

Dr. That was what you needed.

Sp. You gave me so much of it that it is burning my back yet. I got so mad at you! (To Mrs. G.) You made me go in the water. It made me so mad at you! I don't like the water. She took me here and there in that store.

Dr. You will not bother that little girl any more. What is your name?

Sp. My name is Lily. I am a White Lily.

Dr. You must not be so selfish or you cannot find a home in the spirit world.

Mrs. G. Where did you find my little girl?

Sp. I saw this little girl, so I picked up with her. We had such nice times together. There were lots of things to play with.

Dr. You must understand that you no longer have a physical body. Do you know that you are in California?

Sp. I do not know anything.

Dr. What did your father do?

Sp. I did not know much about my father.

Dr. Where is your mother?

Sp. I do not know. I ran away when mother spanked me. I got mad at my mother and ran away. My father and mother put me in a place with lots of other children, but I ran away from there. They put me in a big building. They were mean and so was I. They always teased me. I got so mad at them. I got into a fight and then I ran away.

Dr. Where did you go when you ran away?

Sp. I fell down, and then I can't remember what happened. (Died.) Sometimes it seems like I am a very small girl, but I was different. I was eleven or twelve years old, and after a while I was a little girl again. It seems like I was five years old then.

Dr. What did they call you when you were a little girl again?

Sp. They called me R., but that wasn't my name. After I fell down it was dark for a long time, then all at once I could walk and play with that little girl.

Dr. Some accident must have happened to you when you ran away. You lost your body and became a spirit. We do not see you.

Sp. I don't see you either!

Dr. You are a little spit-fire.

Sp. You are a real bogy man! I am a little girl and can't take care of myself. You let go my hands!

Dr. I'm not holding your hands. I am holding my wife's hands.

Sp. I don't like you!

Dr. You are using my wife's body, but only for a short time. You are an ignorant spirit and have been hovering around that little girl and have now been taken away from her.

Sp. She is my little girl.

Dr. Let me tell you something. You cannot have a home if you do not behave yourself. Intelligent spirits have brought you here and allowed you to control my wife's body so that we might help you. You will find friendly spirits here who will help you and will show you the wonderful things in the spirit world. There you will find happiness which you cannot find by hovering around the earth plane. But you will have to overcome your temper.

Sp. Will they be mean to me? Everybody shoved me here and there. So many boys teased me, then I got mad and had to fight.

Dr. Now you must go with Silver Star, a little Indian girl, who will be the best friend you ever had. Forget your past. Do not be ugly. You will be shown every kindness and nobody will tease you.

Sp. I always got so much whipping.

Dr. The intelligent spirits will help you to progress.

Sp. Why, here comes Happy Daisy. (Spirit.)

Dr. Does she look as if she would scold you?

Sp. No. The boys used to call me "Red Head" and "Freckles," and I used to go for them. Could I go with that pretty lady standing there?

Dr. Yes, and you will not have any more fire or sparks.

Sp. You are sure you are not telling stories? Happy Daisy says for me to go with her and she will take me to a nice home. Will that be Heaven? She says I must learn to do good and be good, and after I learn I can come back and help this little girl, and I'm going to help her in school too.

Mrs. G. Do you like arithmetic?

Sp. I don't like school at all. Now I will go. They say I am going to school -but I don't like school.

Dr. You will go to a different school -the School of Life.

Sp. Can't I have blue eyes and light curly hair? Can I have it? I want to be beautiful.

Dr. You can become beautiful only as you help others. Think beautiful thoughts and do kind acts and you will be beautiful. You will have beauty of spirit. Now go with these friends, and after you have learned how to be of service you can help little R. Think yourself with the others and you will be there. Determine to begin a new life.

Sp. I'm going to help this little girl. Goodbye.

A week after the interview with "Lily," another homeless spirit wanderer came to the circle, a quaint, investigative philosopher who had been drawn into the aura of Mrs. G., the mother of R. G.

This spirit was an orphan who had known Mrs. G. in childhood; she had at that time developed a strong affection for her and this love had attracted the spirit to Mrs. G., although she had not recognized in the grown woman the friend of her childhood.

EXPERIENCE, AUGUST 9, 1922

Spirit: LAUGHING ELLA Patient: MRS. G.

Psychic: MRS. WICKLAND.

Doctor: Why don't you join in the singing?

Spirit: I never saw these people before, so why should I join in the singing?

Dr. Where did you come from?

Sp. I don't know.

Dr. We should like to know more about you. Isn't it strange that you should be here?

Sp. I don't know anything about it. I shall have to find out.

Dr. Tell us who you are and what your name is.

Sp. Somebody said if I came here I would find a home.

Dr. You certainly will.

Sp. I have not had a home for a long time.

Dr. What have you been doing?

Sp. Walking around everywhere and sleeping where I could put my head.

Dr. Are you a girl, a man, a woman or a boy?

Sp. Don't you know I am a girl?

Dr. How old are you?

Sp. Probably -but I'm not sure -but I think I am sixteen or seventeen.

Dr. Where were you staying?

Sp. I don't know.

Dr. Try to think; perhaps you can remember.

Sp. I have been to so many places, I should like to have a home.

Dr. Have you no father and mother?

Sp. No.

Dr. Where did you stay when you were little?

Sp. I always stayed in a big place where there were many children. We were all together. We used to fight and carry on all the time. I don't think I ever had a mother. I think I was born in that big place. I was there as long as I can remember anything. It was a big place, with lots of boys and girls. Some were good and some bad, all kinds. I did everything I could do. I did what they told me to do, and they kept me doing things all the time. I kept on working like machinery.

They said: "Now, Ella, you go there, and Ella, you go there," and after a little while, it was Ella everywhere. I had to fix so many little boys and girls that I think I was a mother to them all.

Dr. Were they fond of you?

Sp. They all came around me and I had to do things for them. That was my work and I helped them all I could. And it wasn't always easy to bathe and dress a dozen little children. They were very noisy, so I said for them to keep quiet. I got mad sometimes. You know I tried to do my very best, but when they stepped on my toes I got mad.

Dr. How long ago was that?

Sp. I don't think it's so long ago. You know, I lost my way. I went out walking one time and I couldn't find my way back.

Dr. What happened after that?

Sp. Nothing has happened. I have been walking to find that Home again.

Dr. Did you have an accident?

Sp. No, but I shall have to keep on walking until I find that Home.

Dr. Do you want to understand why you have been walking and have no home?

Sp. Somebody said if I came here I would have a home, and they pushed me in, and before I knew anything, I was sitting here and you were singing. I was crying, and a girl said you had helped her, and if I came here I would get happy. When I walked it was half dark and half light. I have been trying to find a home. When I was with those children I had to work hard, but it's better to have them than to have nothing to do. I would rather have my children.

Dr. Were they orphans like yourself?

Sp. They thought I was not right in my mind, but I was as good as any of them.

Dr. You are talking to us but we cannot see you. I can see my wife but not you.

Sp. Your wife! For land's sake alive! (Laughing heartily) You know, I always like to laugh, and when all the children began to cry I started to laugh, and I laughed and laughed until I got them still. That was the only way I knew to get them all still when they were crying. Then they got good natured again. If you laugh hard when somebody cries, they will stop crying and begin to laugh. Sometimes they called me "Laughing Ella."

Dr. Where did you get this ring?

Sp. I never had a ring before. (Greatly pleased and laughing again.)

Dr. This is not your hand, and this is not your body.

Sp. What are you talking about? (Laughing.)

Dr. It may seem foolish to you, but it is the truth. Have you ever heard that "He who laughs last, laughs best?" Ask these people whose body this is.

Sp. (To audience.) Is this my body?

Ans. No, it is not.

Sp. Yes, it is.

Dr. This body belongs to Mrs. Wickland.

Sp. Mrs. Wickland! (Laughing.)

Dr. You are laughing at your own ignorance. You are temporarily controlling Mrs. Wickland's body.

Sp. I never heard such funny talk.

Dr. What I am telling you is not so foolish as it sounds. You lost your physical body. Probably you were sick. You have awakened to a new condition of life.

Sp. How could I waken if I had no body?

Dr. You have a spirit body.

Sp. When you say I have lost my body, do you mean I am dead?

Dr. To the world, yes. The world is ignorant of the facts. When a person loses his physical body, people say he is "dead." That is wrong. The spirit has only left the body. The spirit is the real person; the body is merely the house. Nobody dies, it only seems so.

Sp. Yes, they do! I have seen dead people. I knew a little girl that died and she went to Heaven.

Dr. You have only seen dead bodies. You can only stay here a short time, then you will have to leave.

Sp. Where will I go?

Dr. To the spirit world.

Sp. Say, I am a real lady! I have a necklace round my neck.

Dr. That belongs to my wife. You are an invisible spirit and have been wandering in outer darkness. If you want a home you can have one.

Sp. Do you mean Heaven?

Dr. Jesus said: "The Kingdom of God is within you."

Sp. Jesus died for our sins, and if we are good, when we die we will go to Heaven and be with the angels. We prayed all the time in the Home. (Seeing little R. G. sitting beside her mother.) I like that little girl over there. I have seen her before.

Mrs. G. Do you know Lily? She is a spirit who was here last week.

Sp. (To R. G.) You were very naughty the other day when we had company. What made you so naughty?

Mrs. G. That other girl, Lily, made her behave badly.

Sp. That other girl was awfully mean. I felt like spanking her. When she came near, that little girl (R. G.) changed faces.

Dr. She was a spirit and was influencing this little girl. You are also a spirit and are talking through my wife's body. In just that way the spirit of that girl acted through this child.

Sp. Somebody told me to come in here and I would find a home, and that I had a mission to do. What does that mean?

Dr. Probably you can protect this little girl.

Sp. They say I am going to be a watcher; that I must see that nobody gets hold of her. I don't know what they mean.

Dr. That will all be explained to you. Listen to a little Indian girl whom you will find here. She will take you to a home.

Sp. Will they like me? In that big Home all the children liked me because I made them laugh. They say I must stay around this little girl and protect her from influences.

Dr. That means spirit influences.

Sp. I am going to look into that business.

Dr. You will need to have understanding first. Do you see others here?

Sp. I see many girls jumping around and feeling happy. There is a nice lady here and she says her name is "Pretty Girl." She's awfully pretty. There's a young girl and she says I can come with her. She says she brought me here. They say I always tried to do everything I could to help; now they are going to take care of me.

Sometimes when I got a whipping, I thought: "Well, maybe I needed it." I cried for a few minutes and then I went into my little corner, and said: "Now, Ella, you were naughty and you needed that spanking." I thought about it for a while, then I began to laugh, and I never felt the spanking at all. When you feel good inside from laughing, you can't feel things on the outside. You just try it.

Dr. Now you must go with these friends.

Sp. They say when I get understanding I am going to be a little helper. (To R. G.) Don't forget, when you feel naughty, just laugh and then you won't be naughty. When I get to be nurse girl for that little girl, I won't let anyone in. I will see that they stay out -I will show you!

Dr. Where did you live?

Sp. In Kansas. (Mrs. G. had formerly lived in Kansas.) I had to dress ten or twelve of the children, and wash them and put them to bed. Some went to school and some went to play.

Mrs. G. What town did you live in?

Sp. Why -near H. (Verified later.)

Mrs. G. Do you remember the name K.? (Superintendent of orphanage at H.)

Sp. Why, yes.

Mrs. G. Do you know M.? (Assistant Matron, in charge of girls.)

Sp. She was in another room. There were some naughty girls in M.'s room. Sometimes even the Matron could not control some of the girls, even when she spanked them, so I had to go to them. You know spanking isn't good all the time. When the Matron spanked the little ones and they cried, I would go to them after she had gone and make them laugh. A good laugh always made them forget the spanking.

Mrs. G. Do you remember seeing me when I was a little girl?

Sp. (Staring, then excited.) Yes! Why yes, I remember you now! But you were not there all the time. (Mrs. G. came to the orphanage occasionally as a visitor.) You used to come and then go away. You always had such pretty hair, and you used to have such pretty dresses. Do you remember you had a parasol and walked around like a big lady?

Mrs. G. Do you remember the time I fell into the water?

Sp. Oh my, yes, and everybody was so excited, and you got wringing wet, and your Grandmother scolded you. I took a liking to you. The time you went into the water I felt so sorry for you. You spoiled your nice dress. That was a long, long time ago.

Now I remember lots of things. My eyes seem to open! I took an awful cold and I got sore throat, and then I remember I went to sleep. I always liked you, and now I've found you again, I am going to help, and stop walking to find that home.

Mrs. G. I am grown now and married, and this little girl is my child. Spirits have been bothering her for some time.

Sp. I will help you. I have found you and we will be together again. Silver Star, the little Indian girl, says I must learn to protect your little girl.

Dr. The first thing you must do is to go to the spirit world and learn about your new conditions, then you will understand how to help someone else.

Sp. I will do all I can. Now I will say Good Night, but I will come again. Don't forget Laughing Ella.

THIRTY YEARS AMONG THE DEAD

Chapter XI

Materialism and Indifference

The binding influence of skepticism, of mental apathy and unconcern regarding the higher life is so powerful after transition that many are held in a condition of helpless despair, darkness, bewilderment and rebellion, often clinging to mortals as their only means of expression.

Some years ago a friend of ours, Mrs. F. W., was living in New York, very happily married and leading an active, normal life. She had an understanding of the higher laws of life, but her husband, although devoted to her, maintained the viewpoint of a materialist and fatalist.

Believing in no form of religion, Mr. F.W. was convinced that death ended all, and had often declared that if his wife should pass away he would commit suicide, and frequently urged her to promise that if he passed away first she would take her life, but to this she would not consent.

After a brief illness this gentleman suddenly passed away, but his wife could still see him very distinctly, especially at night when he repeatedly awakened her, frightening her so that she could not sleep. Unconscious of his true condition, he still sensed that something strange had occurred, and wishing to remove the barrier which separated him from his wife, he constantly urged her to come to him, calling insistently:

"Kill yourself —you must come to me! I want you, and I will finally get you, so kill yourself now!" The continual cry of "Kill yourself!" was with Mrs. F. W. day and night, until she feared for her own safety. Anxious to prevent any rash act on her part she left New York and came to us in Chicago for assistance.

During an interview, the spirit of F. W. was allowed to control Mrs. Wickland, and when he found himself sitting beside his wife, he grasped her hand, kissed her wedding ring, and asked if she were angry with him, since she would not answer him when he spoke to her.

Then, seizing her in his arms, he kissed her frantically, and crushed her in so powerful an embrace that she could not free herself and called for aid.

I explained to the spirit that he was controlling a body not his own and that he had passed out of the physical life. When he at last realized the situation, his regret for having unintentionally annoyed his wife was profound, and he was eager to learn the higher laws in order to understand how he might help her.

Mrs. F. W. then returned to New York and experienced no further disturbance. F. W. became a loyal member of the Mercy Band, and in several of many communications since received from him he related the bewilderment of one suddenly finding himself on the spirit side of life without understanding.

THIRTY YEARS AMONG THE DEAD

EXPERIENCE, NOVEMBER 22, 1920

Spirit: F. W. Psychic: MRS. WICKLAND

Well, here I am again.

I want to come in to tell you that I have not gone. I have to speak through this instrument, but otherwise I am here to help you all do the good work you are doing, and you know I am always here ready to do what I can to help you, and also to help all who are in trouble.

I want to thank you for having helped me, otherwise my wife and I would be in trouble, and through my own fault. I would not listen to the great wonders of the life beyond. When I was in my parents' home, my parents were so orthodox, so strong in their belief, that they condemned every one who did not believe as they did, and they hypnotized themselves with the idea that nothing was right except what they thought. I could not live in that atmosphere and I left home. I was only a boy when I left home, and why did I go? Because the atmosphere was so strongly orthodox that it drove me away. I could not believe as my parents did, and they said if I did not I was a sinner.

I was not a sinner and I could not believe as they did, so I ran away from home. I am not sorry that I left, for I learned to know something of the outside world. I had my troubles but I learned from them. I learned the condition outside of the church, and I learned how to battle for myself, but I was bitter, and so hard toward churches that I would not have anything to do with any religion. I had heard so much of it through childhood, and had seen too much of what was going on in the churches.

I do not mean that all churches are alike, but you will find that when there is too much orthodoxy the people are hypnotized and feel they are so good that no matter what they do, whether they are right or wrong, they are right, because they cannot do wrong. They are so holy that even the wrong they do is considered right.

I traveled and saw the world, but I had a great longing for home. I came home again after I had seen enough of the world and I thought I would remain with my parents. But the same conditions were still there; I wanted to stay at home to do my duty and work, but I could not. I felt as if I were being crushed by orthodoxy, so I went away again. I traveled still further and I had new experiences. I opened my heart and tried to look for the brighter and happier side of life.

Later on I met one who loved me, one who made a home for me. That was the first time I felt I really had a home, and it was the first time in my life that I was happy. We had only a few short years of happiness together on earth, but those few years will always be with me. I did not think there was a life after this. I did not believe in anything. I was tired of orthodoxy and everything else. I thought when I died that would be the end, and there would be no more.

That was also wrong. Do not let us go to one side of the road or the other, but let us stay in the middle and investigate everything. Find the truth and stay in that narrow path -the path of reason and understanding of God's wonderful manifestations.

I passed to the other side of life with the thought that there was nothing after death. I passed on very suddenly. When death came it was like a sleep. I woke up and saw my dear little wife crying; she was very sad, but I did not realize that the change had taken place. She did not listen to what I said -she did not seem to hear. I called to her and asked what was the trouble, but she did not speak to me.

I wondered what was the matter, for we loved each other dearly. I began to grow stronger and I did not want to leave her. I came in direct contact with her and felt that she must come to me and be with me, for we had never been parted. I was attracted to her through her sadness and I felt she must come to me. I did not realize the change, and I knew she wanted to be where I was, so I made up my mind that she was coming to me.

Before I knew it, I was in her magnetic aura. I stayed there because I could not get away. I was unhappy, she was unhappy. But I thank God she had an understanding of the life hereafter. She knew the condition I was in and she wanted to free herself from the influence I was throwing on her, so she came to these dear people. (Dr. W.'s.)

I was helped and so was she. We would both have been miserable if she had not understood, for I did not know about the life after this and I did not care. I want to give a warning to all of you here -do not doubt the next life. Some day you will all have to go the same way. Let us investigate; let us know the truth before we pass on to the Great Beyond so we may go with open eyes and know where we are going with a definite knowledge.

If my wife had not had understanding I would have made her take her own life -then where would we have been? There are many passing from earth life who are in a similar state. They find themselves in somebody's magnetic aura and cannot get out, and then they obsess that person.

I wanted to get out of my misery but I did not know how, and the only way I could think of was that my wife should come to me. When there is an understanding of life then one cannot be in such a situation as I was when I passed to the spirit side of life. I want to thank you all for helping me. Since I have been helping other unfortunate spirits that cannot see and do not know of the higher life, I am happy. So I am working, and now I can be with my dear wife to help and guide her.

Learn all you can of the wonderful life beyond. I wish every one of you here would do your part to spread the truth that there is a life after this and that we must find it. If we do not learn this while in the body we must do so when we reach the other side. Many, many times we are sorry that we did not look into the truth before we passed out of earth life.

I want to say a few words to the two young girls who are about to leave here. (One had been a patient, the other her companion.) When you leave, keep in your hearts what you have learned. Remember it, and learn more, because you will have to protect yourselves. Learn all you can. Help others in similar trouble and you will help yourself and gain strength. Now that you have found the truth do not put your light under a bushel. Helping others will strengthen you. You will receive strength and power to keep well, and you will not then be obsessed any more.

Each and every one should be proud to help spread the truth, because there is a wave of obsession going on everywhere. Let us all do our part, and do our work while we are here, gaining all the knowledge of the life beyond that we can.

This is F. W. Goodbye

EXPERIENCE, JANUARY 18, 1922

Spirit: F. W. Psychic: MRS. WICKLAND

How do you do? Don't you know me?

I think you should. This is F. W.

The time must come when there will be circles of this kind in every little society, every church. Then people will not be taken to the insane asylum -they will be helped. Many of the poor afflicted ones who are in the asylums are controlled by spirits and should be helped, but most persons think they are not worth bothering about. They prefer to send people to the insane asylum and let them stay there.

We must not condemn the spirits who are controlling sensitives, because they were not taught regarding the higher life while in the physical, and have no knowledge of it. Many believe that after "death" they will go straight to "Heaven" and will see God on a throne, and there they will sit and sing, and eat figs, and all that. When I was a boy, my father and mother were very religious. My father professed holiness, and the environment was such that I felt as if I were being pulled to pieces. I could not stand the atmosphere at home.

My father and mother were good people, but had such a narrow way of thinking that I felt I was in a cage, so I ran away when I was only a child. I had many struggles and many hardships, but I thank God today that I ran away. I learned many bitter lessons during my life, but I also learned not to be a mere believer, and when I reached the spirit side of life and received an explanation of my changed condition, I was not held back by any orthodox religious doctrine.

When I was on earth I made the best I could of circumstances, but when it came to religion I did not believe in anything. I felt that death was all and there was nothing more. I would not, and could not, believe as my parents did. I felt God was the Life of all things, not an angry God who threatened hell and damnation as the churches taught. I felt there was nothing after this, and that after death all would be ended.

I made up my mind to do my best while on earth. I went to church sometimes, I traveled around, saw the world and gained experience which is worth a great deal to me now. After I was married my wife taught me a little about the other side of life -a more cheerful view than the orthodox one -still I did not believe. However, there was a little light of understanding.

I wanted my wife to promise that if I should die first, she would go too, and if she went first I would follow, but she would not make that promise, because she understood more of the next life than I did. The time came when I had to leave, and very suddenly. I seemed to go into a pleasant sleep of rest, and I woke up -where?

It says in the Bible: "Where your treasure is, there will your heart be also." My treasure was my dear little wife and when I woke up I found myself in her magnetic aura. She would not pay any attention to me and I wondered what could be the trouble and why she would not talk to me when I spoke to her. I felt queer, and I did not know where I was.

Death is only a sleep, a sleep as natural as that which you have every night on earth. When one awakes from the sleep of death everything is so natural that you feel you are still with your relatives. Then if you get into a person's magnetic aura, you live right with him, and you are there. I was in my wife's aura, and could not realize why I should have to go wherever she went, and not be an independent individual as I used to be, and it annoyed me. I felt desperate. I felt that my wife must come with me; I did not know where, but I wanted her.

My love for her was so strong that I tormented her against my will, because I had no understanding of the real life on the other side. I loved my wife dearly, yet I disturbed her, for I did not know any better, and she was tormented -tormented by the one who loved and idolized her.

But she came to these kind people (Dr. W.'s) and was freed, and I thank you, as I have many times before, for having helped us both. I had to learn by experience. When we know about the other side we are happy to go and meet friends who have already gone over.

It is very necessary for every one to know the truth, because we all have to take that journey. I know now that God is Love, God is everywhere. Since He is Love and Wisdom, He knows the past, present and future. How could He then have created a world only to lose control of it? For if He later found the people full of sin, He certainly must have lost control of His creation.

Yet the churches teach that, having lost control of the world, God created a person for the particular purpose of being sacrificed, and that those who believe this will win a golden crown. Let us not misconstrue God. God knows everything, and He reveals Himself to Himself. Everything has life in Nature. Where can you go without Life -without God? He is in everything. Humanity should know that each is a part of this wonderful life. Nothing should be condemned, because everything in Nature is perfect. Any disturbances in Nature are only for development. As soon as you have trouble and something disturbs you, you begin to long for a higher life; you want to attain it and you work for that end.

Life goes on, on the other side, and it is always progressive. Teach children the truth. Teach the higher things of life. All is God. Now I must go. Good Night.

In the following case the apathy and characteristics of the spirit were recognized by Mrs. H. W., the mother of the patient, who had known the spirit well during his earth life. He was the son of a neighbor, and his statements were confirmed by the patient and her mother, who were from Chicago, and both present in the circle.

EXPERIENCE, DECEMBER 2, 1919

Spirit: FRANK BERGQUIST Patient: MRS. A.

Psychic: MRS. WICKLAND.

Doctor Who are you, friend? Some sleepy one? Wake up and tell us who you are. Have you found a happy condition, or not?

Spirit No.

Dr. Why not?

Sp. I don't know.

Dr. What was the trouble? Didn't you have any faith, or did you have too much?

Sp. I don't know what is the matter with me.

Dr. Do you know who you are?

Sp. No.

Dr. Can't you recall your name or anything about yourself? Do you know how long you have been dead?

Sp. I don't know.

Dr. Where do you think you are?

Sp. I don't know.

Dr. Have you been sleeping for many years?

Sp. Not many. I don't feel natural.

Dr. Does it interest you to know the reason?

Sp. I can't find out. I have asked many but they do not understand and they do not know. They cannot inform me.

Dr. They have been in darkness as well as yourself. What have you been doing recently?

Sp. Doing nothing.

Dr. Don't you get tired of nothing?

Sp. It is monotonous, but what can you do?

Dr. Acquire understanding.

Sp. How can you find it?

Dr. You cannot find understanding; you have to develop your mind. You are controlling a woman's body, yet possibly you claim to be a man. Are you a man, or a woman?

Sp. I am a man, but have been a woman so long, I do not know. (Confusing himself with the patient, Mrs. A.)

Dr. You have been a woman a long time? Have you caused trouble?

Sp. Not that I know of.

Dr. Don't you find that things do not seem just right?

Sp. It has been queer, I told you that before.

Dr. Did anything disturb you?

Sp. A whole lot.

Dr. What woke you up and disturbed you, and caused you to come here?

Sp. I don't know.

Dr. Have you been disturbed at all? Have you had any peculiar experience lately?

Sp. Yes.

Dr. In what way?

Sp. In many ways. I cannot talk as I want to talk, and I cannot do as I please to do.

Dr. What do you please to do?

Sp. I like to talk and sing.

Dr. Have you not been able to do that?

Sp. No.

Dr. What is your name, if I may ask?

Sp. I don't know.

Dr. Surely you do.

Sp. It seems I have forgotten everything I ever knew.

THIRTY YEARS AMONG THE DEAD

Dr. There probably was not much to forget anyhow. That is very often the case. What did you do in life?

Sp. Any little thing, now and then.

Dr. Did you have religious belief of any kind?

Sp. (Yawning, and stretching lazily.) Why, yes.

Dr. What did you believe in?

Sp. I believed in God and Christ and the devil, and the other things.

Dr. Have you seen any of them? You have probably been dead a long time.

Sp. I don't know. I do not feel dead.

Mrs. H. W. Were you a Baptist, a Methodist, or what?

Sp. I was a little of everything.

Mrs. H. W. Where did you live?

Sp. I don't know. I'm tired.

Dr. You have been sleeping long enough. What else have you been doing?

Sp. Nothing.

Dr. Don't you get tired of that?

Sp. You get pretty tired of doing nothing. It is monotonous. And to be a fool woman all the time! I have seen nothing but women, women, women and women. (Other spirits obsessing patient.) I saw nothing else.

Dr. Don't you get tired of women?

Sp. They do get pretty monotonous.

Dr. Do they know you are there?

Sp. I don't know. I talk, but they do not answer me.

Dr. That is very foolish.

Sp. It seems so to me.

Dr. Do you seem to be in a strange condition yourself?

Sp. I cannot tell what it is, but it is queer.

Dr. You don't care very much.

Sp. No, I don't care.

Dr. Isn't that an unfortunate condition to be in?

Sp. I have been walking from one place to another.

Dr. Why did you do that?

Sp. I had nothing else to do.

THIRTY YEARS AMONG THE DEAD

Dr. Couldn't you find any work?

Sp. Nobody wanted me.

Dr. What could you do?

Sp. Anything, but nothing in particular.

Dr. Where did you live?

Sp. In Chicago, at times.

Dr. Did you go from one city to another?

Sp. I was in Rockford and Galesburg. I was anywhere, everywhere. It is a tiresome job.

Dr. You must have been born tired, you are so indifferent.

Sp. What was the use?

Dr. Did you try to understand the wonderful facts of life?

Sp. Life? No.

Dr. I suppose you only believed that Christ died for your sins, and that is a lazy man's job. That is not enough.

Sp. It's good enough for me. It was good enough for my father and mother, and it's good enough for me.

Dr. Are your father and mother alive?

Sp. Why, yes, I think so, but I don't know.

Dr. Where did they live? Chicago?

Sp. Somewhere around Bethany Home, near the Methodist Church.

Dr. Did your father and mother belong to that church?

Sp. Yes.

Dr. What was your father's name?

Sp. I don't know.

Dr. What was your name?

Sp. It's a long time since I heard it and I don't know.

Mrs. H. W. (Recognizing from the foregoing the traits of a former neighbor.) Was it Frank?

Sp. I don't care what you call me; call me anything.

Dr. We don't want to do that.

Sp. I don't care; call me anything. I am pleased with anything.

Dr. You are mentally lazy.

THIRTY YEARS AMONG THE DEAD

Sp. What's the use?

Mrs. H. W. Do you know anybody by the name of B?

Sp. A long time ago.

Mrs. H. W. Who was he?

Sp. He was somebody.

Mrs. H. W. Were you related to him by marriage? Whom did he marry?

Sp. He married somebody I knew.

Dr. What was her name?

Sp. Names have gone from my memory. Yes, I know -it was my sister. Say, I don't know what is the matter with me!

Dr. You are "dead."

Sp. Dead? Then I'm gone.

Dr. Do you remember how you died?

Sp. I didn't know I was dead. How can I remember how I died?

Dr. Well, you are "dead."

Sp. I am? That's a funny thing -but I don't care.

Dr. You are occupying a lady's body now.

Sp. I've had enough of ladies. I have been walking and walking between ladies, until I am sick and tired of them.

Dr. I think you were born with that tired feeling.

Sp. I think so myself, because I am always tired. I do not care very much for work anyhow. It was just as well not to work. I was born to be traveling around, because I

was never satisfied to be in one place. I liked to see the world. I did not want to do very much except what came along, just enough so I could get along.

Dr. Were you a sort of tramp?

Sp. I was a little better than a tramp, but next door to it.

Mrs. H. W. Do you remember that you had a twin brother?

Sp. Something like that -but what is the matter with me anyhow? I cannot recall anything; everything is gone. I do not know for sure what is my name.

Dr. Sit quietly and think.

Sp. (After a moment.) It is Bergquist. I think it is Frank -yes, it is Frank. I heard that some years ago. It's an awful long time since I heard it. It seems so far away that it is miles and miles away, that name is. It seems like I was walking away from it. The more I walked, the more I forgot. After a while I walked so long that I forgot who I was. I walked with women, women, women, until I thought I was a woman myself, and really sometimes I thought I was. And probably I am a woman, for all I know, and for all I care. What is the use anyway?

Mrs. H. W. Did you live on Paulina Street, Ravenswood? (Chicago.)

Sp. Yes, Chicago; that was where I was some of the time.

Dr. Do you know where you are now?

Sp. In Chicago.

Dr. You are in California.

Sp. California! Well, if I didn't walk after those women clear to California! Well, that was a long walk! I know I haven't been riding. I have walked for miles and miles and miles. At last I got to California! That was some walk! I am pretty tired. Why did you tell me I walked that far? Because that makes me very tired, and now I feel I have to rest.

Mrs. H. W. That is natural for you. Do you know me?

Sp. I thought when I looked at you I had seen that face before. Didn't you go to the Methodist Church? I think I have seen you there.

Mrs. H. W. Do you remember the bakery on W. Avenue? (Across the street from the boy's home.)

Sp. Some time ago that was.

Mrs. H. W. Look at me again and see if I am not the one who had that store.

Sp. Yes, and you had two girls.

Mrs. H. W. Yes, I did. Would you know one of them if you saw her? Would you know L.?

Sp. I didn't know them very much. I liked that girl, but you could only look at those girls with one eye.

Mrs. H. W. Somebody looked at them with two eyes. They are both married.

Sp. I looked at them with a quarter of an eye. They wouldn't look at a fellow like me.

Dr. Has anybody else looked at you?

Sp. I don't know. Women, women, women -I have been with them. It is a funny world anyhow.

Dr. What did they call you when you felt that you were a woman?

Sp. I don't hear anything. Of course I have had a long walk, if I have walked to California. Sometimes I got chased out when I was behind; then I ran fast as I could, and sometimes I got in front.

Dr. In front of what?

Sp. The people. Do you suppose I walked that long distance alone? I was walking with a big crowd. (Spirits obsessing patient.) At times I was before and then I was behind. What's the use? We all talked the same thing.

Dr. Where did you get food when you were out walking?

Sp. I didn't seem to need much. I have learned to fast.

THIRTY YEARS AMONG THE DEAD

Dr. Didn't you go to different houses and ask for food?

Sp. At times, but that was long ago. Somebody said if you fast three or four days you would not feel your stomach. It was a bother to feel hungry if you didn't have anything to eat. I fasted pretty good, and it was a good thing I did.

Mrs. H. W. Did your parents live on the top floor?

Sp. In the basement.

Dr. (To Mrs. H. W.) Is that correct?

Mrs. H. W. Yes, it is. I think his parents are dead now.

Sp. They are? When did they die?

Mrs. H. W. Not long ago. Your mother died a year ago, and your father a few months ago.

Sp. Who told you that?

Mrs. H. W. Your sister.

Sp. Why didn't she tell me?

Mrs. H. W. You are dead.

Sp. Dead? I am dead? I feel full of life.

Mrs. H. W. Didn't you used to go to saloons?

Sp. Oh, don't talk like that in company!

Mrs. H. W. We have no company.

Sp. I went, but don't tell them that.

Mrs. H. W. Why don't you want them to know?

Sp. Because they wouldn't like it. Mother doesn't like me to go there.

Mrs. H. W. You had a good father and mother.

Sp. I wanted to live my life, but they wanted to live mine for me.

Mrs. H. W. What did you do when you were home with them?

Sp. Nothing.

Mrs. H. W. Didn't you help in the kitchen?

Sp. Mother wanted me to, but I didn't do very much of anything. I used to wash the dishes for her, but I didn't want to do it.

Mrs. H. W. She made you.

Sp. You know, she said: "If you want to eat, you will have to work." Say, that isn't

right. I always liked to slip out if I could. That's natural.

Dr. No, it is not. It may be to some, but not to others.

Sp. Everybody likes to get out and do some idling around. You want a little freedom.

THIRTY YEARS AMONG THE DEAD

Mrs. H. W. You wanted all freedom; you wanted to just loaf around.

Sp. I worked sometimes -once in a while. I gave my mother money at times, but it was not often I had any.

Mrs. H. W. You liked best to walk from door to door and beg your food, and get five dollars wherever you could.

Sp. What was the use anyhow?

Dr. We want you to understand that you have passed out of your body. You have been dead a long time. This lady (Mrs. H. W.) seems to know who you are.

Sp. She made good biscuits. I wished sometimes I had one.

Mrs. H. W. Did you ever have any of my doughnuts?

Sp. Yes, sometimes you gave me some. I was supposed to look for work, but some way or other, I did not work, and I didn't care very much either.

Dr. Now then, understand, friend, that you are so-called dead. You have been an ignorant spirit for a long time, in the outer darkness which the Bible speaks of. This is not your body.

Sp. Yes, it is.

Dr. It is my wife's.

Sp. How could I be your wife when I am a man?

Dr. You are an invisible spirit. We do not see you. We only hear you talk. Do you recognize these hands? (Indicating hands of psychic.)

Sp. I have been so strange for a long time. What in the world is it? It has been so strange at times. There was lightning and thunder (electricity given patient) and it bothered me terribly. I have not been left alone for one minute. It was fierce, that thunder and lightning. The lightning is the worst, the thunder is not so bad. The lightning is so bad that it doesn't seem as if I should really see afterwards. I should say it was coming down in torrents. It seemed as if you got knocked in the head, and then got it again and again. It was wonderful how you got it. It was a wonder, for it woke me up. It woke me up good and plenty at times, so that I could not stand it any longer.

Mrs. H. W. I am glad of it.

Sp. I don't see why you should be glad.

Mrs. H. W. I will tell you why I am glad. You have been bothering my daughter for a long time.

Sp. How do you know I have?

Mrs. H. W. That is the reason you were with women all the time. You are ignorant and have been troubling my daughter. You got "thunder and lightning" for it, when my daughter had electric treatments, and you got out. I am glad of it.

Dr. I am the one who gave the electricity to you. We chase ignorant spirits away with it.

Sp. I think you had better be a little milder with it then.

Dr. I do not like to give it, but it is sometimes necessary.

Sp. I do not see why I should need to have so much of it coming down like thunder and lightning. You get it in the head like a sledge hammer!

Dr. But we succeeded in driving you from the lady.

Sp. I didn't bother any lady; I didn't have a chance. I was walking behind them, but it does not seem to me that I had any way of bothering them.

Mrs. H. W. You surely bothered my daughter.

Dr. That was why we had to give you electricity. Were there any others with you?

Sp. There are many with us.

Dr. Are there any more left?

Sp. I don't know. There are some that come and go.

Dr. They will get electricity every time they come.

Sp. I'm not going to have it any more. I don't think I need it.

Dr. If you stay around you will get it.

Sp. I don't care for any more.

Dr. Have you ever been called Mrs. A ?

Sp. No. I never was a woman, so I never could be anybody by that name. I was with women.

Dr. Did you hear that name at all?

Sp. No.

Mrs. H. W. That is my daughter's name, and you got that electricity for being around her.

Sp. Did you order that for me?

Mrs. H. W. Yes, I did.

Sp. Then you are a bad woman to do that.

Mrs. H. W. I wanted you to leave my daughter alone.

Sp. I told you I never bothered your daughter. I walked behind the women.

Dr. You walked a little too close. Were you the only man among so many women?

Sp. There is something like what you would call a line and you have to walk in that line and you cannot go out. I did not want to work. (The patient suffered from a heavy listlessness.)

Mrs. H. W. You were too lazy.

Sp. What was the use when you could get your food without? It is just as well to take things instead of working yourself to death.

Dr. That is a poor argument. People who accomplish something are happy.

Sp. I do not fancy it. If people want to work like slaves they are welcome to it, for me. I would not work.

Dr. (To Mrs. H. W.) Is that like this man's disposition?

Mrs. H. W. Yes, every inch of him. His name is Bergquist.

Sp. How do you know?

Mrs. H.W. Your disposition and actions are clear to me.

Sp. Can you know one's name before you know the person?

Mrs. H. W. I know you by your actions. I used to know you well. I knew your brother, who went to war in Cuba. He came home, had consumption and died.

Sp. I had another brother who died.

Dr. Now friend, I want you to understand.

Mrs. H. W. Listen to the doctor.

Sp. Doctor? I am not sick.

Mrs. H. W. You need advice from the doctor.

Sp. Advice? Then I must go to a lawyer. When I was sick, I went to a doctor, when I needed advice, I would go to a lawyer.

Dr. You are mentally sick.

Sp. I wouldn't say I am sick; I feel pretty good. I feel better than I have for years and years in the past.

Dr. You will not feel yourself so very long, unless you change your attitude. You are controlling my wife's body.

Sp. I can do as I please for that matter.

Dr. You cannot in this instance. Do you think that I want you to sit here indefinitely, controlling my wife's body? Look at those hands. Are they yours? Wake up, and don't be so sleepy. Do you know that hand?

Sp. How did I get it? I have been with women so much that I have a woman's hands.

Dr. You must wake up and listen. The fact is, you are an ignorant spirit. You have been taken away from that lady; you have been bothering her for a long time. You lost your body years ago.

Sp. That doesn't interest me.

Dr. It will have to. You died a long time ago. You are an invisible spirit. You have been hovering around that lady and troubling her. She has been brought to California to be freed from spirits -of which you are one -and I have had to give her the electricity to get rid of you. You have been driven away from her and allowed to control my wife's body. The point is, you will have to leave this body and become sensible.

Sp. I want to ask you this -if I haven't any sense what will you do? Mother used to say I had no sense.

Dr. You have been lazy, but now you will have to use the sense that God gave you, even if it is only a little. You cannot be lazy any longer.

Sp. I will not work either.

Dr. You will have to in the spirit life.

Sp. How do you know? How do you know they will make me work?

Dr. You will be glad to work. You cannot bother people any more.

Sp. What do you mean?

Dr. Ignorant spirits hover around the earth plane interfering with mortals, and make them act as if insane.

Sp. What is a poor fellow to do?

Dr. Use the sense God gave you.

Sp. I have none. What am I to do? You say I am controlling a body that does not belong to me?

Dr. Yes, and you must leave this body and listen to spirits who will help you. My wife allows you to control her body in order to free the other lady.

Sp. What kind of a wife is that?

Dr. She is a psychic sensitive who allows ignorant spirits like yourself to control her body. If you will look around, you will find spirits who will help you.

Sp. Spirits?

Dr. You will find spirits who will help you and teach you how to progress. You can also find happiness.

Sp. My legs are getting numb.

Dr. That body is not yours. We do not see you.

Sp. No?

Dr. You are invisible to us. Can you understand that?

Sp. I suppose I can't get that in my head.

Dr. Look around and you will find invisibles like yourself, who will help you.

Sp. I don't need help.

Dr. You do; you need help to progress to the spirit land.

Sp. Where is that place?

Dr. It is an invisible plane around the earth, and you will find it if you look for it. You will be taught that life is something worth while.

Sp. I think I could go to sleep.

Dr. If you do I will give you some electricity.

Mrs. H. W. Think of the sorrow you caused your mother.

Sp. I was a fool.

Dr. You were not one, you allowed yourself to be one. You were lazy.

Sp. Mother is here (spirit), but I can't see what she wants with me.

Dr. Listen to what she says.

Sp. She says: "You have been a very wayward boy. Now try to wake up and be different, because life is different on this side and you will have to earn your happiness."

Dr. Then you will find that life is worth while.

Sp. Mother seems to be very happy.

Dr. She will help you if you are in earnest.

Sp. I want to go with her. I must learn.

Dr. You must be obedient.

Sp. Mother says she is happy she got me to come to her now. I am happy in my way to see her.

Dr. Try to realize that life means something.

Sp. I will go with her then. She says I must not bother that lady any more. After the last bombarding I got, I will leave that body alone. I thought my head would come off. I got it all right.

Mrs. H. W. You certainly did. Can you see your sister F.? (Spirit.)

Sp. She's here with a lot of people. I think I will go now.

Dr. How will you go? I will explain to you.

Sp. No, I am ready to go.

Dr. How?

Sp. I will get up and go. (Trying in vain to rise.) I can't move.

Dr. You have only partial control of this body now. You will have to think yourself with your mother.

Sp. Think myself?

Dr. You will have to travel by thought.

Sp. You come over there, Mother, (pointing) then I will jump over to you by thought. (Sitting still for a moment, then laughing heartily.) I can't jump! That would be quite a jump.

Dr. You are in California now; how long does it take you to think yourself in Chicago? You can be there instantly in thought, for you have no physical body to take with you. In the spirit world thought is the motive power.

Sp. Now I am going to think quick and jump. But I don't get there.

Dr. You must relax and quietly think yourself with your mother, and then you will lose control of this body.

Mrs. H. W. Can you see F., your sister?

Sp. Yes, and father too. They are coming to get me. They say they want me to reform and be a good fellow. Yes -I suppose I must.

Dr. You must go now. Your first lesson in spirit life is to think properly.

Sp. It seems foolish to me to think. My mother says, Thank you, and please forgive me for my ignorance. Goodbye.

Many earthbound spirits are conscious of influencing mortals but enjoy their power, seeming to be without scruples. Often these have, during earth life, turned away from orthodoxy and become hardened to higher ethics and ideals. A spirit of this type was dislodged from Mr. G., who had since childhood been subject to violent attacks of temper.

During the weeks when this spirit was being "brought to the front," preparatory to removal, Mr. G. was very irritable, especially when driving his automobile, and developed moods during which he wished to be away from every one. After the spirit was dislodged the gentleman's characteristics changed completely and he became natural again.

Both Mr. and Mrs. G. were present at the time this spirit controlled Mrs. Wickland.

EXPERIENCE, SEPTEMBER 21, 1922

Spirit: FRED HAUPT Patient: MR. 0

Psychic: MRS. WICKLAND.

The spirit made violent attempts to escape and when the hands of the psychic were held, fought furiously.

Doctor: Who are you? Come, be sensible. This will not do you any good. There is no

use in fighting. Who are you?

Spirit: It's none of your business who I am! I don't want to be here with you. I didn't want to come here. I will not come any more! You won't trap me again!

Dr. With whom did you come?

Sp. It's none of your business who I came with.

Dr. How long have you been dead?

Sp. I'm not dead. You will find that I won't stand for anything. (To Mrs. G.) You don't care for me any more.

Dr. I don't care for you?

Sp. I don't mean you. I am going to fight you all right. You gave me that awful lightning on my head and back. (Patient's electrical treatment.)

Dr. That was electricity and it evidently put life into you.

Sp. I told you many times that I would never come here again.

Dr. How long have you been dead?

Sp. Dead! I'm not dead, and you're not going to make me come here any more. You think you have me this time, but I'll fix you! You don't trap me any more. I get so mad at you!

Dr. What are you so angry about?

Sp. The world and everybody.

Dr. If you have a grudge on your mind perhaps we can help you remove it.

Sp. You can go your way and I'll go mine! I'm through! You can go just wherever you please! You think you've got me where you have control over me, but you'll find you will get left. I'll not tell you anything, so you don't need to ask.

Dr. We are anxious to know who you are.

Sp. That makes no difference to me. You think you have me in your claws, but you'll get left.

Dr. Won't you tell us who you are?

Sp. I don't want to get acquainted with you and you don't need to get acquainted with me. I want to be all by myself, and I'm going out. I don't want any one around me; I want to be alone. I enjoy my own company best.

Dr. What experiences have you had?

Sp. I will not talk to you any more.

Dr. How do you happen to be here?

Sp. You made me come with those funny lights. (Electricity.)

Dr. It will relieve you if you will tell us what you have on your mind, because we can help you. Where did you get that ring you are wearing? (Referring to ring on hand of psychic.)

Sp. That's none of your business. It needn't bother you where I got it.

Dr. Were you always so sarcastic?

Sp. You keep your hands off me! I will go.

Dr. Where will you go?

Sp. That makes no difference to you where I go, and I don't care where you go either!

Dr. But you have no place to go.

Sp. (Angrily.) Do you think I'm a tramp? I always had enough money to pay for my lodging. I can go where I want.

Dr. Then you were somewhat of a gentleman?

Sp. When I am in gentlemen's company, then I am a gentleman. You don't need to talk to me, for I don't care for you with your electric sparks.

Dr. Are you despondent?

Sp. No, I'm mad!

Dr. Tell us who you are.

Sp. I have no use for you. As soon as you leave your hands off me I will attend to myself.

Dr. What will you do then?

Sp. That's none of your business.

Dr. Tell us how long you have been dead.

Sp. I'm not dead, and never have been.

Dr. Would you understand if I should tell you it is 1922? Would you believe it?

Sp. I won't have anything to do with you! I have no business here. I'll never go to that place again.

Dr. We did not ask you to come here.

Sp. You put me in a prison.

Dr. How did you get into prison? Who put you there?

Sp. You put me there yesterday.

Dr. Is that so?

Sp. I will haunt you until you don't know where you are at.

Dr. I am used to things like that.

Sp. I will attend to all my business and you attend to yours. We part right here. I will have nothing more to do with you. I am going my own way and you can go yours.

Dr. Suppose we will not let you? Try to understand your situation. You are a spirit and have lost your mortal body.

Sp. I don't care if I have lost my mortal body ten thousand times. What of that? I am living just as well as if I had my body. What do I care?

Dr. Whose body are you talking through?

Sp. I have many bodies. I go from one place to another. I can be a lady at one time, and a gentleman another. Nobody can catch me.

Dr. This time somebody has caught you, and you will have to stop interfering with the lives of others.

Sp. I have been attending to my own business for many years.

Dr. Didn't you say you had been in prison?

Sp. That won't last long.

Dr. If you don't change your behavior you will be put into a dark dungeon.

Sp. You'll get left! I've been in tight places before, and always got out.

Dr. Did you ever own a Ford car?

Sp. No, I didn't -what's that?

Dr. I'll tell you a story. A man who owned a Ford machine died, and his last request was that his Ford should be placed in his grave with him.

Sp. What for?

Dr. He said his Ford had helped him out of many a tight place.

Sp. Did they put it in?

Dr. Oh -I suppose so.

Sp. Ha, ha! Such fools! They couldn't have a car with them if they are dead.

Dr. Don't you know there is no actual death? No one really dies.

Sp. You say I am not dead?

Dr. Your body is dead.

Sp. Well, I can be just what I want. Sometimes a man, sometimes a woman.

Dr. No, you cannot; you only obsess men and women.

Sp. No, I don't. If I want, I can boss the whole family. I have a mighty good time. I go where I please; I am my own boss. If I am hungry, sometimes I eat, sometimes I don't. The best thing to work up an appetite is to get hungry. Then you eat everything and it tastes good. If you are not hungry, nothing tastes good. I tell you, I'm no spirit.

Dr. You are talking through my wife's body.

Sp. We are just wasting time, so I will go.

Dr. You and I are going to be good friends, I hope.

Sp. I will have nothing to do with you.

Dr. Come, friend, let us talk things over. Life is a wonderful thing. We can think and act, and yet we do not know ourselves.

Sp. You don't? Well, that's too bad about you.

Dr. Did you ever stop to think how wonderful sound is?

Sp. It's no more wonderful than anything else. Now let me go; I don't want you to hold me any longer.

Dr. No, I can't let you go until you behave yourself.

Sp. If you didn't hold me I would knock you down as quick as lightning! I can get mad! I have a temper.

Dr. Now, Johnnie, listen to what I have to say.

Sp. Johnnie! That's not my name. I will not tell you what it is.

Dr. Did you kill any one, and is that why you are so full of hatred?

Sp. No, I am an honest man. I want to have my own way, and I always do. I get so mad.

Dr. What church did you belong to?

Sp. That's none of your business.

Dr. Were you a minister or a deacon?

Sp. No, I wasn't. I'll not tell you anything, so keep still! (Closing lips firmly.)

THIRTY YEARS AMONG THE DEAD

Dr. Why are you sitting so quietly?

Sp. Be still! I am thinking. I want to be by myself.

Dr. What evil thoughts have you in your mind now?

Sp. You look out, asking me such questions! When I get mad I could knock this house down in a minute. I could knock everybody down.

Dr. Talk is cheap.

Sp. You might as well say big things as little ones.

Dr. Tell us who you are, and how long you have been dead.

Sp. (Stamping feet violently and struggling.) If I could get loose, I'd show you I'm not dead! I've told you that before now keep quiet!

Dr. But you are talking through my wife's body.

Sp. Just let me get free, and I'll show you a few things.

Dr. That is bombastic and does not amount to anything. You are talking through my wife's body.

Sp. I will not listen to you any longer. I have no use whatever for you. Only for that electricity, you couldn't have chased me out and put me in prison! I'll knock you down when I get loose. We can part right here, you going your way and I mine. That will suit me just right.

Dr. But we want to part friends.

Sp. You say friends? You can never find a friend in me when you give me electricity like you did.

Dr. Those were just friendly taps. That was the best thing that ever happened to you.

Sp. (Sarcastically.) You think so!

Dr. Try to understand that you are talking through my wife's body.

Sp. I don't want to have anything to do with your wife. All women can go their way, and I'll go mine. I want nothing to do with women, and I don't want your wife any more than the rest. I never knew your wife. Keep her yourself!

Dr. You are talking through my wife's body. You cannot realize your condition because you are so ignorant.

Sp. You are just as ignorant as I am.

Dr. Be free and open-minded. Try to realize that you are a spirit. You are a foolish spirit and do not know it.

Sp. A gentleman, to call a man a fool!

Dr. You are a foolish, selfish spirit. If you were intelligent, you would listen to me.

Sp. I don't care -just leave my hands alone!

Dr. I am not holding your hands; I am holding my wife's hands.

THIRTY YEARS AMONG THE DEAD

Sp. For God's sake, can't you see I am a man? Don't mix your wife with me. Take her; I'm sure I don't want her.

Dr. If you were not stubborn, you would realize there is something the matter with you. Look at your hands.

Sp. (Refusing to look.) They are mine. If I could get loose, I would show you a thing or two! I have more strength now than I have had for some time. Now I can talk again. Before, someone always interfered with me. Now I am myself and can talk and fight.

Dr. You are talking through my wife's body.

Sp. I'll knock you in the head if you don't stop talking about your wife!

Dr. My wife is a psychic.

Sp. Well, what of that? What do I care? I don't care if your wife is a thousand psychics!

Dr. Intelligent spirits have brought you here to be helped, and unless you are willing to listen to reason, you will be put in a dungeon.

Sp. You can do just as you please.

Dr. What do you gain by acting this way? We are trying to bring you to an understanding.

Sp. I was converted once by a rascal of a minister. He took all of my money and then kicked me out.

Dr. Probably that was a good thing for you.

Sp. What! To kick me out? I just asked him a few questions about life, and he said: "You big sinner, get out of here!" All he wanted was money.

Dr. But that didn't settle the question of life.

Sp. The question of life? Life is life, that's all. We are born here, we stay for a while, and then go.

Dr. Where was the church you speak of? What denomination?

Sp. I will not tell my secrets to you. I will not talk anything about myself. I won't tell my name or the ministers.

Dr. You do not understand that you are among friends. We can help you. You will find we can help you to understand things of which you are ignorant now. I have told you many times that you have lost your body and are a spirit, and yet you do not understand it.

Sp. I have not lost my body, because I have lots of bodies.

Mr. G. How could you have more than one body?

Sp. I don't know about that, but I had enjoyment with others.

Mrs. G. How did you find these others?

Sp. I don't know, but that doesn't bother me a bit.

Mr. G. How could you be a man one time, and a woman another?

Sp. I didn't stop to think anything about that. I don't know myself.

THIRTY YEARS AMONG THE DEAD

Mr. G. Who brought you here?

Sp. They brought me here.

Mr. G. Who?

Sp. I don't know, I was not going to come here at all, but they made me come. I said I would never come here any more.

Mr. G. Have you been here before?

Sp. Sometimes.

Mr. G. Who brought you here?

Sp. I told you I didn't know.

Mr. G. Look closely; don't you recognize the one who brought you here?

Sp. I don't know and I don't care.

Mr. G. Have we ever talked to you before?

Sp. It seems so.

Dr. Do you recognize the man talking to you? You may have been friends.

Mr. G. Is there anyone here whom you have seen before?

Sp. I don't know. With all that electricity on my head, it hurts, and I feel like knocking somebody down.

Mrs. G. How did you get here?

Sp. That's nobody's business. I have a temper that no one can conquer. I get mad as quick as lightning, and it comes like thunder.

Mrs. G. When you get into another body, do you have a temper at that time?

Sp. Yes, I have a bad temper. I don't know why I get mad sometimes, but I get mad like fury at everything. I have to go here and there.

Mrs. G. Can't you stay at a certain place if you want to?

Sp. No; I have to go along, and I get so mad.

Mr. G. You are not independent then?

Sp. I don't know. I get so furious when I have to go places and I don't want to go. I get

awful mad.

Mr. G. Would you like to get over being mad? (Pointing to Dr. W.) There is a gentleman who can tell you all about your condition as he is a physician.

Dr. If you will be sensible we can help you.

Sp. Sometimes I fly off about things that don't amount to a pinch of snuff. I don't know why I do that.

Dr. You allow yourself to fly to pieces over nothing.

Sp. Things don't always go my way, and when they don't, I don't feel right. Sometimes I feel as if I did not have whole control and I am only half and half, and then I get mad.

Dr. You are hovering around people and using their bodies. You are not really dead. The mind is one thing and the body another. You have lost your mortal body, and your spiritual body looks like your mortal body. You are ignorant of your condition and come in touch with mortals who are sensitives; then you try to control them, but they have wills of their own too.

Sp. I always get mad at that machine.

Mrs. G. Don't you like machinery?

Sp. No; I feel sometimes as if I could knock it all to pieces, I get so mad at it.

Mrs. G. Do you mean the automobile?

Sp. I don't know. What does that mean? Is it that machine that runs without horses?

Dr. You have never seen an automobile, have you?

Sp. Is it that machine that goes "Whz-z-z?" (Circling arms around wildly.)

Dr. Have you never seen one of those machines? Who is President?

Sp. I don't know. I haven't read a paper for years.

Dr. Was McKinley the President?

Sp. No -Cleveland.

Dr. Do you remember the Chicago World's Fair?

Sp. No, I don't.

Dr. Where did you live?

Sp. I lived in Kansas.

Mr. G. (Whose early years were spent in Kansas.) In H., or N.?

Dr. You talk things over with that gentleman. (Mr. G.)

Mr. G. Did you know a family there called G?

Sp. Yes, they lived in that pretty house, a big house.

Mr. G. Did you live in N?

Sp. No, a little outside. I was a helper here and there. I never stayed long in one place.

Mr. G. Did you live on farms?

Sp. Yes, where they had horses. I don't like to ride in that "Ch-ch-ch!" I get so mad when things don't go just right.

Mr. G. You can go so much further with a machine than you can with horses.

Sp. I like air, and you don't always have the windows open in that machine -shut up in there!

Mr. G. Were you ever sick, or did you have an accident?

THIRTY YEARS AMONG THE DEAD

Sp. I am not quite sure, but it seems I have something the matter with my head. I do not really know what happened. I lose my temper so often that I know there is something the matter with me.

Mr. G. Do you remember any of the G. boys?

Sp. I have heard of them.

Mr. G. How old were you? About as old as R.?

Sp. He was that stout fellow.

Mr. G. Were you as old as he?

Sp. No, no. He was more lively than the other fellow, and liked to have a good time. The other fellow (Mr. G.) studied. He wanted to go off by himself. I think he was going to study for a minister, or a lawyer, or something, because he always had a book with him. (This was correct.)

Mr. G. Did he ever sing?

Sp. Who?

Mr. G. This other fellow.

Sp. I don't know very much about him. I was just a helper around.

Mr. G. Did you work around at their home?

Sp. No, I lived Southwest. The farm was in the hollow, in the distance. You go up the hill and then down in the hollow -that's the place.

Mr. G. Down toward W?

Sp. Yes.

Mr. G. Did you have an accident there?

Sp. I can't remember. I know I had something the matter with my head. There were a lot of fellows out with the threshing machine -the threshing gang.

Mr. G. You must have been hurt very badly at that time.

Sp. Do you mean when they were threshing on that farm? What is the matter with my head?

Mr. G. You must have been so badly hurt that you passed on.

Dr. Possibly you thought you went to sleep. You lost your physical body. Most people would call you dead, but you are not really "dead."

Mr. G. Did you know Tom? (Another spirit who had previously been dislodged from

Mr. G.). He is a good friend of mine.

Sp. Yes, and he is here. He says he came here to help you. But how is he going to help you?

Mr. G. Ask Tom.

Dr. Ask him why he is going to help this gentleman, and why he needs help.

Sp. Tom says to me: "You get out!"

THIRTY YEARS AMONG THE DEAD

Dr. You listen to him; he will tell you the truth.

Sp. If he tells me anything that isn't true I'll knock his block off! Tom says that I -for God's sake, no! (Excitedly.) Tom says that I -he says that I have been sponging on that man (Mr. G.) for years!

Dr. It sounds strange, but it is true.

Mr. G. Tom did it too. He bothered me a great deal. Now he is a good friend of mine, as you are. You and I are going to be good friends, are we not?

Sp. Why did I get so mad at things?

Dr. When you hurt your head you may have disturbed your mind.

Sp. Tom says he is trying to help you get rid of me -that's what he says. He's going to get left! Why does he want to get rid of me?

Mr. G. Then you will be free. He is a good friend of ours. We are all going to work together. You will have your own body and you will not have to get out of anyone.

Sp. I don't understand what you folks mean.

Dr. I will explain. Don't contradict me, no matter how foolish it may seem to you. I will tell you nothing but the absolute truth.

Sp. If you don't, you look out!

Dr. You lost your mortal body some time ago. It is now 1922.

Sp. You mean 1892.

Dr. That was when Cleveland was President the second time. You have been so-called dead all these years. There is no actual death. The mind is one thing, the body another. It is the physical body which dies, but not the mind or spirit. You are not talking through your own body now.

Sp. I'm not?

Dr. No; you are speaking through my wife. She is so constituted that spirits can control her and speak through her, and we are having these investigating circles to come in contact with spirits like yourself. Ignorant spirits often influence mortals and disturb their balance. You conveyed your temper to this gentleman (Mr. G.) and made him act as if he had a bad temper.

Sp. I did?

Mr. G. Did you ride in that machine?

Sp. Yes, but I hate it.

Dr. I'll tell you about those machines. About 1896 they began to invent what they call automobiles; these machines go without horses, for they run by their own power. We have millions of them now.

Sp. What have they done with their fine horses?

Dr. They do not use them now. Automobiles are very convenient; you can travel one hundred miles an hour, but the average is twenty or twenty-five miles an hour.

Sp. I wouldn't ride in one that goes that fast.

THIRTY YEARS AMONG THE DEAD

Dr. You can travel two or three hundred miles a day. These machines have been invented since you lost your body. We have aeroplanes now that fly in the air, and we can telegraph without any wires. We can even talk across the ocean without any wires.

You cannot realize what wonderful things have happened since you passed out. Do you know that you are in California now?

Sp. I feel so weak.

Dr. Don't lose control, friend, until you give us your name.

Sp. I don't know it, my head is in such a mess. Don't bother me and I will tell it to you in a little while. For a long time I have had so many different names that I don't remember my name at all.

Dr. Look around; your mother may be here.

Sp. I heard my mother call me one time. Sometimes I am Charlie, sometimes Henry, sometimes a man and sometimes a woman, so I don't know what name to give you. It's so long since I heard my own name that I seem to have forgotten it.

Mr. G. Ask Tom what your name is.

Sp. He says my name is Fred. Yes, that's it -Fred?

Mr. G. Fred what? Ask Tom.

Sp. How can a man forget his own name? There must be something the matter with him.

Dr. What did they call your father? What did your father do?

Mr. G. Was he a farmer?

Sp. No, he was not a farmer, but he had some land. We were further down from that college, where that church was. My father was a German.

Mr. G. Was he a Mennonite?

Sp. No, my father came where they were, but went further back. What is the matter with me? Why can't I think what my name is?

Mr. G. Tom will tell you, if you ask him.

Sp. I can get certain places and things, then I can't go any further. I remember Fred, because everybody called me that.

Dr. Well, I wouldn't worry about it any more. Your memory will come back to you. You are a spirit and when you leave here intelligent spirits will take care of you.

Sp. Tom says he is going to take me to a home for rest. I have been so worried, and I get so tired out that I get mad at everything. I will not be angry any more. Whenever I got mad I suffered terribly after it. I always felt so bad because I could not control myself. I always felt so sorry I said such mean things, and I was too proud to acknowledge it, but I knew it, just the same.

Tom says: "Come on, we must go." I want to go now. (To Mr. G.) Tom says I must ask you if you will forgive me for making so much mischief for you.

Mr. G. We are going to help you, and let bygones be bygones.

Sp. You are not mad at me, are you?

Mr. G. Not at all.

Sp. I feel so weak, what will I do? I am too weak to go with Tom.

Dr. That weakness is a common experience with spirits when they begin to understand. It is only a temporary sensation; you are merely losing control. Think yourself with Tom and the Mercy Band of spirits.

Sp. My head feels so funny! Am I going crazy? You had better get a doctor because I think I am going to die.

Dr. You will be all right as soon as you leave this body.

Sp. I need a doctor, for the blood is all coming up in my throat and I can't breathe! I feel so choked. Maybe I can get to sleep. Doctors always say if you can sleep it is better, when you feel weak. I am not going to die, am I?

Dr. You must remember that you are a spirit and are controlling a mortal body.

Sp. Fred Haupt is my name. Tom says I must ask you to forgive me because I have made so much trouble in getting you in a temper.

Mr. G. Certainly I forgive you. Thank Tom for helping both you and me.

Sp. Goodbye.

Silver Star, the Indian guide of Mrs. Wickland, then came in and said to Mr. G.:

"We got the man! Now we are going to take him to a hospital. We worked hard to get him; he was so in your magnetic aura that it seemed like taking a piece out of your body to detach him from you.

"He had been with you for a long time; he was with you when you were a child. When things did not go right for him he flew into a temper. It will be a great relief to have him away, and you will feel like a new person. You will not feel so irritable.

"He has been working on you nearly all your life, but lately he has become stronger and stronger, until he almost had control of you.

"Now we have him and he won't bother you any more. He is very weak and needs hospital care; he can hardly walk. He will have to be nursed. He has been living on you, and with that strength taken away from him he is very weak, but he will he taken care of."

THIRTY YEARS AMONG THE DEAD

Chapter XII

Selfishness

Those whose earthly interests have been superficial, who have been dominated by pride, vanity, greed, ambition and selfishness, are held in the earth sphere after transition until these tendencies have been conquered and love and sympathy have been developed through service for others. Frequently spirits whose earth lives were spent in pursuit of pleasure and the pastimes of wealthy society have attained realization of a higher life through our psychic circle. Among these was one who sank with the "Titanic" in 1912.

EXPERIENCE, OCTOBER 22, 1916

Spirit: JOHN J. A. Psychic: MRS. WICKLAND

After the spirit of W. T. Stead had visited with us a few moments, another spirit came in, struggling desperately, as if swimming, and called loudly for aid.

Spirit: Help! Help!!

Doctor: Where did you come from?

Sp. That man who just left told me to come in here.

Dr. Have you been in the water?

Sp. I drowned, but I have come to life again. I cannot see that man now, but I heard him talking and he told me to step in. He said that you know the way and would teach me, and that I could go with him afterwards. But now I cannot see him. I'm blind! I'm blind! I don't know whether the water blinded me or not, but I am blind.

Dr. That is only spiritual blindness. When a person passes out of his physical body without a knowledge of the laws of the higher life, he finds himself in a condition of darkness. It is the darkness of ignorance.

Sp. Then I will not always be blind?

Dr. You must realize that you are in the spirit world and that spirit friends are here who will teach you how to progress out of your condition of darkness.

Sp. I can see a little now. For a while I could see, but the door was shut again and I could not see through. I was with my wife and child for a time, but no one noticed me. But now the door is closed and I am out in the cold. I am all alone when I go to my home. Changes seem to have taken place. I do not know what I shall do.

Dr. You have not realized your own situation.

Sp. What is the matter anyway? What is causing this darkness? What can I do to get out of it? I never was so handicapped as I am now. I was all right for just a minute. I hear somebody talking. There, now I see him again. Was it Mr. Stead?

Dr. Mr. Stead was speaking through this instrument just before you came. Mr. Stead probably brought you here for help. It is our work to awaken earthbound spirits who are in darkness.

Sp. This darkness is terrible. I have been in this darkness for a long time.

Dr. Understand that there is no death. Life continues in the spirit world, where each one must serve others in order to progress.

Sp. I really was not what I should have been. I just lived for self. I wanted amusement and to spend money. But now all I have seen is my past, and I have been in the darkness, and it is terrible. Every act of my past stands before me, and I want to run away from it, but I cannot. It is there all the time and accuses me, because I could have done differently. I have seen so many places where I could have done good, but now it seems too late.

Dr. When a person lives for self alone he usually finds himself in darkness when he passes over to the other side of life. You must obtain understanding of the glories of the spirit world and realize that life there is service to others. That is the true "Heaven" -it is a condition of mind.

Sp. Why are not these things taught in the world?

Dr. Would the world listen? Humanity as a whole does not look for the spiritual side of life, but looks for other things. The world is seeking for amusement and for selfish gain, not for truth.

Sp. There is such a queer feeling coming over me! Mother! Mother my loving mother! (Spirit.) I am a man, but I feel like a child in your arms again. I have been longing for you, but I have been living all by myself in the terrible darkness. Why is it that I should be in the dark? Cannot my eyes be cured? Will I be blind all the time? Isn't it strange that I can see you, yet I seem to be blind?

Dr. You have a spiritual body now, and when your spiritual eyes are opened you will see the beautiful things of the spirit world.

Sp. I see Mr. Stead there. We were both on the same boat, but he does not seem to be in the dark.

Dr. He understood the truth of spirit return and life on the other side while he was on earth. Life is a school and we must learn all we can about the spirit side of life while we are on earth, for the only light we have when we pass to the other side is the knowledge pertaining to life's problems which we have gathered here.

Sp. Why did no one ever tell me these things?

Dr. Would you have listened to any one who would have tried to talk to you on these subjects?

Sp. No one ever approached me with such ideas.

Dr. What year do you think this is?

Sp. 1912.

THIRTY YEARS AMONG THE DEAD

Dr. It is 1916.

Sp. Where have I been? I have been very hungry and cold. I had a very great deal of money, but lately when I have wanted some to spend I could not get hold of it. Sometimes I seemed to be shut up in a room, very dark, and I could see nothing but a procession of my past life. I was not a bad man, but you probably know what society people are. I did not know until now what it was to be poor. It is a new experience to me. Why should humanity not be taught differently before death? Then there would not be such suffering as I am in now.

Dr. If you will go with your mother and other spirit friends and try to understand what they tell you, you will feel much happier.

Sp. I can see Mr. Stead. I met him on the boat but I had no use for his teachings. I thought he was old and that he had a hobby. You know when people get old they have hobbies of one kind or another. I never had time for such things, because all I thought of was my money and society. We do not see the poor people and we do not care to see them. I could do so differently now, but money is of no use to me any longer. My mother is waiting for me and I should like to go with her, for I have not seen her for years, and it is so good to see her. She says she could not reach me, for I was like a crazy man and would not listen to her. Bless you all for the help you have been to me, and for having opened my eyes. It is misery to be blind, yet able to see the procession of your past life, and not be able to see or hear anything else.

Dr. We should like to know your name.

Sp. I am John J. A., and I am glad I met you all. I am so grateful for what you have told me. Now I can see and hear, and understand something that I did not know existed. My mother and friends are coming for me, and now I am going through that beautiful gate into what will be to me Heaven. I again thank you all, and hope some day to come and see you again. Goodbye.

A few weeks later the foregoing spirit brought a friend, another member of New York's aristocracy, who had met his death at the sinking of the "Lusitania."

EXPERIENCE, NOVEMBER 5, 1916

Spirit: ALFRED V. Psychic: MRS. WICKLAND

Spirit: Somebody told me to come in here and I would get warm.

Doctor: What is your name?

Sp. Alfred V. I was on a boat. John J. A. came and told me he would try to help me get in here. He said if I would come in here I would get help. Say, I have never been hungry in my life before, but I am both hungry and cold, and my clothes are all wet.

Dr. That is only a condition of your mind. You have lost your physical body and should not feel the need of food.

Sp. I know I drowned and I have been in misery ever since.

Dr. If you had an understanding of the life hereafter and of progression in the spirit world you would soon find happiness through serving others.

Sp. I never was happy. I suppose I had my own way too much, yet sometimes I felt, what was the use. But I thought: "Just forget yourself and have a good time." You may not care for society life, but in society you can drown yourself in gaiety. I really did not care for society life.

THIRTY YEARS AMONG THE DEAD

I used to forget myself with my horses. If you have a beautiful horse he is faithful to you through life. But when you get into society, women just show you one side -smiles, and sometimes they hate you.

The love I know most is the love of a beautiful, faithful horse. Horses were my pleasure and I felt they loved me. Women liked me only for what I could do for them; they wanted money and pleasure. Women wanted all the money they could get from me. I let go of things and tried to lose myself in pleasure, but I was not happy.

Society does not know anything about honor and respectability. If I could find people as faithful and true as my horse was to me, I tell you I would thank you for that society. But go into the kind of society I have known, and men and women are nothing. I was a sport myself, but there were things that drove me to forget that little thing within me, conscience. I longed for something that was good, but where can you find it?

Not amongst society, but amongst horses. Society is all right if you want that kind of a life. You will probably realize that I developed a great deal of selfishness.

Dr. You must try now to forget your past life with all its sorrow and bitterness. Look for higher things; then your spiritual eyes will be opened.

Sp. Friends that took an interest in me brought me here, and my eyes have been opened since I came. I feel that probably -but I am not sure -a time may come when I can be happy. I have never been really happy, for when a child I had my own way too much. I thank you for allowing me to come here. If I ever am truly happy I will come back and tell you so.

A sequel to the above occurred several years later, when John J. A., and Alfred V., brought to our circle a friend of theirs, Anna H., stage celebrity.

EXPERIENCE, SEPTEMBER 8, 1918

Spirit: ANNA H. Psychic: MRS. WICKLAND

Spirit: Water! Please, water! (A glass of water was given and eagerly taken.) Thank you so much! I have been very sick and am still weak. The doctors really do not know what is the matter with me. They said I must be kept quiet. My legs and arms pain me so.

Doctor We will relieve your pain. (Manipulating arms of psychic.)

Sp. Be very careful about my bones. I want to retain my beautiful form. I want to get well and return to my work. I have been very sick, and I am still very weak.

Dr. What is your name?

Sp. My name is Anna H.

Dr. How did you come to Los Angeles?

Sp. I am not in Los Angeles. I am in New York.

Dr. Who brought you here?

Sp. I thought I had a dream and that Alfred V. came and spoke to me. He always liked me, but he is dead. Now he says that I must wake up. I am so sick. My bones, my bones! I don't want to lose my beautiful form. I feel that I am commencing to get better and stronger. Will I live now, and can I perform again and do my work? I do not want to lose my beautiful form.

Dr. You will never perform on the physical plane again.

Sp. I hope to. Alfred V. bothered me so much, but he is dead.

Dr. Does he look as though he were dead?

Sp. He seems to be very well, but I thought I was dreaming. Why, here is John J. A., too! They are both dead.

Dr. So are you.

Sp. When did I die?

Dr. A short time ago.

Sp. Alfred says that they do missionary work to wake up spirits. But they do not believe in such things as spirits. I don't want to die.

Dr. Nobody actually "dies."

Sp. Of course they do. The doctors said I could never get well. I fought and fought to live. I want to live. I want to overcome my sickness and get well again, and I want to retain my beautiful form.

Dr. From now on you must try to develop a beautiful spirit.

Sp. The two men want me to go with them to find understanding.

Dr. They have found the truth through this little circle. They were very poor spiritually before they came here, but became rich, through an understanding of a more beautiful life than they had here on earth.

Sp. What is this place? They say it is the Gate to the Understanding of Real Life -The Gateway.

(Noticing dress.) This dress does not fit well. (Touching neck and shoulders.) This is not my neck, or face, or form. They say I am weak yet, but I am to go with them and they will show me the way, but that I have much to learn.

Dr. Did you ever ask yourself: "What is Mind?"

Sp. No. I just wanted my beautiful form. If it were not for my beautiful form and acting I could not have attracted people to me and earned my living. There are quite a few people here. (Spirits.) Alfred said if I came here he would bring me to my relations, and to a beautiful home beyond the grave.

Dr. What do they call that place?

Sp. I do not like the name, but they say, "The Spirit World." They say that is the home beyond the grave. They say I shall have to overcome my earthly condition before I can open my psychic eyes. I do not know what they mean. They say if I go with them I will find beautiful conditions after I have understanding, but that I shall have to overcome a great deal of self and live for others. Alfred says that we lived for society and ourselves, and we have to suffer for it. He says I must go, but I cannot, for I am very sick.

Dr. Your body was sick, but you have lost that body. It is in the East.

Sp. I feel better now than I did a while ago.

THIRTY YEARS AMONG THE DEAD

Dr. My wife is a psychic sensitive, and you are speaking through her body. Alfred V. and John J. A. at one time controlled her body as you are now doing.

Sp. My bones are so sore.

Dr. That is only in your mind. Mind is not the body. Mind is invisible. We do not see you at all; you are invisible to us.

Sp. (Touching face.) This is not my face, and I don't want this form. I want my beautiful form.

Dr. It will be your duty to serve others in the spirit world.

Sp. These people want me to go with them. They took quite an interest in me and my work. My pains seem to be leaving me. Will you please tell me how I could come here when you are all strangers to me? I do not know why I should be here tonight. I feel so well now.

Dr. We are carrying on experimental work to learn what becomes of the dead. My wife is a psychic and you are controlling her body.

Sp. Alfred says I must go. I thought I had a dream and that I was going to die, but I fought and fought for a long time. I did not want to die, so I used all my will power to live as long as I could. One day I felt very weak and I went to sleep for quite a while, but I woke up again, as I wanted to live. They thought I was dead, but I was not. I had only gone to sleep. I wanted to live because life is dear to me, but I was sick so long and suffered so severely.

I went to sleep again and I slept a long time, and when I woke up it was all dark, and I could not see anything at all. Everything was dark, dark, dark. I could not find any light and it was so dark. I felt so distressed -all dark. I thought then I went to sleep again, and as I slept I dreamed Alfred V. and John J. A. came to me and said: "Anna, wake up! We are here to help you. Come with us. Come!" I thought I was waking up, but I was so sick, so sick, that I could not go with them. My crippled body was so sick.

They said: "We will take you to a place where you will have a new body, and you will be well and strong. Come with us to a more beautiful world than this." Here I am, all well and strong. Will I not have those terrible pains again? They are so hard on me. I felt I must not eat too much, or drink too much, or I would not be able to retain my beautiful form. I would not eat meat, because I would get too fat, and I must eat just enough to retain the roundness of my form.

What have I now? Why did I not do more helpful things? Life was so sweet. I liked to be flattered and I liked to have admirers. It is so hard to lose your admirers.

Dr. Do Alfred V. and J. A. flatter you now?

Sp. No. They do not look as they used to. There is a seriousness about them. They look so sincere that I feel different with them. While to me they look much younger, I know they are older. They do not say to me as they did once: "Come along and have a good time."

Life was very sweet while I had admirers. But I suffered for my vanity. The doctors said if I had not laced so much I would not have been so sick. I would not mind the doctors either. They wanted me to eat to get strength, but I was afraid if I lay there and ate, and did not get my regular massage and baths, I could not keep my form, so I starved myself.

When I was in the dark Alfred came to me and said: "Come I will show you something far more beautiful than a beautiful form and selfishness and vanity. They are only shadows. Now come, and we will show you why we should live for others. You will be beautiful again when you have served others, but you must forget self and overcome all selfishness."

Now I must serve and I must help.

Suddenly the spirit lost control and was gone.

Two years later, after Anna H. had brought the spirits of Olive T.20 and Anna D. to our circle, she spoke to us again.

EXPERIENCE, SEPTEMBER 22, 1920

Spirit: ANNA H. Psychic: MRS. WICKLAND

Good Evening. I came here tonight to thank you for what you have done for me. I am now very happy. I only lived for myself and for my body and beauty. I lived only for a good time.

When you live for a good time you are not really happy. You are always afraid that some one will shine brighter than yourself, or that some one will take your place and charm away your admirers. Here in this room I found harmony, when I was in such darkness. I could not see anything except all the promises I had made and broken, and I felt sad.

Now I have understanding of the real life. The real life is to serve others, to do good for others, to help others; then you yourself will have help. This brings happiness, which is "Heaven" -it is the Heaven of Contentment. When I first came here I was very sad and gloomy. I had only thought of self, with never a thought of God, our Maker. We should all think of Him and learn to know Him.

He is the, one we should pray to and we should try to realize what life is. We should learn to know, not be satisfied with blind belief. Learn to understand God in His truest sense. I was once quite a church-going girl. I believed and believed and condemned others, and thought if you did not do so and so you would be lost. That is the reason many fall by the wayside.

People only have time for amusement. They do not go to church. Why are they not taught to understand the real Christ spirit? Give them innocent amusement of one kind or another, and do not keep them wrapped in gloom, praying and praying all the time. They fall. They want to go to church and they want to have a good time, but they are taught that if they do not go to church and pray they will fall lower and lower and they will be condemned, not by God, but condemned by the people.

If a girl falls, who will raise her up? Does the church do this work? No; churches will not have anything to do with her, because they say she is bad. They say: "We do not want our daughters to go about with her or be seen in her company, because she will make them bad."

Since churches teach the Gospel of Christ, why should they not help such a soul to rise? Christ did not accuse the fallen woman. He said that he who was without sin should cast the first stone. Because a woman had fallen, accusers stood ready to throw stones at her. When Christ spoke, the accusers went away. Then what did Christ do? He took her hand, lifted her up and said: "Where are your accusers? Go and sin no more."

He meant she should try to enter a new life and do better. But society will not have her. The churches will not have her. She is down. Where will she go? Where can she go? She has not sinned against any one but herself. Her own self accuses her for what she has done. How can she rise? If she goes to church she will not be helped there. She can only go to the lowest condition where there is a good time and champagne, and try to drown her conscience.

THIRTY YEARS AMONG THE DEAD

Suppose we tell the people that this unfortunate girl has fallen, has had to go into a wild underworld, has been bad, has had no chance to rise, and that her character has gone -will they help her? No, they will not.

We should always try to help others, especially the weak and fallen ones, and try to raise them as Christ taught us. Do not condemn, but raise them to society again, and help them to be honest and sincere. Then we shall convert the world of men as well as women.

Men are also greatly to blame for trying to ruin poor innocent little girls. Just because a girl has a beautiful face and has charms men should not praise and flatter. They ruin the girl. The man goes back to society but the girl goes lower and lower. She cannot go back to her former life but has to remain where she is. If you could see the lower life of Paris you would shudder and realize that that is hell. People who go there have lost their pride, their senses. The women there have lost all modesty.

They do not believe in God; they do not believe in the Christian religion any more, because the Christian religion and its people have driven them to what they are. They think there is no God and so they can do whatever they wish. Let us try to help these unfortunates. I am now working in the slums of earthbound spirits. I am serving. There was a time when I would not soil my hands to help anybody, because I had to be waited on. I had my maid, and if I were not waited on at once, just when I wanted things, I scolded and was very irritable.

Now I wait on the lowest with the true spirit of Christ, who taught us to serve others and love others as ourselves and God above all things. When the one who has fallen by the wayside is given true understanding, then that soul will serve, and his love for his fellow man will be much stronger than that of the one who does not have that understanding. One who has always had a good home, gone to church and is pure and good, knows nothing of evil.

Let us all understand our Maker, the God of us all. Our Maker is God for the one who has fallen just as much as for the pure. God is Love. When you have shining in your heart that light of love which is the love of God -not love as people understand it, lukewarm, sentimental love, but love which has suffered and which understands, which does not ask anything, which sacrifices and will serve from the lowest to the highest -that is real, true love.

When people are crushed we should raise them again with love and sympathy, then we could not condemn any one. God does not condemn. Why should we? God loves all his children. He has given them all free will to go their own way for a while until they are ready to say: "Not my will any longer, but Thine."

Each one of us has had experience in one way or another, but let us all look to God, and let the love of God and understanding so shine in our souls that each will he a part of that divine spirit of love. No minister, no one, can reach you, but you yourself will have to see and feel what God really is. Then you will sin no more.

That is Heaven; that is Bliss. It is beautiful, it is harmonious. When each understands the other in God's love, then there is peace and harmony; but you will have to feel this beautiful condition, which we call Heaven, within you. You cannot be contented in this beautiful condition unless you help others. We stand by our brothers and sisters. We call them so through love of God.

Say to those in misery: "Let me reach my hand down to you and I will help you to an understanding of the true love of God and you, too, will shine in this Heaven of Love." From your own home in the spirit world you reach down to the lower plane and you see some here, some there, in all kinds of agony. Some have taken their own lives because of disappointment in love. Others are overcome by sickness. Others are all crippled.

Others are being punished by conscience. Through lack of understanding they pray and pray and sing. They are only ignorant. They pray to the personal God they believe in, but the poor things do not understand the truth. Others are earthbound because of their belief. They do not want to talk to you because you do not belong to their church. They say: "I do not want to have anything to do with you. You stay there, and I will stay here," and the praying and singing goes on.

They do not know that they have passed out, neither do they know of the wonderful God of Understanding. When you have understanding, the knowledge of God will shine in your heart. I am in the spirit world now, and it is all so beautiful, but I would not have had all this happiness so soon had I not come here and been given understanding. I would not have had it if I had not served. I have brought many here who were crippled through lack of understanding and they received light.

These two young girls, Olive T. and her little friend, Anna D., who both took their own lives, are ones whom I will look after. I could do nothing with them, because they knew I was dead. Their fear of me kept me from them. They shunned me. I could not reach them. I did not want them to go to any other place. I did not want them to go to earth life and obsess some one.

I brought both of them here tonight and I shall take them to my home in the spirit world. I will take care of them and help them to an understanding, and some day they may come and thank you as I have come to thank you tonight. Let us all have an understanding of truth. Do not only believe. Belief is all right, but to your belief add knowledge and understanding of God's wonderful love.

Do not let others tell you they will save you, because they cannot do it. You will have to find the saving spirit within yourself. When the love of understanding shines in your heart you will realize the wisdom of God. Then you will not need to think that God is in His "Heaven." He is here, there and everywhere. He is in the drop of water, He is in the flowers; all are a part of His wonderful work. Let us worship Him and let us see Him with open eyes, and we will be happy.

Thank you for allowing me to come.

Goodbye.

In Chicago we had known two Jewish ladies, Mrs. Sr. and Mrs. Simons, who were excellent friends, although the latter was somewhat tyrannical in her exactions. She particularly disapproved of the automatic writing which her friend was experimenting with, declaring that Spiritualism was a fraud, since after death everyone became a flower, a bird, or a tree.

Mrs. Simons passed away in the presence of her friend, suffering from dropsy and intense lumbago pains. A number of years later, when Mrs. Sr. was in California, she developed melancholia and was afflicted so severely with pains in her back that she could not walk erectly.

After spending three weeks in the hospital without any improvement she came to us and after the following experience, during a circle at which Mrs. Sr. was present, she was entirely relieved.

THIRTY YEARS AMONG THE DEAD

EXPERIENCE, OCTOBER 27, 1919

Spirit: MRS. SIMONS Patient: MRS. SR

Psychic: MRS. WICKLAND

The controlling entity groaned and immediately placed hands on back, apparently in great pain.

Doctor: Are you in trouble? Have you lost your body without understanding it?

Spirit: I don't know.

Dr. We can relieve your pain. Tell us who you are.

Sp. I don't know.

Dr. Surely you know your own name.

Sp. I cannot think.

Dr. How long have you been dead?

Sp. I don't know if I am dead.

Dr. What did your friends call you?

Sp. Mrs. Simons.

Dr. Where did you live?

Sp. Chicago.

Dr. Where did you live in Chicago?

Sp. It's a long time ago, and I don't know. I have not felt just right.

Dr. In what way?

Sp. I felt so small, and was so uncomfortable.

Dr. Do you realize that you were interfering with some one?

Sp. I know that I am in such a stupor. I don't feel natural.

Dr. Do you know the reason for that?

Sp. No.

Dr. You did not believe in spirits, did you?

Sp. No, and I don't believe it yet.

Dr. Then you do not believe in your own self, do you? You thought any one who believed in spirits was foolish. Is it not foolish to be an earthbound spirit? Do you realize that you have been one?

Mrs. Sr. Do you know me?

Sp. I know that voice; it belongs to a friend of mine.

Dr. Where is she?

Sp. In Chicago.

Dr. What was her business?

Sp. I don't know. Everything is so dark and I cannot remember anything. I know that voice, but I cannot tell you who it belongs to. I cannot remember her name at all, but I knew her in Chicago. She used to call and see me. My friend was always like sunshine to me. She helped me.

Dr. What did she do?

Sp. She always came with such a nice cheerful disposition, but she got interested in Spiritualism once. I told her not to bother with it because there was nothing in it. I would not have anything to do with that. I miss her so. I only see her once in a while. I feel so little and uncomfortable. To save my life I cannot think of her name.

Dr. What was her first name?

Sp. It comes to me now! It was R. Something ails my memory and things are so queer to me. Once in a while I get a glimpse of light, then I feel I am locked up in a small place. You know I am a big woman and in that little place (aura of patient) I was so crowded that I had no feeling.

Dr. Did you get warmed up occasionally?

Sp. Yes, once in a while. I do not know what is the matter, but something burns me sometimes. (Static treatment given patient.) Now it is all dark, dark. I do not see a thing. I do not know which is the best, the fire, or being crowded so that I got no breath. I could not breathe. I do not know why it is. But I seemed to have gotten a shock.

Dr. Did you die from a shock?

Sp. I cannot tell that I am dead because I do not feel dead. I have had fire, and sometimes it was like thunder, shooting pain.

Mrs. Sr. Do you remember Dr. Wickland?

Sp. Yes.

Mrs. Sr. Do you remember that machine he had?

Sp. The one that shot fire?

Mrs. Sr. Yes, and that is the fire you feel.

Sp. Why, I didn't take treatments from him.

Mrs. Sr. You have been bothering me all these years.

Sp. Why did I bother you?

Mrs. Sr. Have Doctor explain it to you.

Dr. It is not hard to explain. You are now a spirit and have been hovering around your friend. That is why you feel uncomfortable. You are not in Chicago now, you are in California. You are in Los Angeles, California. Don't you remember Mrs. Sr?

Sp. Yes, she was in Chicago.

Dr. You are both in Los Angeles now.

Sp. I was in Chicago. I always had pains in my legs, and very often in my head.

Mrs. S. You gave me those pains lately.

Dr. You loaned Mrs. Sr. your pains.

Sp. No, you are mistaken in that.

Mrs. Sr. Do you remember Mrs. Wickland of Chicago -Dr. Wickland's wife? Do you remember she was a psychic?

Sp. I don't seem to remember. It is strange I don't know anything.

Mrs. Sr. You thought you knew so much.

Sp. I supposed I knew. You meddled with that foolish thing, Spiritualism, and I did not want to have anything to do with it. Have you been fooling with it again?

Mrs. Sr. No, you have been fooling with me.

Sp. No, I did not want to have anything to do with that; there is nothing in it. I didn't like that fire -I could not stand it. It chased me away. I suffered terribly. When I was chased out I was locked up in a new room.

Dr. You were locked up in a room of ignorance.

Mrs. Sr. It is a long time since you died.

Sp. I am not dead.

Dr. Look at this hand. Is that yours? You are using another body now. You are proving that what you thought was humbug is true.

Mrs. Sr. Do you know what year it is Mrs. Simons?

Sp. I don't know anything. Where is my home? Where is my girl?

Mrs. Sr. Your girl is not here. You are in Los Angeles, California.

Sp. No, now you are a little off. Mrs. Sr., don't you know you are in Chicago?

Mrs. Sr. I have been here in California for six and one-half years.

Sp. We are in Chicago. Such a foolish woman! She is hypnotized and wants to have me believe such a story.

Dr. Wouldn't you like to understand matters? You have been dead a good many years, and were hovering around your friend, Mrs. Sr. You were driven away from her by electricity. Now you are allowed to control my wife's body temporarily so you may acquire understanding. Do you know anything about the purpose of life? Did that ever interest you? No, therefore you think there could not be anything in a higher life. You call yourself Mrs. Simons. This body belongs to Mrs. Wickland and she is in Los Angeles, California. You claim you are in Chicago and we cannot convince you of the facts. You have been obsessing Mrs. Sr.

Sp. I came to her because it was so dark. It seems I had been sleeping for a while, then I woke up. I saw a light, then I was here. I could see just a little light if I could be with her.

Dr. You got into her magnetic aura and made her suffer. In order to get you out I applied electricity to her.

Mrs. Sr. Do you know what I told Doctor? I told him to give you that electricity.

Sp. You have no sympathy for a poor old, lady like me.

Dr. Would you have liked to have an earthbound spirit control your body?

Sp. I will not listen to you.

Dr. You are willing to bother your friend.

Sp. I do not know whether I have been bothering her. I have only been around her to see light.

Dr. Then how did you happen to get the electricity when I gave it to her? I have never treated you.

Mrs. Sr. By right you ought to pay Dr. Wickland for that treatment, Mrs. Simons.

Sp. Tell me one thing -how did I come here? I do not think you are right, Mrs. Sr., but if you should be, how did you come to California?

Mrs. Sr. By paying my railroad fare I came here. Did you pay anything?

Sp. I never paid anything, so how did I get here? I don't believe it anyhow -you cannot say that to me! I am in Chicago, and Mrs. Sr. was never in California.

Dr. Do you hear that rumble? That is a train leaving Los Angeles for Chicago.

Sp. That is the Northwestern train.

Dr. There is no Northwestern out here. What do you gain by arguing? When you understand the situation you will appreciate what I am trying to tell you. What would you think of a person who refused to understand life, who has been dead seven or eight years, whose body is lost and in the grave, and who is an ignorant spirit, bothering one who was formerly a friend?

Sp. I cannot see how that is.

Dr. We are telling you facts.

Mrs. Sr. Your body was buried in Waltheim Cemetery six or eight years ago.

Sp. I have been sleeping. I woke up with very severe pains and I could not move very well, and I felt so crowded.

Dr. That was because Mrs. Sr.'s body is smaller than yours, and you have been obsessing her.

Sp. How could I get in that body? I felt I could hardly move. I have to find out what you are talking about. I don't believe it. I want to know what object you have to say such things?

Dr. Did you ever study Life at all?

Sp. I studied trees and Nature.

Dr. Did you ever observe how the tree grows? It is wonderful. God puts life into it and it grows. What is life?

Sp. God, I suppose.

Dr. Have you ever seen mind?

THIRTY YEARS AMONG THE DEAD

Sp. Mind is mind.

Dr. Have you ever seen mind?

Sp. No, you could not talk if you had no mind.

Dr. Mind is invisible, isn't it?

Sp. I haven't seen it.

Dr. Suppose we tell you that you are invisible to us. When I speak to you I can see only my wife's body.

Sp. Your wife's body? Mrs. Sr., what is the matter? Have I lost my body?

Mrs. Sr. Yes, you have.

Dr. Only your stubbornness keeps you in the dark.

Sp. I haven't seen or heard anything. There was a time, I tell you, when I walked on and on, but always in the dark, and it seemed like I never could get there. I rested, then I kept on walking. At first I could see just a little light, and it seems like it came to me in a flash-"Mrs. Sr.!" I thought, "Yes, she was a friend of mine" and then I could see her.

Dr. You transferred yourself by thought.

Sp. Then I had a terrible pain. I thought I had lost all my pain for a little while. I woke up and felt no pain at first, but when I got to that light all the pain came back.

Dr. You had pain when you had your body. You must understand you are a spirit, invisible to us. When an earthbound spirit comes in touch with a mortal body he again has the pains he passed out with. You got in touch with Mrs. Sr., and had your mortal pains again. You have caused trouble. You were selfish and you have not gained anything by it. In the spirit world you will have to serve others. Realize that you are now a spirit; you no longer have a physical body. Why did you not become a tree as you expected to?

Mrs. Sr. Your body is buried in Waltheim Cemetery, Chicago. Go to the cemetery and see if you have a tombstone there.

Sp. I don't want to go and examine my tombstone in the cemetery.

Dr. Did you go to church?

Sp. I believed that when I died there was nothing more. I didn't want to have such foolish thoughts as you had, Mrs. Sr. I had my own ideas and did not need yours.

Dr. God created the world but you did not investigate anything.

Sp. (In great excitement.) My God! My God I see my mother! (Spirit.) Why, she is in her grave -yes, many years ago! It must be a ghost. She looks so beautiful.

Dr. She did not limit her mind as you did. She did not want to be a tree. You must be willing to learn. Jesus said: "Except ye become as little children ye shall not enter into the kingdom of Heaven."

Sp. (Of Jewish faith.) I do not believe in Jesus.

Dr. What you believe, or what you do not believe, has nothing to do with the fact of life.

THIRTY YEARS AMONG THE DEAD

Sp. Mother, is that really you? Why, look at that beautiful road, with beautiful trees and flowers! See that beautiful garden and those beautiful houses, and my mother walking around.

Dr. Your mother is not a tree, is she?

Sp. Now she is walking on that beautiful road. She says: "Come, this is my home." Her home, but not mine. Can't I go with my mother?

Dr. Ignorance cannot enter the "Kingdom of Heaven."

Sp. Look at that steep hill which I have to climb! I cannot climb that hill with the big body I have. Mother says: "No, you cannot climb it with your body, but you have to climb the hill of understanding, and you must forget yourself. Forget that you have existed in your selfishness. You must serve." I know; I. know. Yes, I was selfish. Mother, I will try, but help me! Help me up there! I cannot do it alone. (Crying.)

I cannot stay in this misery any longer! Take me, take me, Mother, with you. Take me with you and show me! She says I must work and not be lazy as I was in life and expect everybody to do something for me. If they did not do what I wanted then I got angry.

My mother says: "Now you have to serve. You have to work to climb this hill of understanding to a higher life. You have now to learn the first lesson of life, the lesson of understanding, and you will have to go up that hill until you have gotten away from all selfishness, jealousy and envy. You must do that.

"You must also ask forgiveness for what you have done to your old friend. You will have to do it," my mother says. "You will have to be forgiven. (Crying.) No, you must ask for forgiveness, because you have been selfish, very selfish. All thoughts of self must be thrown away, and you must live for others. I am your mother, but I cannot take you to my home yet, because you must learn."

(Doubtfully.) She says she is my mother -but I do not know. Yes -I believe it must be, but she looks so beautiful.

Dr. That is because she is filled with the spirit of truth.

Sp. Mrs. Sr., if I ask you to forgive me, will you forgive me?

Mrs. Sr. I surely will. You didn't know any better.

Sp. You have helped me to light, and it was because of you that I reached this understanding.

Mrs. S. You must thank the Wicklands for it.

Sp. I don't feel like thanking them for it. Mother says I must, because I would still be in that terrible pain and agony but for them. She says I got into your magnetic aura with a mind full of pain and selfishness and envy. Love was not in me, except selfish love, and she says now I must have love for others and not self. Forget self and work for others, then, she says, I will be happy.

Dr. "Love is the fulfillment of the law."

Sp. I don't know. I didn't have much interest in those things. I now see myself as I was. I was a bundle of selfishness. Mrs. Sr., I must also ask you to forgive me because many times I spoke to you in a very rude way, and I was selfish. I felt people should always come to see me and they had to do it. I see now my selfishness.

THIRTY YEARS AMONG THE DEAD

Mrs. Sr., please forgive me. I ask it now from my heart. I see now, but before I did not want to see it, because that was putting my past life before me, and how I had lived for self. I do not want that evil, ugly, homely body of mine, which they (guiding intelligences) show me. That is not my body.

Dr. That is your spiritual body, for you have made no other. You have made a spiritual body of only selfishness and jealousy.

Sp. It is all crippled and wrinkled.

Dr. You will have to alter it by your good acts for others. You will have to wear the garment you made until you have earned another.

Sp. To think I should have to wear such an ugly, homely, old fool thing! That -that spiritual body of mine -just because I did not do anybody any good!

Dr. You will have to wear that and be happy until you have learned how to earn another, and to climb the hill of understanding and wisdom.

Sp. So I have to live now in that awful body of mine. I have to get in.

Dr. Serve -serve your fellow man.

Sp. I will be brave, and I will try, because now I see what I should have done, but I did not do it. They say it is not too late, and I will try to wear that body, all wrinkled and so homely. They tell me I can soon wear it out by good acts, and each time I do some good act, some wrinkles will be taken away, and there will be a change for the better. I will try to be happy. It is hard. Mrs. Sr., help me!

Dr. We will all help you.

Sp. Give me some little sympathy because I have to be in that terrible, homely body of mine that I have made only by selfishness and hate. I will wear it until I can do better. I need help and strength so that I can stand it.

Mrs. Sr., forgive me. They say I have done harm to you, and that now I have to wear that homely body and have to serve you. I will serve you and help you. My first lesson will be how to be kind. I will, I will.

Dr. You will find many good friends who will help you. Ask the intelligent spirits to help you. Will you ask them?

Sp. Yes, I will. They say I must thank you for those thunder shots.

Dr. Do you believe in spirits now?

Sp. I must, I suppose. Don't be like I was, selfish, but do what you can so that you will not have to get into a crippled-up body like mine. They say, no one can help us to work out our own salvation. Make your spirit body more beautiful than mine. Now I will go and begin my work. Goodbye.

Miss F. H., a talented young musician, of gentle disposition, was a student in college when she suddenly became violent and destructive, tore her clothes into shreds and struck every one who came near her.

She was finally placed in a sanitarium, kept in a locked room for some time and her case diagnosed as dementia praecox. When brought to our Institute she had become almost a skeleton.

At this time she declared constantly her name was not Miss H. but that she was Margaret Young, of England, and had two children.

One noon, as Miss H. was seated at the table, Mrs. Wickland clairvoyantly saw the spirit of a newsboy take possession of the patient and reach eagerly for food, exclaiming: "Gee whiz! I'm hungry! I haven't had anything to eat for a long time."

His hunger satisfied, the newsboy left, and after this occurrence the spirit of Margaret Young ceased tormenting the patient.

Miss F. H. had with her as companion a younger sister, Miss C. H., who understood obsession and was of great help to her. One afternoon while Miss F. H. was seated at the piano, she suddenly became controlled by a strange entity, but the sister sharply ordered the intruder to leave, and the patient again became herself.

This spirit controlled Mrs. Wickland during a physic circle held that evening, and after this the patient improved rapidly. Within four months she returned to her home, entirely well, graduated from college and later took up music professionally.

EXPERIENCE, OCTOBER 6, 1920

Spirit: ALICE Patient: Miss F. H

Psychic: MRS. WICKLAND

Doctor: Where did you come from?

Spirit: I came here as a visitor.

Dr. Would you please introduce yourself?

Sp. I must find out where I am. I do not know any of you people.

Dr. Will you please tell us who you are?

Sp. I do not know whether I want to tell you who I am.

Dr. Then tell us how long you have been dead.

Sp. Dead?

Dr. Do you understand your situation? Why are you here?

Sp. I do not know what I came here for. Somebody told me to come in here but I do not see any object in coming.

Dr. Perhaps we may learn something from you. You could tell us about your life and present condition. Tell us who you are; introduce yourself.

Sp. Oh, I do not know.

Dr. Who told you to come in here? Do you know the party?

Sp. No. I was walking around trying to find some place. Everything had been so dark and I have been walking such a long time, and I am very tired. I do not want to be talked to. I want to rest.

Dr. You cannot do that because you are a stranger here. Are you a man or a woman?

Sp. That's a very strange question to ask.

Dr. It may seem so to you.

Sp. Can't you see whether I am a man or woman? Don't they dress differently?

Dr. This is a lady's body in this chair. Are you a lady?

Sp. I most certainly am not a man!

Dr. Were you a woman or a girl?

Sp. I have not changed to a man, I tell you.

Dr. You evidently changed your bodily form. If I tell you that this is the body of my wife you would be surprised. Evidently you are still asleep.

Sp. Asleep, this time of day?

Dr. Why not try to understand matters? You know you are in a strange situation. Try to understand it, try to learn the reason. This body is not your own.

Sp. How you talk! I came into this room, and I certainly could not come in without a body. I did not come in like a feather, floating around.

Dr. Do you recognize these hands?

Sp. Those hands belong to me.

Dr. I want you to understand that you are using some one's body temporarily. You do not recognize these hands.

Sp. I am not used to such treatment. (Haughtily.) I used to be in society. (General laughter.) Oh, dear! Everyone is laughing at me. I do not know what to do, it is so provoking.

Dr. Did you have a great deal of wealth when you had your own body?

Sp. Why should I tell you of my affairs?

Dr. Were you only pretending to be aristocratic?

Sp. I never heard such talk before.

Dr. You are a spirit but do not understand your condition.

Sp. I can't see how I happened to come here. (Struggling to leave.)

Dr. You must be sensible and listen to reason.

Sp. Oh, dear! What shall I do? Why should you hold my hands?

Dr. I am not holding your hands. I am holding my wife's hands.

Sp. I am not your wife!

Dr. Ask these persons if this is not my wife.

Sp. I do not know these people and I do not care to.

THIRTY YEARS AMONG THE DEAD

Dr. When you are ready to talk we will talk sensibly.

Sp. You need not dictate to me!

Dr. How long have you been dead?

Sp. Dead? What are you talking about? I have never died.

Dr. You have lost your physical body and have evidently been wandering around for a long time. You are allowed to control my wife's body and you must behave sensibly.

Sp. I do not like that girl with the yellow waist. (Miss C. R., the patient's sister.) She bothers me so very much. She drove me away when I was getting along so nicely. (To Miss C. H.) What right have you to do that to me? I do not like you one bit.

Dr. She probably drove out an earthbound spirit. You do not realize your own condition.

Sp. She chased me away, and I don't like her.

Dr. You were controlling her sister, and she did not like it. You are an earthbound spirit.

Sp. I am no such thing! (Stamping.)

Dr. You are a spirit, ignorant of your actual condition.

Sp. You need not talk to me! I will not listen to you.

Dr. Do you realize that you are using another person's body?

Sp. You certainly are crazy!

Dr. Do you not wish to be helped?

Sp. Do you think I need your help? Why, I came in here just to see what things were. I have been walking so long, and then there was a little light (aura of sensitive) and that girl in the yellow waist talked to me as if she owned the whole earth. Talking to me like that!

Dr. Does it not seem strange to you that you are in the dark?

Sp. I was lost and have been walking around for a long time. It has been very dark and I have felt so badly. I have not seen anything.

Dr. Strive to understand why you are in the dark.

Sp. I heard music (patient at piano) so I thought I would listen to it, and then before I knew it I saw a light, and then came this thing to me (Miss C. H.) and talked as if she owned the earth.

Dr. Let me tell you something. This girl's sister is a psychic sensitive, and has been controlled by different spirits who have disturbed her life. Today she was playing the piano, you listened and got in touch with her magnetic aura. Through that you saw a little light and then you controlled the girl.

Sp. I have never seen you before today, young lady! (To Miss F.H.)

Dr. At the present time you are controlling my wife's body.

Sp. I am sick and tired of hearing that.

Dr. Can't you understand what I am telling you?

Sp. I do not understand it one bit, about controlling. How can I control another body? That is such nonsense.

Dr. My wife is a psychic sensitive and allows spirits to control her body.

Sp. Spiritualists, then? I suppose you are all Spiritualists. I see, I see. They are all crazy, all crazy.

Dr. You are proving the fallacy of your thinking at the present moment. You are a spirit and are using my wife's body.

Sp. Keep still with that wife business. I was never married, and I certainly will not marry you.

Dr. I said this is my wife's body.

Sp. There you are again, insinuating about the wife business! This body belongs to me.

Dr. For a little while only.

Sp. Have you ever seen a person change bodies? What are you talking about?

Dr. Did you ever stop to consider what mind is?

Sp. That belongs to the soul, and the soul is part of the Divine God.

Dr. That sounds very well. Do you understand what God is? I am trying to reach your understanding. You have lost your body, and are now a spirit, absolutely invisible to us.

Sp. Crazy, crazy, crazy! You are the craziest person I ever saw.

Dr. How would you explain the situation?

Sp. That girl came to me with such force and told me to get out, and before I knew it I was gone. I stayed around and tried and tried to get back, because I was not going to be driven out as she thought. I have been watching for another chance to get in again, and here I am, and now you can't drive me out.

Dr. Should not such an experience cause you to think?

Sp. Why should I?

Dr. You realize that you are in a strange condition. You are very selfish; you know that I am telling the truth.

Sp. You have not told me any truth yet.

Dr. Ask one of these gentlemen whose hands I am holding.

Ans. The doctor is holding his wife's hands.

Dr. You are a spirit and are invisible to us. I am holding the hands of Mrs. Wickland.

Sp. How in the world am I Mrs. Wickland?

Dr. You are not Mrs. Wickland. You are only using her body.

Sp. Now you know we cannot change bodies. I know this.

Dr. You have lost your own body and are a spirit.

Sp. Then why did I lose it? If I were dead and had lost my body how in the world could I have been walking around as I have been? I was so hungry for a while and I wanted to get something to eat, but that thing (pointing to Miss C. H.) chased me out. I put up some fight, because I was so hungry.

Dr. It is your body that is dead; you have lost that, but you yourself are not dead. Paul said: "There is a natural body, and there is a spiritual body." You have lost your natural body.

Sp. When did I do that?

Dr. I do not know. After you stepped out of your physical body you continued to live in your spiritual body. You were brought here to obtain an understanding of your condition. When you have that you will not need to walk in the darkness any longer. You will then have an understanding of the spirit life.

Sp. I have been walking but I am on earth, not in Heaven.

Dr. What do you understand "Heaven" to be?

Sp. That is where God is.

Dr. The Bible says: "God is Love," and "Ye are the temple of God and the Spirit of God dwelleth in you." If you have love in your heart then you are a part of God.

Sp. I have always done the very best I could.

Dr. Do you know what year it is? It is 1920. Can you realize that you have been in the dark for some time?

Sp. I have been in the dark and cannot remember things very well.

Dr. That is because you have lost all physical contact, and have no understanding of the higher life. You have been brought here for the purpose of being helped. You can only stay for a short time.

Sp. But where will I go?

Dr. To the spirit world. What is your name?

Sp. I do not know.

Miss C. H. You told it to me this afternoon. You said your name was Mary Bulwer and that you were from Germany.

Sp. I did not say that. You were speaking to my friend at that time. (Another spirit controlling patient.)

Dr. Do you realize where you are now? Do you know that you are in Los Angeles, California?

Sp. No.

Dr. Where do you think you are?

Sp. My friend and I were traveling on the railroad.

Dr. Did something happen?

Sp. We were going to -now I can't remember where. Oh, Mary! (To a spirit.) Don't go! You know you were my companion, my traveling companion. I always paid your way and you must not leave me now.

Dr. What does she say she is going to do?

Sp. Mary, won't you please tell me my name? Look! Look at that fire! The whole thing is on fire!

Dr. You are again going through the condition under which you passed out.

Sp. Mary, Mary, look at that fire!

Dr. Were you in a railroad accident?

Sp. Yes, yes!

Dr. That has all passed.

Sp. Look at Mary! She's dead! She was crushed!

Dr. They are revealing to you the conditions under which you passed out. That is all in the past. You must quiet yourself.

Sp. I only got a glimpse of it for just a minute.

Dr. What does Mary say? Does she understand that she has passed out?

Sp. She is lost and so am I. We are both lost. We lost our way.

Dr. That is because you are ignorant of the real life. If you had had understanding when you had your physical body you would not have been lost.

Sp. I have been walking and Mary is dead.

Dr. She is not really dead; she only lost her physical body. Mary is no more dead than you are. You are both spirits.

Sp. I died in that terrible fire. Look at them all! All those people are burning up! (Greatly excited.)

Dr. Forget the accident and collect yourself. Try to calm yourself and forget the past.

Sp. (Agitated at sight of several spirits.) I don't want to see them -any of them! Look at that one! He is coming -he's coming! I don't want to see you! I don't want you and I told you I did not want you.

Dr. You probably wronged these persons in life and are now having to meet the consequences.

Sp. I just had a good time with you, but I don't care for you. I only wanted to see how much you loved me, but I don't love you. Now they say they come to accuse me. I do not want any of them. There are three.

Dr. Men or women?

Sp. I do not love a woman. Why do they come here?

Dr. What does your conscience tell you?

Sp. (Sneeringly.) He killed himself because I would not marry him -the fool!

Dr. Didn't you play vampire in the first place?

Sp. That's my affair.

Dr. You will now have to strive to do better.

Sp. Let me remain in darkness -it is far better than this. There I just walked. I did not see anything, but I am tired of walking.

Dr. What does your conscience tell you?

Sp. Do not talk to me about conscience.

Dr. Jesus said: "Except ye become as little children, ye shall not enter into the kingdom of heaven." You will have to start a new life; you will have to develop a newness of spirit. Sacrifice self. You will have to sacrifice self and become as a little child; you will have to correct your mistakes.

Sp. (To another spirit.) What have you to do with me now?

Dr. You have wronged these men you speak of.

Sp. There is a woman here too. What have you to do with me, I said? No, I never paid her for my dresses. Accusing me, just because I did not pay!

Dr. Was that the right thing to do? Your conscience told you what you should have done. Now you will have to serve others. Selfishness is the root of all evil.

Sp. I was taught nothing except to have a good time and spend money. Money was just what I was taught in my childhood to be proud of. Not a serious thought for any one that was beneath me. Why should I have been taught that and now have to suffer for it?

Dr. Was truth in your heart?

Sp. I was taught always to have the respect of others and to remember that I was rich, and that I should have all the world could give me. I wanted money, and when I broke a heart it was good cheer to me. (To spirits.) I said, Don't come, don't come!

Dr. You have been brought here for help. Be quiet and listen to me. You will now have to try to undo your mistakes.

Sp. I could never do that.

Dr. You can and you will. Others are here to help you, and they will show you a better way. Don't be selfish.

Sp. I am very selfish and I have always been very selfish. I was never taught anything else. My mother was a proud woman and she was very pretty.

Dr. Unfortunately for you. You must quiet yourself; you have been allowed to come here for help. Do you see any one else you know?

Sp. I do not care to look around any more; I see only those whom I have wronged. They are all standing here! Oh! (Shrinking back.) Why should I suffer so?

Dr. You created that suffering yourself. There is help for you if you will be sincere. Intelligent spirits will help you.

Sp. I thought that I could live and have a good time. I traveled everywhere I wanted to go. I saw everything and had everything I wanted that money could buy. Every wish I had was gratified.

Dr. You stupefied your soul. You will now have to undo your own follies by kindness. You will have to serve others.

Sp. I cannot serve anybody. They will have to serve me. I have never done anything in my life. I have always been waited on.

Dr. Understand that unless you help these spirits you will continue to suffer. You will

have nothing but the torment of your own conscience until you ask for mercy and say, "I will serve."

Sp. I never can wait on any one; that would be a step beneath me. What would my mother say if I should wait on any one beneath me?

Dr. There is nobody beneath you. Money does not make intelligence nor merit.

Sp. Nobody beneath me? Would I associate with my dressmaker?

Dr. When you go to the spirit world you will probably find that your humblest servant has a higher position than you have. You will often find that the people you think beneath you have the most beautiful homes in the spirit world. You have much to do to overcome your own disposition. There are many advanced spirits here who will help you. Jesus taught us that we must humble ourselves.

Sp. You do not know what that would mean to me.

Dr. My wife allows spirits of all kinds to control her brain and body. Would you be willing to sacrifice yourself as she does? She allows you to control her body so we can help you to a better understanding. Look around and you will find spirits here who will help you.

Sp. Oh, Rudolph! (Spirit.) I loved you, but you know that my pride and my mother would not consent to our marriage. I know you suffered, but you did not know that I suffered also. You know you could not give me the social standing I was used to. I loved you, and I love you yet. Rudolph, will you forgive me? I would have liked to have married you, Rudolph, but I could not.

Dr. Why should pride and money be obstacles to love?

Sp. I was not happy, but I had to crush that. I did not dare go contrary to my mother. I had to shine in society with a broken heart. I had to smile at all those fools. I had to be another person when my heart and love were with you, Rudolph, but forgive me! I know you suffered.

I went to your funeral but mother did not know it. I wished I were dead and could go with you, but I had to close the door to love. From the moment you had gone, I said I would conquer and shut out love and sympathy, and I would now live for selfishness and let others suffer as I had suffered for the love I had to shut out of my heart.

Rudolph, forgive and help me. You were such a good man, but religion and money and mother stood between us and love. You were poor but you were good.

He says if he could have been with me he could have taught me to be a good woman. Yes, Rudolph, but the good influence you brought with you was shut out for me; then I did not care what became of me. I went into society and had a good time trying to drown my sorrow. I tried to lead every man on so that I could get him down at my feet. I did not care if I crushed men. I wanted others to suffer as I had suffered.

Dr. That was selfish.

Sp. I was taught nothing but selfishness.

Dr. What does Rudolph say?

Sp. He says: "Alice, come with me to the spirit world." (Crying.) He says in Heaven there is no pride to interfere; all is love and harmony.

Dr. We can help you. Strive to understand. When you realize the better life you will have much to do to correct your mistakes. You can undo your mistakes by kindness to others. You will have to work out your own salvation.

Sp. (Stooping forward.) Carl, don't go. I know you meant well, but I could not love you when my heart was with another. I knew I was at fault when you killed yourself. See he just lies there! (Crying.)

Dr. He, too, will find understanding. Others will help him. Spirit is indestructible.

Sp. Look there! That cannot be! My mother! Look, look, how wrinkled and homely she is! That cannot be my mother. She says she is -but it cannot be. Oh, she is so homely! She was very lovely and beautiful. That cannot be mother. She is so homely, so homely! Mother, what is the matter with you? You had such a beautiful form, now you are all shriveled.

Dr. That is the spirit form which she developed by her selfishness. Her spirit body is of her own making. "As a man thinketh in his heart, so is he."

Sp. Mother, Mother, what is the matter with you? She says: "Alice, I am at fault in the way I brought you up. I am at fault for not bringing you up to be a better woman than you were. I am at fault for breaking up that true love with Rudolph, which probably would have brought out your better nature." She says that she closed the door, that she did not do any kind acts in life, so her spirit body was all crippled because of her bad deeds. She says she is now serving, and when she does a good act some of her crippled condition disappears.

She is so crippled and she has ragged clothes on. She says she is now serving with the body she earned when she was in earth life. She is now showing me the body she has earned in spirit. It is better than the other, but her face is all wrinkled.

Dr. Her face was her pride.

Sp. She says she has to serve and help every one she wronged, that she must do good acts, many of them, before her face will be beautiful. She says: "Alice, try to be different. Here is your spirit body, Alice." Oh, no! Not that! Rudolph, come and help me! You know how I feel.

Dr. What is your name? Ask your mother.

Sp. My mother cannot tell me; she cannot remember.

Dr. Can you remember who is the President?

Sp. McKinley.

Dr. He was killed in 1901. Did you know he was dead? He was shot in Buffalo in 1901. You must have been dead twenty years or more.

THIRTY YEARS AMONG THE DEAD

Sp. Have I been walking all that time?

Dr. You must have been.

Sp. I was born in Milwaukee. I wish I could tell more, but I cannot. The door is shut and I cannot even think. Why cannot I get my name? My memory is gone. Please remember Alice.

Dr. Your memory will come back to you. Realize life as it is. Think yourself with Rudolph now.

Sp. I will. I also want to thank you. Goodbye.

Haughty superiority and pride of station had long kept the spirit of a cultured English lady in the earth sphere, but with an understanding of life's higher purpose came spiritual discernment and progress.

EXPERIENCE, OCTOBER 4, 1922

Spirit: ESTHER SUTHERLAND Psychic: MRS. WICKLAND

The controlling intelligence was very arrogant and gazed disdainfully about.

Doctor: Is your condition strange to you? What has happened to you?

Spirit: Many things have happened to me, but that is not strange.

Dr. We should like to know who you are and where you came from. You are a stranger here.

Sp. (Condescendingly, with marked English accent.) I fancy I am a stranger to you.

Dr. May I ask to what nobility you belong?

Sp. What sort of a gentleman are you to ask such personal questions?

Dr. Do you not like this gathering?

Sp. (Greatly bored.) I do not know anything about you.

Dr. Do you belong to royalty?

Sp. Why are so many looking at me? Some are standing, some sitting.

Dr. Some must be spirits.

Sp. Spirits! I fancy it is only imagination. I see people sitting and standing. It may be you have no glasses to see with. I fancy you are of the more common class.

Dr. We were not fortunate enough to be born in the upper class. You have not introduced yourself to us yet.

Sp. I would not care to have an introduction to any of you here. (Loftily.) I do not think you belong to the set I am used to going with.

Dr. We are not particularly anxious to belong to that set, but unless we know who you are we cannot pay you the honor due you.

Sp. I do not know if I should like to have honor from you.

Dr. We should like to treat you with proper respect.

THIRTY YEARS AMONG THE DEAD

Sp. You have joked so rudely.

Dr. Lady, at least please tell us your name.

Sp. I do not know if I should do so. (Looking her questioner over from head to foot through an imaginary lorgnette.)

Dr. It would not do you any harm, you know.

Sp. (Pointing to reception room.) Who stands there? (Invisibles.) There are quite a few people here. It seems like a meeting of some sort. I do not know why I should have come here.

Dr. Won't you please ask those people in the other room who they are? I cannot see them. Ask them why they are here.

Sp. I fancy that is a select crowd, and I think I had better go with them. I fancy they are more my set. (Attempting to rise.)

Dr. Please remain seated and ask those people who they are.

Sp. I do not see why I should ask them that.

Dr. Introduce yourself to them.

Sp. I do not think I should introduce myself. We do not do that.

Dr. You are a total stranger to us; you might be an imposter.

Sp. (Turning frigidly away, and speaking to the gentleman at her right.) Recently I have not been able to express my thoughts as well as I would care to.

Dr. Just ask those people who they are.

Sp. I told you I do not want to talk to them. If you feel like talking to them you are welcome to go there and speak.

Dr. But we cannot see anybody there. How can we talk to them?

Sp. I cannot help it -I cannot help it.

Dr. Ask them if they are spirits. What do they do when I say they are spirits? (To the invisible assemblage.) Are you all spirits? (To controlling spirit.) What do they say?

Sp. Some nod their heads, Yes; some do not answer, but I cannot see why they should do that. Most of them answer in the affirmative. I see a soldier in uniform.

Dr. That might be one of your relatives. Are you of English descent?

Sp. I am English.

Dr. Do you know that Queen Victoria is dead?

Sp. Queen Victoria was the English Queen. She was a wonderful, wonderful woman. She died a long time ago.

Dr. I think it was in 1901.

Sp. Yes, I think it was, was it not?

THIRTY YEARS AMONG THE DEAD

Dr. King Edward is dead, too.

Sp. They used to say he was a wonderful King. Everybody respected and loved him. He was very much for everybody. He mingled with the common herd as well as with fine society.

Dr. That is a good suggestion for you. You should feel more at home with the common herd. Do you remember the Great War.

Sp. What Great War?

Dr. Do you know Lord Kitchener? He died in the Great War.

Sp. We had war with the Boers.

Dr. That was about 1898. Did you know Lord Kitchener?

Sp. He was a good man but not much in any war. I do not know anything about the Great War you speak of.

Dr. There were twenty-three or four nations fighting each other. England was fighting Germany.

Sp. I fancy that is remarkable. I do not know anything about that. I used to read a great deal at one time.

Dr. Do you remember the Kaiser?

Sp. He was a strange man.

Dr. Do you know that the Kaiser is deposed? Do you know that the Czar and his family were killed?

Sp. How?

Dr. By the Bolshevists.

Sp. What? Who are they?

Dr. They are the ones who upset the royalty business in Russia.

Sp. No, they did not call them that. They called them -what is that word I wish to say?

Ques. Nihilist?

Sp. Yes, that is it. They were sent to Siberia.

Dr. The Czar was sent that way, and then killed.

Sp. Fancy that!

Dr. Do you remember the Emperor of Austria? He has passed on.

Sp. Where have I been all this time not to know about the things of which you are talking?

Dr. The Hapsburg House is no longer in power.

Sp. No! What is the world coming to?

Dr. Coming to democracy.

Sp. All royalty gone! Then the common herd is starting in to do wrong.

THIRTY YEARS AMONG THE DEAD

Dr. There may be no aristocracy in time.

Sp. We have noble blood in our veins.

Dr. Suppose a commoner were made a King; would that change his blood? Do you remember that the King honored Napoleon and gave him a title? That did not give him blue blood.

Sp. I was born of noble blood and I will stick to that all my life.

Dr. What is your name? Were you a member of the English royal family?

Sp. My name was in olden times -well, I have not had my name for a long time. It seems to me -yes, my name was Esther Sutherland.

Ques. Were you the Duchess of Sutherland?

Sp. (Indignantly.) No, I was not the Duchess, but one of the distant relatives. They all had more money, while I only had the title. That is worth a great deal.

Ques. Do you know you are in America?

Sp. I am still in England.

Ques. Do you see any of your old friends around here?

Dr. Look in that crowd you spoke of; can you find some one you know?

Sp. I never knew that Kitchener had passed away as you state.

Dr. He was drowned when a war vessel was torpedoed on the Scottish Coast. Do you know him?

Sp. Yes. He is here, and he says that I must try to understand my situation.

Dr. That is why you were brought here.

Sp. (Pointing to further end of hall.) Why, there's an old gentleman (spirit) lecturing that I heard many years ago! Just fancy! I never thought I would hear him again. He is talking to a great many people. (Spirits.) It seems we have many here who just came to investigate what kind of a meeting this is, and what is going on. They all seem to be trying very hard to find out what they really are.

He is now standing on that platform. He is lecturing just as he used to in England some years ago. I went to hear him, but he talked Spiritualism. I did not really know what he meant. He spoke well. He said his name is Dr. Peebles. (Famous lecturer on Spiritualism.) He said to me, "You go in there," so I came.

He says: "I want you to get understanding, and I do not" no, no, what does he mean? He says he does not want me to stay in the earth sphere, but to lift my soul up to God and understand the real spiritual meaning of Him.

He has a big crowd around him; some he is trying to lift up to higher things, others he is trying to wake up, so he tells me. They are not sleeping, are they?

Dr. Yes, mentally. The Bible says: "Blessed is he that hath part in the first resurrection: on such the second death has no power."

Sp. What does that mean?

THIRTY YEARS AMONG THE DEAD

Dr. It means that for those who have a spiritual understanding while in the body there is no death.

Sp. Of course there is.

Dr. No one ever "dies." The spirit, or mind, is not the body.

Sp. It is not?

Dr. You are dead to the world and your own relatives, and evidently have been so for many years, but we know that you yourself are not really dead.

Sp. I have been walking about a great deal, and I have traveled extensively, but I have felt very strange. Whenever I wanted to go anywhere, all I had to do was to think, and it seemed that I did not need a train or anything, but I was there. At times I felt I must be in America, because I always heard they run their trains much faster than in England.

Dr. You are in Los Angeles, California.

Sp. California! How did I get here? The old gentleman is talking to a big crowd. He says he has to bring them here to get them to understand, and to have them open their spiritual eyes to see.

Dr. You are having yours opened now.

Sp. Why should I come here and speak? Why do the rest not speak? The lecturer says he could take me quicker than any of the others. Still I do not look different than they. He says he could take me more quickly to control a psychic.

Dr. He is right.

Sp. What does he mean by that? He said it was necessary to bring this crowd here. He met most of them in England when he was lecturing there many years ago. He says some will listen to his lecture, but many he cannot reach, nor even waken, so he brought them here.

He says he did not bring me here to waken me, but I had come with others in that room over there. There are so many there. Some are crippled and some cannot speak at all. It seems as if he speaks and lifts them up, and then they waken. He has a wonderful power for healing.

Dr. They are lifted up by his thought. He makes them understand that their crippled bodies are in the grave.

Sp. Now he says that I must thank you for the privilege of meeting you and of talking with you. I do not see why I should do that. He says also that I shall have to put all my pride aside. Yes, but the rest are the same as I.

Dr. You might see Queen Victoria or King Edward21 in the crowd, and I am told that you will find them very common now.

Sp. Of Queen Victoria they always said she talked to spirits, and everybody thought she was a little crazy on the subject.

Dr. She was open-minded.

Sp. She had spirit communications very often.

Dr. She is not a Queen any longer.

Sp. Some said she had a medium with her a great deal to ask what things to do and what not to do. His name was Brown, I believe.

Dr. Yes, John Brown.

Sp. She said she always had to ask her husband about things.

Dr. What more does Dr. Peebles say?

Sp. He says I had better say Good Night to you all, and he also says that he will take all the crowd away with him, and that he will show them the spirit world and try to help them. That is his work.

Dr. He passed out about six months ago. Now he is active on the other side.

Sp. I think I am growing weak; I feel strange.

Dr. You are losing control. This body is not yours; it is my wife's.

Sp. What do you mean?

Dr. She is a psychic through whom you are talking. You are experiencing only a temporary sensation.

Sp. There is my mother! (Spirit.) I have not seen her for many years.

Dr. How does she look?

Sp. She looks very young.

Dr. Ask her if she has understanding?

Sp. She says, yes, she was very much interested in Dr. Peebles' lectures, and also she used to go and listen to Mrs. Britten.

Dr. She was a wonderful woman. She is now showing object lessons in spirit life.

Sp. Mother says she used to go and hear her quite often, and also some man who lectured.

Dr. Was his name Mr. Wallis?

Sp. Yes. He was quite a young man at that time.

Dr. He has also passed on. They all pass along to the better land.

Sp. (With transfigured face, gazing raptly upon some vision.) Look at that open door! It is so beautifully engraved. It has engraved on it:

The Door of Life.

Understanding of Life.

Understanding of God in the True Sense.

The door is opening, very slowly, and we look in. What a beautiful Hall! The altar in the front is so beautiful, so beautiful! On the altar, in the center, is a beautiful statue which represents Wisdom. There is a statue of Truth, one of Love, one of Understanding, one of Honesty, one of Life and one of Modesty.

Wisdom is the center statue. There are seven statues in all, each holding a light, each one of the seven colors. Three on each side of Wisdom, each with a light, all blending into Wisdom, the beautiful White Light.

Wisdom

Truth Honesty

Love Life

Understanding Modesty

From these colors come the seven musical notes. Each note corresponds to a color, and then goes toward the center and lends into Wisdom. There the real truth of life and an understanding of God is learned.

Dr. The Bible says, "God is Love," and "God is Spirit, and they that worship Him must worship Him in spirit and in truth."

Sp. That is beautiful. See those colors blend! They go on and on, blending in all ways, into all forms, into all kinds of shapes, into stars and flowers, and then they become music. Now they form into leaves, buds and flowers -music taking form and color. The music itself -I never heard such beautiful music! Is that Heaven?

Dr. You may call it Heaven, or the spirit world. Heaven is a condition of mind. The Bible says: "Ye are the temple of God and the Spirit of God dwelleth in you." God is Love and Wisdom.

Sp. They say to me: "This is the Gateway to the Higher Life. You have had a glimpse of it, but you cannot be there." Why cannot I go there?

Dr. You are carrying a load of which you must rid yourself -your pride and your ignorance of spiritual laws.

Sp. There is one who says: "We have to learn our lessons, to be humble, to be charitable, to serve. Learn to be honest and sincere, then you can enter that beautiful hall. Take up the cross and follow me.

"That cross represents the crucifying of self -selfishness, jealousy, envy, bigotry, dogma, creeds, false belief and pride. Take up your cross and follow me." That means that I must crucify self, learn to serve, learn the lesson of life, learn to love others better than myself. "Selfishness is the cause of all trouble. Crucify self-conceit." Oh, I have much of it. I have much to crucify. I must take up my cross and learn my lesson down there. (Pointing downward.)

Dr. Jesus said: "Except ye become as little children, ye shall not enter into the kingdom of heaven."

Sp. (With meek humility, and a beautiful expression of resignation, hands uplifted.) Take me -I am ready to serve, and also to seek for truth. I will begin here and now to do the will of Heaven.

Whatever is the will of God, find me there doing it. I must not go to church to find God, I must find Him within if I wish the opening of the door to that beautiful Hall of Understanding, Wisdom and Glory. Now I have to start at the bottom, at the very bottom, to serve. Is that to be my mission? Is it?

Dr. Yes; every one must serve.

Sp. Amongst all those crippled and blind people -I am to show them the way. The door was opened for me to have a glimpse of what I am to work for, but it was closed again, and I -I have to serve.

I have never served. It will be very hard, for I have always been waited on. I have never had to dress myself or comb my hair. I never have done it in all my life, never. Now I have to serve, and comb the matted hair of those cripples down there -I -but I have to do it.

Dr. Jesus said: "My yoke is easy and my burden is light."

Sp. (Earnestly.) It is worth it, to gain that crown of wisdom. It is worth all I must go through with to enter that beautiful hall and listen to the wonders there. I will serve, yes, I honestly will. I will do that and more, for all. God help me in my great struggle. Yes, I promise I will serve and do all within my power. I must go. Good Night.

THIRTY YEARS AMONG THE DEAD

Chapter XIII

Orthodoxy

The science of religion should teach an intelligent realization of the nature of God and the life hereafter, but humanity is still kept in subjection by fear, superstition, dogmas and creeds, and has not yet attained liberation through a full understanding of what becomes of the dead.

Passing through the change called death, a great majority remain in entire ignorance of their condition, and are bound for a time to the earth plane by their false doctrines. These cling to their orthodox ideas, often influencing those still in the body, and the mental derangements which frequently follow in the train of revivals are examples of these obsessions, as are the phenomena known as "The Gift of Tongues," and "Seizure by The Power," which accompany many revivals.

Religious exhortations readily lead to mental aberrations since invisible religious fanatics are always present who are unconscious of their transition and, having found no higher life, retain their mortal bigotry, and by their presence add to the insane fervor. These spirits often make themselves audible to excited sensitives, for at such gatherings many are encouraged to listen to "the still, small voice," supposedly of God.

During religious excitement the psychic faculty is highly sensitized, giving mischievous spirits, as well as fanatical spirits, the proper opportunity to impress credulous persons with their whisperings.

Such entities, for their own deceptive purposes, may pretend to be angels, the "Holy Ghost," or "The Spirit of God," and the thoughtless victims, elated and unwilling to listen to reason, heed these whisperings, which so frequently lead to obsession and possession, resulting in madness, insanity and other psychoses.

The most difficult to enlighten of the earthbound spirits are the religious fanatics. Dominated in earth life by one narrow, fixed idea, opposed to logical analysis and independent thinking, they are found, after passing out of the physical, in a state of self-hypnosis, ceaselessly repeating their empty "religious" jargon.

Nothing exists for them but their dogmatic creed; they are adamantly set in their self-assurance and it is often many years before they can be brought to a semblance of sanity.

EXPERIENCE, MARCH 28, 1923

Spirit: SARAH McDONALD Psychic: MRS. WICKLAND

The spirit who assumed control of the psychic tonight was vigorously singing a religious hymn.

Doctor: Have you been here before?

Spirit: Let's sing some more.

Dr. We are going to talk now.

Sp. I think we'd better sing another song.

Dr. If we did, you might become too enthusiastic.

Sp. We are in church, and you know you have to sing. Sing! Hallelujah! Tell the story!

Dr. We are going to be sensible.

Sp. You have to sing. You have to do that. That belongs to church. Let us pray, in Jesus' name, for evermore!

Dr. That would be very tiresome.

Sp. Let us sing and pray to the Lord. Hallelujah! Jesus Christ!

Dr. Now stop; that is enough. What is your name?

Sp. Let's sing and pray!

Dr. You must be sensible or leave. Tell us who you are and where you came from.

Sp. What church is this anyhow, where you talk in this way?

Dr. Be sensible, otherwise you will have to go. How long have you been dead? You know something happened to you. You have been hovering around the earth, probably for years, and have never gotten anywhere. Be sensible.

Sp. I am sensible; I'm not crazy.

Dr. You are religiously insane.

Sp. We all pray to God and the Holy Ghost. (Loudly.) Hallelujah!

Dr. We do not need that shouting.

Sp. I am doing work in the name of Jesus Christ.

Dr. We have heard such talk before.

Sp. Not from me, you haven't. I am working for the Lord Jesus Christ.

Dr. This is not the place for such talk as that.

Sp. Are you a sinner?

Dr. Listen to me. Whoever you are, you have lost your body.

Sp. What church is this?

Dr. It is no church.

Sp. I am glad of that, because I thought the church must surely have changed. Let me talk, in Jesus' name!

THIRTY YEARS AMONG THE DEAD

Dr. You have been brought here by kind spirits so that you can understand your condition. You are a spirit and probably have been for a long time. You will not listen to any one who tries to enlighten you.

Sp. Go ahead then, and say what you have to say. Then I can talk, too.

Dr. Understand your condition. You are temporarily controlling this body. Some friend brought you here for help. Do you realize that something happened to you?

Sp. No.

Dr. You would if you were honest. You know that you are in a strange condition. You are not honest enough to pay any attention to it. Do you know that you are in Los Angeles, California?

Sp. How did I get there? I suppose I sang and prayed as a missionary. A missionary must have taken me away.

Dr. You were brought here because you are an ignorant spirit. What did your mother call you?

Sp. I don't know just now; I can't think.

Dr. You have lost your physical body. Ignorant spirits often lose the memory of their earth lives. You do not even remember your name.

Sp. My name is Sarah, in Jesus' name!

Dr. Sarah what?

Sp. McDonald, in Jesus' name!

Dr. You know that all that shouting is useless. Do you not realize that you have been "dead" for some time?

Sp. Hallelujah!

Dr. You do not even know that you are dead. You are only using this body for a short time. Do you hear me? Do you know what year it is?

Sp. In Jesus' name, I do not care.

Dr. Religious fanatics never care.

Sp. I am a Christian woman, in Jesus' name. Glory to God! Hallelujah!

Dr. Do you know what Jesus said?

Sp. Yes; He said: "God forgive them, they do not know any better." I will pray for you.

Dr. We do not need your prayers.

Sp. Glory to God!

Dr. Do you know that you are dead?

Sp. That doesn't interest me.

Dr. You are controlling the body of a mortal sensitive.

Sp. Jesus is my friend! Glory!

Dr. We carry on experimental work to learn what becomes of the dead. We always find that the most ignorant, stubborn spirits are the religious fanatics, shouting and singing all the time. Jesus said: "Know the truth, and the truth shall make you free."

Sp. God forgive them, they don't know better! I will pray for you all.

Dr. You need not trouble yourself. You do not understand your condition at all. What you say is nothing but foolish talk. In your heart you know you are a pretender.

Sp. God forgive! Let us pray!

Dr. We do not need your hypocritical prayers.

Sp. I never was in such a place before. I never saw anything like this. (Crying.) I do not know what will become of me!

Dr. Try to understand what I am saying to you. Stop your foolish religious talk. You say "Jesus" and "Lord," and you have no understanding of true religion.

Sp. God help me! God help me! God forgive!

Dr. He does not need to. Listen to what I say.

Sp. (Drawling.) What more do you want?

Dr. Why speak with such affectation? Do you know that you are controlling a body that does not belong to you? Aren't you ashamed of yourself? You know that you are not sincere. Tell us how long you have been dead. You must realize that something has happened to you. Intelligent spirits have brought you here and allowed you to control my wife's body, and we are trying to help you understand your condition, but that does not seem to interest you.

Sp. I don't care! (Trying to bite.)

The spirit would not listen to any line of reasoning and was forced to leave. She was immediately followed by a little child, who came in crying dismally.

EXPERIENCE, MARCH 28, 1923

Spirit: MARY ANN McDONALD Psychic: MRS. WICKLAND

Doctor: What is your trouble? Don't cry. We are going to help you.

Spirit: Where is Mamma?

Dr. Have you lost your mother? We can help you find her. Tell us who you are. What is your name?

Sp. Mary Ann McDonald. (Coughing, choking and crying.)

Dr. You must not do that. Why do you cry?

Sp. What's the matter with my Mamma?

Dr. Have you lost her?

Sp. She's gone. I don't know where she is now.

Dr. We can help you. What was your mother's name?

Sp. Sarah McDonald. Will you bring Mamma to me?

Dr. We are going to help you. Where was your home?

Sp. I don't know. I can't remember. All my Mamma does is to pray and sing, and she says if I do not do the same, I will go straight to the devil.

Dr. You will not go to the devil.

Sp. I cannot pray and sing in my heart like they do.

Dr. You do not have to pray and sing. There is no religion in that. We can help you; our work is the helping of unfortunate spirits.

Sp. I don't know what to do!

Dr. You have lost your body, just as your mother has lost hers. We could not see your mother and we cannot see you. You are using the body of another for a time. Your mother was here and controlled this body before you came.

Sp. Have I lost her?

Dr. She is being taken care of. She has been taken to a spirit hospital. She is insane on religion and would not listen to what I said.

Sp. She says if she does not pray and sing all the time God will not forgive her.

Dr. There is no religion in that, only insanity. That is not what Jesus taught.

Sp. Do you see that big fire?

Dr. No, we cannot see it. Where is it?

Sp. The whole house burned all up. My mother was praying and singing. I didn't know what was the matter. I was sleeping and did not know anything about the house burning up.

Dr. Don't worry about that.

Sp. When I woke up I was all choked. I couldn't breathe.

Dr. That is all past now. What town did you live in?

Sp. I don't know. Just wait a minute while I try to think. I was so scared that my mind can't remember. We prayed and sang all the time, and I am so sick and tired of it that I don't know what to do. We did not get anywhere. We just prayed the same thing over and over again. I do not know what will become of me, because I cannot feel like my mother does at all.

Dr. Our work is to help spirits who are in trouble, and you will find happiness when you leave here.

Sp. I will tell you. The minister at the church we go to, he says: "If you do not do so and so, and pray every night, and sacrifice everything, you will go to hell." He says we must not eat, but must lay on the floor and torture our bodies for Christ's sake.

Dr. That minister is insane.

Sp. He said we must not eat anything except dry bread with water. He said I had been a sinner, and I must give all the money I make to the Lord, and I must be His slave. I asked him if the Lord was so poor that He needed all my money, and he said that question was from the devil. I worked very hard and Mamma took all my money away from me for the church. I went out sewing in a shop, but my Mamma took me to church every night. All I got was a hard crust of bread and some water in Jesus' name.

Dr. How old are you?

Sp. About sixteen or seventeen.

Dr. What kind of a shop did you work in?

Sp. I sewed overalls.

Dr. In Chicago?

Sp. No, but we were in a big town. I can't remember. That minister preached and preached.

Dr. That is all over now.

Sp. Sometimes I asked Mamma why we had to sing and pray all the time. It came to my heart that God is Love, and we are His children, so why does He let us work so hard and sacrifice our bodies so that we hardly have any strength, then give all our money to Him. Is He so poor?

Dr. The Lord has nothing to do with any of that. Only ignorant, insane persons say such things.

Sp. He is a minister.

Dr. What church did you belong to?

Sp. The minister said if we did not do as he told us to, we would go to hell. He talks and talks, and we have to listen to him. I don't know why, but I haven't sewed since I was in that fire. It seems like a fire and an earthquake. I felt so bad because I choked and coughed. My Mamma and I have not had any house to sleep in.

The minister told us we could sleep most anywhere, but if we worked and gave all our money to the Lord we would be all right. Sometimes I wanted a new dress awful bad. I didn't earn so very much money, but if I could have kept it I could have got a new dress sometime. Mamma took it all.

She said: "Mary Ann, you must sacrifice for the Lord." Sometimes I said: "I may go to hell for it, but I think it would be better to go to hell than to hear about the Lord all the time." I don't know if it would be better, but I thought it would be.

Dr. All that fanaticism is wrong, every bit of it. God is Spirit, and God is Love. God has nothing to do with such fanatical talk. He does not need any one's money.

Sp. Then why do they give it to Him?

Dr. God doesn't get it—the ministers do. God doesn't need it.

Sp. Doesn't God need our money?

Dr. No. God is Spirit. Spirit is invisible. I am talking to you and you are talking to me, but you are invisible to us. We cannot see you. Mind is invisible. You see my body, but not my mind. God is invisible and He is not in a certain place as we are. He is the Soul of all things.

Sp. But the minister says He sits on a throne with Jesus on His right hand. Why did he tell us that if it is not true?

Dr. Because "the truth is not in him." He is not honest.

THIRTY YEARS AMONG THE DEAD

Sp. But Jesus died for our sins.

Dr. No, he did not.

Sp. He said: "Take up my cross and follow me, and go to church every day."

Dr. Jesus never mentioned going to church. His teachings were about the higher life.

Sp. Heaven?

Dr. Not as you understand it. Heaven is a happy mental condition. If you could have had a new dress, as you wished, you would have been happy, wouldn't you?

Sp. Yes, I should like to have a new dress. I don't care so very much for fancy things. Once in a while I wanted a nice new dress, and not what the minister told us we should have. But we had to give our money to the Lord.

Dr. No, you didn't. You gave it to the minister.

Sp. He gave us some old dresses that had been given to the church, and my Mamma said we must sacrifice. When I kicked, Mamma said: "You will go to hell if you don't do what the Lord says you should do."

Dr. There is no such place as "hell."

Sp. No hell?

Dr. Of course not.

Sp. Isn't hell a burning fire? I have seen it burning, and I see it yet.

Dr. Possibly your mother, in her religious insanity, set fire to the house.

Sp. No, I don't think so. It seems like there was an earthquake, and then after that there was the fire.

Dr. Who is President?

Sp. I don't know. I'll tell you, I didn't have so very much school. I went to work when I was nine years old.

Dr. Did you have a father?

Sp. I did not know my father.

Dr. Your schooling does not make any difference. You have lost your physical body and are now a spirit.

Sp. I lost my physical body? But I have a body.

Dr. This is not your body; it belongs to my wife.

Sp. Where did I get these clothes from?

Dr. They belong to my wife.

Sp. But I should like to have my own clothes.

Dr. You will have your own soon.

Sp. I do not like to take them from your wife. I am sorry, but I must not wear them.

Dr. Look at your shoes.

Sp. I must be in Heaven!

Dr. You feel better, do you not, than when you were praying all the time?

Sp. I feel strong. Did I get something to eat, because I feel so strong?

Dr. You are controlling a healthy body. This is my wife's body.

Sp. I don't like to have your wife's body.

Dr. You will only stay here for a short time.

Sp. Then where will I go? I won't have to go back to that minister, and hear all those crazy people sing all the time, will I? When the minister talked about hell and damnation, I saw a big fire, and I saw the devil with his pitchfork, and he pushed people in.

Dr. When that minister was preaching, he was thinking of hell fire, and made a picture which the rest of you saw, and it appeared like a reality. But it was only a phantasm which he created.

Sp. He scared us with it.

Dr. As he talked it would appear to you as a reality.

Sp. But it looked like real. I suppose they have those things in hell, but I want to go to Heaven.

Dr. Your mother and the minister are spirits, but ignorant of the fact.

Sp. Do you mean all those people are spirits? There must be a thousand all singing and praying, all the time. Sometimes we got just bread and water, and we lay down on boards. We must be there all the time, otherwise the minister is not pleased with us, and he says if we do not get down on our knees, we go into the fire.

Dr. That is all nonsense. All those people have lost their physical bodies, and are in the outer darkness that the Bible speaks about. They are in blind, religious ignorance. They will remain in that condition for a very long time if they do not change their way of thinking. They are filled with religious fanaticism. Your mother was brought here for understanding and controlled this same body.

Sp. Someone pushed her in, and then I could not talk to her any more. The whole crowd down there will not listen to any body; they just sing and pray.

Dr. They can stay there for years and years, and their "Lord" will not care anything about them.

Sp. There, that hell is not there any more!

Dr. The minister thinks of hell and devils, and creates phantasms, which seem real to ignorant spirits.

Sp. Will you help my mother?

Dr. Intelligent spirits will take care of her. It was they who "pushed" her in here, to bring her to an understanding. The difference between you and your mother is that you will listen and she would not.

THIRTY YEARS AMONG THE DEAD

Sp. Then you do not think God would be angry with me?

Dr. Of course not.

Sp. Sure?

Dr. God knows everything. He is All in All. He is the Creator and Creation both.

Sp. Don't we fall in sin?

Dr. No, never. If you say we fall in sin, you say God made a mistake when He created us. He is All-Wise, All-Powerful and everywhere present. When such a God as that created the world and mankind, He did not make a mistake, allowing man to "fall in sin." Otherwise He would not be All-Wise.

Sp. Why do they say that then?

Dr. People worship creed. The truth is given allegorically in the Bible.

Sp. Didn't Jesus die for our sins?

Dr. Of course he did not.

Sp. The minister said there is power in the blood.

Dr. No, there is not. Some of those people you speak of have probably been dead a long time. We cannot see them.

Sp. Can't you see all those people over there? (Pointing.)

Dr. No; they are spirits and have lost their bodies long ago. They are blind to the higher life. You are not satisfied to be with them and you ask questions, therefore we can help you to an understanding. We must add understanding to our faith. You lost your own body, perhaps many years ago.

Sp. Everything was all mixed up. I got hurt in the head.

Dr. Don't you remember any of the streets in your city?

Sp. No, I can't remember. It seems like I was in San Francisco.

Ques. (By a former resident of San Francisco.) Did you go across the Bay to Oakland?

Sp. Yes, and we went to Oakland to the prayer meeting.

Ques. Did you work at Strauss Brothers Overall Factory? Was it on Mission Street?

Sp. Mission Street! I remember now. We lived on Mission Street.

Ques. Near Daly, toward Golden Gate Park?

Sp. No, it was near the depot.

Ques. Toward the Ferry?

Sp. Near the Southern Pacific Station. They had a Mission House on Mission Street.

Ques. Was that toward the Bay?

Sp. I don't know. We lived in a little house we rented. My mother went to the factory too, but she got sick because she sang and prayed all the time. I had to do her work too. We did not get much, just kept enough so we could live. The minister said it was a sin to eat meat, or milk, or butter, or eggs. He said they cost too much and that we must sacrifice our bodies.

Dr. Was your father dead?

Sp. I think he died when I was a little girl; I don't really know.

Dr. Look around and see whether there is anyone here whom you know. Other spirits are here who will help you and take you to the spirit world. That is the invisible world around the physical world.

Sp. I see such a pretty garden. Look at those beautiful flowers, just look at them! I never saw anything so beautiful! There's trees and flowers. Hear the pretty birds, how they sing! Look at that beautiful lake, and all the children swinging on the shore!

Dr. That is the spirit world.

Sp. It is so much better than over there, where they sing and pray. Sometimes I was so hungry that nothing satisfied me. Isn't this different from those crazy singing people? Can't you see them all? Couldn't you help them to see this beautiful place?

Dr. Your mother was here, controlling this body, but we could do nothing with her.

Sp. Oh, look at that nice little house over there! It has two rooms and a beautiful garden full of flowers.

Dr. Do you see any one around there?

Sp. Somebody says my grandmother lives there, and it's going to be my home, too. They say she is waiting for me. I only know grandmother a little. She visited us once but she could not stay, because Mamma was carrying on so and grandmother didn't believe in it. So she went far away, I think East somewhere, and after that she died.

Mamma got some money from grandma -I don't know just how much, but I think she said a little more than a thousand dollars. I thought then I should get a new dress, but the Lord got it all.

The minister said the next Sunday that she would go up into the Seventh Heaven, because she gave the Lord all that money. She would not eat one thing all that day. I thought sure I would get a new dress, but I didn't. Can you hear that beautiful music? Listen!

Dr. We cannot hear it.

Sp. I never heard anything so fine. All the flowers bow to the music, and when they hear it they look happy. The music seems like colors, and it seems to go with the flowers. When the music changes the flowers have a different color.

Dr. You will find many beautiful things when you leave here.

Sp. There is a gentleman standing there, and he looks at me and says: "Come, little child." We are many, because each mother had her children that she took to church with her. One time -I'll tell you. There was I, and Bertha, and Clara and Joe -Joe's a boy -we all went into a corner and we just sat there and talked.

The minister saw us, and you don't know how mad he was! He said he would have to punish us all, and he did. He said: "The Lord will punish you all," but the minister did it -and his hand was awful hard.

My grandmother is here, and she says: "Mary Ann, you can come with me and we will try all we can to help your mother." This gentleman who stands there says he is my father. Grandma was my father's mother. Grandma says he died East.

Mother joined the Salvation Army, but the Mission Friends got hold of her. We came from Kansas when I was a little girl. The money my grandma sent was to be given to me, but my mother said we would put it in the Lord's keeping. So the Lord kept it -and I didn't get any new dress.

Dr. The Lord did not get that money either.

Sp. Whether he got it or not makes no difference now; I will get my new dress. I have one, but that is not mine, because you say this is not my body. I will have a new dress, but I don't want sackcloth. I must not say that, it isn't nice.

Dr. Now you are going to serve others, and be where there are trees and flowers and beautiful music.

Sp. This gentleman comes; he says he is my father, but I don't remember him. He says he will help me. You know my father died -or passed out. Sometimes people say that.

Dr. "Passed out" is right. There is no actual death; nobody ever "dies." Your father only lost his body.

Sp. Isn't that dead?

Dr. His mind, or spirit, being invisible while in the body, is still invisible to mortals when he steps out of his body. His body is only the house where his spirit lives, and when the spirit leaves the body, the body is placed in the grave. But the spirit is not dead.

Sp. Sometimes I prayed for my father, because mother said he went to hell. Father says there is no such place. He looks awful nice, and he's all dressed up. I wish my mother would understand.

Dr. Don't worry about your mother. After spirits like she control this body, they are placed in a spirit hospital.

Sp. Can you talk to the Lord too? I wish you would talk to Him, because He takes too much money from the poor.

Dr. The Lord does not do that, it is the minister.

Sp. Why, here comes a little Indian girl. (Spirit.)

Dr. Isn't she nice? She will show you beautiful things.

Sp. Can I go with her? What is her name?

Dr. Silver Star.

Sp. Is that her name? Will you play with me, little girl, and can I play with you? She says, yes, and that she will take me to her home and show me pretty things. Won't I be happy! I will have a new dress, not this sackcloth -but probably the Lord would not like that.

Dr. Forget all about that. Go with the intelligent spirits and they will help you and teach you.

Sp. Silver Star says I should come with her, and she will take me to my grandmother, and my father and my brother. (Surprised.) Oh, my brother! I forgot all about Lawrence. He was so little when he died.

Dr. How old was he?

Sp. I don't know. He was only a little baby. I don't know much because I couldn't go to school when I wanted to. I had to work for the Lord.

Dr. After you leave here you will learn many things.

Sp. But my mother said the Lord did not want us to learn, because we must sacrifice everything. If you read and write you get away from the Lord.

Dr. Just remember I said that was all wrong teaching.

Sp. I will find it out, and I will find out if the Lord gets all the money. If that minister took all that money, I will tell him he is not nice.

Dr. You will find that belief about the Lord is not true.

Sp. And I thought it was gospel truth. They would not let me go to school. I saw lots of children learn but I could not. They said I would not go to Heaven if I learned. I cried when I could not have a new dress, and the minister told me I would go to hell.

Dr. Now you will learn the truth. You have been dead probably many years. Have you seen "Heaven"? Why are you not there?

Sp. That's true.

Dr. The Bible mentions the "outer darkness"; you were in darkness, but it was all of your own making.

Sp. How can they sing and pray all the time when they are dead? These people have churches. Once in a while they go to other churches (on earth) when God wants them in some other church. Sometimes, before the minister (mortal) knows it, the people in the church do something like that (swaying motion of the body) and every one gets up and jumps and sings. (The mortals having opened themselves, through wild emotionalism, to spirit obsession.) Their minister says that is the influence of the Holy Ghost. Some of our crowd get into that other crowd and make them all jump.

Dr. Spirits such as you speak of often go to churches on the physical side and unbalance the people, making them demented. Then the people say they are controlled by the "Holy Ghost."

Sp. Silver Star says she will take me along, and that I will have a new dress. Maybe it is not right, but it feels good to know I will have one. Silver Star says that I must thank all of you for being patient with me. Some day I will come and tell you how I like things, and then probably I can remember more. If you do not come there, then I will come to see you.

Mary Ann McDonald is my name. I will see you some time. I feel like saying "God bless you," but I suppose I shouldn't.

Dr. That is all right. Now go with Silver Star.

Sp. All right. Goodbye.

That conscientious church attendance, faithful meeting of obligations and upright living do not in themselves insure spiritual enlightenment hereafter has often been evidenced.

EXPERIENCE, JULY 19, 1922

Spirit: HENRY WILKINS Psychic: MRS. WICKLAND

The controlling intelligence was apparently crippled, with body bent over knees.

Doctor: Can't you straighten yourself? Wake up.

Spirit: I'm not sleeping.

Dr. Why are you bent over?

Sp. My back is broken.

Dr. You are mistaken; it is not broken.

Sp. Oh, yes, it is.

Dr. It may have been broken but it is not now.

Sp. I tell you I cannot straighten up; my back is broken.

Dr. We can change that condition.

Sp. Many times they told me that, but they never could.

Dr. But we are going to do it for you this time.

Sp. I will give you ten dollars if you can straighten me out.

Dr. Where is the money?

Sp. When I can stand up I will give it to you. If you can cure me it is worth all of ten dollars.

Dr. Just think, "I can walk," and you will be able to walk.

Sp. You will have to show me.

Dr. Move your legs and you can walk.

Sp. I did that many times, but it never helped.

Dr. Nevertheless you can be cured.

Sp. But I have no money. I haven't had money for some time. Every time I see money I grab it, but it gets away just like it had life.

Dr. I will explain. Do you know that you are a spirit? Do you know you are "dead" yes, dead to the world?

Sp. Then I don't know it, and I haven't been in Heaven. I was a good Methodist. I went to church every Sunday and also to Sunday School. I prayed and prayed that I might get well. I was a shoemaker.

Dr. Where did you live?

Sp. Down in Texas.

Dr. What is your name?

THIRTY YEARS AMONG THE DEAD

Sp. My name is Henry Wilkins.

Dr. How old are you?

Sp. I am an old man in the sixties. One time I was driving a horse and he ran away. I fell off the wagon and broke my back. I used to be a farmer. After that I could do no farming. At that time I was in the thirties. After I was hurt all I could do was some cobbling. I earned my living but it was surely hard sometimes.

Dr. Have you any idea what year it is?

Sp. I can't remember.

Dr. Who was President?

Sp. Let me think a little -I ought to know that. I think, if I remember right, it was Cleveland.

Dr. What was the cause of your death?

Sp. I did not die. I did some work but I never got any money for it, because as soon as I was going to take the money, somebody else grabbed it. I heard many times that my shop belonged to somebody else. I have been working there a long time, but the young fellow there he always takes the money all the time and I never get anything.

Dr. Did you start the shop?

Sp. Yes, many years ago. Some young fellow came to my shop and helped with the work, but I had to show him how to do it, and I had to teach him how to do lots of things. He got all the money -I never got a smell of it.

Dr. The fact is, my friend, you have passed out, and are so-called dead.

Sp. I have done nothing for some time except help that young fellow get rich.

Dr. Now listen to me. You lost your physical body probably while you had that shop, and now the shop belongs to somebody else. The young man did not know you were there, but you may have impressed him how to do things. He did not know you were there.

Sp. He did not know, because I did the work. I sat there working, and once in a while he would sit right on me. I could not chase him out.

Dr. Do you know what year it is?

Sp. It is 1892.

Dr. That was, thirty years ago. Do you know where you are? You are in Los Angeles, California.

Sp. California !

Dr. Look at these clothes you are wearing.

Sp. Who put these clothes on me? I don't want to be dressed in a woman's clothes!

Dr. Let me explain.

Sp. Bring my pants, please!

Dr. Look at these hands.

Sp. They do not belong to me. I have a ring on, but I never owned a ring.

Dr. Suppose you sat here mending shoes. Do you know what people would say? They would say: "Why is Mrs. Wickland sitting there, mending shoes?" Mrs. Wickland is my wife, and you are using her body.

Sp. I am no woman, I am a man. I was engaged to be married, but when I had my accident and became a cripple, the girl said she did not want to marry a cripple, so she married some one else. I told her I could earn just as much money by mending shoes as I did when a farmer, but she said she would not marry a cripple. I loved her just the same, and I love her still.

Dr. What was her name?

Sp. Mary Hopkins. She said she was ashamed of me. I could not help my accident. I felt that if she loved me she would have thought more of me because I needed her more. Of course I did not look so nice. I could not dance and do the things she wanted to do. One day she said to me: "I am ashamed to go out with you all crippled up." I felt so bad because I did not think she could be so cruel. I suffered terribly. It was not enough that I had a crippled body, but my heart was broken as well. From that time I said: "Women are all devils." I had no use for them; I hated them.

Dr. There are many good women.

Sp. Sometimes I felt there is no God, because He would not have let me suffer such mental and physical pain. I tried my very best to be patient.

Dr. You will have your reward for it now.

Sp. I gave money to the church. They said I must give money because God needed it. Sometimes they made me give so much that I hadn't enough left for bread and butter. They said if I didn't, I wouldn't go to Heaven.

Dr. There is no such "Heaven" as the preachers teach.

Sp. Then why should they preach that way?

Dr. For a living. Do you realize that the teachings of Jesus were wonderful? "God is Spirit," Jesus said, and we should worship Him "in Spirit and in truth." The orthodox Christians think Heaven is a place up in the sky. "Heaven" is a mental condition, not a visible place.

The fact is, we are spiritual beings, invisible while occupying the mortal body. When we step out of the mortal body we are still spiritual beings, and if we are free-minded those gone before will meet us and will show us the way to the spirit world. God is not a visible spirit, but God is Spirit, God is Love. You say you loved a girl. Did you ever see love?

Sp. No, but I have felt it.

Dr. "He that dwelleth in love dwelleth in God." We are talking to you, but we do not see you. I do not see you -I see only the face of my wife.

Sp. I don't see why you keep calling me your wife. You say we never die, yet you tell me I am dead, and I still have my crippled body.

Dr. If you had had understanding you would not have been crippled all these years since your "death."

Sp. Could I have been well all these years?

Dr. Yes, if you had been taught the truth. Jesus said: "The people honoreth me with their lips, but their heart is far from me."

Sp. People believe that Jesus died for our sins, and that if we are good we will go to Heaven when we die. I am not there.

Dr. You will never go to any orthodox "Heaven." And if there were such a place, you would be lonesome after you arrived there. Heaven is a mental condition attained through understanding. Think of the wonders of Nature and God's revelations. Do you like music?

Sp. I used to. I used to sing in the choir. My girl sang too. We were so happy. I always felt when we were singing there was such beautiful harmony, but then the minister got up in church and condemned everybody that did not give enough money to the church.

He said we would go straight to hell. I could never see the justice of that, that when a man does the best he knows how and lives a clean life, that he should go to hell if he does not give enough money to the church.

Dr. Do you know who was the founder of the Methodist Church? John Wesley. He understood the real life on the other side and lectured on spirits and spirit communion. He knew the truth -he did not just believe -and he wrote of it, but his people do not follow the teachings of the founder of their own church.

Christians do not understand the teachings of Jesus. They do not want to understand, because that causes them to think. It is easier to merely believe. Spiritual things must be spiritually discerned.

Sp. When I was in my shop, once in a while I saw my father and mother, but they are dead and I knew I could not be with them.

Dr. Why not?

Sp. Because I was in life, cobbling in my shop. Mother said to me: "Come along with me!" I could not go because I had my crippled body, and I had to earn my living. When I did not work I did not get anything to eat, and I was awfully hungry. Once in a while I got a smell from the restaurant, but that was all, unless I worked.

Dr. You were a spirit so could not eat. Your parents came to you because they are spirits. All these years you stayed around your shop, because that was your greatest interest. You did not know the higher laws of life.

Sp. I was taught that if I did not go to church I would go to hell and burn for ever and ever.

Dr. There is no such thing as burning for ever.

Sp. Thank God for that!

Dr. Look around; perhaps you will see somebody you know.

Sp. I am sick and tired of mending shoes.

Dr. After you leave here you will not have to mend any more shoes.

Sp. I would like to play and sing. I love music. I was getting along very nicely with my singing lessons until I got crippled.

THIRTY YEARS AMONG THE DEAD

Dr. Perhaps Mary is here now.

Sp. Mary? She gave me up and married, but she was not happy. She married a drunkard. She suffered. (Seeing a spirit.) Oh, there is my mother! She was good to me.

Dr. Does she speak to you?

Sp. She says: "My son, you need not be crippled any longer." Why, I have a new body, Mother -but, oh, Mother, (crying). I am a woman now! Such a foolish thing -to be dressed up like a woman!

Dr. You are only talking through my wife's body.

Sp. Can I talk through another person's body?

Dr. Yes. My wife is a psychic instrument through whom spirits can talk. She is entirely unconscious while you are speaking through her. It is strange, but true. Did you ever ask yourself what life really is?

Sp. No, I had no time. I had to use my mind to make shoes.

Dr. That is no excuse at all.

Sp. My mother says -. At this point the spirit was removed and his mother assumed control.

2nd Spirit: Henry, life is real. There are no mysterious things as we were taught. I believed in the same church as you. You know father never cared for church, and do you know, he progressed more rapidly than I in the spirit world. My belief and dogma held me back. You remember father studied, and we called him crazy, because once in a while he went to Spiritualist meetings, but he was right. You know he had that book "Heaven and Hell," by Swedenborg, and we used to look at each other and think he was going out of his mind.

We went to church and he did not, yet he was the one to open my eyes to see better things when I reached the spirit side of life. If he had not opened my eyes I would still be bound in my former belief, and that means I would be in the earth sphere. I was always afraid if he died he would go to hell, and I was in misery. You remember father died before I. He came to me after I passed out but I thought it was imagination.

He tried very hard to get me to understand. I want to tell you that creeds and dogmas of the church cause many earthbound spirits. These spirits do harm to mortals.

Henry, the Bible says: "Where your treasure is, there will your heart be also." Your treasure was your workshop. You have been in your shop helping that young fellow, unknown to yourself. We could not get you.

First you were crippled, and we could not get you to realize that your spiritual body was not crippled, but your mind was so set on your crippled body that you could think of nothing else. We have been with you for some time, trying to get you to come with us, but we could not.

One day we were passing by this place and we heard singing, so we came into the meeting. We saw that spirits were made to understand when nobody could reach them otherwise, so I said: "Let us bring Henry here." That was a long time ago. We had to wait our turn before we could bring you here.

Now, Henry, open your spirit eyes and see that your spirit body is fresh and new. Don't think of your old crippled body, because then you will be crippled. Think of your young spirit body and you will be young. You will be happy.

You were a good man. You had your sorrows but you tried to do the best you could, It was only ignorance, false doctrine and belief that held you back.

Henry, we have a beautiful home in the spirit world, and I will take you there, where you will have to learn many things. The first thing is to throw away all selfishness, ignorance, self-pity and jealousy. Come with me with an open heart. Open your heart to God in a spiritual way, and you will find the Kingdom of Heaven within you.

You have much to learn. When you are happy you will find that happiness and love are Heaven. Selfishness and ignorance are hell; darkness is hell. People make hell for themselves and others. Let us do all we can to help others and forget self. If you think only of self, when you pass to the spirit side of life you will find yourself shut up in a room, alone, and all you will see will be your ignorance and selfishness.

You will be kept in this condition until you cry out: "God help me to forget my selfishness." Let us do the work that is always waiting for us to do. We must say: "Get thee behind me, Satan." "Satan," or the "devil," as he is often called, is not a man. "Satan" is only selfishness, ignorance and bigotry -these are the devil. I was a good woman but I had to suffer, because I lived only for self. I worshipped my church. My husband was taken away from me. I worshipped my family more than I did God. I loved my church and when I passed away I clung to it.

I had a daughter, and I got into her magnetic aura and clung to her, and she was sent to the asylum. I could not get away from her. She died; then she was free and so was I. Then father came and told me what I had done by my selfish thoughts. Then I had to serve. All my work was with little children -not my own children, for they were taken away from me. They told me I would have to develop as much love for other children as I had for my own, and when I reached that point I was very happy.

Now I have children, not my own, but any child is mine, because one child is as much God's child as another and we should love them all. We should care for one as well as the other.

I have, my reward now. Every one loves me and I love them, and my home always has a new child in it. I take a new child, one who has not known love. I tell him of the life beyond. I want him to have an understanding of God. Love should govern all, not one child, but all. The great Universal Love -that is all, everything. One child should be loved just as much as another.

Therefore, be very careful in concentrating your love on one child or just your own family. Do not put your mind on one child, because when you pass out you will be in hell. You will stay around and disturb that child, and sometimes, as in my case, the child goes insane.

My poor girl was called insane because I was with her and could not get away. I was crying all the time because I wanted only my child. I did not realize I was controlling her. I could not see her. They told her she was not married and that she had no child. I was the one who was crying for my child, my daughter. Because she asked for her child, when she had none, they said she was crazy and sent her to the asylum.

So you see, friends, how necessary it is that we should all learn to know these things before we pass to the spirit side of life. Let us be wise and learn all we can while here. The more we learn here about the other side of life, the better and happier we shall be. The spirit body is only a counterpart of the physical body. As we progress in mind we grow.

If we intended going abroad we would do all we could to find out about the places we were going to visit and what hotels to stop at. How much more important it is that we should find out all we can about the next world. You will all be there some day.

Find out all you can, then when you are ready to go you will just say goodbye and wake up in the spirit world. You only say goodbye to the physical body and find yourself in your spiritual body. If you have lived only for self, as I did, you will stay right where you have been, just where you left off, as I did, and suffer. This is a lesson and you can profit by my experience.

Do not love and worship your own children more than others; that is selfish love. Many children have no mother. Why not try to help them? Divide your love with some child who has no mother. I have over one hundred to care for now. I have tried to bring them up and give them a mother's love. They never knew the comfort of a home.

I have worked and worked for Henry because I loved him, but I could not reach him. My husband was not held down as I was, so he has progressed much higher than I. Some day I shall probably reach where he is. He studied deeply, while all I had was belief. Friends, take advantage of what I suffered and learn from it. I thank you for allowing me to bring my son here. I also have my daughter with me. I have found the light and am now doing missionary work among the little children.

Remember, do not be selfish enough to worship your own children, but have a mother's love for all children, and above all things, worship God first.

Mrs. A., a patient from Chicago, was unusually sensitive to psychic influences, and her mother, Mrs. H.W., had for some time noticed in her daughter's actions a similarity to the mannerisms of a minister, former pastor of a church which she had attended, who had been killed by a train a number of years before.

Mrs. H.W. had spoken to Mr. A., her daughter's husband, of this similarity, and both were in the psychic circle when the patient, also present, was concentrated for.

EXPERIENCE, NOVEMBER 18, 1919

Spirit: J. O. NELSON Patient: MRS. A

Psychic: MRS. WICKLAND

The controlling spirit was dazed and seemed to be suffering from severe chest pains.

Doctor: Think strength and you will be able to talk. Who are you?

Spirit: I don't know.

Dr. Where did you come from?

Sp. I don't know that either.

Mr. A. Can't you tell us where you came from?

Sp. I don't know, but if I should say anything, I would say that I came from hell.

Mr. A. What kind of hell?

Sp. Real hell. I was burning up.

Mr. A. What caused that?

Sp. I don't know what it was but it came like fire. (Static treatment given patient, which is felt much more keenly by the obsessing spirit than the patient.)

Dr. It woke you up all right. Where did you come from?

Sp. I don't know what I have been doing for a long time. I think I must have slept and then I woke up in hell. I saw all kinds of sparks. I guess I did not pray enough.

Mr. A. What were you doing when you were living?

Sp. I don't know. I don't know what I did. If I could only know what is the matter with me.

Mr. A. What were you doing, the last you recall?

Sp. I have such a pain here. (Rubbing the chest.) I feel as if I had been sick. I can't remember yet what I have been doing.

Dr. Your memory will soon return.

Sp. You know when a man walks and walks, and does not know where he is going or what he is doing, it's bad.

Dr. Were you on a journey?

Sp. I don't recall things yet. I think I have been in a coma state for a long time. When I was walking everything was so dark. I couldn't see anything. I have such pain here. (Placing hand on chest.)

Now I remember something -I got into a crowd, and they pushed me and pushed me. (Earth sphere condition after death.) Then I saw just a little star of light. (Magnetic aura of psychic sensitive, the patient he had been obsessing.)

They seemed to be crowding me in and in until at last I got to hell. The crowd was pushing me forward, and I did not know where I was going; then I got these sparks. I always thought I had been chosen to save others, and here I was in hell myself. The fire was awful. I had it for a while, then I seemed to get lost again. I don't know what is to become of me.

Dr. What is your name?

Sp. I do not know yet, I am so dazed. I can't recall anything. I seem to be getting somewhere. I must have gone through a very severe sickness. People crowded me and they came after me, and I felt I had not done right. I was always sincere.

Mr. A. Did you believe in hell?

Sp. Yes, I did.

Mr. A. Did you believe in Jesus?

Sp. Yes. I was one chosen to save others, but yet I went to hell -and I was to save others!

Dr. Now we will try to help you out of it.

Sp. There are so many people around here. They seem to want so much of me.

Dr. They must be the people you tried to save but did not.

Sp. They all ask me to save them now, but I cannot save myself.

Mr. A. Did something happen to you?

Sp. I think so. My head hurts me so much and I have pains here. (Chest.) I don't know where I am. I wish you could take away this dark gloom. At times I have felt that I did not know anything.

Mr. A. Who are you? Are you a man or a woman?

Sp. I am a man, and I do not know anything except that the crowd pushed me and I got to hell.

Mr. A. Did anything happen to you?

Sp. I don't know.

Mr. A. Where did you live?

Sp. In Chicago, I think. I seem to be blind and I feel so strange.

Mr. A. Were you going to any particular place while you were walking?

Sp. I don't know, but I see a train coming so fast, and then I remember getting into a crowd. Say -do you think my name is Nelson? Sometimes that seems to be my name and sometimes it doesn't.

Mr. A. Were you Pastor Nelson? Were you a minister?

Sp. It seems I was at times. That's my name! My name is Nelson.

Mrs. H. W. Do you know me?

Sp. I recall the voice.

Mr. A. Where did you know her?

Sp. In Chicago. I can see a train coming so fast, and then everything got dark, but I remember something hit me in the chest. Didn't I have a wife?

Mr. A. Yes, and several children.

Mrs. H. W. Don't you know me?

Sp. Yes, you used to come to my church. You were a good church member, but you got away.

Dr. Do you know that lady? (The patient, Mrs. A.)

Sp. No.

Dr. Did you know L. W.? (The patient's maiden name.)

Sp. Yes.

Dr. That is she.

Sp. She was much younger.

Mr. A. Do you remember coming from Western Springs?

Sp. Yes, I had been preaching.

Mr. A. You were hit by a train and killed.

Sp. I cannot recall that I am dead, but I know I have been mixed up. I am in such a crowd. What is the matter with my head?

THIRTY YEARS AMONG THE DEAD

Mr. A. Do you know a Mrs. Nelson who used to live on Foster Avenue?

Sp. Yes, that's my wife. There was somebody else along with me when I came to the trains and they pushed me ahead of the train. The train was coming this way, and I was going over there. Somebody got hold of me and then there was such a big crowd. I remember the big crowd after I was hit by the train. That big crowd has been after me all the time. (Spirits.)

Dr. That is because you did not teach them correctly.

Sp. Somebody says: "These are your followers that you have misled in the wrong path."

Dr. Why did you mislead them?

Sp. I taught them God's truth.

Dr. Possibly, as far as you knew.

Sp. I tried to save humanity from hell.

Dr. And then you went there yourself.

Sp. I was only in it for a little while, but it was terrible. I did not imagine it that way. I thought hell would be different than pouring down fire -fire and brimstone -and it smarted like everything. I cannot see why I should have been in hell.

Dr. It must be because your teachings were wrong. All these people accuse you of having misled them.

Sp. I gave myself up to God.

Dr. Did God ask you to do that? Or did you do it for a living?

Sp. I tried to save people from sin. I suppose I did save some.

Dr. You did not save yourself.

Sp. That lady over there (pointing to Mrs. H.W.) should go to hell. She did not stick to the church as she should.

Dr. You stuck to the church, and yet you say you have been in hell.

Sp. Yes, that's so.

Dr. Then how do you know your church and your teaching were right? You were a "Servant of God," yet you went to hell. You were supposed to be better than the congregation.

Sp. (Pointing.) Is that Mrs. W?

Dr. Yes.

Sp. (To Mrs. H. W.) Why don't you go to church?

Mrs. H. W. I do, sometimes.

Dr. She doesn't want to go to hell, where you say you have been. You went to church and yet you went to hell. You taught the wrong thing. You do not want her to follow in your footsteps, do you?

Sp. I don't want her to go to hell where I have been.

THIRTY YEARS AMONG THE DEAD

Dr. Then the church must be wrong.

Mr. A. Was your name Nelson -J. O. Nelson? Your wife is living in the same house on Foster Avenue.

Sp. Yes, that's my name. Now I remember.

Mr. A. You were killed eight years ago.

Sp. I have not seen my wife and children for a long time.

Dr. You did not preach the truth when you were trying to save souls, and you did not save your own. For years you have been in the purgatory of ignorance.

Sp. How is my wife? She loved me.

Mr. A. She is well.

Sp. How could my wife leave me as she did?

Mr. A. She did not leave you; she buried your body in Graceland. Do you know Graceland Cemetery?

Sp. Yes.

Dr. Do you believe in spirits?

Sp. What do you mean?

Dr. Ghosts?

Sp. No.

Dr. Doesn't the Bible speak of them?

Sp. Not particularly.

Dr. Yes it does. Jesus used to cast out unclean spirits, and the apostles did also. Have you met Jesus?

Sp. No. I have not met any one. I have been in the crowd, and they have been pushing me all the time.

Dr. Those were people whom you had taught falsely before they died.

Sp. One day I saw a little light.

Dr. You got into the aura of this lady, Mrs. A.

Mr. A. She is my wife. Why are you bothering her? Why don't you go to the Heaven you taught? Why do you stay around the earth?

Sp. Are you in hell too?

Mr. A. No, we are on earth. Your "hell" was static electricity that we gave you.

Dr. That was the only way we could drive you away from this lady.

Mr. A. Why didn't you go the way you taught?

Sp. I do not know.

THIRTY YEARS AMONG THE DEAD

Mr. A. Why didn't you teach the truth when you lived on earth?

Sp. I taught the way I learned, and the Bishop told me what to do. I taught the religion taught on earth.

Dr. That is a misconception. You yourself have proven that it is a fallacy. You have been dead eight years and yet you are an earthbound spirit.

Sp. I certainly expected to be in Heaven.

Dr. You did not teach the truth. That lady (Mrs. H. W.) will reach "Heaven" quicker than you will.

Sp. She will! How do you know that?

Dr. She has learned the real truth, the truth of the spirit world and spirit existence. Paul taught about spirits. Jesus cast out unclean spirits.

Sp. We cannot compare ourselves with Jesus. Jesus was the son of God.

Dr. The Bible says, "Ye are all the children of God" and Jesus said, "I and my Father are one."

Sp. He was God's Beloved Son. God sent Him to save us from sin.

Dr. I will tell you who said that. In the year 325 A. D., at the Council of Nicea, Italy. Constantine declared Jesus to be "The Son of God, and very God," and his declaration was officially accepted by the Christian Church.

Sp. Christ was God's Beloved Son, and if we believe in Him, we shall inherit salvation.

Dr. Why didn't you do it?

Sp. Jesus is God's Son, and if you believe in Him, you will be saved.

Dr. Then where are you now?

Sp. I don't quite understand it yet.

Dr. But you said you had been in hell. Does your conscience not tell you that you were wrong? I think it does.

Sp. It accuses me.

Dr. If you will listen carefully you will realize that you were wrong. You never felt quite satisfied with the story of God's creation of the world, did you?

Sp. We should not argue about God. God is perfect, and we are His children and if we believe in Him we shall inherit salvation.

Dr. You say God is perfect. You say God created everything and that He knows everything, therefore, He must have known beforehand that His creation would be imperfect, and that man would "fall in sin." Would you create a world and then destroy it?

Sp. People fall in sin and God's Son came to save us.

Dr. Did God know that the world would fall in sin? Did He know it, and yet create it? Does that sound reasonable? Did He know that "fallen angels" would obsess people? Was He All-Wise? The preachers are at fault in their teachings.

Sp. We were taught that. When we are teachers of the Gospel, we must live up to it, and we must believe it.

Dr. You did not use your reason or you would not have believed what you were taught. The people who are crowding you now are evidently the very ones you tried to save, and they too, are in darkness. They did not find Heaven. What does the Bible say? "Ye are the temple of God and the Spirit of God dwelleth in you." "God is Love, and he that dwelleth in Love dwelleth in God." According to your teachings you should have found God before this. But you have not. The teachings of Jesus contain wonderful truths, but they are not understood. It is easier to teach that Jesus died for our sins and that we will be saved and everything will be all right. Now you will have to obtain understanding.

Sp. If I am dead, then I should see God.

Dr. You will never "see" God. God is not a person on a throne. God is Spirit and God is Intelligence. Have you ever seen music?

Sp. I have heard it.

Dr. Did you love your wife and family?

Sp. Yes, I did.

Dr. Have you ever seen that love? If you understand the Love Principle in the higher sense you will understand that God is Love. That was Jesus' own teaching.

Sp. We have to teach as I did. Don't you think, Mrs. W., that I did all right?

Dr. She left your church.

Sp. She went astray.

Dr. You say you are a man, and yet here you are, controlling my wife's body. Did you ever believe in mediumship?

Sp. That is all humbug.

Dr. There must be some truth in it. You are proving it yourself.

Sp. I didn't feel that anybody should give up church for that humbug.

Dr. You yourself are proving that it is not a humbug, for you are talking through a medium now. Look at these hands and see if they belong to you. Did you have a wedding ring?

Sp. That's a woman's ring.

Dr. You are using my wife's body.

Sp. How did I get into it?

Dr. You are an invisible spirit. We do not see you. You are talking through my wife's physical organs. Now you see how little you really know of the laws of Life, and Love and the Hereafter.

Sp. Things seem so strange. There was a time -I recall now -I am getting some of my memory back. I recall I got hurt.

Dr. When the train struck you, you were driven from your body.

Sp. I remember going home, and I stayed at home, but my wife didn't seem to notice me.

THIRTY YEARS AMONG THE DEAD

Dr. Your wife did not know you were there. You were invisible to her.

Sp. I tried to talk to her and the children, but they took no notice of me, so I thought, what's the use? I prayed and prayed. I went away from my wife and I could not get back. I was parted from her and everything was so strange. Then I got into this crowd, and they followed me, and again I tried to go home, and after I got there I talked to, my wife and children, but it seemed as if no one cared for me, because they would not talk to me and took no notice of me.

I put my hand on my wife and it seemed as if my hand went right through her. I talked to my wife again, but no response, so I went out again, and got into that crowd, and I was with them until I got into hell. There were so many in the crowd that we were like sardines. One came after another, and then I was pushed ahead. (Controlled the sensitive.) I saw a little light and after that there was fire and brimstone.

Dr. You were in the magnetic aura of that lady (Mrs. A.) and obsessed her, and finally controlled her body.

Sp. How could I do that?

Dr. I am going to answer your question in true Yankee style by asking another -How could you control this body? You see how little you know about the mysteries of God. You preached only a doctrine but did not understand the truth.

Sp. When you go to a Seminary and learn what they teach you, you have to preach it whether you like it or not..

Dr. You "sinned against the Holy Ghost" because your better judgment told you it was not right. Jesus did not teach what you taught.

Sp. I was not very successful in my ministry, (this statement was afterward confirmed) as many others are not, because it seemed as if the audience, my followers, did not stand by me, and then I was discouraged and felt what was the use. No one seemed to care for my preaching. I was very discouraged. I felt sometimes as if I should give up the whole thing.

Dr. Why didn't you?

Sp. If I should tell you the truth and tell you why I didn't, I should say it was because I had a wife and family to support. But I was not successful as a minister. I wish I had never studied for the ministry, but had been more of a mechanic; I would have had a happier life. (It was later learned that during his earth life the spirit had made this same remark to a fellow minister.) I could not provide for my wife as I wanted to, and she is a good woman. My salary was small, and when you have a family to support, and have to get your salary "by your mouth," it is hard when you don't get any encouragement from your followers.

Some found fault with me. I would go into the pulpit and my heart would not be in my work because I knew they did not like me. I was not happy. I wished that I had not studied in my younger days but had earned an honest living.

I see things now that I did not see before. I was blind, and I see now that I was greatly at fault. I should not have followed in the path I did. They found fault with me here and there, and the Bishop sent a poor fellow from one place to another, and sometimes it meant a whole month's salary. Sometimes I had to borrow money so that I could move. At last I got tired of being moved around. I would get a few friends in one place, then we would have to move, and I got discouraged.

THIRTY YEARS AMONG THE DEAD

Finally I got a house and I said I was going to stay there, and told them if they did not want me, or they could not find anything for me to do, I would go to work. I never could get enough together to properly support my family, because they changed me so often. The Bishop would move me from one place to another. That is not the right life to live. I would not wish my worst enemy to be a minister. It's pretty hard on a fellow. Now I am in a worse condition that I was, because I'm blind.

Dr. Before you leave here we will open your eyes and send you on your way rejoicing.

Sp. First tell me if there is any cure for my blindness.

Dr. We will open your eyes. The Bible says: "Eyes have they, but they see not; they have ears, but they hear not." Yours is only spiritual blindness.

Sp. I wish I could open those spiritual eyes.

Dr. It is not the fault of Jesus' teachings that you are spiritually blind. It was wrong to teach as you taught. That is the cause of your present condition. If you say that God sent Jesus as a special Savior, you infer that God made a mistake when He created man, and He did not.

Sp. Jesus was God's Beloved Son.

Dr. That conception is wrong. Jesus said: "I and my Father are one," and we are told in the Bible "Ye are all the children of God. Are we not strangers to ourselves?

Sp. We fall in sin. Do you believe in the Devil?

Dr. In the first place God is not a person. He is Spirit, All-Wise, All-Powerful, everywhere present. We accept that as the first principle in the Universe. God is All in All.

If God is All in All, as the Bible says, would He make the big mistake which Christianity implies he made when it asserts that God's creation was so imperfectly planned that man was doomed to fall in sin, and that the sending of a Savior was the only means of rectifying this mistake?

The church teaches that some of the angels fell. That means they became something inferior. How could that be if they were created out of God's own substance? That Something Supreme created the world and placed us here -had He not forethought and foresight enough to see what would happen?

Sp. We were born into this world and fell in sin.

Dr. Didn't God know what would happen?

Sp. I suppose so.

Dr. I am showing you that the orthodox teaching is wrong. Much of the Bible is simply a collection of allegories. Jesus always spoke in parables.

Spiritual things must be "spiritually discerned." When Jesus wished to teach the people that they should love their fellow man as themselves, what did He say? He told them the story of The Good Samaritan -the story of a certain man who went from Jerusalem to Jericho and fell among thieves who beat him and left him half dead.

A certain priest came that way, and when he saw him he passed by on the other side. Then a Levite came and he passed by on the other side. But a certain Samaritan came, and when he saw him he had compassion on him and bound up his wounds and brought him to an inn and cared for him. And when he left the inn he paid the host to take care of the man. Then Jesus asked the lawyer which one represented his fellow man, and the lawyer answered, "He that showed mercy."

Sp. But that is history.

Dr. No; that is allegory.

Sp. How do you know?

Dr. The very Bible tells us so. Jesus told that story simply as a parable -to show what? The principle. Your doctrine blinded you.

Sp. Then don't you believe that really happened?

Dr. No. Jesus spoke in parables.

Sp. I was not taught that way. When I was not taught that way how could I know more than I did? Ministers teach as I did all the time. The way you say it is all new to me.

Dr. That is the true teaching of Jesus.

Sp. Don't you believe he died for our sins?

Dr. No, I do not. Did Jesus die to please God?

Sp. No, he died to save us from sin.

Dr. Do you mean to say that God created a special son for people to kill so they could be saved?

Sp. We must not talk against God.

Dr. I am talking against erroneous teachings.

Sp. Do you believe in such things, Mrs. W?

Mrs. H. W. I do now.

Dr. Jesus said: "Except ye become as little children ye shall not enter into the kingdom of heaven." What do children do? They ask questions. They want to know. Did you seek to understand? No. You only tried to teach the doctrine of belief. Did you ever understand flowers?

Sp. They belong to Nature. We must not worship Nature.

Dr. God made Nature. We must not worship Nature, we must worship God. But God is in Nature, He speaks to us through Nature. The corrected translations of the Bible tell us that Jesus said "God is Spirit." He did not say, "God is a Spirit," but "God is Spirit, and they that worship Him must worship Him in Spirit and in truth."

Sp. I never heard things explained like that before.

Dr. We want to open your spiritual eyes so that you can see. "God is Love; and he that dwelleth in Love dwelleth in God." Where are you going to find God outside of yourself? What is love? What does love look like?

Sp. I cannot describe how it looks. You feel it.

Dr. "Love is the fulfillment of the law." "Thou shalt love thy neighbor as thyself."

Sp. Are you a minister?

Dr. Not as you understand the term. I honor God, but not dogma. I realize that the Universe did not make itself. God is Spirit, Power, the Soul of the Universe. He is a Practical Something in which the heavenly bodies all move. If we want to understand God we must understand ourselves. We must try to understand why we are living beings. What is the size and breadth of mind? How large or small is mind?

Sp. You say that I am a spirit, and that I am talking through this lady's body. How is that possible? You also say that I bothered that other lady. (Mrs. A.)

Dr. There is a psychic law whereby spirits can control mortals. When correctly followed we have spirit communication of the highest order. Perversion of this law results in obsession.

Mrs. A. is a natural psychic, and you and other spirits came into her magnetic aura and interfered with her life. She came to California to be helped. She is in California now, and so are you.

Sp. California! How did I get here?

Dr. By another wonderful law. You followed her. The obsession of mortals by spirits is a fact that has been known in all ages.

Sp. You do not mean that I have been bothering that lady?

Dr. Yes, and would have helped to ruin her life.

Sp. How did I get to her?

Dr. How did you come here? How are you controlling the body of Mrs. Wickland?

Sp. I don't realize that I have ever done any wrong.

Dr. We had to give the lady the electrical treatment we did in order to expel you from her aura. You are not the only one that has been removed. When many minds try to function through one body, it creates a disturbance. Others would say that my wife is insane just now because she is a woman and yet you, speaking through her, say you are a man and a minister. Another mystery is that Mrs. Wickland is entirely unconscious at this time.

Sp. How did I come to this body?

Dr. Spirit helpers brought you here and allowed you to control my wife, because she is a psychic sensitive.

Sp. I did not mean to do anybody harm. I just followed the crowd and they pushed me in. I did not know any one in particular in the crowd. I was blind and could not see, so I just kept with them.

Dr. Do you know why you were blind? You had lost your physical eyes but were not aware of the fact. You were in the spirit world but you knew nothing of the spiritual laws. You were in what the Bible calls "outer darkness."

Sp. Does outer darkness mean when you don't understand?

Dr. Yes. When you lost your physical body you lost your physical eyes, but you did not know it, and since you did not understand the higher life your spiritual vision was not open.

Sp. I have had a body and I have had eyes.

Dr. You have a spiritual body, but you were mentally blind. Do you remember that Paul spoke of a natural body and a spiritual body? "First that which is natural and afterward that which is spiritual."

Sp. Do you mean to say that I was spiritually blind when I was a spiritual adviser?

Dr. Yes. When you have your spiritual eyes open you will realize what Jesus meant when He said: "I and my Father are one." Jesus said: "Be ye therefore perfect even as your Father which is in Heaven is perfect." The Bible says. "Add to your faith . . . knowledge," and Jesus said: "Know the truth and the truth shall make you free."

The Bible states: "Blessed . . . is he that hath part in the first resurrection" -that is, obtains understanding while in the body -"on such the second death hath no power," meaning that when ignorance is replaced by understanding spiritual light is obtained.

Sp. Do you mean to say that I had no real comprehension of the truth?

Dr. You had faith, but you did not have knowledge; you only had orthodoxy.

Sp. Then you mean that all my followers and the church people who came to hear me will all be spiritually blind?

Dr. Many of them may be if they follow your teachings. If you look you will probably see others here.

Sp. There is a big audience here and they are all listening. (During a psychic circle of this nature, many earthbound spirits are brought to profit by the experience of the spirit who is controlling the psychic.)

Dr. It is our own stupidity that keeps us back. We should use the wonderful mind that God gave us. We have the marvelous universe to study and try to understand. Did you ever stop to think how fruit grows? You plant a seed in the ground, it decomposes and out of it grows a tree.

Sp. That belongs to Nature.

Dr. Nature is the body of God. God is All in All. You taught that in church.

Sp. I have said that many times but I did not see it as you do.

Dr. If God is All in All would not creation itself be a part of God?

Sp. I never thought of it in that light. It seems strange that while I gave truth to my people I should find myself in this darkness. Say, are you a minister?

Dr. No, I am not, but I try to understand God's wonders and the meaning of existence.

Sp. You have studied the Bible pretty well. You seem to know the Bible much better than I did myself.

Dr. I regard its teachings differently.

Sp. You seem to quote the Bible by heart. I should like to have you write down all you have told me. I should like to have your statements written down, and if I could give it to the people as you have given it to me, I should be very glad.

Dr. Now your spiritual eyes will be opened and you will see others who will teach you the same things. Advanced spirits will teach you how to progress in a rational way in the spirit world, and you will be taught much more than I tell you. You will not be in the dark any longer. If you will look around you may see some one you know, who has passed on.

Sp. Should we call them back?

Dr. Call them back from where?

Sp. From Heaven.

Dr. Jesus said: "The Kingdom of God is within you," and in the Bible you will find: "Ye are the temple of God and the Spirit of God dwelleth in you."

Sp. Don't you think we should all go to Heaven?

Dr. "Heaven" is not a place.

Sp. We must have some place to stay.

Dr. "Heaven" is a condition of mind. When you are happy, is that not Heaven? The more happiness you create around yourself, the more "Heaven" you will have. Happiness is Heaven.

Sp. But we have to be in some place.

Dr. You are in the spirit world; I have told you that. You can only attain "Heaven," or happiness, as you develop.

Sp. Where is that place -the spirit world?

Dr. It surrounds the physical world. You will be taught all that. Jesus said: "Seek, and ye shall find; knock, and it shall be opened unto you."

Sp. There are many people here. (Spirits.) Some are very happy and contented, and they seem to be asking me to come to the home of understanding, life, happiness and the spirit world. What is the spirit world?

Dr. That is the world of the spirits who understand Nature's higher laws.

Sp. Before I go with them, I should so like to send a message to my wife. Will somebody take it to her?

Mrs. H. W. I will be glad to.

Sp. Tell my wife I have found that life is more serious than I thought and we should try to understand more of God's wonders and not only believe. (Spiritual vision opening, with a flood of understanding, face upturned and arms outstretched.) I want to tell my wife that I have learned more about the wonderful world beyond than I ever knew before. My spiritual eyes are open. I wish so much that she could accept the proof that has been revealed to me.

All this time, as you have told me, I have been dead. I have been in darkness but, as this gentleman tells me, it was a spiritual darkness. My eyes are open and I can now see. A beautiful world lies before me. I want my wife to understand these things so that she will not be in the dark as I have been. Tell her not to have belief alone. Investigate, and find out what the life beyond is.

I do wish I could teach about the beautiful land beyond as I see it before me. There are wonderful landscapes and homes of all descriptions. My eyes are open and now I see. Here is one beautiful home, and there another.

A man stands here and he says to me that the homes in the spirit world are not bought with money, but are acquired by good acts done here on earth. This man, this teacher, says: "Be unselfish, and have love for others, then you will have a beautiful home in the spirit world. If you live for yourself alone you will have only a little shanty, for you have done nothing to help your fellow man. Give help to others and serve the ones who need help. These are also the teachings of Jesus." I see beautiful homes around, but where is mine? I have none. I have not seen it yet.

Dr. By helping and serving others you will soon have one.

Sp. I want my wife to know that we should live so on earth that when we come to the beautiful world beyond we shall have a home. We must do as our better nature tells us to do.

Dr. Now you are preaching an excellent sermon.

Sp. I am not preaching it. This man (spirit) tells me that. He stands right here by me. He says: "The Bible states, 'It is easier for a camel to go through the eye of a needle than for a rich man to enter into the Kingdom of God'."

He says: "I will illustrate to you what a home would be if a man sells his soul for money and does not help others." There is the home of a millionaire who has taken money from the poor people and grasped all he could. In the spirit world his house will be a mere hovel in the ground, for he could not enter one of those beautiful homes. Those homes were built by good deeds done for others and not for self. He will have to work, through service, to an understanding of a higher condition.

There are homes of all descriptions, and castles, too. This teacher says that many times there are in these beautiful castles poor old widows and men who were outcasts, but who lived for others and not for self.

Their acts were acts of kindness, not selfishness. They made many sacrifices. There are many homes, from castles down and down, until they are made of dirt, many surrounded by snakes a miserable condition through which the selfish must pass. Now he points to a house and says: "This is yours -this little, tiny house. You were honest in what you taught, so you have a house, even though small. Some have none.

You did not seek for the truth; you accepted things as they were presented to you. "Now you will have to work for others, and make a home for your wife and children. You must work now and try to help them realize the beauties of the life beyond. "Is it not more beautiful to see the spirit world in the true sense of life than to preach the gospel of condemnation? Why should we not open our spiritual eyes and understand God as He is, instead of picturing Him as a monster of cruelty?"

He says: "Christians murder their fellow men. The war has grown out of selfishness. The churches will soon fall, and there will be a new religion that will bring true understanding, and all people on earth will open their eyes and see the real truth of God's wonderful manifestations."

Isn't it wonderful? How I wish I could come back and tell people the truth as I see it now. I would tell my people that I had not taught properly and so had not helped them. Now I could give them the truth and help them.

I would not need to tell them that if they did not live the right kind of life they would go to hell. "Hell" is only ignorance and selfishness. If only I could give this truth to my followers! How I wish I could go back and preach what I know now. I would work to help them to a spiritual understanding and I would not teach condemnation, as I sometimes did. I would try to help them open their eyes and understand what life really is. I wish that they could see the beautiful land and homes that I have seen.

I will work, and work hard, to make a home for my wife and children. The home I want is not mine yet, but I have a small beginning. I will work to give my wife and children the home I have always wanted them to have. What is this? (With great excitement.) This man says this is the lower sphere I see, where ignorant spirits travel in darkness.

Here is another scene which is the result of my work. How sick these spirits are, and how crippled! They are blind and grasping.

Dr. They are showing you the lower earth sphere.

Sp. This man says they are showing me the result of orthodox teaching. Look at those drunkards and murderers!

Dr. They are now showing you these scenes so when you leave this body and begin to progress you can better help others.

Sp. He says this is a condition which false teachings and human selfishness have created. These spirits look like snakes. Look at the nails on their hands! This is terrible! Some are on their knees, crawling, and some are on all fours.

That -and that -and that -is my work! Oh, God! This is the result of wrong teaching. It is terrible! Now this man shows me an asylum of crazy people, and there are crazy spirits around them all. Oh, that is hell -hell! They shout and howl! What a sight, what a horrible sight.

They are showing me the real things. Here is a human being with three or four spirits crawling on him! Now he shows me another place -it is this place, here. (Institute Hall.) There is a Spirit Home built within this room an Inner Hall. There are many spirits here. He says: "We take them from obsessed mortals and bring them into this Hall and keep them there until we can convert them. Often we must have them control this psychic to bring them to an understanding.

"By bringing one to an understanding, the door is opened for many others. One or two are allowed to control and the others see how they are enlightened, and then they learn that they also must go with friendly spirits to the world beyond. "Let us preach the gospel of truth so there will not be this earthbound spirit condition, caused by ignorance and selfishness."

If only I could return to help preach this great truth that I have found!

Dr. Now you have been shown the way and you must go with these advanced spirits who will help you.

Sp. Will I go with that man?

Dr. Yes. He will teach you many great truths.

Sp. He says that it is false teaching of ministers which brings people to this hell. He says I must go, but before I go I want to thank you all for helping me to a home in the spirit world.

(To Mr. A.) He also wants me to ask you to please forgive me. I meant no wrong to your wife; it was only ignorance on my part.

(To Mrs. A.) I want to ask you to forgive me. I will help you all I can, but not before I know how. I will do all within my power to help you become free from the condition you are in. Now I see those around you. Fight, and we will help you win. I also want to thank you, Mrs. W., for helping me, because this man says you helped me to an understanding.

God bless you and my dear wife. Please bring this message to her.

Three years after the above experience, when Mrs. H. W. was again present in our circle, the spirit of Pastor Nelson returned and spoke through the psychic.

EXPERIENCE, MARCH 14, 1923

Spirit: J. O. NELSON Psychic: MRS. WICKLAND

I have come here tonight to thank you all for the help I received in this little circle. You gave me the truth, and I also learned that I had unconsciously been obsessing some one.

I wish all could understand and know the laws that govern the spirit conditions on this earth life. I was not a bad spirit, but I was ignorant of the laws. I should have been much more enlightened, because I used to preach to people and try to help them understand the real life, but how few ministers who stand in the pulpit today give out the truth? They all know there is a life after this, but they cling to the old orthodox belief. Some are ready to grasp the truth and some are not.

I thank you for helping me. I felt like saying I was in hell because of those electric sparks, for I thought the devil himself was after me, but I was brought to a realization of what I should have done when in life, and that I should not obsess any one.

(To Mrs. H. W.) I also want to thank you, Mrs. W., for helping me, and to ask your forgiveness for having obsessed your daughter. But I assure you I did it unconsciously. I did not realize the laws that govern.

I was not taught myself. I thought I was teaching my people about the real life, but I was not. I preached about Christ dying for our sins, that you must believe, and faith will make you free.

That is not so. To faith, we must add knowledge, and that will make us free, so the Good Book says. I did not preach that. I taught, to faith add belief and you will be saved.

How very little ministers do to help uplift people or to give them a right understanding of God. We always tell them to believe, believe. We do not want people to have knowledge, because then they begin to ask questions that we cannot answer, so we tell them to believe and have patience, and they will be saved. Why should we not teach them the real truth and have them understand God and life in the true sense?

The time is coming when the ministers cannot preach the old dogmas to the people. They will have to change if they want the people to fill their churches. I know I was not a good minister -I mean I was not popular. I could never hold my people because I did not have my whole heart and soul in the work. I felt that we should believe, but at times a strong power came to me and I felt that I should have more real knowledge of the life hereafter, but I shut the door to it. Now I am sorry that I did not try to investigate more.

When I went out of my body I went so quickly that I did not realize the change. You know, Mrs. W., there was quite a company of us and we were all rushing to get home. I stepped over to the other track and another train, which I did not see coming, killed me.

I did not even realize that I was hurt. When the rest of them went home, I went with them. I went to my home but I did not realize that anything unusual had taken place. I could not understand things. I went first to one, then another, but nobody seemed to notice me. It was very queer.

I did not know what to do. Where should I go, where could I go? I went to my church and stayed there, still I did not realize that I had passed out.

One day, Mrs. W., you came to church. In your thoughts of me I saw a light, because I was in darkness. I did not feel sick, but I did not feel quite myself, so I followed you to see if I could get an explanation. When you reached home, suddenly I seemed to be closed up in a room, and I was in very close quarters. (Obsessing Mrs. W.'s daughter, Mrs. A.)

After a while I went to sleep. I slept in a way, and still I felt weak and had such a strange sensation. There were several others with me, but I cannot describe the condition except to say that we seemed to be in a room too small for us. We were all packed in like sardines. I could hardly get my breath. Then I fell asleep and I slept for a long time. I did not realize anything after that until I got fire all over my body. (Static electricity given patient.) There seemed to be fire all over me and I could not realize what it was. All I could see was this fire -and how it thundered!

At first I thought I was really dead and in hell, because I could not imagine anything else. I thought: "I, a minister, trying to save people from hell, and here I am, right in it myself!"

Then I woke up and there was more fire, but before I knew it, I was alive again and I could talk, which I could not do before. (Having been transferred to Mrs. Wickland.) While I did not know I was dead, yet I felt I had to come to life again. I found I had been brought to this little circle for help, and I want to thank you all for waking me up. I have no grudge against you for having given me that "hell fire." It helped me from "hell" to "Heaven," or as we like to call it, the spirit world. I found the hereafter very different from anything I ever dreamed of. What do we think, we ministers?

I want to say that we do not think at all. We preach, but we do not practice. We do not realize what we are doing when we try to "save" people -save them from what? Since I left you and you gave me the true understanding of life as it is, I have seen much. I have learned much.

In the three years since I woke up -I do not say three years since I passed out, because the rest of the time I was in a dream state -but in the three years since I have had an understanding of life, everything has been so beautiful, and I have been very happy and busy. I have my hands full with my work.

My mission is to go to the religious fanatics in the spirit world and preach to them the truth. They are in darkness. They pray and sing and they think that Christ died for their sins. All they do is to pray and sing, and they do not get anywhere. There are many people on the earth plane who go insane, but they are only controlled by crazy spirits who are religious fanatics, and all they do is sing and pray. They are wild. Some I cannot reach; some I can turn to an understanding of the higher life. I hope the time will come when the ministers who preach the gospel will preach a true interpretation of the Bible, not the one Orthodoxy teaches.

Mrs. W., I want you to tell the Pastor of your church that I said he must not hide his light under a bushel, but must teach the truth. He must study and learn the true lesson of life. He must give out the truth to his people. Tell him I said he can give it out, little by little, and before he knows it he will have given them the whole truth, and he will have many more people attending his church than he has now. People do not believe now in the old dogmas, but they want something -the truth.

Tell him that I wanted you to say this to him. I have found my home in the spirit world and am happy, but I have a great deal to do. I have to undo the wrong teaching I gave to the people when I was on earth. I taught dogma and now I have to give them the truth.

Mrs. W., please forgive me for having obsessed your daughter. I had no intention of doing what I did, for I did it unconsciously. Before I go I want to ask a favor of you, Mrs. W., and that is, tell Rev. W. to study and look into the truth before he comes to the spirit world, so he will not be in darkness as I was. Tell him he can give the truth to his people because the majority are ready for it. It is very monotonous to sit and listen to the old time dogmas over and over again.

Tell him I said if he does not do this, people will leave his church. He is a good speaker and a good man, and if he teaches the real truth, as he will find it if he studies, he will have many followers, but if he keeps on with the old doctrine he will not have many attending his church.

If he interests his congregation and has a revival meeting to tell them he has found the real truth, he will see things will soon be different. Nearly every one in his church has been to some Spiritualist meeting. They want the truth, so tell him to give it to them.

Tell him the old people in the home should be rightly taught, because they will soon come to the spirit side of life, and it is better that they should know about the land they are going to.

The young men of the present day do not want to be orthodox ministers. They want other doctrines. They know the old dogma is not the real truth, and they do not want to preach contrary to their knowledge. There are not many applications for the ministry now.

Tell Rev. W. if he will preach the truth he will have many young people in his church. Tell him to present the ideas of the founder of his church. John Wesley, the founder of the Methodist Church, lectured on spirit phenomena. All he has to do is to present Wesley's doctrine. Now I must go. Good Night!

Chapter XIV

Christian Science

The domination of any one fixed opinion to the exclusion of further mental growth holds the spirit in a state of non-progression, as has been attested by intelligences who on earth had held strongly to the Christian Science teaching regarding the non-existence of matter, and who have told of the difficulties encountered in freeing themselves.

A friend of ours had been a deep student of Christian Science and at the same time an investigator of the facts concerning spirit return. Shortly after he had passed away he was brought to our circle to be awakened through controlling Mrs. Wickland, and has since told us something of the conditions in the spirit world.

EXPERIENCE, JANUARY 27, 1918

Spirit: MR. H. M. Psychic: MRS. WICKLAND

I am pleased to come here again. I felt that I must take advantage of this evening to say something to my dear wife (present in the circle). I am so glad I can talk to her as we always talked. I am happy she is here.

God bless you, my wife. We were so happy together. I would not care to come back here at all if it were not that she is still on earth. This world is only a school where we gain understanding through experience. In the spirit world we go on and on progressing, but before we can progress we must have understanding of the spiritual laws. If we have not the right understanding then we remain in darkness and hover around the earth plane.

I am pleased that I had even a little knowledge of the higher life, for when I reached there my spiritual eyes were open and I could see and realize the beauties of the spirit world. I have met many of my dear friends on the spirit side of life. Many whom I knew are still in darkness and I have tried to help them understand their transition.

If I could only express the conditions on the spirit side of life so that you would get the full meaning! There is such beauty, such harmony. I have to thank little Silver Star (one of Mrs. Wickland's guides) for having awakened me when I reached the other side. Even with my knowledge of the other world I might have slept a long time, because when I passed out I was in a heavy sleep from an opiate which was given me on account of the nature of my sickness. But this little Indian girl called me by name and woke me up, and brought me to the spirit world.

You know I had been sick for a long time and I was very sick before I passed out. I made my mistake in trying for so long to cure myself. Christian Science says we should overcome matter.

THIRTY YEARS AMONG THE DEAD

We cannot overcome matter by will. When we are in the physical body and the body needs certain forces of which it is made, if we do not get them in our food we must get them through medicine and so build up the body, because will cannot conquer substance.

God has given us a will to use as a force in Nature and we should use it rightly. When as Scientists we refuse to do this we must suffer the consequences. I was an example of such a consequence. I went into Science with full will power and full faith that there is no such thing as matter and that we should overcome it. I tried and failed.

Mrs. Eddy is suffering now for advancing that idea. When you have a dress that is wearing out you try to get some material of the same color and quality with which to mend the dress. We do not do that with our bodies. We think the body should develop the substance it needs when it wears out. I did not get enough elements in my food to build up my physical body, my organs became atrophied and sluggish and were inactive because I did not take the right food to give them proper activity.

I should have gone to a physician to have them put in normal condition, but instead I tried to use my will to make them work. I tried by intelligence to overcome and build up the weak part of my body. That is just as if one refused to mend a worn place in a dress, insisting that no hole could come in that dress. I was just as foolish about my body, and I had to suffer the results.

When the body needs toning up we must do something to tone it up and to get the electric forces set right. I passed out because I wore out my body with my mind and did not feed it or take sufficient care of it. God gave us our bodies and He also gave us minds to take care of them. If we become one-sided and think mind is all then we get into trouble.

I took good care of my clothes, but how little I took care of my body. If I had paid half as much attention to my body as I did to my clothes I feel that I would have been on earth today. Probably some day things will be so understood that there will be no death -I mean that we will merely step out of the physical body into the spirit world.

If one would prepare himself for passing out of the body as he does for a journey he would be able to say: "Now I am ready to go. I am through with this world. It is time for me to go, and I want to go to the spirit side of life." Then there would be no dread. Many Christian Scientists ruin their bodies by lack of right care and often go as far as I did; they use will, no reason, and take improper nourishment, or not enough. I knew about ten years ago that I should attend to my inactive organs. If I had had them attended to, I would not have suffered as I did. I suffered a great deal and I used my will to make inactive parts act.

I should have liked to remain on earth long enough to do the work I felt I should do; but I will do the work on the spirit side of life, and when my wife comes we will work together. My dear wife, if I had thought less of mental, or Christian Science, and given more thought to the material side of things, then you would be in a better position than you are now. I really lost all thought of things material and I guess I thought we could live on air, and I always thought conditions would change some time. I did not realize. I was so hypnotized in my work that I hardly lived in the material world.

If it had not been for my wife I think that sometimes I would have forgotten that I should eat at all. I thank God she was not so deeply interested in the work as I, because then there might be two dead people.

Before leaving I must tell you of a little experience.

THIRTY YEARS AMONG THE DEAD

When I passed out I was awakened by hearing somebody say: "How do you do?" I listened, and once again I heard the quaint voice of my little friend, Silver Star. Then I thought I must be in California, because I remembered that Dr. Wickland and his wife were there, and I thought that Silver Star was speaking through Mrs. Wickland. Nobody says "How do you do" like Silver Star. I did not realize that I had passed out of my body. Again I heard Silver Star say "How do you do" in her strange way, and then I began to wonder where I was.

All at once I seemed to be alive again. Then I felt better. I thought, "I must have gone through the crisis of my sickness and now I am feeling better and am waking up." That was the time Silver Star brought me in to control Mrs. Wickland. I realized that I was weak from my sickness, but, having no pain, I thought I was getting better. I felt so light and strong that my first thought was that I could finish my book, but when I really came to myself I heard Dr. Wickland talking to me.

Then I thought, "Well, how did I get to California? How did I get here? I must be dreaming." It was some time before I realized where I was. I did not even then realize that I was controlling.

Doctor asked me who I was. I thought it strange that he did not know me, but I told him that I was Mr. M., and asked whether he did not know me. Doctor was very much surprised and explained as gently as he could that I had passed out of my mortal body a week before and was now a spirit. That was the first time I realized that I had passed out of my physical body into a spiritual body. It was very pleasant to think that I had wakened in a mortal body instead of in darkness.

Afterwards I saw many of my friends and I felt that there is no death. Doctor talked to me for a while and then my father, mother, sister and brother all came to me, and they brought many relatives and friends, and we had a happy reunion, one that can never be forgotten. Only, I wanted you, my wife, to be with me when I met all my relatives and friends.

When I realized that I was using an earthly body I felt sick again and my will power seemed to fail me. I began to feel very weak and a sensation of sickness came over me.

I at once thought of my little friend, Silver Star, and she said I must throw away my old clothes because I had no use for my old body, for I had new clothes now. When I thought of my spiritual body, I arose; I felt I had new clothes and I received strength and left the physical altogether. The magnetic current was cut and I dropped my old clothes entirely. I was then lifted bodily, so it seemed, and I felt I was floating, and we went through

conditions of all kinds. I felt so strange and saw so much that I grew fearful, so they told me to shut my eyes and keep them shut, which I did.

I did not know anything after that until they placed me on a beautiful bed. I was very tired and all I wanted was to rest, just rest. When I awoke from that sleep of rest my relatives and friends were around me. Somebody said: "Now you are well and strong and we will take a journey to our home in the spirit world."

We went to many of their homes. Each had a little home. We were united and happy, for here only harmony exists. We traveled from one place to another.

When I had been to visit quite a few friends, they said: "Now you have seen the spirit side of life. Here we are not idle. This is not a world in which one is idle; it is a world of busy minds. It is each one's duty to work. Now you are strong and we will take another journey -to earth." I wanted to see my wife so much. You were in my mind so much, my wife, and I wanted to see you. We passed through the spirit world and earth sphere to matter again. The earth is a little globe. The globe has a sphere around it. The distance between the spirit world and the world of matter is about sixty miles. This sphere is the world of the spirits in darkness.

Christ went to the spirits in darkness and prison -the prison of ignorance. We passed through conditions that cannot be described, the most hideous, the most fiendish, so ugly that I cannot describe them. It made me shudder to see the condition of the crippled minds, the selfish minds, the jealous minds. Each had the countenance of his mind. They were dressed as when on earth, but only because of their minds.

They were like vermin. They were like a lot of worms stirred up and crawling over one another. Talk about hell -that surely was hell! They told me that was the earthbound sphere. Then we came to matter again. We saw the people walking around in a life of matter, each one in some kind of business. It looked like a world of ants, and each one seemed to have some of these evil-minded spirits clinging to him. They are like the barnacles on boats; some are shaken off, but others come on. I cannot describe the sight.

I have been with you, my wife. You have felt me. I could not impress you because I was not strong enough to use my mind for that purpose, but still you have felt me. It has only been a little, because I had not strength enough to come closer. I am with you a great deal. After I learn in spirit how to overcome matter then I can come to you and help you.

I will build a home for you in the spirit world and when that home is finished and your work here is done then I shall be the one to meet you, and we will have a real home. I want to thank you all for the privilege of coming to your little circle, and would like to come again some other time.

An extract from another communication from Mr. H. M. follows the same line of thought as the previous remarks.

EXPERIENCE, NOVEMBER 3, 1920

Spirit: MR. H. M. Psychic: MRS. WICKLAND

I wish that I had had less belief that I could cure myself by thought. Everything that God has put in Nature is for man to use, not misuse. We should not condemn anything that God has given the world to use, but we have so many beliefs and creeds that we forget the principle of our Maker.

If we would understand His wonderful work through Nature we would love others better than we do. Do not condemn anything but teach men and women to love each other, teach them to know what their duties are in this mundane sphere.

Those on earth have so many creeds and fads that they drown themselves in their faith, forgetting that it is their duty to help the weak ones instead of stepping on their feet. So it is also with the body God gave us to take care of and not misuse. For my part I should have done more to learn what was the matter with me instead of only thinking there was nothing the matter, that I only imagined it and that there was no such thing as sickness.

If I had not hypnotized myself in that belief of Mrs. Eddy's that mind should overcome matter, and that it is only our mortal mind that is so-called sick and we have not the right understanding -if I had tried to find out what was the matter with me and called on some physician, one who had studied anatomy and the philosophy of life, one who had spent years in studying human nature and the human body, I should have been better off.

Christian Scientists condemn physicians, yet physicians have devoted their lives through centuries to the study and control of all sickness. Should we condemn them and say there is no such thing as sickness? Why should anybody condemn another who has devoted his whole life to study? Christian Science says there is no such thing as sickness and that you are not in the understanding.

Suppose that in olden times we had held the theory that there is no matter. How about Harvey? He discovered the circulation of the blood. Poor man! He was killed because of his discovery; he was killed by ignorant people who did not believe the truth. So one thing after another has been discovered in human anatomy. Yet Christian Scientists discard that altogether, and also say that there is no such thing as the body. I did not take care of the body that God gave me. I thought mind should overcome it. If I had consulted a physician I might even be with you today.

Do not let yourselves be hypnotized by ideas. Every theory has some good in it, but let us take the good and discard the rest. As Mrs. Eddy now sees these things, she wishes she could correct many of her statements. She now has to suffer for her mistakes, and it is very hard for her. Her followers come to the spirit side of life and expect to find things as she taught them. Mrs. Eddy herself has spoken in our circle several times, and has brought invisible audiences which she endeavored to free from the misconceptions acquired from her teachings relating to the problems of life and matter.

EXPERIENCE, FEBRUARY 24, 1918

Spirit: MARY BAKER EDDY Psychic: MRS. WICKLAND

I am here again and I feel so sad. Do not doubt me, do not doubt me! Why will people doubt me? Help me! God help me! I am in a terrible condition. I knew about the wonderful truth of the life beyond. I knew it well while in life, but I shut the door because I wanted a religion of my own. Spiritualism belonged to the past days. I wanted something new, something higher, something better than spirit return. I taught that you must not let any entities control you, or influence you, or give you any inspiration, but that you must be yourself and develop yourself, and be one with the Infinite.

Shut the door to the spirit world and be selfish -that was I. I had the truth of healing the sick. I was a medium, and in my younger days, my childhood, I was obsessed. As I grew older no one knew what was the matter with me, for I had such queer spells. Now I know what it was -an influence was controlling me whenever I had the spells. I was of a very nervous temperament and I was cured of those spells by Dr. Quimby. He believed in the work of obsession.

I took some of his doctrine and used it for my own. The doctrine would have been all right if I had not denied the finer forces in Nature. I denied matter, but friends, as I told you one time, I had a vision, and I saw how they treated patients in the other world, but at that time I thought it was a dream. They were teaching the spirits that there is no such thing as matter. They said: "Forget it, it is only imagination. You are not sick, you just imagine it. That belongs to matter.

That is only your mortal mind. You should overcome and develop the spirit within you." I thought that this vision meant that I was to teach that on earth, and I set to work. Now I see my mistake, because there is matter, and so long as you live on the material plane you will have to recognize matter. When you reach the spirit side of life your mind has to be taught to overcome matter, not cling to it, because spirits in darkness are clinging to matter as much as we cling to matter when we have our physical bodies.

I took this and taught it, and started on my work. It was so misunderstood, because I could not myself explain why matter was not. If only I could get people to recognize matter and recognize the truth of life after this! If I could only go back to my Church and teach the truth, the genuine Truth of God! God is the Spirit of the Universe and we are a part of that Great Spirit. Understanding this, we can overcome matter.

You are in the material body and you become sick. You become sick because there is a lack of something in your body which you must have, some element that helps in some way or another. But your mind can help to overcome. If I had taught that instead of denying matter altogether, it would have been so much better.

I wanted money and we concentrated to have the grandest churches in the world. My aim was to have churches of my own teaching all over the universe. I lost the opportunity to develop people's finer nature, the finer nature of men and women, because I shut the door of love and sympathy.

Do not doubt who this is -do not doubt me! I am here, I am here. I am no more than any human being. Mine was a life which did not do what it ought. I want to be helped. My people come to me and want help, and I need help myself. They cling to me and hold me down, and I shut the door for their happiness. We have only one mind. You understand where I got the mortal mind part from? I thought that should be taught here, but it should only be taught beyond the grave, beyond the veil, and only to the earthbound spirits who are in darkness and cling to matter. That should be taught on the spirit side of life and not on the earth plane.

Have love and sympathy and do the very best you know how for others. I could not leave this matter alone and I do not feel that I should, because it crushes me so. I came to this circle because so many have been helped here. I go from one place to another, and you will hear of me at different intervals because I can explain to a few at each place, and in that way people will wake up.

We cannot do much yet, but will you allow me to come here once in a while, when I see I can be helped? You know I have so many people who hold me down, and say: "Why did you teach this? Why did you shut the door for us? Give us light, give us light and understanding!" So many people are here, but they cling to matter. So many of my people are here and in talking with you I talk to them. You understand, I knew the real truth, but I shut the door. I cannot open the door to many of my followers because I shut the door for them and closed the door for myself, and when they pass out the door is closed. They want me to help them and when I explain things to them in the true light they doubt me, and say that I am not Mrs. Eddy because she did not preach such lessons.

I thank you for giving me this little time. Tonight many of my followers came with me, and through my talk to you they will be helped. Their sub-consciousness, which is asleep, must be awakened.

Question: Is the little pamphlet, recently published, called "Confession by Mrs. Eddy, from the Spirit World," authentic?

Spirit: Certainly it is. I am trying through every avenue to speak; I am not going to stop here. I will take advantage of every chance there is for me to tell the truth and reach my people.

You may hear from others that I have talked with them. I will bring up the above subject here and there. People doubt me now, but I shall keep on; I will not rest. We will have centers for the work. I want you here to help me spread the news, not much, just a little thought now and then will help. I will get my people together and bring them here and talk to them, if I may come once in a while, for I can reach them more easily when I control a mortal body.

THIRTY YEARS AMONG THE DEAD

God bless you all, and again I thank you for the privilege of having this opportunity of speaking to some of my people and helping them.

Further evidence of the fact that Mrs. Eddy, when on earth, knew the truth regarding the spirit side of life and the earthbound condition is found in one of the early editions of the Christian Science text book in the chapter on "The Science of Being."

"If the Principle, rule, and demonstration of Being are not in the least understood before what is termed 'death' overtakes mortals, they will rise no higher in the scale of existence at that single point of experience; but will remain as material as before the transition, still seeking happiness through a material instead of through a spiritual sense of Life, and from selfish and inferior motives. So long as the error or belief lasts, that life and mind are finite and physical, and are manifested through brain and nerves, so long the penalty of sickness, sin, and death will continue. To the other, the spiritual class, relates the scripture: 'On such the second death hath no power.' "

A spirit who had become fanatical over the Christian Science teachings was brought in by Mrs. Eddy as an example of the difficulties which she encountered in the work of enlightening her followers.

EXPERIENCE, JUNE 16, 1918

Spirit: NAME UNKNOWN Psychic: MRS. WICKLAND

Spirit: What kind of a meeting is this?

Doctor This meeting is held for the purpose of helping ignorant spirits -spirits in darkness.

Sp. We should not sing so much as we do, for that belongs to the mortal mind. We should be quiet and concentrate our minds to understand.

Dr. To understand what?

Sp. The true understanding.

Dr. What is that?

Sp. The Spirit of God.

Dr. And what is that?

Sp. If you do not know then you had better study and understand.

Dr. If you can tell us something about God or Spirit we should all be glad to hear it.

Sp. God is All in All, and we are a part of that great Divinity. We should concentrate and put our mind toward the Great Spirit. We should develop the finer forces within us but I am not here to talk to any one.

Dr. Should you not like to enlighten us?

Sp. I do not know if you belong to The Church.

Dr. Did you not say that God is All in All? Then we are a part of Him also.

Sp. If you have the right understanding, you are. If you do not have that understanding then you are not; you are more of the mortal mind.

Dr. Are we not a part of God, if God is All in All?

Sp. I do not care to answer your questions.

Dr. Is the mortal mind also of God? What happens to people after death?

Sp. I have nothing to do with death.

Dr. Have you found God?

Sp. God is within you when you have the right understanding of His wonderful works.

Dr. How is it with yourself?

Sp. I am one with that Great Spirit because I have understanding.

Dr. Understanding of what?

Sp. God, and how to develop your own self.

Dr. As far as I can tell, you have developed selfishness.

Sp. That all belongs to the mortal mind.

Dr. What happens to people when they lose their bodies?

Sp. They go back to the Infinite.

Dr. Where do they go?

Sp. Don't you know? I know, but I do not care to speak of it. I do not argue. I know myself, but I do not like to teach. I am one of His Elect.

Dr. Then you do not like to teach ignorant people?

Sp. No, I do not.

Dr. What church do you belong to?

Sp. I belong to The Church of Understanding.

Dr. Where does it exist?

Sp. It is the church that should be all over the world, the church where the people understand and know they can overcome matter and overcome mortal mind and be one with the Infinite.

Dr. Are you a Christian Scientist?

Sp. Yes. Why do I have to come down to such mortal minded people?

Dr. Don't you think you must have made some misstep which brought you down to such people as we are? Don't you think if you had read and studied the Bible, and had acquired an understanding of the real mystery of life, it would have given you more peace of mind? Isn't it strange that you should come down to such common clay as we are?

Sp. I suppose I have come here to do some missionary work among you. I suppose I came to teach you to forget mortal mind. You should all be loving and kind -one with the Infinite. You are not in the understanding. I may have come to lead you up to God -to the right understanding. I must help you all to understand. You must take the first step and read Mrs. Eddy's books, then you will be one with the Infinite and leave all mortal mind behind. You go on and on. You have to go through a great deal to get understanding. You can be led up to the Infinite God if you read and study. You have not understanding of the Infinite.

Dr. What does that "Infinite Understanding" call you?

Sp. I do not care to talk or argue with you.

Dr. What did they call you when you had a mortal mind?

Sp. Call me? Names belong to the mortal mind and I have nothing to do with that. It degrades one and drags one down. I came to teach you regarding the Infinite, the Spirit within you.

Dr. Do we have to give you two dollars for your teaching?

Sp. That belongs to the mortal mind. Develop the Spark of the Divine within you, then you will rise to the Infinite God.

Dr. Do you suppose we could ever climb so high?

Sp. Yes, by studying and studying. It is the only salvation for you.

Dr. You seem to have gone so far that you cannot join in anything with us.

Sp. I have passed beyond mortal mind, and we do not need to go back; we go forward.

Dr. It hurts to come down to mortal mind again, doesn't it? There is an old saying that "What goes up must come down."

Sp. What kind of people are you?

Dr. We are just common sense people, just "mortal-mind" people.

Sp. Then I must raise you to a higher level.

Dr. What is your name?

Sp. Just call me "Infinite."

Dr. Christ went among sinners. Are you better than He?

Sp. I am one with the Infinite God myself.

Dr. Have you seen God?

Sp. God is within you. You are a part of the Infinite. You are happy with Him -the God of the Universe; just beautiful Bliss and Harmony.

Dr. How did you happen to come here?

Sp. I suppose I came to be your teacher.

Dr. You spoke of going forward and that God is All in All. Is He within you?

Sp. I am one with the Infinite. I am in love with the Lord and the Infinite. You people here are still in your mortal caskets. You do not know anything.

Dr. That is a very elaborate statement.

Sp. We have to overcome; it is just an error.

Dr. On your part or ours?

Sp. I must help you to climb higher. I came to be a teacher to you all, to help you to understand and become one with the Infinite.

Dr. Probably an exchange of ideas might be helpful.

Sp. I do not need any teaching. I am one with the All in All.

Dr. What do scientists think will happen when they die?

Sp. They shall be a part of the Divine. I was a follower in one of the churches of Christian Science. I belonged to the Mother Church in Boston. I am one of the Elect.

Dr. Did you ever see Mrs. Eddy?

Sp. Mrs. Eddy is Christ Himself. She is my Christ; she is God Himself. She is the most wonderful woman on earth and she is the one we should worship.

Dr. How long have you been so radical on that subject?

Sp. I will not answer you.

Dr. How long has Mrs. Eddy been dead?

Sp. I do not care to argue with you.

Dr. Who died first -you or Mrs. Eddy?

Sp. (With asperity.) I will not answer your questions!

Dr. I did not think you had so much "malicious magnetism."

Sp. Mrs. Eddy never died. She never will, because she is the Teacher of the Infinite Spirit.

Dr. Have you ever seen Mrs. Eddy?

Sp. She is in Boston.

Dr. She is dead.

Sp. She is not dead and she never will die.

Dr. Mrs. Eddy died several years ago.

Sp. Her teachings were that she would never die. She will go from the mortal casket into the Infinite.

Dr. How long is it since you died?

Sp. I did not die; I only left my mortal casket. I was a fine practitioner.

Dr. How did you come to Los Angeles, California?

Sp. I am not in Los Angeles; I am in Boston.

Dr. Some intelligent spirits have brought you here to be helped. But the entity was so wrapped in her own ideas that she would not listen to anything else and was taken away, after which Mrs. Eddy came.

THIRTY YEARS AMONG THE DEAD

EXPERIENCE, JUNE 16, 1918

Spirit: MARY BAKER EDDY Psychic: MRS. WICKLAND

Good Evening. I am Mrs. Eddy -Mary Baker Eddy. I wanted to come back here again to give you one demonstration of what I have had to deal with. (Referring to preceding spirit.) I cannot do anything with people when they are like that until they contact matter again.

I feel so sad and sorry, for I shut the door myself. I want you to let me come here and extend help to a great number of spirits (by speaking through the psychic to an invisible audience) that have the same understanding of my doctrine.

If I had only opened the door of the real spiritual understanding and taught the real truth on earth, things would be different. I knew I had the truth. We should unite and be one strong body, because I know there is power in concentration, and I only wish that I could have the whole world understand this doctrine.

If I could only come back and tell my people what I now have to do. You saw the demonstration you had here tonight. I asked the Band of Mercy to bring one of my followers in to show what I have to deal with. With this one we could probably demonstrate to a hundred similar spirits the folly of the mortal mind idea.

Concentrate your mind over and over, again and again, round and round, and read and read -that was the way I taught one was to reach understanding. I said my followers should read my books, and read them and read them until they became second nature. When you are in matter the mind has to have some food. But when my people pass to the spirit side of life and matter is no more, and they have thrown off the mortal error, you see just where they are.

What can I do with them? How much could you do with them under similar circumstances? There is my work and more is coming. Every day there are more and more people coming. I try to help them because I taught mortal error and did not teach the truth.

I feel so sad, and I do wish I could tell them to open the door for the spirit of understanding, and not keep on just reading and reading and concentrating. In every church, all over the United States where we have churches, they use the same lesson on the same Sunday. They form a circle, round and round, and you must know they form a very strong magnet and draw people into the same condition. When they come here they cling to me, cling to me so closely, and what am I to do? If I tell them the common sense things I should have taught them, they will not believe.

I knew I had the real truth and I had power, but I was selfish. I wanted to have a religion of my own. I wanted one that the whole world should know. What have I now? When my people pass to the spirit side of life the door is closed and I cannot open it. What progress could you make with the spirit you had here tonight? I thank the Mercy Band, and all of you here, because through this experience we took this spirit to the spirit world, and they will teach her through object lessons.

There were many Scientists here tonight and they saw how foolish it all is; their eyes were opened and the spirit friends took them away with them. The one here we could not do much with, but she was an object lesson to teach the others, and in time she will be helped. My people read and read, and the majority come over here without any understanding. I closed the door for my people and it is hard.

It is easy for them so long as they are in the mortal body, but when they have lost the mortal body they see nothing. For them there is no spirit world, it is all "Infinite." I taught them to close the door to the spirit world, and I taught them to read only my books. I wanted a religion of my own. I was a trance medium and I gave readings, but I must confess I felt that was too common. I wanted to reach more intelligent people, because I found that Spiritualism would not reach the people I wanted to reach, so I took Quimby's doctrine, and also, as I told you previously, the vision I had of mortal mind in the spirit world, and combined the two.

I want it understood that I used to give readings in Boston. I was very selfish and wanted to be somebody and have some kind of a religion where I could have a following. I wished once that on my birthday church bells all over the United States would ring, and before I died I had that wish. I wanted to be one that would be looked up to.

I was brought up in such orthodoxy that I would not have anything to do with any of the churches. I went into Spiritualism first, and found that was much better than Orthodoxy, so I followed it for some years, but I felt I could not get very far with it, and in the end I was obsessed. What I saw in visions I put in "Science and Health." That book was written through the visions I had. It was not from my own brain.

If only with that I had given the truth which my brother wanted me to -he was in the spirit world -but I would not. I did things Albert (brother) said I should not do, and I closed the door for him. During the last of my days I was not myself very much. All through life I was back and forth on the invisible plane.

You know I was a psychic and I could have been a very good one, and have done more good to the world through my psychic power than I did. At the last I was too obsessed to be responsible for all I was doing. If I had used my psychic power I could have helped thousands.

Now I have to deal with what you saw here tonight. So long as my people are in the mortal body they are all right, but once the body is lost things go round and round. My followers are in just as bad a condition as are those who followed orthodoxy. When they pass out of the body everything they see is "mortal mind."

Possibly you felt sorry you did not convert the spirit you had here tonight, but while not successful with her, hundreds of others were converted through seeing how foolish it all is, and were helped through your talk. This room was crowded with people, and I hope you will all be liberal enough to never shut the door for the beautiful truth of spirit return.

I bless you all and give you my solid support and help and I hope you will allow me to bring more unfortunate ones sometime. I thank you for keeping the door open for me to come. I am only mortal and I am not of the "Real Infinite" either. We all have our ups and downs, here as well as on the other side of life. People think that they change their condition when they die, but they do not. My people are especially fixed because everything with them outside of themselves is "mortal mind" and their own mind is "Infinite."

Many who were followers of my Church have gone into New Thought. From New Thought they come into a more spiritual understanding. New Thought is more liberal. In New Thought they branch out and, being liberal, will look into spirit return. They are more liberal in their reading of books. I forbade my people to read anything but [Christian] Science books. That was because of my selfishness. I wanted a church of my own with my people under my thumb.

(Comment: Eddy was a greedy and egocentric control freak.)

How I do wish I had taught obsession, which I knew was true, but I did not. When I used to go into trances I wrote a great deal, and when I came to myself I would deny what I got. I was obsessed by some spirit who wanted me to do such work and I could not really help myself. If I had written the books as they were given to me, and credited their source, I might have revolutionized the world.

I again want to thank you and hope I can come another time. I also want to thank you, lady, (Mrs. M. mentioned in the first experience of this chapter) because your husband helped me in the very beginning. (In the spirit world.) He was one that helped me to a better understanding, and brought me here where I could get help. I hope you will have all the success you wish. Concentrate your mind on success and have no fear that you will not succeed, and all over the world will spread this wonderful truth of spirit return and obsession, and through your obsession work you will cure many more people than I did.

In our work, often when a healing was instantaneous, it was an obsession being relieved. You understand also that all the healers are in the circle of concentration with the power of the whole church to aid them, and that power of concentration is so strong that an obsession cannot live in that atmosphere.

Many I cured were obsessed, but they concentrated that they were not sick. How are they helped? I will tell you. The average doctor tells a patient that he has such and such a sickness. He creates a fear in his mind. Let us take a case of gall stones. It is very hard to diagnose such a case correctly. The doctor says the patient has gall stones; sometimes he operates when that should not be done.

Sometimes the patient gets well without an operation. That is due to his mind. He concentrates his mind on gall stones, gall stones, until he can think of nothing else. You understand, you have in your mind a creative power. We have a spark of the Infinite within us. In that Divine spark God created the world, all in it, and you as a part. Each of us has much of that creative power and when you set your mind working with that power you create your condition.

When you go to one of my practitioners, the first thing that is done is to take your mind off your sickness. You are given absent treatment to get rid of fear. You have the same creative power within yourself. In a case of diphtheria the mind can help, but we cannot kill germs. There are many things we fail in, but we have success with chronic cases.

We have more success because so many are obsessed. When you have fear you are negative. I will be with you to teach obsession to the world. Teach the real truth and do not care for people's opinions. If only I could go to my Mother Church and teach them the truth! Thank you each and every one of you, and sometime I shall come again. That the mind has power to create the condition in which a spirit finds itself after transition is illustrated in the following experience.

A former patient of ours, Mrs. Anna R., who had at one time been under our care and had been entirely restored to health, many years later left her home to care for a sister-inlaw, Mrs. Jessie R., who was very ill. The latter was a Christian Scientist and denied that spirit obsession had been the cause of the former illness of her sister-in-law, claiming that Christian Science and her own concentration had cured her. She was a masculine type, a very large woman, preferring to assist her husband with his oil station rather than care for her home.

After a long illness she died in the arms of Mrs. Anna R., who then remained in the house to care for the widower, and also keep house for him. She occupied the room and bed of her sister-in-law, and not only attended to all household duties but spent much time working in the garden until her strength failed when she became negative and was again disturbed by spirit interference.

She acted in a masculine manner and a brother, Mr. Herman M., realizing that some spirit had taken possession of his sister, at first thought the entity was a man. But Mrs. Anna R. began to talk as though she were Mrs. Jessie R. and authoritatively ordered everyone to leave the house. Mr. M. urged his sister to come to us for treatment but this she refused to do, insisting, under control of the obsessing entity, that "Christian Science cured me the last time."

Mr. M. then telephoned us regarding the situation and attended a séance in our home, mentally commanding the spirit that was troubling his sister to come with him. We concentrated for the patient and when Mrs. Wickland became entranced a corroborative conversation with the controlling spirit ensued.

Spirit: MRS. JESSIE R. Patient: MRS. ANNA R

Psychic: MRS. WICKLAND

Doctor: Can you tell us something about yourself? (Touching arm.)

Spirit: Leave me alone.

Dr. We want to enlighten you.

Sp. I am enlightened enough. They thought they were going to get me but they got left. (Intelligent spirits.)

Dr. To whom do you refer?

Sp. Those people. I don't want you to hold my arm. You have no right to touch me.

Dr. I have a right to touch the arm of my wife.

Sp. (Struggling.) I don't want to be held down!

Mr. G. Be a nice fellow.

Sp. Fellow! I'm not a man, I'm a woman. Can't you see that?

Dr. When I look at you I see my wife.

Sp. I don't care. There must be something the matter with you. They all think they are smart! (Evidently referring to intelligent spirits who had been endeavoring to free patient from influence of this entity.) I tell them they can't fool me. I don't want to talk to any of you.

Dr. To whom are you talking?

Sp. (Flourishing hand.) I'm talking to all of you. This is my house and my home.

Dr. Can you tell us your name?

Sp. I don't think I need to tell you my name.

Mr. G. The gentleman on your left is Dr. Wickland.

Sp. Oh, so that's it! (Dramatically.) Now you can all get out of here. This is my home and I'm going to stay right here.

Dr. Just now you are in our home. Do you know me?

Sp. Yes, I knew you some years ago. (When visiting the patient, Mrs. Anna R., who had been restored to health while under our care.) But I never believed in you. I was a good Christian Scientist. Now all of you get right out of here! This is my home. What right have any of you here?

Mr. G. You speak as if you were omnipotent.

Sp. I am not God but I am next to Him. When you are a true Christian Scientist you come next to God!

Dr. What about the lady whom you have been bothering?

Sp. She can go to the dickens. When I get well I'll show her! That's my home.

Dr. Did you buy it?

Sp. I worked and helped pay for it. Now others are occupying my home but when I get well I'll chase them out!

Dr. Who is occupying it?

Sp. My husband is there for one.

Dr. Do you want him to leave?

Sp. I want everybody to get out.

Dr. Did you pass out?

Sp. Oh, no, you'll find out that I'm not dead yet. I scared one woman.

Dr. Who was that?

Sp. She laid down on my bed, but I made her get up. I scared her!

Mrs. N. W. (Remembering that upon a recent visit to the patient's home she had lain down to rest upon the bed which had belonged to the former mistress of the house but had been unable to remain there because of an unpleasant influence.) I wasn't at all frightened.

Sp. Just the same I made you get up!

Dr. What satisfaction do you find in staying around the house? Don't you realize you are a spirit?

Sp. I don't believe in spirits and never did. Several years ago you talked spirits to me but I didn't believe you and would not listen to you. (This had been the case.)

Mr. M. Do we know you?

Sp. I am Jessie R. (Sister-in-law of patient, Mrs. Anna R.) You thought you would chase me out, Herm, but you got left.

Mr. M. I think we succeeded in getting you away. You are at Dr. Wickland's home now.

Sp. All of you tried to chase me out, but you got left.

Dr. No, they didn't, because you are now at our home.

Sp. I never liked you. You believe in spirits and I don't.

Dr. You believe in the continuation of life, don't you? What are spirits but those who have passed on to a continued existence?

Sp. (Angrily.) I tell you I have not passed on. I live in my home and I want everybody chased out!

Dr. Christian Scientists die just as other persons do.

Sp. Not if they are in the understanding.

Dr. Mrs. Eddy died. Where does a Christian Scientist expect to go when he loses the physical body?

Sp. Body! The body is only imagination.

Dr. Then why do you object when I touch your arm?

Sp. Because I feel tied up. I was a big, fat woman and here I am with a little body. I have told you before, I don't like you and I never did.

Dr. Why?

Sp. Because you always talked about spirits.

Dr. Yes, we often talked about the subject. You are now proving the fact of spirit return.

Sp. (Addressing patient's brother, Mr. Herman M.) Herm, why did you bring me here?

Mr. M. I thought you needed a little education. You were not doing the right thing where you were.

Dr. Did you come here in an auto?

Sp. I don't know how I came. Herm made me come with him.

Dr. Did you bring anyone else with you? (Referring to spirits obsessing the patient.)

Sp. Three of us came. They help me. They are all good Christian Scientists. They don't associate with anybody but their own people because it causes cross-currents. I was the leader.

(Laughing.) They all thought I was a man. I did a man's work, so why shouldn't I have the honor of being a man? My husband was sick, but he is well now. Just as soon as Anna came he braced up.

Dr. Because your sister-in-law took proper care of him.

Sp. What business had they to bring me here? I said I would never go to Wicklands' again. (Patient had made similar statements the day before, although normally very friendly.)

Mr. M. I heard last Sunday that the Christian Scientists take the credit for curing Anna some years ago, when the Wicklands straightened her out and got rascal spirits away from her.

Sp. (To Mr. M.) I will get you yet.

Mr. M. Don't worry about me. You had better try to get understanding.

Dr. This body belongs to Mrs. Wickland.

Sp. I used to talk to you folks when I came to your house to see Anna but I had no use for you. If you had become Christian Scientists I would have been interested in you.

Dr. You are controlling the body of Mrs. Wickland and she is unconscious while you talk through her. You claim you are Jessie R., but when I look at you I see the face of my wife, hence you are a spirit.

Sp. How could I get in this little body when I am a big, fat woman?

Dr. You are a spirit and spirit does not need a big body. You must realize you are a spirit and understand your situation. When spirits are ignorant of their condition they often cause much trouble.

The spirit of Mrs. Eddy has spoken through this same instrument several times and she has always expressed regret that she failed to include in her teachings the truth of spirit communication, which she knew from her own experience to be a fact.

Sp. Where is Wes? (Wesley R., her husband.)

Dr. On the ranch, because that is his home.

Sp. He likes it there much better now than he used to. Why is Mel R. bothering me? (Referring to spirit husband of patient.) He is here now. He says I have no business to bother his wife.

Dr. Ask him whether you are so-called "dead"?

Sp. He says, yes, and that everything you have said is true. He bothers me all the time.

Dr. He is not in the physical; we cannot see him. You know that he has passed out. You say he bothers you?

Sp. Yes. He is here and he says I shall not stay around the house but must keep away and leave my husband and Anna alone.

Dr. Does any one ever talk to you?

Sp. No, they take no notice of me, and that's what makes me so mad. (Listening to some invisible.) You tell Anna that I feel sorry for what I have done to her. Her husband (spirit) has opened my eyes. I am also sorry for Wes.

Dr. You must acquire understanding.

Sp. Pray for me. Tell Anna how sorry I am that I have disturbed her. I did not have a proper understanding and I was angry. I had a quick temper. Herm, you know that.

Dr. It was wrong to upset Mrs. R. She thought a great deal of you.

Sp. (Penitently.) I can see how selfish I have been. My Christian Science belief was only a cloak.

Dr. The higher ideals of Christian Science are excellent, but should include the whole of life.

Sp. Help Anna!

Dr. Are there any more spirits troubling her?

Sp. Yes, there are.

Mr. M. Isn't Mel trying to get them away?

Sp. He chased me all the time and I didn't like it.

Dr. He wanted you to realize your condition and leave his wife alone.

Sp. Will you help her, Doctor?

Dr. That is what we are trying to do.

Sp. I liked my home very much. I was taken very sick and I went to sleep (died) and after awhile, when I woke up, things were changed. Anna was taking care of my home and I stood it for awhile, then I wanted my place as I had always had it. I commenced to bother Anna. Poor girl! I wouldn't let her come here. Please help her, and help me, too.

Dr. Yes, we will, but you must also help yourself.

Sp. They (spirits) tell me I have to go -but where, I don't know.

Dr. Mrs. R.'s husband and other spirits will take care of you and teach you how to progress in your new life. Forget the past. You must broaden your mind. Realize there is a spirit world. We are all spirits whether in the body or out of it.

My wife allows spirits to control her body in order that we may enlighten them and learn the facts. If the future life were more clearly understood such conditions as yours would not exist. If you had understood the truth of spirit existence, spirits could have helped you at the time you passed on. But your mind was on the earth plane. Now you have an opportunity to learn and advance.

Sp. Clint is here. (Spirit, a brother of the patient.) He says I should come with him. I had him on one side and Mel on the other; you can imagine how I have been bothered. Where shall I go when I leave here?

Dr. These spirit friends will take care of you.

Sp. (Addressing Mr. M. in audience.) Will you forgive me?

Mr. M. Surely; we know you did not understand.

Sp. Tell Anna I will do the best I can to help her when I learn how. I bothered her because I did not like the way things had been changed in the house, then, all at once, I lost myself. (Obsessed patient.) Doctor, I never liked you because you believed in spirits, but now I have to thank you for helping me.

Dr. Be open minded; think yourself with your spirit friends and you will be with them.

Sp. Goodbye.

The following day a sister of Mrs. R. telephoned that a noticeable change had taken place in the patient and that the latter had that morning said: "I want to go to Dr. Wickland for treatment."

Upon her arrival Mrs. R. was extremely exhausted and between static treatments slept for two days but upon the third day awoke clear in mind.

Further records of statements made by the founder of Christian Science follow.

EXPERIENCE, DECEMBER 2, 1919

Spirit: MARY BAKER EDDY Psychic: MRS. WICKLAND

I wanted to come again to speak of the work you are doing. What a blessing it is to humanity to help the mortals here on earth and the spirit who has passed on in ignorance, with no knowledge of the life beyond. I closed the door I should have opened wide to give my knowledge to the world. I had the power and gift that God gave me to do work to help humanity, and to teach humanity that there is a life after this.

THIRTY YEARS AMONG THE DEAD

I was a medium and could have helped open the door from the spirit world to earth life, but I closed it because of my selfishness. Also I liked to have something new that was not known before, and to establish a religion of my own. I taught the wrong religion of life, and I denied the truth of spirit return, and tried to give out other things which suited my own fancy -my own self again.

I shut the door for myself and for my followers hereafter. If you could only help me to open the door again to tell them that I am trying my very best to open the eyes of my followers. Tell them not to shut the door to the truth. Truth will stand wherever you find it, but do not deny it when you find it. I denied it, and so I suffer.

Here are my followers coming to me one by one. Every day there are some coming over to the spirit side of life, and I am trying to tell them of the beautiful spirit world. But they say, "No, you are not Mrs. Eddy, because she did not teach that when she was on earth. You are only a false person." And then they go away.

You see what I have to deal with, and I cannot progress -until I can help all these to open their eyes. We should not deny God's wonderful manifestation of matter. It is real, not imagination. You could not live without matter. You could not have manifestations without matter.

I denied the wonderful manifestation of matter and called it only imagination and error. We have only one mind -the mind that God gave to every mortal being. Matter belongs to material things. Still we have matter in the spirit world, but more ethereal. I denied it. What is my spiritual body now? It is in a very crippled condition, because my mind was so closed and I denied the truth.

I prayed to God, and I said that God was All in All, and His manifestations beautiful, and said that we should look up to Him. Where is God? What is God? I said to my people that "God is Love, and Love is God," but that phrase became only empty talk with my followers.

We must realize God and where God is. God is Life; God is Electricity, because electricity is life. Electricity is only one part of God's wonderful manifestation. Flowers and colors of all kinds are manifestations of His wonders. Go into chemistry, go into the wonderful mystery of life, go into the microscopical world. These I denied entirely. I denied there was such a thing as disease and denied the existence of germs. When you get into the microscopical world you will find a world in itself, and a very wonderful one.

Now I am talking of what I have learned. Body and spirit are the nearest to His wonderful manifestation, yet a little microbe can kill the body but not the spirit. Why should we not be powerful enough to overcome a little microbe? I denied God by denying matter. Let us go into chemistry and see the wonderful things there. That is matter. Did I go into it? No, I did not. It is easy to say there is no such thing as matter, that it is only mortal error. Let us study. Anything that is in matter, study in every phase.

I have my eyes open now. I wish I could come back to teach my people the wonders of Nature, and the wonders we can do to help humanity, and the spirits that are in darkness. I am here myself. I have to serve for what I have done, and I speak, not here alone, but everywhere. I came to tell you this.

Let everyone open the door to the spirit world when he has once found it. Do not deny it, do not deny it. Christ said, do not hide your light under a bushel. Let it shine for others. Christ said: "I am the light of the world; he that followeth me shall not walk in darkness." Christ was the Truth. When you find the truth do not deny it but give it out to the world.

THIRTY YEARS AMONG THE DEAD

I shut the door. I wanted to keep the people under my control, and I did. I am now suffering for what I did. Tonight I feel so happy to think I can be of help to earthbound spirits that are doing very much mischief to humanity. If you could only see how many spirits there are in darkness who cling to human bodies and obsess people and send them to the asylums, or to the spirit world by shortening their lives. There is so much work to be done.

Let us all join hands and work together to spread the truth of the life hereafter, and also to help the earthbound spirits. Do not cast them away and say they are devils. They are only ignorant spirits -like myself. I wanted to be something in the world and sold my soul, for money. Let us all join together and pray to God to open the hearts of all my people to look into the higher life of spirits.

If all my churches could be turned into sanitariums for earthbound spirits what great good could be done! We could empty the asylums and help people out of their misery.

Let us help the unfortunate ones instead of sending them to the asylums where they are mistreated, for it is not understood that the poor ones who are obsessed have to suffer because of the spirits who control them. Let us try to do all we can to spread the truth and help every one who is obsessed.

I wish all could realize and understand how beautiful and simple conditions are if people would only open their eyes to see them. I mean they should open the soul eyes, but they are so material. And everything that is being taught is only matter. People cannot grasp spiritual things. The Bible is a beautiful book if it is read spiritually, not taken literally, and not as history. I wanted to study and learn what is in life, what is the aim of life here on earth.

If you would only stop to think and study yourself a little you would see how wonderfully God has manifested in you. First, there is your material body -how beautifully and wonderfully it is constructed. But how much more wonderful your mind is. How few understand the real meaning of life; it is always theory or dogma. It seems hard to get people to understand. When they get a little glimpse of light they add dogma and theories of various kinds.

If they would only be natural and look at Nature. Everywhere you look it is so simple to understand. There is no dogma or theory in Nature's finer forces. These forces are hidden, but they are for you to discover. It is for you to find God's wonderful manifestation in Nature. Let us worship God in that way. Let us worship Him in that wonderful spirit which is everywhere. Let us send out love to His children. We are all children of God, not just my child or your child, but all. Do not think there is no one for you but your own child. That attitude is a sin and very selfish, for it is all only for self.

Let us give out love as God gives it to us all. Let the sun shine every day on us and on everybody -not one or two, but all. Let the sun of understanding bring out beautiful thoughts of love. I want to know the real life. I have had many difficulties and I still have, because I wanted to shine and I wanted to be a light. I wanted to be known as one of The Teachers. I had my difficulties before I attained my ambition. I followed studies of various kinds but most of all the secret of suggestion.

If you knew how to apply and concentrate! Get one thing in mind and do not let anything else come into your mind; just concentrate your thoughts on that very thing. Suggest and suggest and concentrate, then you will gain strength and power. When you talk try to suggest things, keep them in your mind and hold them, because you have power over them. There are meetings of various kinds but in a meeting for concentration and suggestion there is power and strength.

THIRTY YEARS AMONG THE DEAD

A man can hold his audience by his hypnotic power, and you follow along and presently you get strength and power. I studied that because I wanted to have such power and I got it. I got that, but another much more important thing I did not get, which was to study Nature's finer forces instead of clothing myself with one idea and just circling around and around. I held people in that circle and did not let them get out.

If I had only done what was first given to me in a vision! That is what I should have done, but I closed the door because I wanted to hold my people through suggestion. I felt that I had the power to conquer everything, even the world. I did a great deal, but selfishness crept in. I meant well in the beginning and I did well, but I was selfish. I thought I had it all.

Others had power before me and others will have it after me in the same way, but I felt I had it all and that I had found it all. I was not true. I should have said I had found the truth and I should have given it to others as it was given to me, but I did not. I called it my own, and I closed the door for the real truth. I found the truth in the beginning, but I clung to theory, and that is the way with all of us who try to be leading lights. We are always clinging to theories and not to the truth.

Theories seem to hold the people better than does the truth. We do not teach it as we should. The truth would always stand if we did not deny it. All leaders want a little theory of their own, and want to gather the people around them and hold them. They succeed for a while only, for truth will spring up and spread. Do not be afraid of the truth, do not be ashamed of it. Some day or other every one will have an understanding of truth. It is there and it will blossom. Do not clothe it with dogma and theory. If I had taught the truth I should be so much happier and it would have been so much better for my Church.

I thank you for what you have done in publishing my little article. It will shed a little light here and there. People may say no, and scoff, but they cannot do so truthfully, because my spirit will be there and impress the truth upon them. I never felt that I was a little woman; I felt that I had the power to conquer the world. You can have that power too if fear does not interfere with you. Concentrate and shut the door to fear. Do not let fear come in.

If you feel fear, say "No, no, no, I am not afraid. I shall conquer," and you will be surprised at your power. In a moment you will feel you are a giant. Shut the door to fear and open the door to spiritual power and the strength of God will flow in and give you strength and power to conquer.

You can never accomplish anything when you have fear. Take five minutes each day and concentrate on fear. Say, "I shall never be afraid, I can conquer," and keep on and on, and you will be surprised at the result. There is always worry and fear. Worry is the sister to fear. When you have conquered these two you will have strength and power, and you can help in healing. You can help everybody by just speaking a word to them.

When I had conquered fear and worry I sent my thoughts for strength and health to the persons who were sick. That was power and removed the fear of sickness from them. When you treat persons, the first thing is to take away fear and worry. Let them forget themselves. Forget self and you will be surprised how strong and well you will be. That is the secret of health.

It takes time to conquer; do not be discouraged. If it looks dark, overcome fear and worry. When you once have conquered you will be well. You will be well and you will do well in every way.

Now I will say just a few words about my experience in the spirit world.

In the first place, when I passed into the spirit side of life it was in one way surprising to me, because I had concentrated that I should live forever, and had gotten the idea in my mind that I would not die. I had the idea that there is no death, and that I would never die. I took it literally. I thought my body would never die and that I would stay on earth forever. There is no death when you have understanding; we only change the physical body for the spiritual.

My body began to grow old. I concentrated and suggested, but I used too much energy in my work and I wore out. Finally I lost out and another stepped in; at the last I was obsessed. Of course my people did not know it, but there were times when I was not myself. I thought I would never die but I had to go just the same. Now I can see how ridiculous the thing was.

You know I did not believe in matter. There was no such thing as matter, still my body was placed in a casket and sealed so well that my body could never get out of the casket. It was sealed in many ways so nobody could get it. If there is no matter why should all that money have been used to put my body into the grave? That was against my teachings, but we are material nevertheless. When I woke up to life -remember, I say life, because that was the real life -I had a spirit body. In my visions I had been to the spirit world many times and had always returned to earth. This time I felt that I could go back again, but my body was not there.

It had been interred. Still I did not realize the change because I had closed the door for spirit return. I did not want to teach it. I knew it, because I was a medium in my early days. I gave readings in Boston for some time, and I gave lectures as well, but after a while I denied it all -the truth was not in me. When I woke up in my spirit body I still did not realize that it was not my material body. It was very hard for me to understand that I had gone through the change called death because I had concentrated and concentrated that I should never die.

The realization took much time. Then I had much to do, and many difficulties to overcome. First of all came my brother Albert. When he came I felt that I did not want to have anything to do with spirits. You see, I said in my book that there is no such thing as spirit return. I had so hypnotized myself with that theory that it was real to me. Albert came and told me that I had not taught the whole truth. There was a time when I was a medium and he talked through me, but after a while I refused to allow this.

Now he came to me again and said. "Come, I will show you that what you have taught is not true, and that you did not tell the truth." After that my first husband came. He understood me better than the rest. He showed me the way. One by one many friends came. Then came Quimby. He said: "You took my theory. Why did you not give me a little credit for the help I gave you?"

Then I saw how selfish I had been. I was accused. I was helped but had not given credit for it. I was obsessed when I was a young child and often had spells of obsession. For many years those obsession spells came over me.

Quimby helped me; he took the spirits away and taught me the true religion. He taught me to know myself. He taught me spirit return, but I did not listen. After he had gone I took his theory as my own.

In the spirit world I had to go through a great deal to over come selfishness. I had to serve and learn the lesson of life as a little child. I had to be taught about God in a different way. Mental healing is something we should all learn, It is of great importance. Let us all learn to overcome by suggestion and concentration. Get your mind centered and learn the art of concentration. Take some object -say that table -concentrate and concentrate and try to hold your mind on that table, nothing else, for five minutes. You cannot do it. Try, try very hard, and after a while you will succeed.

THIRTY YEARS AMONG THE DEAD

That is the secret of health -concentration is the secret of power. You must be able to concentrate your mind on one object for five minutes. This will require a long, long time of practice. It does not come to you at once because as soon as you try to concentrate and keep your mind absolutely on the table there will be a dozen other thoughts coming into your mind. Keep them out, and keep your mind on the object and you will find in time that I am right.

When you can concentrate your mind for even one or two minutes you have gained much. Say to yourself, "I can concentrate, for I have no fear or worry," and keep on concentrating. Shut other things out and keep on shutting them out, and before you know it you will have strength, and you will feel powerful, because you have a part of life itself -God. When you have gained that power you can say to a sick person: "I send you power, and you will have strength and health," and you will be surprised how quickly recovery follows.

Before you try to send out that power concentrate your mind on one object for fifteen minutes. Do not think, "Now I have the power in my hands and I can heal," for you cannot heal if your mind is not there. For that reason many healers are not successful. The mind must be centered on one object before you can heal. That is the secret of healing. Now learn the lesson and conquer.

When you are sick, or you go into a sick room, concentrate your mind on some object. Hold your mind on that object for a while and you will feel that you have great power and that you can heal because you will receive strength from God to heal. That is another secret. We should all understand it.

By concentration, without fear and worry, you can all heal, but remember, settle your mind first before you begin to heal, for otherwise it will be of no use. Now I have taken up too much of your time, but I wanted to say a few words and to thank you for having my article published. It will awaken some people and teach them to think and understand that the real life is on the other side.

Do not try to lean on others but stand by your own self and conquer self, then you can help others and bring them together in one circle of harmony and you will have true happiness.

This is Mary Baker Eddy. Thank you for letting me come. Good Night.

THIRTY YEARS AMONG THE DEAD

THIRTY YEARS AMONG THE DEAD

Chapter XV

Theosophy

That the belief in reincarnation on earth is a fallacious one and prevents progression to higher spiritual realms after transition[24] has been frequently declared by advanced spirits, while numerous cases of obsession which have come under our care have been due to spirits who, in endeavoring to "reincarnate" in children, have found themselves imprisoned in the magnetic aura, causing great suffering to both their victims and themselves.

A little boy in Chicago, Jack T., had been normal until the age of five when he began to manifest precocious tendencies and acted strangely. Formerly he had had the natural disposition of a child but began to fret about things ordinarily foreign to a child's mind and acted in many ways like an adult. He worried over trifles, lay awake at night with strange mutterings and presentiments, and at times had an uncontrollable temper.

He was a boy of good appearance but talked constantly of being old, homely and ugly looking, and was so intractable that efforts at reprimand and correction proved of no avail. This condition became so aggravated that his family despaired of restoring the boy's reason.

A relative who knew of our experimental work in abnormal psychology wrote to the Institute requesting us to concentrate for the boy. This was done and an entity, whose actions and expressions were in every way like those of the boy, was attracted to the psychic, Mrs. Wickland.

This entity said his name was Charlie Herrman; he was aware of having died and declared he was a very homely man, with ugly features and a face covered with pock marks. Nobody had cared for him and this fact preyed on his mind. Someone had once told him that after death individuals could reincarnate and become whatever they wished to be. Since his only desire was to be good looking, so that others would not shun him, he decided to try and reincarnate.

As a result, he became entangled in the magnetic aura of a small boy and was unable to free himself. Finding that he was helplessly imprisoned, and incapable of making himself understood, he had outbursts of temper and "felt like flying to pieces."

"They called me Jack at times, but I am not Jack. That was not my name, and I could not understand."

Our concentration for the boy had freed the spirit and for this he was very grateful. After instructions were given regarding spiritual progression and he had been assured that he need no longer be homely if he would discard old ideas from his mind, forget self and strive to help others, he expressed great eagerness to go with the spirits who, he stated, had come to help him.

In a letter written a few days later by the boy's mother we were informed that a remarkable change had occurred in the child.

"Jack is now a boy again and has been very good this week, really like he used to be." He remained normal and received excellent grades in school, where his progress from that time on was unusually rapid.

At one time we concentrated for a crippled child in Hollywood with interesting results.

EXPERIENCE, NOVEMBER 19, 1916

Spirit: WILLIAM STANLEY Psychic: MRS. WICKLAND

Spirit: Is it really true that I am well now? Can I talk? Can I move my arms and feet?

Then reincarnation is true, because before I could neither talk nor walk. How did I get out of the child?

Doctor: Intelligent spirits brought you here for help.

Sp. I wanted to come back and reincarnate in a child, and I got in and could not get out. I was so paralyzed that I could not express myself and I was in an awful state. I was a Theosophist and I wanted to reincarnate to be great. I got into a child's body and crippled it, and also crippled my mind and that of the child. I stayed in the child because I did not know how to get out. I acted as a child and I could not talk.

I know I passed out of my mortal body some years ago, far away in India, but I do not realize when it took place. I wanted so much to reincarnate and to come back to this earth life to live my other Karma. Do not hold on to the thought of coming back, but look for something higher, for the state I was in was the worst torture anybody could have.

I lived in Calcutta and wanted to learn to be a Master and go through my Karma, but instead I am as you see me to be. I reincarnated in a child and became crippled, and I also got into the vibration of the mother. It was very hard and I want to warn others never to come back and try to reincarnate through a little child. Leave reincarnation alone, because it is only a mistake, but the philosophy of Theosophy is very fine.

Look upward; don't think of the astral shells, for they are of no use. I was very selfish and wanted to come back to earth life just to be something great, but instead I got into a very low state. I had intended to show the Theosophists that I could come back and reincarnate in a child.

Madam Blavatsky should have taught differently. (Pointing to an invisible.) I will tell you, Madam, you are the one who is to blame for the condition I am in today. Madam Blavatsky stands here trying to help me now. She is the one who gave me the teachings and thoughts of reincarnation, and now she is trying to show me the right way and states there is no such thing as reincarnation. One gets all mixed up trying to enter another's body for reincarnation.

Dr. What is your name?

Sp. I cannot recall my name just now. Madam Blavatsky was in India and taught Theosophy, had many followers and I was with her. I have also met Anna Kingsford and Dr. Hartmann, and he also was to blame for my condition.

They pushed me in here that I might be taught and freed. I am so pleased that I can talk again; that is something I have not been able to do for years. Madam Blavatsky, Anna Kingsford and the Judge were all great lights, and now they have found out their big mistakes. They are all working to get their victims free, and so they brought me to this place for instruction and guidance.

I was in India, having been there for many years. My father was an officer in the Army. I spent most of my time in Calcutta, where I met all the great lights of Theosophy, and I joined the Theosophical Society. I liked Colonel Olcott; he was a great fellow. I remember being very sick in India for some time. I have no desire to reincarnate again because reincarnation is a wrong doctrine. It creates a selfishness to come back. One can learn without being reincarnated. What I suppose did I learn in my last reincarnation in the child? What did I learn ?

I believed in Theosophy and my Karma, and I thought I had to go through with it. Colonel Olcott belonged to the Great Masters. He belonged to the spirit of Fire and Water -I mean the elementals of Fire and Water.

Dr. Have you ever heard of mediums?

Sp. They are only astral shells. Madam Blavatsky says we must all help those who try to reincarnate. She and the others have come to say they are trying to help and for that purpose have formed a big society. I thought I had come to life when I came here, and that I could reincarnate and talk to them as I did in life. I did not know they had passed over. Teaching as they did, why did they not reincarnate the same as I?

Madam Blavatsky was a great missionary, as you know. She says she is now trying to make all her victims understand about the life after this as it really is. She says that she was a medium at one time, but that she did not want anybody to control her. She thought you should develop your own self and mental faculties, and go through your Karma. I should not have been taught the falseness I was.

Madam tells me that I should listen to this gentleman, (Dr. W.) and that he will explain things. Explanations were given regarding life on the earth plane, the preparation for the life that is to follow, and the fact that the knowledge and wisdom gained here will be the light of understanding each one carries to the other side of life.

The spirit finally gave the name of William Stanley, and departed, grateful for the enlightenment he had received.

J. A., a listless, crippled boy of seven years, with an adult manner of speech, was a patient from Chicago, who suffered from convulsions and a slow, hesitant stammering, was notional about his food and subject to violent attacks of temper. Through concentration, a spirit was dislodged from him, a superficial Theosophist, who was peculiarly self-hypnotized.

EXPERIENCE, APRIL 28, 1920

Spirit: EDWARD JACKSON Patient: J. A.

Psychic: MRS. WICKLAND.

Doctor: Have you been here before?

Spirit: (Slowly.) Myself-do-not-know.

Dr. How old are you?

Sp. (Drawling.) Me-do-not-know.

Dr. Where did you come from?

Sp. Where-they-shot-fire-at-me. (Static treatment given patient.)

Dr. How old are you?

Sp. Myself-do-not-know.

Dr. Don't you understand that you have lost your physical body and are a spirit? Listen to intelligent spirits who will help you.

Sp. Me does not know anything about spirits.

Dr. Don't you want to know something about them? Where did you expect to go after "death"?

Sp. Me does not know.

Dr. Would you like to know anything?

Sp. That takes care of itself.

Dr. If you had been more concerned about the facts of life you would not be in this condition; you would be in the spirit world. Do you know anything about the spirit world?

Sp. No.

Dr. Would you care to know?

Sp. I do not know.

Dr. You must want to know. You have lost your mortal body and do not understand it.

Sp. I don't care.

Dr. You will have to care. Are you happy in your present condition?

Sp. No.

Dr. Were you sick?

Sp. I was.

Dr. What was the matter with you?

Sp. Crippled.

Dr. Where did you live?

Sp. I don't know. It is a long time since I was born.

Dr. Were you a man or a woman?

Sp. I suppose I am a man.

Dr. Were you married?

Sp. No.

Dr. Why?

Sp. No one likes a cripple, and I stuttered and stuttered a great deal. I also studied.

THIRTY YEARS AMONG THE DEAD

Dr. What did you study?

Sp. All kinds of books that came my way.

Dr. On religion?

Sp. Why, yes.

Dr. Were you orthodox?

Sp. No, thank God.

Dr. Did you have any fixed opinions at all?

Sp. Once, for a time, I studied. Then I was shut up in one place one time and another place another time. It is the fourth time I have been reincarnated. (Obsessed sensitives.)

Twice I got in a cripple.

Dr. Were you a cripple in the first place?

Sp. I do not remember anything about it. People told me to remember about my lives, but I do not. I know I was once a cripple, and then I got into somebody and was more crippled. But I got out. I do not know how I got out. I feel stronger now than I have before, I thought when I reincarnated I should be a nice young man, but instead I got crippled, because I suppose my mind was crippled.

Dr. What did they call you when you were a cripple?

Sp. I had so many names, but you know, I liked the last time. I liked it very much to be a rich man's son, so I did not need to work. I had my father to work for me. I had a good time.

Dr. Did you become a rich man's son?

Sp. In a way, yes, and in another way, no.

Dr. What is your name?

Sp. My name was, once upon a time -I do not know. Some time ago, when I was studying Theosophy, I was a cripple born. Some friends brought some books to me about Madam Blavatsky. They called me Edward Jackson.

Dr. What other names did you have?

Sp. The other was J.

Dr. Was J. a grown man or a boy?

Sp. I do not like that fire shooting and someone talking all kinds of things. Why cannot I reincarnate and not be a cripple all the time?

Dr. I suppose when you found yourself in a rich man's family and thought of reincarnation you believed you were experiencing your former condition again.

Sp. It is Karma to develop one's highest self, so the Theosophists say. They chased me out, so I tried again, because I wanted to know if that theory is true or not.

Dr. It is very true in one way -earthbound spirits can control mortal sensitives. That is very true.

Sp. They must live out their Karma which has been put out for them; it is the only way.

Dr. Where did you come from?

Sp. Chicago. I was going to be a rich man's son, but I was turned out.

Dr. Did you like that?

Sp. I was fighting and when I get mad I do not care what I say, and I get mad once in a while. Sometimes I get so mad because I shall be a cripple all my life. When I reincarnated I got into the same crippled state again.

Dr. Don't you think you had better stop trying to reincarnate?

Sp. I must live out my Karma, and must not interfere with it.

Dr. Then you must continue suffering because of your foolishness.

Sp. I was trying to get to Devachan. I was not well educated, but I read up on Devachan, which is the resting place where they reincarnate again.

Dr. You came back too soon.

Sp. Theosophy appealed to my mind, and then I wanted to have a good time. You must not interfere with your Karma. You can choose your life and I was going to have plenty of money, but I got crippled again. But my mind was good. They said you should not think of your former life.

Dr. Who told you that?

Sp. They said you should progress and not interfere with your Karma, then you would get to Devachan. I suppose I must be an astral shell. I did not study enough.

Dr. Would you like to use a little discrimination and progress in the right way to the spirit life?

Sp. I want to go to Devachan -that is the best place for me. Then you can be a Master.

Dr. You should become a Master of your own destiny.

Sp. I want to be a Great Master. Then I would not be a cripple, and would have lived out my Karma.

Dr. How were you crippled?

Sp. In my legs.

Dr. Could you not walk?

Sp. No, my knees were too weak and my ankles were weak. I am crippled all over now.

Dr. Could you think and talk?

Sp. Yes.

Dr. Do you like corn meal mush? (An especial aversion of the patient.)

Sp. I don't know what you mean.

Dr. Are you particular about eating?

THIRTY YEARS AMONG THE DEAD

Sp. I will not eat meat and not much fish. I like to have some raw vegetables. I want my food more sun-kissed. I want to go to Devachan and be a Master.

Dr. Master of what?

Sp. Master of Higher Things. I want to be a Master.

Dr. Madam Blavatsky denies reincarnation now and says it is folly.

Sp. She doesn't know what she is talking about.

Dr. Do you want to be perfectly well again?

Sp. Then I have to reincarnate again.

Dr. Now wake up and be sensible. Understand you are a spirit. You are now controlling the body of my wife.

Sp. I did not reincarnate in another person's body. I thought next time I would reincarnate differently. You say I am a woman now. I do not want to be a girl -I want to be a man.

Dr. You are using a woman's body just now.

Sp. I have to be born again, even if I am crippled.

Dr. Don't be foolish. Realize you are no longer crippled.

Sp. How can you tell any one not to be a cripple when they are?

Dr. You are now a free spirit, temporarily controlling a woman's body.

Sp. I do not understand what you are talking about.

Dr. Your Devachan does not work at all. You did not study thoroughly.

Sp. Yes, I did, but I disregarded it.

Dr. Do not talk such nonsense. It makes nice earthbound spirits.

Sp. We have to reincarnate to learn and get all kinds of experiences.

Dr. I suppose you could not progress to Devachan if you did not have all the different experiences?

Sp. You have to come back and learn them.

Dr. Do you know what you have been doing? You have been controlling different persons, and disturbing their lives.

An ignorant spirit ruins the life of a mortal sensitive by clinging to him. You have been brought here for help and are now controlling my wife's body.

Sp. I have to reincarnate in your wife? No -I must reincarnate in a child, and be born again.

Dr. This is not your body. It belongs to my wife and you are using it temporarily.

Sp. Then I have to reincarnate in your wife.

Dr. You are controlling her body for a short time only. Look at this hand -do you know it?

Sp. I have reincarnated again in your wife's body. No -you must reincarnate again in a child and be born again.

Dr. You do not know what you are talking about. If you understood the truth you would not talk as you do. You are an earthbound spirit, making cripples of children.

Sp. That is my Karma. I have to so live until I get Devachan.

Dr. You live so only because of your ignorance.

Sp. When you have a chance to reincarnate why should you not do it?

Dr. When you have a chance to take possession of the body of another and ruin his life, is it right to do so?

Sp. I would just as soon be that spirit in that body.

Dr. The asylums are full of people who are controlled by earthbound spirits like you. You have been ruining the lives of children. Evidently you have come from a boy we know. When we applied static sparks to the boy we got you out. Now you are allowed to control my wife's body temporarily and we are trying to make you understand your condition.

Sp. That has nothing to do with my Karma.

Dr. You have lost your physical body a long time ago. Do you realize that you are controlling my wife's body?

Sp. It is my Karma, and I don't care.

Dr. You have been bothering a little boy and you should now listen to what is being told you.

Sp. I know the only truth is reincarnation. I have reincarnated, and I will again.

Dr. You will have to leave at once if you cannot be sensible.

Sp. You cannot frighten me out. I am reincarnated.

Dr. Where is your mother?

Sp. She is in Devachan. She is ready to reincarnate again.

Dr. You will soon see spirits who will show you something different.

Sp. They are only astral shells.

Dr. They will put you in a dark dungeon. You do not know the A-B-C of Theosophy. You do not want to know.

Sp. You cannot stop my talking if I want to talk. I am reincarnated again. I am going to live out this Karma. If I am a woman now, I will live it out. If I get killed, that is part of my Karma. I will just have to study and get in the Inner Circle, and know that God is my Creator. I have reincarnated and I will reincarnate again, then go to Devachan and be happy. I will finish my Karma.

Dr. You get out and take your Karma with you.

Sp. You think you are going to take away what is my Karma, but you will not. I am happy and I am going.

Smiling beatifically, the spirit departed.

Several extracts are given from remarks made in our circle at various times by the spirit of

Ralph S., son-in-law of a lady who attended our circles. He and his wife in former years had been deeply interested in Theosophy, and when he reached the spirit world he had found it difficult to free himself from preconceived ideas.

EXPERIENCE, MARCH 17, 1920

Spirit: RALPH S. Psychic: MRS. WICKLAND

Spirit: I have been here before and I was so anxious to come again.

Doctor: Who are you, friend?

Sp. Don't you know who I am? I am Ralph S. I studied a great deal about Theosophy and the law of developing myself regarding the higher things, but forgot to study the truth.

My wife and I studied to develop ourselves, aiming for the highest, but we forgot to learn the simple lesson of life everlasting. How little we know of the world beyond. How I do wish we had both understood more of life.

There is so much dogma. Now I have so much to unlearn, so much to overcome.

Dr. "Love is the fulfillment of the law."

Sp. Yes, we have to serve.

Ques. Are you happy?

Sp. In one way, yes, but not in another. If only the door were not closed!

Ques. Which door?

Sp. The door of communication. My wife would be afraid if I tried to manifest myself to her. It hurts me.

We studied and studied so much, and it was very hard to find that when I reached the spirit side of life I knew so little and was in darkness. I am pleased to know, Mother, that you are not ashamed to stand for the truth. Give it to others as much as you can, for it will help you in return.

EXPERIENCE, APRIL 14, 1920

Spirit: RALPH S. Psychic: MRS. WICKLAND

Here I am again. This is Ralph, Mother. I want to come to my wife, but cannot, as the door is shut. I know it is as much my fault as it is my wife's. The door is shut for me and will be for some time, because of the dogma and creed there is in the mind. If only my wife would realize the truth -it is so simple, but the simple truth is always rejected. Something mysterious is always accepted.

We thought that by working out our Karma everything would be all right, but we developed selfishness. It is selfish to shut yourself up and try to be a Master.

Master of what? We should try to master ourselves, try to learn about all things, look up to all things, because God is in all things and is Love and Wisdom.

We should not feel that because of a little learning we are better than others merely because we studied to be "Great Masters." We speak of things of which we do not realize the full import and we make ourselves sensitive and become obsessed.

THIRTY YEARS AMONG THE DEAD

I realize now how dangerous the doctrine of Reincarnation is. According to that doctrine, this would be the time for me to reincarnate. Should I reincarnate and obsess a child and tie both of us up in one body until such time as the child leaves the mortal body? Why should I "reincarnate" and make a child become an idiot?

All creeds should be set aside and we should seek the simple truth of life. Love God above all things and your neighbor as yourself. There would be great rejoicing if everybody tried to live up to that teaching; then there would be true happiness. Creeds and dogmas interfere and make us selfish, and selfishness is the root of all evil.

I am to blame for the present conditions surrounding my wife. (Her refusal to receive spirit communications.)

My work now is to come down to earth to help the ones who believe in the same theory as I did, and are engaged in the same study I was. I have to work hard trying to bring them to realize the truth.

I must also work to try to bring my wife to the realization that she must not go into that dogma any further. If she does she will become more psychic and will be obsessed by some theory or other. I do not mean obsessed by spirits, but ideas.

I was more deeply steeped in the dogma of reincarnation than my wife, because I was further advanced in my studies. I went into the subject deeper than she. We were both so selfish in our theory that we could not see anything else, and we condemned all other theories. We felt we were better than many others because we lived to sacrifice. (Having adhered to a restricted diet, a supposed requirement for spiritual attainment.)

The body is only a dress for the spirit. We should eat what comes before us. Let us not put our minds on eating and drinking. We should not sacrifice our bodies and crucify the flesh to become more spiritual. That was never meant to be.

Take care of your body but do not rob it of its needs. God gave it to you to take care of. Keep it in a healthy condition so the spirit can work through it to the best advantage.

It does not make us spiritual to abstain from certain foods. We need specific elements for the body, so let us strive our utmost to take care of it.

My wife is hard to reach. We had agreed not to try to call each other back after death. We were hypnotized by our theosophical theory that we must go on and clear our Karma, and that we cannot open the door to the higher life unless we go very slowly. This makes it much harder for me.

(The two made an agreement that should one pass out the other would not try to establish communication, considering this to be a hindrance to the ego in its progression to Devachan.)

I am to blame as much as she is. I shut the door for her as much as she shut the door for me. I condemned Spiritualism, because I thought the theory we held was the real one and that everything else was false. Of course there is some deception in Spiritualism, but there is good as well as bad in every movement.

Let us not be carried away by anything; let us use reason in all things.

THIRTY YEARS AMONG THE DEAD

EXPERIENCE, NOVEMBER 8, 1922

Spirit: RALPH S. Psychic: MRS. WICKLAND

It will soon be three years since I passed away, but in those three years I have learned a great deal. I did not find conditions as I had believed them.

I am sorry that I was so set in my mind on the theory of Theosophy that we must come back again and again in order to reach the higher plane.

Since I have come to the spirit side of life I have not had any thought of coming back except to help my dear wife. We both studied to learn about life, but after I came here I tried to impress her that there was nothing more to learn about the religion we had both studied, because it is not the true religion.

If I came back I could not reincarnate as I thought. I would rather come back to help my wife and learn all I can about spirit return than to come and stay in one state for a certain time, then come back again as a baby.

I had said to my wife that I would not come back to her because I wanted to go on and be a Master. We think a Master is one who is very highly developed and cannot do anything but be holy.

You do not want to become such a "Master" -the greatest masters serve. The more we learn in the spirit world, the more we want to serve. Here we want to help, to learn, to teach others.

Christ is worshipped as a Master. Did He come back? He went among the poor and lowly, trying to teach and serve people, and to help them to a higher life and understanding.

Learn the truth, give it to others and serve others.

Be a master in learning, but humble in serving.

When we have learned to serve others we have learned the lesson Christ taught.

When we have reached that state we can love our enemies as ourselves and God above all things. Then we are masters. That does not mean that we are so high that we cannot come back to serve, to teach, to help others.

It means that we must all be masters of ourselves and conquer all desires.

In a little talk given one evening by one whose writings were well known to many, reincarnation was also mentioned.

EXPERIENCE, JANUARY 28, 1920

Spirit: ELLA WHEELER WILCOX Psychic: MRS. WICKLAND

Good Evening. I have not been here before. But I heard of you while I was on earth, and I also heard of your work and had read your pamphlet.

We should all try to understand the true meaning of God, but how few try to understand the actual truth. Truth is always crucified. Truth should be known, and not clothed with all sorts of creeds.

When I was in earth life I was once a bond servant, with wrong ideas and foolish thoughts of truth, but toward the last the simple truth and an understanding of the real life beyond were shown to me and I accepted them.

The truth had to come to me through sorrow. We do not seek for truth until we have had a deep sorrow, such as losing a dear husband or friend, then the heart seeks after the truth and will not let dogmas and creeds stand in the way.

We are hungry to know about the life beyond, and to learn if our dear ones and friends are with us to guide and help. I felt the loss of my dear husband so keenly that I was broken-hearted. I could not think that I would not be with him and near him again, but the light of truth and the understanding that there is no death came to me and I felt him around me.

This beautiful truth will come to everyone who earnestly seeks after it, and after finding it we must stand for it in all honesty and sincerity because, if we do not, doubt will come in, and fear, and shut the door for our dear ones, who have only gone ahead to prepare our home everlasting.

How we mortals are clothed with doubt, and when the truth of continued existence is presented to us, even then we doubt. The Bible is full of the beautiful truth which is revealed to us, but still we all doubt.

When I found the truth I wanted to teach it to the world, but my physical body was not strong enough to do what I should have liked. I tried to tell it to the soldiers, because I knew that to them the truth would be a Godsend, because they were here today and tomorrow there.

Should I not, when I had found the truth, give them the understanding that there is no death? They then felt that they could go right on and fight because they realized that death was not the end of life. It would only be the clothing -the body which would be destroyed. How courageous and how happy they were when I said to them that there is no death, only a transition to a happier and more beautiful state, and I wished so much that I could give them more.

I spent my life in dogmas; all my life in trying to do good. I did good, but my thoughts were clothed with dogmas of different kinds. At last I found the truth.

Oh, my dear Robert had to go to open the door before I could realize what was awaiting me! I did some good after I found the truth; let us all do the same.

People will scoff at you at times, but never mind, never mind. By so doing you will become stronger and you will find that it will help you to grow in understanding.

I found the truth, but by a dangerous method; I had to struggle as well with that. The Ouija Board is a dangerous thing, and I found it out. It greatly weakened me.

Be very guarded in seeking for the truth, for it is a dangerous road. You must learn the way in order to have help and guidance.

I had struggles with others because I went into the midst of earthbound spirits as well as the soldiers. If you could only realize the dreadful pressure around the soldiers! They wanted light on one side as well as on the other. (Spirits yet in ignorance of the higher life.)

It was too much pressure on my physical body and I gave out. I could not stand it, or the thoughts that were centered on me.

I taught the truth to the soldiers on earth but I did not realize how many I lectured to who had gone before. The strain was too great for me so I came home, not weak in spirit but in body.

Still I feel happy that I was enabled to help. I found the world of spirits where I could be with my dear one whom I loved the most.

You wonder where the real life is. The real life is on the other side of the grave, as you call it. This life is only a temporary school -the school of learning to know ourselves, and for what object we are here.

People think that when they die they will see God, but how few realize what God means. God is the Life of all things. How little people think of this earth plane and what it really is. It is only an infinitesimal part of the Universe.

Once I thought of reincarnation. I was at one time a Theosophist. Theosophy is all right so far as it goes; the thoughts and teachings are beautiful, but why should we reincarnate on this little planet?

I would not care to come back to the earth plane except to tell you of the higher and real life which lies before you. I would not like to come back to this earth plane again to be a little baby and I do not see why I should, for what would I learn? Could souls like we come back into children again and feel satisfied?

After you have learned the higher things of life, you do not care to come back to matter another time. You want to learn while here and gain sufficient knowledge so that when you pass on you will not want to come back and learn it over.

You can learn much about the other side of life while here, and when you pass over there you will learn more and more of things which you could not learn while here because you could not understand them.

Oh, the world of worlds! If you could only travel to the beautiful worlds beyond and see the grandeur there!

We also have to serve, to bring others to the same harmony we enjoy. We cannot return and be babies again, but we step down to earth life to help our loved ones and friends.

There was a time when I thought I had reincarnated, because when I would write I felt that I had been here before, but I find that it was only spirits who sent the thoughts to my mind, and gave me strength to write, and in that way I felt that I had been here before. It was only another's mind reflecting on my mind.

The work you are doing here is one I wish I had known about and could have helped with, because it is so much needed. So many need help and enlightenment. We cannot reach many from our side of life because they are bond servants to creeds and desires of different kinds which attract them to this earth plane.

We must have stations like this where we can bring them and open their spiritual eyes that they may see. Then they will see us and we can help them to a better understanding.

Let us all try to concentrate for training schools where earthbound spirits can be brought for enlightenment.

You may be surprised to think I came tonight. I have tried to come through Ouija Boards, and I have tried to come other ways, but here I can step in and talk as you talk. It is like talking through a telephone, and I feel strong. I feel now that I am amongst you really in body and in spirit. We must all unite, and do all we can to further this work, because we want stations like this, here, there and everywhere.

THIRTY YEARS AMONG THE DEAD

In time you will have receivers which will record messages from our side of life. It will not be long before a message will come over this receiver from the other world that will awaken the people from their creeds. It will awaken the churches.

Churches will be empty, but it will only be for a short time, because a new religion will spring up, a religion which will be founded on the truth of spirit return, and not on dogma. People will live for others and will not grasp all for themselves. The churches will be for the people and not for creeds.

People will pay money to the church but it will be to further the work of the beautiful truth of the life beyond. There will not be any salvation, but you will learn to know that we are with you. There will be churches which will have open doors for the spirits as well as the mortals.

I wanted to come to California to see your work while I was on earth, as I had heard of you and was very much interested in your pamphlet and your work.

I wrote a little about it but I thought I could do more if I could see you in person. However, I went to the spirit life before I could meet you.

Now I am here to see your work. If you could only realize what vast numbers (invisibles) there are outside the door who are waiting for a chance to come in to learn the truth of life, and how they are crowding each other for help!

Now, I cannot take more of your time, but I do thank you for letting me come. I am glad if I can be of some service to you in your work. Have courage. People refuse to recognize the fact of obsession because they think it hurts the cause -spirit return. I believed in it thoroughly because it is true, and I knew it.

I am Ella Wheeler Wilcox. I wanted to come here to give you encouragement in your work. Go on with the work of obsession because it is so much needed, and we will give you help from this side of life.

Please understand I would have been here in your concentration circle before, but the door is crowded with people who are waiting for an opportunity to come. We have to come one by one. This evening, I am very happy to say, was my turn.

This work is so much needed to help humanity. There is only one other that I know of who has such concentration circles where the medium allows earthbound spirits to control.

There are very few indeed who will allow earthbound spirits to come in and control. For my part I know only one other, and I have been hunting for some time to see where the work could be done.

The work of obsession, as carried on by you, should be done in every town and city. Every medium should be willing to do this line of work. The time will come when every minister will speak regarding the philosophy of life and spirit return, and all isms will be done away with.

I cannot stay any longer but I thank you very much for the privilege of coming, and shall come again some time, I hope.

A venerable family friend, Dr. J. M. Peebles, former Consul to Turkey, world traveler and for sixty years an international lecturer on psychic science, passed on at the age of ninety-nine and has since spoken through Mrs. Wickland upon various occasions, sometimes bringing earthbound spirits for enlightenment.

THIRTY YEARS AMONG THE DEAD

EXPERIENCE, OCTOBER 4, 1922

Spirit: DR. J. M. PEEBLES Psychic: MRS. WICKLAND

Spirit: Good Evening, my friends. I thank you for opening the door so I could bring in the ones that are in misery and have them find understanding. I like to be here with you and I like to help you with your work.

Doctor: Whoever you are, you are very welcome.

Sp. You know who I am -you know. This is Dr. Peebles.

I am young now. I was always young in spirit but my body commenced to grow old and I could not always do as I wished. I should very much have liked to live to be one hundred years old, but I could not. I had a most beautiful celebration on my hundredth birthday in the spirit world among friends.

I was very glad to go. When I reached the spirit world I was glad to find such glory and happiness and beauty. I understood about the spirit world but it cannot be described. I cannot tell you how it is when we have understanding.

Even though I had been a Spiritualist for many, many years, still I clung to dogma as well. I was a Spiritualist on one side, but I could not give up the dogma of the Christian religion -it was my hoodoo.

I traveled around the world five times, saw many conditions of life and heard many different lectures on the Great Truth. Let us not have beliefs. Let us only learn to understand the grandeur of God.

Realize that this little earth is only a grammar school. It is not a University, not even a High School; it is only the first lesson of life. Many do not learn in that school. Dr. (Who had been discussing reincarnation with a member of the circle, jestingly.) They reincarnate again! Sp. (Earnestly.) No, they do not Why should you want to come back again? Why should you go back to be confined in a small body and have no will of your own?

In the spirit world you are free to travel everywhere; you do not need a physical body. Why go back into that prison again? Why should a child, ready to enter High School, go back to the Sixth, Seventh or Eighth grade?

Those of you who are here at the present time, when you have learned the primary lesson of life, would you like to go back into a small body, and know nothing?

When you travel, you learn. You can learn in one day here what it takes ten or twelve years to learn on earth. If you feel like seeing things, you travel.

During my life I studied Reincarnation, and also Mrs. Cora Richmond's Reembodiment. Ques. What is Re-embodiment? Dr. It is a projection of self into the physical to acquire certain experiences. Sp. She believed you had to have many experiences; that you had to be a murderer, a thief, a salesman, a tailor, that you must learn all the trades and professions.

Why can't you learn these experiences through others? If you come in contact with a man, you do not need to be perfect to profit by his experience. You can learn by object lessons. We teach children by object lessons and so it is through life.

In the spirit world, if you wish to see a big factory making all sorts of machinery, you can, as a spirit, go there by thinking and can learn all about it.

If you want to learn what they are doing in other parts of the world, in Russia, Germany, England, Indian, Australia, think and you are there, and so learn your lessons. Should you then be born again?

All you learn in life is only like a day in spirit. I do not mean you grasp it all at once. You have nothing to hold you when you are free -remember, a free spirit, free and open to learn. Dr. For instance, here, when we want to know what is in a book, we have to go through it. In the spirit world, I presume you sense the contents. Sp. Yes, you sense it by feeling. When you are in the body, you have to act through the brain, and it is difficult, but in the spirit world you are free. You have no brain to interfere.

Life is everlasting. Everything you have learned through life that belongs to the soul is stored in your memory, but so long as you live in the material body the cells clog up. You lose your memory because the spirit cannot work on the brain cells as well in old age as in youth. The cells are not so active, and there are times when memory is shut out.

There are times when you feel like a drowning man; everything stands before you, things which have been forgotten.

As spirits we have our memory, but when we come back and control a medium, sometimes even our names are forgotten. We get into another body, very much like obsession. Dr. That must be a form of obsession. Sp. No, it is not. When obsession takes place, the spirit clings to that body and it is hard to let go. I would say that there is not one person on earth who is not obsessed in one way or another.

You know, in olden times, when I was a young boy, life was very different from what it is now. We did not hurry, because there was nothing to hurry for. Now, life is all hurry. People are living too rapid a life. If a man does not work fast, they say, "Quit him"; if he does not do that and that, "Quit him." Nowadays people have to be so keen that the nervous system fails and they lose themselves; then the spirits step in. If you were a clairvoyant and walked down some busy street, you would be surprised to find how many persons have invisible company.

Very few people, on entering the spirit side of life, even among the Spiritualists who preach it, understand the condition of the higher life. Dr. They usually care only for phenomena; they do not care for philosophy. Sp. Tonight I brought about one hundred spirits here. At first I lectured to them and tried to waken them, but could not. Then I saw the English lady (spirit who preceded him in controlling psychic) and from her actions I thought she would listen, but she would not.

So she was allowed to control Mrs. Wickland and served as an object lesson. The other spirits were watching her, as they thought she acted so strangely. They were curious, so they roused themselves and woke up; then I could talk.

You may think that sometimes we bring in strange spirits, but it is to help many others, as well as to give the controlling spirit an understanding of spiritual things.

Forget reincarnation, because it is a sandbag around your neck. You will have that so centered in your mind that you will think and think about only that, and then you will stay just where you are. You cannot progress because your mind will always revert to the earth again, and that gate which was opened for the English lady could never be opened to any one who believed in reincarnation.

THIRTY YEARS AMONG THE DEAD

The thought of it is so self-hypnotizing and so self-satisfying that there is nothing in your mind except coming back, and those are real selfish thoughts. You wrap yourself in those thoughts and you remain just where you are.

You cannot reincarnate. I have seen the effect of such thoughts, and have also talked with people who believed in reincarnation. Ques. What does Madam Blavatsky think about reincarnation now? Sp. We had some dispute about it when I was on earth, and we have had more since I came here. She does not believe in it now. She has had her lesson. It took a very long time, but now all she would like to come back for would be to correct her mistakes. Dr. That is hard to do. Sp. I had my hobby. I thought I should see Christ. I have not seen Him and never will. "Christ" is the Principle of God; "Christ" is the Principle of Life; "Jesus" is Truth and "Christ" is Enlightenment and Understanding. When you have found yourself and learn to be one with your Maker that is At-Onement with God.

Through "Jesus" you find the Truth, and "Jesus" has to be crucified that "Christ" may live. We must overcome earthly things. Crucify selfishness and jealousy on the cross. Truth cannot be selfish or jealous; selfishness and jealousy belong to the lower part of man.

Do not become hypnotized in any way by dogma, creed or belief, but find God within yourself and be free. Ask to hear, to see, to feel and to know God, then your eyes will be opened to spiritual things and you will not want to come back to this earth life again.

You could not live on earth more than once -no, no! You cannot light again a candle that has burned out. Life is progression not retrogression. You go from one degree to another, and so on and on.

In the spirit world your time is so taken up with duties that you have no time to think of coming back. You want to see your friends and you want to travel, because you can see all you want to when you are free and have understanding.

Many ask, "How about children who have passed out and have not had earth life experience?" They have it. The spirit of the mother's love brings the children to her, often they are around her and in this way learn of earth life.

They are also taught. We have, in the spirit world, teachers of higher things, and they teach by object lessons. We take children to schools of various kinds and teach them God's wonders. There they learn the real life, not merely reading and writing.

They learn the real lessons -anatomy, astrology, astronomy, and many other subjects. Those are the studies of the children, and the masters therein are teaching the lessons.

Our schools teach progression to a higher life. I wish you could open your eyes to see how rapidly the children progress by object lessons.

I want to tell you that I am with you in your work. I want you to understand that I have not left you.

People are lost for lack of a real understanding of life. Obsession is very, very bad. Insane asylums are filled and the doctors do not know what to do to stop insanity.

Let us have more love for each other; let us all help the weak ones and reach the point where all are brothers and sisters.

When that time comes everybody will work just half the time they do now; they will have more time for themselves and will have more pleasures. Now half the people are idle and are a detriment to themselves and the world at large. If all would work for others and not have such unrest it would be better for everybody. Now I must not say any more but must go. Good Night.

Very unexpectedly we had a visit from the one whose teachings and writings have made world-wide the theory of Reincarnation.

EXPERIENCE, NOVEMBER 1, 1922

Spirit: MADAM BLAVATSKY Psychic: MRS. WICKLAND

I wanted to come to you this evening. I believe in the work this little circle is doing, and I am very pleased with the work you are carrying on. I wish there were more to help us, to meet us on a half way basis to understand there is no death.

I do wish I had taught this truth more, and also that I had tried to look further into it. I knew about it. I also had many manifestations.

I do not know why, but when truth comes to us we shut it out. Truth is always hidden. We have to search to find it. Theories and dogmas seem to have more chance in the world than truth. Every one has some manifestations but hides them instead of acknowledging them.

I wanted to be a leader in some way or another. Now I want to bring the truth to the world. I knew of spirit manifestations and I had them myself. I did a great deal in my early days along this line but I commenced to investigate Theosophy. Philosophy and Theosophy should go hand in hand.

To me came Reincarnation. It appealed to me for a time. I could not see the truth clearly. I felt that it was very unjust some should be rich and have such good times and that others should be poor and have so much trouble. Others did not get enough earth experience -at least so I felt.

I studied Reincarnation, and I thought there was truth and justice in the theory that we come back and learn and have more experiences. I taught it and wanted to bring it out to the world and its peoples.

I felt that I remembered far back in my past. I felt I knew all about my past, but I was mistaken.

Memories of "past lives" are caused by spirits that bring such thoughts and represent the lives they lived. A spirit impresses you with the experiences of its life and these are implanted in your mind as your own. You then think you remember your past.

When you study, especially when you study Theosophy, you develop your mind and live in an atmosphere of mind. You remove yourself as much as possible from the physical. Naturally you become sensitive, and naturally you feel the spirits around you.

They speak to you by impressions and their past will be like a panorama. You feel it, and you live over the past of spirits and you make the mistake of taking this for the memory of former incarnations.

I did not know this when I lived. I took it for granted that these memories were true, but when I came to the spirit side of life I learned differently.

I studied a great deal. Theosophy is the best and highest philosophy of life intrinsically, but let us study the truth, let us live up to the truth of it and forget theories.

Let us develop the truth within us -find ourselves. Do not let us look far away; do not let us look in the past, do not let us look into the future, but let us find ourselves in our present condition and let us be true to ourselves. Let us forget all theories and dogmas. Let us know and feel the nearness of God.

Reincarnation is not true.

I did not want to believe that. They told me here in the spirit world that I could not reincarnate. I have tried and tried to come back to be somebody else, but I could not. We cannot reincarnate. We progress, we do not come back.

Why should you come back to live another life when you have gained experience and an understanding while you were here, and, furthermore, since this is only a preliminary school on earth?

Let us learn to find ourselves. While I am sorry to say many have not found themselves, let all of us here acquire knowledge so that when we go to the spirit side of life we shall go on to a higher life.

In earth life you have your material body to hinder you. If you want to write a book you have to look up data here and there and go to the library to find some book that contains what you wish to know. You may have to go from one place to another and yet not find it. It all takes time, and time is limited; you are hindered.

In the spirit world, if we want data on a certain thing we think of it and it is all before us. There is no time, no matter, to hinder.

In the spirit world, if we want earthly experience, do you think we have to reincarnate to get that experience? No, we do not.

For illustration, say one wants to know more about medicine. He then goes to a school as a student, hears everything, sees everything, and comes in contact with everything, learning it much quicker than he could grasp it on earth, and he has it much clearer in his mind.

In earth life you have to study for years, and then you do not get it as clearly as we do.

Suppose you want experience in the spirit world with machinery or anything else -you can get it easily. We have everything in the spirit world, because everything that is invented on earth has first been invented in the spirit world.

Suppose an inventor passes on before completion of his invention. He will not give it up. He studies it on the spirit side of life because it is easier to study there, as he has more time. When he has everything ready he finds some sensitive and impresses the invention on his mind. Then that one commences on it, perfects it, and gives it to the world.

If I impress a sensitive with an idea, in one sense I reincarnate -not in his body, but by impressing him with what I want done.

In this way we come and go, if we are attracted to earth life and want to be here.

When you have once reached the spirit world, where all are congenial, where all is life, where all is bliss, where there is no jealousy, no envy, where all is one grand harmony, do you think for one moment that you would want to leave that beautiful condition to come back to earth and be a little baby, restricted in mind and knowing nothing -nothing whatever?

Furthermore, you might get into a sickly, crippled body and be worse than you were before.

No, reincarnation is not true. I believed it, I taught it, and I was sure that I should come back and be somebody else. But I will not. I can do far more good now.

If I want to do some missionary work, or some good, I go down to the earth sphere, the earthbound sphere, where the spirits are in all kinds of misery. I preach to them and teach them; I try to rescue them. So I find my work.

Why should we go down from the harmony in the spirit world to what I might call hell? Here we have one group, singing and praying and praising God from early morning until night, and they are so self-hypnotized that we cannot talk to them.

We go to another group and there we find the misers. They are so busy counting money, money, which is their God, that we cannot reach them.

We go to others who have been ruined in life; they are bitter and jealous, they have nothing but revenge in their minds. They have no love or kindness. They are like sponges which have been dipped in muddy water; you would not even know they were sponges. Their love has turned to hate and they cannot be taught love and kindness.

They will spit at you, they will laugh at you, for they feel that there is no God, no kindness, no love, but all is jealousy and selfishness.

But we are not disappointed; our mission is to turn these souls to better things. We may have a hard time. We cannot go there and pray for them -no, no! They would shut the door and say they did not want us, and so we cannot go there and talk and lecture.

You may ask how it is possible to reach them. First we try to concentrate on them. Then we have music. Sometimes we have to play very softly so they can hardly hear it, then we play a little louder. No matter how evil, how mean, how low souls have been, they will listen to music. When they have given their attention to the music, we concentrate on them to waken and look up to higher things.

Artists then paint pictures of the higher life for them, object lessons, little stories. Their life history can be seen by us and we put this in pictures, one by one, and let them see the mistakes they have made. Presently they ask questions and then we come a little closer to them. After that we take them to the higher life.

In another group are those who are self-hypnotized. They have gone to sleep. They were taught that death is a sleep and that they will sleep until the Last Day when God will sit on His throne and judge them. They are difficult to reach, especially if they have put themselves into an actual death sleep.

Sometimes we have to bring them to control a medium and waken them in that way. When we cannot reach the earthbound spirits at all we have to bring them to earth life to a circle like this where they get understanding through matter.

In one sense you can call this reincarnation, because we have to bring them to matter to find themselves.

I wish we could have more circles like this to waken these spirits and make them understand about the life beyond.

Some may say this is not Madam Blavatsky, but do not doubt -it is. They may say, She would not say so and so, she would not talk so and so,-but it is Madam Blavatsky.

If you have any questions you would like to ask I will try to answer them. Ques. Will you tell us about the "Masters"? What do you think of them by now? Sp. We talk of "Masters" -yes! We are all masters when we try to study higher things, but a "Master," as we understand it in Theosophy, is some big and great mind.

A master is one who can master matter, can overcome matter, one who can live a pure and good life, and master the conditions of life.

Learn the lessons of Nature; learn how to progress.

I am sorry to say that most of those who want to be "Masters" on earth fall. It is not they themselves who fall, but they become so sensitive, so psychic, that, although they do not know they are on the borderland, earthbound spirits step in, control them and they fall.

We should master matter first before we try to master new ideas.

Take myself -what did I really do that was good for humanity? Ans. You led many out of orthodoxy. Sp. Yes, but I only gave them more theory. I could have done, oh, so much more if I had stayed with my mediumship and worked to bring this world and the other together. I was a medium and I could have done a great work, but I became obsessed. I am sorry to say that Theosophists are breaking up. You live now in a time when things are breaking up; there is a general restlessness. All theories will go down and philosophy will rise. Dr. There should be more simplicity in life. Sp. That is a very good word to apply. You have found the truth. You have good workers on the other side connected with this medium.

You have no theories, no mysterious things, as Theosophists have. They think the more mysterious they are, the greater "Masters" they are. Where are they? Where are they?

I am sorry to say that they are so self-hypnotized that their imagination runs away with them.

One may look back and say: "I was Julius Caesar."

He has probably read some book about Julius Caesar and become so wrapped up in it that he feels he has lived in that time. Then he receives spirit impressions and is sure that this was his former life.

You can make people believe almost anything. They do not build their houses on the rock of reason, for a storm will blow them down.

All denominations have some truth. You have heard the story of the elephant? Of the blind men who examined an elephant, and each declared that an elephant was like that part which he had touched -like the trunk, the leg or the tail. Every one had the truth, but none the whole truth.

We do not seek for the whole truth, so one hangs on to the tail, another to the trunk, and so on.

Let us all join together, then we will find the whole elephant, and we will all be together in one great truth.

Ques. Will there be psychics to carry on further investigations?

Sp. When the time comes and the people are ready, the psychics will be ready also. We can all join together then and there will be psychic circles in every church.

THIRTY YEARS AMONG THE DEAD

Ques. Why are there not more inspirational speakers to teach the truth?

Sp. The public lecture work will be inspirational. Lecturers and politicians often think they are going to say what they have written down, but before they know it they speak of something altogether different. They are speaking inspirationally, for there are always those on the spirit side of life who are interested in this life and are ready to inspire a speaker.

Ques. Will a psychic be protected?

Sp. One should always be positive in ordinary life, cure disappointment, never let anything disturb one. No anger or sorrow may creep in, because anger comes from the other side the lower sphere.

Everyone must be positive. When we open the door to the spirit side of life there are crowds of earthbound spirits who want to see the light which they can see through a mortal body. Having lost their physical sight they are blind, for there is no material light in the earth sphere, and without an understanding they have no spiritual light. Ques. Should not a psychic be well informed on all subjects? Sp. Suppose a great musician had to play on a poor piano. He could not bring out the shading of the music in any way. He must have a fine instrument. So it is with a psychic. A psychic should be informed on all topics regarding the world. An uncultured psychic cannot be used to speak properly on scientific subjects. Ques. What becomes of the spirit of a psychic while another spirit is controlling? Sp. You understand that in spirit we can be large or small as we think. The spirit of Mrs. Wickland, at the present time, is in her magnetic aura. There can be a number of spirits in one aura. Some come and some go, but only one can control at a time.

Mrs. Wickland just now is in a coma state. She does not function on the mental plane. She is the live wire; she is the battery. She is the motor, and we have many lines from that motor. If she left we would not have the electrical force to control. In this case the psychic is the battery through which we work. Ques. Theosophy teaches that during sleep one develops mentally and spiritually; that the body will stay at rest, but the soul will leave the body, connected only by a slender thread, And gain experience on the mental or astral plane. Is that true? Sp. Yes, it is. When you sleep you often dream. Some dreams are meaningless; others are real experiences.

When you study Yoga you learn to leave the body. Hindus study Yoga and leave the body at will. Most persons do not know that they leave the body and travel in the spirit world. Ques. Would it be desirable to have continuous consciousness? Sp. If humanity had continuous consciousness it would be a big factor in the welfare of this world.

God is All in All, even to the little microscopic things. He is all Life. If all were taught this simple truth earth life would become ideal. There is no death, only progression. All should be taught that. Selfishness, ignorance and jealousy would be gone then; doubt would be buried. Love and charity would rule.

Suppose you go out of your body. You pass through the first strata -what do you find? Selfishness. You have to pass through this first strata before you can reach the higher. Ignorance, selfishness and jealousy must be passed through before you can reach the better life. It is a case of development.

The Hindus have peace and harmony. They live for higher things, although I do not mean every one in India does this. But when the more advanced leave their bodies no one can get in and disturb them.

THIRTY YEARS AMONG THE DEAD

What I want to say tonight is that we should study life as it is. Let the dreamers and thinkers of the past take care of themselves. I see now that I had many earthbound spirits around me.

I never saw so many religions in one city as in Los Angeles. People go from one church to another and they do not know where they are at. Cranks and others sing and pray, and everybody loves Jesus.

"Jesus" is the Truth. Read Anna Kingsford's works and you will find many interesting things there. She was not a crank. We read many books together. She was a wonderful woman. Dr. Wasn't she opposed to mediumship? Sp. She was a medium herself. Her writings were not her own. Writers have a hard time. When they think they are getting along very nicely their thoughts suddenly change. They are influenced by some spirit writer. All Anna Kingsford's writings were inspirational. Ques. What about Olcott? Sp. Olcott has found the truth. Let us be sensible and learn not to be foolish. Let us find the simple truth.

I have greatly enjoyed this talk with all of you and I will certainly come again. Do all you can to further this noble work.

This room is full of spirits who have listened to what was said tonight. Many have been helped and will go with us to the spirit side of life.

May strength and power be with you all. Let God's light shine in your soul and go on with this good work.

Good Night.

THIRTY YEARS AMONG THE DEAD

THIRTY YEARS AMONG THE DEAD

Chapter XVI

Philosophy

The philosophy of life and descriptions of conditions in the higher realms have been given by spirits who have attained enlightenment and are desirous of helping humanity to an understanding of the spiritual laws.

A friend of many years standing, formerly a Methodist minister, had followed our work with great interest and had been a constant attendant at our circles, in which his daughter took an active part.

Five days after he passed away he controlled Mrs. Wickland, and several months later spoke to us again, telling of his experiences in spirit life.

EXPERIENCE, OCTOBER 27, 1920

Spirit: WM. Y., SR. Psychic: MRS. WICKLAND

Well, I am here again. I have been here before, many times. Do you know who I am? I am Doctor Y.

I am glad that I can be with you here tonight and I am pleased this circle is continuing. We are here every time you have a meeting, and I wish you could see the spirits who are waiting to come in for an understanding of life. Life is a great problem to the world. I wish people would study life and its existence in matter.

It is a shame to send so many spirits out of their bodies into the darkness of ignorance. They only believe; they sing and praise God and we cannot reach them. They are so self-hypnotized by their religion, in the first place, that they do not know they are dead, and, in the second place, by their praising of God and singing, that we cannot reach them with the understanding that they must praise God in a different way.

We must act; we must work for humanity. We must learn the first lesson that Christ taught, to serve others, and to love God above all things and our neighbor as ourselves.

How many do really love God? They pray and sing, but they do not do what the Bible teaches.

I understood a great deal about the other world and still I was like a child regarding that understanding, because I had not learned to control matter and the conditions that surround us. When we pass through the material sphere of ether, the sphere around this world, we pass through the sphere in which are most of the spirits of darkness, which we call earthbound spirits.

THIRTY YEARS AMONG THE DEAD

There all is selfishness and ignorance. These spirits must serve to help themselves to a higher understanding, for they have not served but have been served in their earth lives.

They do not know what it is to live and do for others; they have lived only for self. They are waiting to be served. Their minds have not been developed to do for others.

I wish I could take you to the sphere of suicides, the sphere of the churches, the sphere of the slums, the sphere of the misers, and so on. Here they are in darkness, crying for help. Many of them do not know what to do. They go to mortals and try to control them, upsetting their lives, and they are ignorant of what they are doing.

Frank and Charles (relatives in the spirit world) have taken me to all those places and shown me many things. If you could actually realize what that means. I wish I could make a picture for you of all those conditions and the agony of despair the spirits are in.

They will have to find themselves and waken to a realization that they must not look for God outside, but within themselves.

When you find this wonderful understanding of life, and realize what the object of life is, that is glory. No one can do this for you; others can only teach you, but you have to work for yourself.

There is no time in the spirit world; you have all the time in eternity to find yourself, and as soon as you understand God in His glory you will have happiness. Then your spiritual eyes will be opened and you will awaken to a world of grandeur. You will awaken and realize harmony and glory.

But this is not "Heaven"; Heaven must be found within you.

There is a world of spirits, and there is a future life everlasting. There you have your homes as you have made them while here.

Nearest to the earth is the City of Ignorance and the conditions in which many awaken. No matter how good you have been, nor how well you have lived your life -that alone is not sufficient.

If you are ignorant of the life and system of the other side, you are in darkness for the time being until you awaken and realize that there is a life after this.

Each has a home in the spirit world made by service to others during earth life. As you have made it here, so you will have it there. If you have done good acts and lived a pure upright life, doing the best you know how, your home is beautiful. But you will not know how to reach that home if you are ignorant of the laws governing the spirit world.

If you have lived a life of selfishness and lived only and entirely for self, your home is a little place that you can hardly creep into, and you see nothing but self.

You have no company but your own self. You have your thoughts of self, you have lived for self, and you have to live in that state of mind until you ask God for help, and say: "Not my will any longer, but Thy will. Give me help."

Then your spirit comprehends the results of your actions during earth life. You go back to the earth plane again and there you have to serve those whom you have harmed through your selfishness.

THIRTY YEARS AMONG THE DEAD

If they are still in earth life you have to watch and help them all you can, and you will have to serve them until you have atoned for the harm you have done them while you were on earth.

If they have passed out and are in the dark, you will have to find them and help bring them to an understanding of life, and you will have to serve them until you have paid your debt.

After you have done that, you step out of that sphere into a higher sphere where your home is. Your home is given to you after you have earned it. Then your friends come to you and help you, and there is a reunion like which there is nothing on earth, because that reunion with your relatives and friends is a reunion in reality.

All are like one, all are in tune, all are in harmony with each other. Just to be able to say, "I live in the hearts of my friends" is great happiness.

The reunion that they had for me at the time I passed out and came to an understanding of life can never be described. Many of my friends I met later, and I have been helping to waken them to the glory of understanding.

Let us not believe but let us act. Let us all do our duty while we are here, and let us understand the wonders of Nature and the wonders of God.

We could not worship more than God, for God is everything. You are one part of His grand work, the flowers are another part of His grand work, the animals another part, so how could you be outside God? Why should you not worship His manifestations in every way? You are in the very midst of Him. When you are one with God you have great glory.

I want to say "Hallelujah!" (A favorite expression in earth life.) That is grand, that is beautiful!

This is a step every one has to take; every one has to pass through this. I learned my first step in a few months. When I woke up from the sleep of death -we call it a sleep of transition -I was really awake. I had understanding. I was told about the grand things in spirit but I never could have imagined it as grand as I found it.

Let us visit the "churches" of the earth sphere, the place of the spirits who pass out with religious belief and dogma. These gather in a group and do not try to waken to the realization that they are still sleeping spiritually, because they have never asked: "Who am I? Where did I come from? Where do I go? Where is the real life? " They are self-hypnotized by their belief in Jesus Christ, and in God sitting on a throne with Christ at His right side, judging the people, good and bad. Some, they think, have to go to a burning hell, and some will go in glory to God in Heaven.

That is the belief they have, and, although "dead" the majority of those who only believe are still on earth, going to church. They, want to be on earth singing the same songs, and praying the same prayers. They think that all they have to do is to sing and pray.

Many do not know they have passed out. They do not even stop to think that their relatives and friends do not talk to them as they did formerly. We have a very hard time to reach them.

Some sing and pray, others walk alone, trying to find out what is the matter; at other times they become attached to mortals and hypnotize them so by their belief that the mortals become obsessed and are sent to the asylum for religious mania.

It is a great pity that men cannot understand God. When they have that understanding they cannot live for themselves; they will want to work for others and give every one of their happiness.

I have still to see the depth of misery to which the wretched ones go because of hate and selfishness. These hate all humanity. That is the worst condition. They are so crippled that you can hardly believe they are persons.

They have to be taught to realize, but how can they be reached? They are afraid of themselves, and they have to remain in that condition until they pray in all earnestness to be freed.

I have learned this in the few months I have been on the spirit side of life. I have a very nice home in the spirit world. I have my relatives and friends, but everything is very different here from there.

I have to help many of my friends because, even though some passed out long before I, they are still in darkness regarding an understanding of the real life.

The teaching of children should be very different from what it is. Children should be taught about God in Nature, taught that God is Love. If they were properly taught you would not have any crime. They would love Nature, they would love animals, they would love humanity at large. But they are taught not to worship Nature. How could you worship God more beautifully than to worship Him through His manifestation?

I am glad to be with you tonight and I want you all to go on with your work. If you could only see, every evening when you have your meeting, how many crippled and unfortunate spirits listen and try to get help so they can pass into the life beyond.

Humanity should rouse itself and not send so many ignorant spirits to the other side, because these only stay near the earth and do harm to those who are here on earth.

Humanity will have a difficult time for a little while, because of crime and selfishness. All that people live for now is money and self. They will have to change their viewpoint some time. Then peace will go over the earth. Now it is war -war with everybody, but when peace and harmony prevail, you will find a glorious condition.

I say "Hallelujah!" Let that time come as quickly as possible! Just now it is fighting and laws. Unless this is changed people will rise because they want freedom, but God speed the day when the peace spirit will come over all.

Frank is a good fellow to be with, and he is not afraid to make inquiries. At times I feel like saying: "No, I can't do that," but he says there is nothing which can harm you if you are not afraid.

Fear is what we must avoid; we must develop power. When you develop fear you create conditions of fear around you. You should develop within yourself the power of God, the power to conquer, the power of Love. Then you will conquer, no matter what comes.

I wish you could all understand God, not as a person, but as the Life of the whole Universe, and realize that there is no life without God. He is the Divine in everything, but we are clothed with selfishness, jealousy and ignorance.

If you are troubled by obsession, say to yourself: "I am master over my own body and I shall be." Repeat it over and over again, and you will find that you have power.

Do not send out thoughts of evil because they only hinder your own self. They create more thoughts of anger and you will not have gained anything. Develop within yourself power and strength to conquer.

Say to yourself, over and over again: "I am master, and nobody else can interfere." When you do that you will be free. Do not think of the other one (obsessing spirit) who is trying to bother you. Send out a kind thought to him.

Doctor, I want to thank you and your wife for that nice little party (funeral) I had -that is what I call it. It was a nice little party at the time I passed to the spirit world. I do not think there was one in that little church who thought it was a funeral. It was a party.

I was with them during the service. I do not think any one thought of the coffin. I thank you all for letting the service be held in that fine little church, and also for suggesting that they all wear white.

That was glory, and I felt like shouting "Hallelujah!"

I wish all funerals could be like that. Sadness and sorrow bring to the spirits sadness and sorrow and gloom. They cannot get out of that gloom for years.

Now I must go.

Another old friend, a physician and metaphysician who had been a lecturer among the Spiritualists during his earth life, visits with us occasionally.

EXPERIENCE, OCTOBER 20, 1920

Spirit: DR. ADAMS Psychic: MRS. WICKLAND

I am heart and soul in this work. I was in this work when in life, not so much doing the obsession work as does Doctor, but I was in the work of spreading the truth that there is a life after this.

It is a real life, not an imaginary one; it is a life of understanding, not a life of belief.

If you only believe, you will be in darkness, with a closed door, because you have only belief, not knowledge, of the other world.

The Bible teaches so much, and if people would only understand it as it was really meant, not take it literally or historically, it would be so much better.

You must understand that at the time the Bible was written the people were not as enlightened as they are today, and there was so much selfishness.

When the first church was formed it was the church of the understanding of life, and the teaching was to live for high thoughts and to sacrifice self for others. When you study, and study deeply, earth conditions have no existence for you.

Religion is often used as a whip for ignorant people. The leaders say: "We want these people to obey us, we want them to do as we tell them to do, we want them to be slaves."

Look back in history and you will find that people were easygoing, very lazy, did not care; they did not care to do anything. The women were the ones who did the work; they did the farming, for the men were too lazy. The women had to do the work and be the slaves.

Then along came a shrewd man who thought, "We will make these men work," and the leaders got up a scheme to scare people. They told them that if they did not do so and so the devil would get hold of them when they die, and they would go to hell and damnation.

THIRTY YEARS AMONG THE DEAD

Then they painted hell in the worst condition they could. They painted it as a big oven, burning. There were skeletons here and there, and hot fire, and the one that put people in the fire was the devil, and he put them in with his pitchfork.

That made the men wake up! That picture gave them energy, strength and power. They were afraid -afraid they would get into that hell when they died. Humanity tried to do everything possible to escape that hell, and the leaders were able to make the people do whatever they told them.

One conceived the idea that he wanted to be leader, then another wanted to be the leader, but how could both be leaders in one circle?

Then another conceived the idea that religion would be better if he had a little clique of his own, so he preached in his way and called it whatever he pleased. Along came another, and he had his idea, because he wanted to be leader, so he gathered some people into his corner and preached in his way.

So we had one group here and another there. One wanted to rule the world, but along came another sect, and they called themselves by a new name, and felt they wanted to rule. They fought and had wars.

Then followed other religions and all had adherents. Each tried to be a greater leader than the other. Some were more crabbed, but all tried to get the people together and hold them, some by the picture I spoke of regarding hell. They could not get them together much in the beginning unless they held them in bondage.

That has gone on for years and years, but now there has come a new era and all will be at least partially broken up. There will be a different condition.

Nowadays some of the people believe and some do not, and some think they do not want to have anything to do with religion, and so we have a state of turmoil. They are all fighting and fighting. Each one fights to see if he cannot get the best of others. The idea is to get all the money you can, all the power you can, and then be the leader.

People want to get all they can now, as this is the time to make money, and they say they will make it regardless of the method. They have become so selfish in their money making that their true citizenship is lost.

Things are very different now from what they were when I was a boy. It will be very hard for some time because capital wants to rule, and labor wants to rule, so we have friction and trouble.

The churches are trying to make people go to church, but if they continue to keep people down there will, in time, be a war that will be terrible, because holding people down kills the better nature in them.

People get all they can from each other. The spirit of the day is to get all you can, no matter how you get it.

When I lived on this earth plane it was an honor to do your work well and to be faithful to your employer. Now if the employer does not like your work he can easily get another man to take your place.

How can you expect such people to feel right when they pass out of their bodies? They leave their bodies and take possession of any one they can reach on the earth plane, and therefore we have insanity and all kinds of suicides.

They had war for four years and killed thousands and thousands of people. These left the world they loved filled with hatred and they come back and try to crush this world.

The time will come when conditions will be very serious, but after that things will be better. People will reach a better understanding and will learn through sorrows, and try to comprehend the mystery of life.

There will be great inventions which will be remarkable.

At this time people are being crushed, but after a while there will be an awakening. It is said, "The mills of the gods grind slowly, but they grind exceeding fine," and that is what the world is going through now.

The time will come when people will know that we are not dead when we pass to the spirit side of life, but that we live. We are trying to help and guide you all, and we hope to have more sincerity among the people. Death will only be like a journey which they take to another country where they will be with their loved ones, if they have understanding.

You have flying machines now, but after a few years you will have air inventions that are not dreamed of at this time. This is only the beginning. You will use more electricity, and atmospheric conditions will be used as power.

You will get power from the sun which will be of great benefit to humanity; then the capitalists cannot buy things as they do now. They crush the poor people now because they can buy everything, and the others cannot have it. They say: "God did not give it to you, He gave it to me."

Machinery will run by that power. Any one with a little instruction will be able to use it and can take all the power he wants from the atmosphere.

Selfishness will then be done away with and people will learn to live and love as Christ taught them. They will not live a life of belief as they have during the past centuries.

In the future, people will know that if they do not do right they will suffer for it. They have already taken away most of the pictures of burning hell and therefore the churches no longer have the control of the people they had in the past.

When ministers teach the truth regarding the life after this they will have their churches full. People will then go to church to worship and will not only believe.

We all make mistakes and we should learn through those mistakes. God wants us to be wise and understand Him. It is not that God made a mistake and did not know what He was doing. He has given you power; you are a part of Him, and after you learn to understand God in all His wonders you will be in the happy state that we call "Bliss," and that is "Heaven." You have to search for that understanding.

People should gather together and unite and be in harmony. Always selfishness and jealousy creep in. Let us try to conquer them and put them away, and have love in our hearts. If only people would understand what love means. They talk it with their lips but they never practice it.

I had a very hard time of it when I was on earth, because I believed in a life after this and preached it. They called me crazy; they said I would go to hell. They said there is no such thing as the spirit world; when we die we go to the grave and stay there until the last day.

Then we shall be awakened and God will sit on His throne and call the sinners on one side and the good on another. One lot will go to hell and damnation and the others will be in Heaven and glory.

Isn't that terrible? They say God made them all, some to be condemned and others to go to glory! Imagine some going to Heaven and seeing the others lie in hell and burn!

I had many struggles and troubles in life. Of course I was a physician, but I also practiced magnetism, and I taught the truth of the life hereafter because I felt it was my duty. I did all I could to build up the church of Spiritualism, and I worked very hard. I wanted to preach the philosophy of spirit return, not phenomena.

Do all you can to open the door to the unseen, but always with understanding of the governing laws. The average Spiritualists of today have not even studied the philosophy of life and do not know the laws that govern between this world and the next.

Spiritualism is the Science of the Bible. The Bible says: "The letter killeth but the spirit giveth life." If you understand the Bible, it becomes a grand book. Many go blindly to church only believing, and have no knowledge or understanding.

I shall be glad when all phenomena will be buried and philosophy will take its place, and preachers will preach the true gospel of God, not of the Savior, but God, the Divine, the Life in each of us. We must understand God better and learn to know Him, as we have the power to do.

Do not let us condemn anything through ignorance, selfishness and jealousy. These we should crush under our feet and we should live up to the best of our Love, Wisdom and Understanding of our Maker.

Good Night.

Many years ago Mrs. Wickland had an intimate friend, Mrs. Lackmund, whose little girl, at the age of two and a half, became an imbecile after one sudden convulsion. The mother was convinced that this condition was caused by spirit obsession, and together with Mrs. Wickland began to investigate the subject.

Mrs. Lackmund and Mrs. Wickland had made an agreement that whichever one of them should first pass to the spirit side of life would try to return and communicate with the other, saying, as a test, "Spirit return is true."

A year after this Mrs. Lackmund died, and two weeks later, during the night, appeared to Mrs. Wickland, so life-like that the latter did not realize she was a spirit.

Mrs. Lackmund touched her friend lightly on the cheek and Mrs. Wickland sat up, exclaiming, "Mrs. Lackmund!"

Then Mrs. Lackmund spoke. "Anna, spirit return is true. I will develop you. Go on with the work of obsession."

Shortly after this she appeared to Mrs. Wickland again at a materialization séance, giving unmistakable proof of her identity, and repeated her former words: "Spirit return is true. Go on with the work of obsession. I will develop you."

Subsequently she joined the band of invisibles who guard Mrs. Wickland and since then has very often spoken through the latter.

THIRTY YEARS AMONG THE DEAD

EXPERIENCE, SEPTEMBER 29, 1920

Spirit: MRS. LACKMUND   Psychic: MRS. WICKLAND

How few people understand life or God in the right way. Instead of believing in God and using His name so much, and calling on Him to do what they should do themselves, they should realize that God is Love and the Light of Understanding.

How can we live and not understand Him in the right way?

If people would only understand God as it was meant they should understand Him they would not have so much selfishness, worry or fighting, because people would have more love for each other and not think so much of self.

They would worship God, not money. People think the more money they have the happier they will be. They do not know what happiness means; they do not know what true happiness is. They think they will be happy when they have plenty of money to get things, things to eat, and things to drink, and live a life of injury to the body. These are the things most thought of at present.

In time, however, the world will understand God. The churches will soon waken and teach the true gospel of God, teach people not to believe but to understand, to understand His wondrous works, to understand Him and how He manifests in everything.

Every flower is a manifestation of God. The odor of a beautiful flower is God, and He sends it out to everyone that His presence may be felt. You can see God's manifestation through the beautiful spirit of the odor that shines -I call it so -through that flower. You do not need to touch it. If you were blind you would know there must be a flower because of the odor, for it permeates the atmosphere.

Shall you not worship God and see how wonderfully He manifests Himself to you in the exquisite odor of flowers, that make you feel happier for having them around you?

See the Master's work in one flower and another. Can you make them as they are? Can you paint them with their odor?

In your garden you plant one flower here and another flower there -why do they not mix? Why do not green leaves grow among the petals of the red flower?

The green leaves take from the atmosphere what they need and the red flower takes what it needs and colors itself. The flowers clothe themselves from the colors of the sun. One is purple, one red, another yellow, another blue, and each has its place in the beautiful Nature of God. All is perfect in God's Nature.

When you go from the kingdom of flowers and vegetables to the animals you will find something that you do not often find in men and women -faithful love.

Men and women should be the crown of God's creation, but they are bound by doubt and creed. Many think themselves holy, but the holiness is only superficial. They make no effort to be honest in their every day life.

They go to church on Sunday, pray to God and tell Him how good they are, then condemn another man who does not go to church at all, but who tries sincerely to live the right kind of life as best he knows how.

Probably the latter is nearer God in his way than the one who worships outwardly and does not live a sincere life.

Earthbound spirits who torment mortals by obsessing them are man-made "devils." Selfishness has made them what they are. They go out of the physical in ignorance of the real life, full of hatred, because they were crushed in one way or another. They have hatred for all mankind, and the first persons they can attach themselves to they try to harm, and there you have obsession.

You must all be on your guard; you must, every one of you, try to fight obsession. Humanity is fighting sickness, but does not fight the actual cause of insanity.

Insanity is nothing but obsession by spirits who are sent to the spirit side of life without understanding the truth of God.

Christ taught us to love God above all things and our neighbor as ourselves. People do not love their neighbors as they should.

Teach children the right way of living; teach them the right understanding of God and of the teachings of Christ. Teach them to live according to high principles, not to worship Christ as a person but as the True Understanding and the Light of Life.

Then you will not send earthbound spirits to the spirit side of life to obsess sensitives who have to be sent to the asylums.

People do not know what to do with the insane. They are sent to the asylum, but that is all. They are given morphine, closed up in a room and left there. This is done only to protect humanity, so that the insane will not harm themselves or others.

Instead of that they should be taught the Golden Rule, and be given an opportunity to develop higher ideals.

This is Mrs. Lackmund. Good Night.

In the first years of Mrs. Wickland's psychic work a friend, Mrs. Case, was deeply interested in the furtherance of the same.

Recently this friend came as a spirit to review those early days.

EXPERIENCE, MARCH 15, 1924

Spirit: MRS. CASE Psychic: MRS. WICKLAND

You do not know me personally but I feel that I am one of you. I knew Mrs. Wickland before she was married and, as Miss Anna Anderson, she first convinced me of the truth of spirit return.

I had investigated the subject slightly and had read one of Dr. Hartmann's books, as well as some theosophical writings. I was interested in various studies, but not sat in any.

One evening, in 1890, during a circle which I attended in Minneapolis, Miss Anderson became entranced by the spirit of my daughter, Alice. My daughter Alice and son Willie and my husband had all died in one month.

Alice came over to me and throwing herself in my arms said: "Oh, Mamma! Oh, Mamma! I am so glad that I can come to you! This is Alice."

THIRTY YEARS AMONG THE DEAD

I was greatly astonished but very delighted, and after we had talked with each other for a little while Alice said: "Mamma, Willie is also here and he wants to say a few words to you." Then my son spoke to me.

This surprising experience converted me and from that time I was eager to know more regarding the truth.

My daughter, Mrs. Z., and I often had little séances in my home with Miss Anderson and had many delightful visits with our spirit friends -my mother, an aunt and several others.

I was anxious that Miss Anderson should bring her work out to the world, but she was very modest regarding her mediumship.

I wanted people to know this great truth so I went to Stillwater, Minnesota, and rented an opera house, intending to lecture on the subject of spirit return and then have Miss Anderson give demonstrations.

We advertised widely and many people were present at the meeting. I had my lecture prepared but at the last moment lost my courage and could not face the audience.

We could not have the meeting a failure so I insisted that Miss Anderson go into a trance and let the Russians (spirits) give their drama.

She consented and the play was well given. Then Pretty Girl (guide) came and the evening was quite a success.

This was how Miss Anderson -now Mrs. Wickland -was first brought before the public.

When I became very sick Miss Anderson was with me a great deal.

Through her I spoke often to my spirit friends and asked them when I would go to my home in the spirit world.

I was told that I could not live much longer but that it would be some time before I passed to the other side.

I was taken sick before Thanksgiving and on the 5th of February, 1894, I left my earthly body for my spirit body. I went to sleep about 12 o'clock, Saturday night, and passed out Monday, at 3 o'clock in the afternoon.

At the time my daughter sat watching me and the sun was shining brightly in the room. I felt and knew I was going, and my daughter Carrie saw my soul leaving my body.

My spirit children, Alice and Willie, came to my bedside and my daughter saw them take me away.

When there is understanding there is no death. You only go to sleep in your earthly body and wake up in your spirit body with your friends about you. It is a very pleasant sensation.

I was very happy to think I had had such a peaceful transition. I merely went to sleep and woke up in the spirit world, with my relatives and friends around me.

But my husband was not there. When I asked, "Why is my husband not here with the rest?" I was told that he had been drawn back to earth life where the children and I were. His home was his attraction. We had not been able to see him there and he did not know how to speak through a medium, so he had remained in a stupor.

I went with my spirit relatives to find my husband and when we woke him we were both very happy. We went back to my daughter Carrie to tell her that we were reunited and she saw us clairvoyantly and was very pleased.

After that I often came back and talked to my children through Miss Anderson until she married and left Minneapolis for Chicago, but I have retained my interest in Mrs. Wickland and am one of the Mercy Band.

Mrs. Wickland's work has grown very much; she has developed and has had a great many experiences. She is doing a noble work for humanity.

This work has helped many in earth life but many, many more on the other side. Every one who has been converted goes into the Mercy Band as a helper and helps here as well as on the other side.

If only there were more on earth who would carry on the work of obsession. Humanity wants to have more knowledge and is looking for the truth.

Later on instruments will be invented through which spirits can speak.

Spirit philosophy will come to the front, for the spirit world is helping to bring the truth before humanity.

Those who have passed out as children continue their development in the spirit world and often acquire earth experience by contacting mortals as their protectors.

One of Mrs. Wickland's guides, Pretty Girl, came to her as a gay, playful child spirit, and has since become a discerning philosopher, with a practical knowledge of the principles that govern life.

EXPERIENCE, MARCH 12, 1924

Spirit: PRETTY GIRL Psychic: MRS. WICKLAND

I was five years old when I passed out of earth life and had been eight years in the spirit world when I was appointed as a controlling spirit to protect Mrs. Wickland, through life, against mischievous spirits.

A guide is a teacher and I am a guide now, but then I was only a control.

At that time Mrs. Wickland was often asked to give help and advice to persons who came to her in trouble, and she saved many from suicide by urging them to be more cheerful and to search for the bright side of life instead of the gloomy one.

I was sent as control and adviser because I myself had seen the dark side of earth life and could sympathize more fully with persons who were in trouble than could one who had never known sorrow.

I was born in London, in the Whitechapel district, on the 21st of August, 1875.

My parents were drunkards and many times when they came home I had to hide, otherwise I would have had a whipping. My father and mother swore at me and called me all kinds of names, and most of the time I was playing on the streets.

I had light, curly hair and blue eyes and passers-by used to pat me on the head and say: "Pretty little girl -pretty girl!"

THIRTY YEARS AMONG THE DEAD

Those are the only kind words I remember from my earth life, and I heard "Pretty Girl" so often I thought that was my name.

A neighbor lady was the only person who ever helped me; she was very kind and took care of me. When I was five years old I died.

Eight years later in 1888, I came to be Mrs. Wickland's control because I needed further earth experience and because a youthful spirit brings to a psychic a feeling of youth and strength.

It is often asked why mediums usually have children or young people as guides.

When a spirit who has lived to an old age on earth acts as guide, through his contact with matter he is apt to sense his last physical condition and this often leaves an old and tired feeling with the medium, while children bring a youthful magnetism.

For this reason many mediums have children as guides. Then also the children learn earthly conditions and through this experience progress in the spirit world. They do not need to reincarnate because they gain earth experience through contact with mortals.

Advanced spirits -say such as Abraham Lincoln -do not need to come to earth for further experience. They do their duty in the spirit world, often helping earthbound spirits and giving lectures on the spirit side of life.

If a medium in earth life should happen to be properly tuned in, as a radio, such a lecture may be received and delivered.

In such instances the medium often thinks the advanced spirit is his guide. But a spirit like Lincoln is a guide to no one; he does not need to return to control a medium in order to progress. If mediums are in tune they may receive and repeat lectures given in the spirit world, but they are only receiving instruments and are speaking inspirationally.

The first time I controlled Mrs. Wickland I thought I had come to life again. I acted as a girl of the street, with no knowledge of anything. I was very jolly and boisterous and the people in the circle told me if I did not behave myself I could not come again. So I tried to behave and do my very best.

I wanted to learn so that after a while I could be a teacher, helper and adviser. I went to school on the spirit side of life to learn the lessons of earth, and these lessons I gave many times to persons in earth life.

When Mrs. Wickland first developed her mediumship she also studied Theosophy, Christian Science and Psychology. She questioned whether, during her trance condition, a spirit was actually speaking, or whether it was her own subconscious mind.

Wishing to learn the facts she took up the study of Astrology and had Dr. Wickland ask me what my birth date, birth place, general appearance, last sickness and date of death were.

Then Mrs. Wickland cast my horoscope, which indicated that a person born on the date given would have light curly hair, blue eyes, and a happy, sunny disposition -which I had.

She also found that five years after birth this person had Saturn, Uranus and Mars in Taurus, the sign that rules the throat, which indicated death at that time from throat disease. I had died from diphtheria.

This proved to Mrs. Wickland that it was not her subconscious mind speaking, for she was much older than I, and she also learned that what I had said previously was true.

Everyone in earth life is guided by a spirit. But sometimes an earthbound spirit steps in and takes control and then there is obsession or possession.

Mortals live in the slum of earthbound spirits. Few realize what is on the other side. How many try to learn where they will go after they pass out?

The majority, after leaving the body, remain for some time just where they have been during earth life. It makes no difference whether they are intelligent or ignorant -if they have no knowledge of the other side they stay just where they have passed out.

Many are in a heavy sleep, or in a coma state following the use of narcotics, and will remain so for some time unless some relative or friend in the spirit world finds them and wakens them, or someone from either side sends a messenger by thought waves to rouse them.

Some have hypnotized themselves into a coma condition by a religious belief that they will stay in the grave until the Last Day, or by thinking that death is the end.

There are many with various religious beliefs who do not know they are dead; they go about preaching and singing because they have not found Jesus, and they gather around the churches on earth and continue to sing and pray.

There may be persons in the churches who are sensitives, or of nervous temperament; some of the spirits take control of them and pray and sing until those persons are called insane and sent to asylums.

Other spirits exert a bad influence on humanity. They may want revenge and they hypnotize or obsess sensitive persons and influence them to commit murder or suicide.

Often a murderer knows nothing about the crime of which he is accused, for the deed was done by a revengeful spirit.

What right have the wise men of earth -such as the judges and lawyers -to condemn that person and take his life?

The person who is executed goes out of earth life filled with hatred and comes back for revenge, impressing others to kill or commit suicide.

The judges and lawyers should ascertain whether the accused person is actually guilty or influenced by some revengeful spirit who has acted through him.

Jesus said: "He that is without sin among you, let him first cast a stone."

Instead of condemning criminals, the judges, the lawyers and the ministers should teach them -teach them higher truths and bring out their better nature.

If those in prison knew that when they are released people would help them and give them a chance they would be greatly encouraged to do better.

Many call themselves Christians but will not help those in need, as Christ would have done.

When an employer learns that a man has been in prison he will not have anything to do with him. The man cannot get work. Where can he go? Nowhere but back to crime.

When we go to the lowest sphere to help we try to reach the better nature of men and women. We give them object lessons and when their love and sympathy are won they become true friends, no matter how low they have been.

When those who have lived only for self and for enjoyment reach the spirit side of life they have to serve others.

Serving is progression in the spirit world.

Because of their simplicity of life and religion and their knowledge of the laws of Nature, the American Indians are seldom bound in spirit after leaving the earth plane, and are often sent, as was Silver Star, Mrs. Wickland's Indian guide, to guard sensitive mortals.

EXPERIENCE, MARCH 12, 1924

Spirit: SILVER STAR Psychic: MRS. WICKLAND

Mediums so often have Indians as controls, guides and helpers because Indians have no beliefs or dogmas to overcome when they pass to the spirit world. From early infancy they are taught regarding The Great Spirit and The Happy Hunting Ground.

They believe in The Great Spirit of all Things, and the Medicine Man has taught them how to control Nature.

We Indians are sent to earth to guard mortals because we know the law of protection, and so we are often the doorkeepers to protect mediums from earthbound spirits.

The pale-faces die from all kinds of diseases but the Indians do not. There is little sickness among the Indians; they live in Nature and they die a natural death. So when they come back to control they bring an influence of strength and health.

Indian spirits seldom obsess people; they do not make people crazy because they know the laws governing the control of a mortal.

I am a Chippewa Indian and was born near Shell Lake, in 1883, on an Indian Reservation, in Northern Wisconsin.

I was four and a half years old when I was hurt on the head by a fall and passed to the spirit side of life, and when Mrs. Wickland cast a horoscope for me she found that death resulting from an injury was shown.

I came to Mrs. Wickland in 1893 at Eau Claire, Wisconsin. I am the Doorkeeper. When I first controlled Mrs. Wickland I could only talk the Chippewa language and what

English I know I have learned while being in control of Mrs. Wickland. Different persons in the circles have taught me English.

Some people think Indians do not know anything because they have not had much schooling, but they have true love for The Great Spirit and a true love for helping others.

Of course there are evil Indians as well as good Indians, but the bad ones are only those who have no understanding of The Great Spirit, and most of their bad habits are acquired from the pale-faces.

Before the pale-faces came to America there was no fear among the Indians. The Indians of different tribes fought with each other but were fearless.

Then the pale-faces came and hunted them down like animals. Fear and anger crept into the hearts of the Indians and then came trouble and war.

Many pale-faces wanted Indian land and some stole the land from the Indians, and then the Indians got angry and fought. They thought all the pale-faces were the same and then came trouble.

If the pale-faces had treated the Indians kindly in the beginning they would never have had wars with them. Treat an Indian with kindness and he will do much for you.

The Medicine Men are those who study Nature's forces and have power over them, and the Indians are often able to make rain.

When they pray they use the higher forces of life. They do not do what the pale-faces often do -pray with the mouth and only talk. They say little, but dance around in a big circle and concentrate.

Sometimes they have a Snake Dance. They have learned to charm snakes so they will not bite, because the Indians have no fear.

If the pale-faces would overcome fear they could do wonderful things.

In olden times the pale-faces had no fear, but they were scared by the stories of hell and the devil and this fear grew so that the people lost control of Nature's finer forces.

There are no religions in the spirit world; all are brothers and sisters in Truth.

All are alike in the Higher Life after they have an understanding of The Great Spirit.

Another one of Mrs. Wickland's guiding spirits is Movilia, an Eskimo, who brings strength and power to the circle. He lived in Greenland and was a traveling lecturer, doctor and entertainer, a Medicine Man of high order with a profound knowledge of Nature.

He journeyed among his people as an organizer and a philosopher, accompanied by his wife, a poetess and singer, and his children, who danced symbolical dances.

Some of the Eskimo songs, when given through Mrs. Wickland by Movilia and his wife, have been recognized by an Alaskan traveler as being a part of certain Eskimo ceremonies. These Eskimos do not speak English but one evening Movilia brought another Eskimo who acted as interpreter for him and told us something of the Eskimo religion.

EXPERIENCE, MAY 12, 1921

Spirit: ESOVILIA CHEVILIA speaking for MOVILIA AND WIFE Psychic: MRS. WICKLAND.

My name is Esovilia Chevilia, Eskimo, and the ones for whom I talk are Movilia and his wife.

We believe in the Great Spirit of Love, Wisdom and Knowledge, and that we are a part of that Great Spirit, and that when we pray from our hearts we shall receive what we ask for.

The Medicine Man is the one who knows the Secret of the Universe, the Secret of Love, the Secret of Knowledge and the Secret of Wisdom and Truth.

It is in that Spirit we live, and each tries to do the best he knows how.

Sometimes there comes a missionary who thinks we are not Christians and that we do not live right, and does not think we love God, as they call The Great Spirit.

THIRTY YEARS AMONG THE DEAD

We love the Great Spirit of Love, the Great Spirit of Truth, The Great Spirit, and we worship Him. We do not believe, we know. We know the truth and we know that we are a part of that Divine Spirit that is within us, and when we are in contact with that Great Spirit of Truth we have much in our hearts. We can understand His meaning of Life, His meaning of Love for His children here on earth.

Some of the missionaries who come to us say that Christ died for our sins. Dear friends, we do not have sins for Christ to die for, for God is Love and Power; He is Wisdom, Knowledge and Truth. We are a part of that wonderful Being. When we are a part of that wonderful spirit how could we be full of sin?

We could not fall away from Him because we are a part of Him; we live in Him and are a part of Him. We could not get away from Him because He is everywhere. He is the whole Universe, the whole Love, the whole Life of everything.

How can anyone think we could believe in such a doctrine that He, the Great Spirit that knows everything, is everywhere, and knows the past, present and future, could, in all His power and greatness, let us go down and down and fall in sin? How could He?

The missionary says we must be born in His image, and must believe in Him, that He died for our sins, and if we believe that we will go to Heaven when we die.

We pray to the wonderful Spirit that you call God. You have dogmas and dogmas, and creeds and beliefs. We put ourselves in rapport with that Great Spirit and we believe in His power. We try to get the power from the Great Spirit for healing and for other purposes. We have Hope in that power; we have Wisdom in that power.

The Christians believe and believe that they fall in sin and that somebody must raise them up.

If you step outside of the Law you know what will happen. If you put your hand in the fire you know you have broken the Law and must suffer.

If you have the belief that you have fallen in sin you have transgressed the Law and you will suffer.

We must find the Great Spirit within, not look outside. Find ourselves and we will find Him, for we are a part of that wonderful Mind, that wonderful Power. Let us all try to get in rapport with Him in His wonderful, wonderful glory.

When you are in rapport with the Great Spirit you will feel happy. You have then learned your lesson and will go on your way and not overstep the Law. You will get out of your ignorance.

You travel on the pathway of Life; if you walk out of the pathway you may remain as long as you wish, but you must finally get back on the road again. What made you go from the pathway? You overstepped the law of Nature.

You finally get so weary of breaking the laws of Nature that you will ask, "What am I here for, and where am I going?"

Then you will find you are a Truth-Seeker; you will knock and the door will be opened. You will look within, instead of, as before, without.

You have been living in the material with all its dogmas, here one, here another. And then there is so much condemning. You are all Christians, and yet you condemn and fight, and fight each other, and you have so much turmoil.

This condition will continue until you ask yourself: "What is it all about?" Then you will try to find out. When you seek for things from your heart, you will find. Ask God to reveal Himself to you. Ask God to manifest Himself in your heart before you leave the broad road of Experience for the narrow road of Reason.

When you get on the narrow road you will feel happy and contented, and you come into the Glory of the Infinite. There all is beautiful. There is no selfishness. The narrow road is only for Love, Kindness, Knowledge and Wisdom of God.

The Christians look for God outside; we look for God within ourselves. Within ourselves we look for the Great Spirit. We do not have so many creeds and dogmas, and so many religious speculations. We do not have to speculate for we know.

One gets the truth one way, one another, and so they go, all divided, nothing definite. People must change, for they have had enough of dogmas. Let them get more of the Wisdom of God, on the narrow road of Reason, and find themselves. When they have found themselves, they will have no sorrow and no unhappiness, because they will be happy with the Love of God.

When they love God they will love others, for they cannot keep it to themselves. You want your friends to love God with you. You want them to see the glory of God.

We never saw such a thing as you Christians call The Devil; we call it Selfishness and Ignorance.

Find yourself now. If you do not you will have to stop here, there and everywhere. When you have that beautiful knowledge all is happiness. You must experience this feeling within yourself before you can teach it to others.

This is the Religion of the Eskimos.

I was a Medicine Man on earth, and I was also a teacher.

Eskimo Movilia was the one that came to me and wanted me to say to you what he wishes to say. I have only repeated what he told me to say.

We have no wars. We try to live as near Nature and the Great Spirit as we can. We are not a pretty people, and we do not have so much changing as you do in dress. We have our beauty within us. Prettiness is only skin deep, so we do not care.

The Christian has to be awakened through suffering and trouble. Then you begin to look for what is called the truth. You think that Jesus died for your sins. He could not, and He did not.

The sins that are committed now are many more than when He was on earth. Many things have been discovered that were not known then, so how could he die for something that was not known? I think that is very strange.

God made us and He knew. When you find God within yourself you cannot do wrong. You sing and are happy, and happiness is something we all want.

We had one man come to us and preach. He took away with him one of the best men we had and tried to bring him up with your Christians. He returned to us a ruined man, full of diseases. We do not have such diseases, because we live up to the highest laws of Nature. He came back and told us how you, who call yourselves Christians, live.

THIRTY YEARS AMONG THE DEAD

We all felt so horrified to know that the Christians were so diseased in mind and body.

That is what the Christians did for our fellow Eskimo.

So I felt that I wanted to come and tell you of our religion.

Let all in this little circle find themselves and God, because you and God are one.

Here is a big light, say a candle, which stands in the center. Around it are smaller candles, but they are all a part of the same material as the larger candle. You take the smaller candles and light them from the big one, then you have the spark of Life. Can you then understand what is meant by being a spark of God?

When you die, as the Christians call it, you only blow out the candle. The tallow has gone back to the elements.

Find God within you, then you have Power, Strength and Love, and are learning to get Wisdom. Then you have learned to get strength and conquer material, to conquer sorrow and sickness. You cannot be sick for you have the light of understanding, and the more understanding you have the more strength you have.

All of you here are a part of that Universal Light, and you must all have that light from the candle. Do not worship the candle, but worship the Light of Understanding and God. Do not let anyone come in your way and make you think you cannot reach God.

The Christians do not truly understand God. They must have somebody to talk for them - their "Savior," as they call him. They worship Christ.

"Christ" is Truth, and when you find Truth, that is "Christ." Worship God. When you understand how to worship God you will have strength and power, and success will be yours.

We say: "Find God within your heart and all else will come to YOU."

We do not believe, we know.

Have the true knowledge of God in your heart and you will be happy.

Good Night.

From the time Mrs. Wickland first developed as a psychic she has been especially under the protection of the spirit, Dr. Root, who has fostered this obsession work and urged us to bring it before the public.

He has come often to speak with encouragement and to lecture to invisible, as well as visible, audiences on the higher philosophy of life.

EXPERIENCE, DECEMBER 24, 1919

Spirit: DR. ROOT Psychic: MRS. WICKLAND

As we are gathered together in this little hall I wish you could open your psychic eyes to see the many spirits who have come here for an understanding of the life hereafter.

There has never been real happiness on earth and there will not be so long as people are kept in ignorance of the truth of religion. In all times there have been many different kinds of religion, and always there has been selfishness.

You now live in the Twentieth Century, and since this is an enlightened age why should not people be more intelligent and know more about the world here and the world beyond?

People worship the Golden Calf more than they worship God. The churches are falling to pieces, because they cannot make people believe as they used to in olden times. People now want knowledge, not belief, and if the churches would teach true religion people would be better.

Many ministers know in their hearts that people do not believe the old stories. It is the Golden Calf again -they worship money and they stand in the pulpit and talk against their better nature.

Some day this world will conquer selfishness, but I am sorry to say that at present most of the people are insane regarding money making. They seem not to be able to get money enough. There is little honor, only money, money.

There is little sympathy; all want only what they can get from others through moneymaking schemes. In time this money scheme will fall to pieces.

We should study the other side of life as well as this, when we are on earth. If you want to become a minister, doctor, lawyer or lecturer you have to study to acquire knowledge. Why should we not study ourselves?

It is very important that all on earth should know where they are going after passing out of the physical, for they will then go to the right place and will not stay in the homes they have left.

Without this knowledge many do not realize they are dead and they remain in their earthly homes. Some one of the family may be sensitive and may become obsessed. Then the doctors will declare that person insane and send him to the asylum, for there is no pity for one who is controlled by earthbound spirits.

People should be taught the truth, then, when they pass out, they will look for the spirit world and a happy place beyond instead of a fictitious "Heaven."

Heaven or hell is only a condition within yourself and "Heaven" must be found within before you can be happy in the spirit world.

Some say : "What is the spirit world?"

The spirit world is a counterpart of this with only one exception -here you are thrown together with every sort of person, while there you cannot go anywhere unless you have understanding of where you are going.

The spirit side of life is like a school -you progress by degrees. There is no belief. You learn where you belong and where you are going. It takes time to understand, but there is plenty of time in eternity to study and learn.

The time is not far distant when people will open their eyes and see, and the churches will have circles and try to understand life.

This is Dr. Root. I wish you all happiness and success in your work. Good Night.

THIRTY YEARS AMONG THE DEAD

EXPERIENCE, MARCH 23, 1921

Spirit: DR. ROOT Psychic: MRS. WICKLAND

I am glad I can be with you tonight to tell you of the beautiful conditions we have on the spirit side.

The greater number think that when death comes they will go to a certain place and stay there until the last of this earth.

The "Last Day" is every day that you throw away selfishness and ignorance. That is "Death."

Life is Love and Wisdom. Let us die daily to our ignorance and selfishness. Let us awaken to the truth and an understanding of God who has given us that truth, and who has sent forth His messengers to tell us what life is on the other side. It is a life which is more spiritual, more congenial and more beautiful in every respect than the one on earth.

When you have Truth in your heart you are happy. When you have selfishness and ignorance in your heart you are sorrowful. Sorrow will follow you until you say: "Not my will, but Thine."

When others come in your way and try to keep you down, rise and say: "No, I will be firm, and I will conquer," and then you can create happiness and contentment in your soul, and you will have happiness around you.

When you think only of selfishness and creeds you have sadness and sorrow, and you will have to burn these out by suffering, and say: "Not my will any longer, but Thy will."

Let us pray to God, because He is All in All. He is with you all. We could not live one minute without that wonderful power. Do not let us pray to anyone else, because God is within ourselves. You do not need to go anywhere except your own heart to pray to Him.

Have communion with God in your heart and you do not need to take communion outside. When you have learned the truth then communion is within you. You do not need to be reminded to take communion with God because you know He is there to help you.

You have opened your heart to God and He has heard you and you can then commune with Him. Communion is not understood as it should be.

You take communion. It is only a reminder that you should be united with God. When you have learned and have progressed higher and higher you do not need a physical reminder, because you understand. When you have communion with God you do not need bread and wine.

You cannot go anywhere without God. God is in the air; He is everywhere. You cannot walk on the earth without stepping on His creation, and you should try to understand His work.

There has been so much theorizing. One has one theory, someone else another. One goes into this corner, another into that corner, and one says this is the proper way, and the other says that is the proper way; one has one creed, and one has another.

They go around in a little circle and forget they are in the midst of life, of God Himself.

When you do a kind act to another you do it unto God, because he is one part of God and you another. We only serve God when we serve others. Live to serve and do all you can for others, then you will progress in understanding.

To go to church to serve God is only to remind you of what you should actually do. Act, and do good to those who are in trouble. Why should you go to any place to worship? "Enter into thy closet and pray to thy Father which is in secret."

Pray earnestly and your prayers will be heard. Do not pray idly, but pray earnestly. Live so that people will know you have done your duty in life.

On the spirit side we find it is difficult to open the spiritual eyes of many. They are all so blinded by creeds and dogmas that we have to do all within our power to help them understand that God did not make dogmas and creeds, but that God made the Universe, and the people in it should worship Him alone, without any creed or dogma.

When we understand and realize love -not what people call love here, but the love which springs out everywhere -then love is like the sun.

When there is love in your heart you are like a sun to others. You have found God in your heart and this shines forth just as the sun shines on all.

Those who have only creed, dogma and selfishness, and are ignorant, feel gloomy; they have a fear of God, a fear of everything around them. They have not opened their souls' eyes to ask for the light, for understanding of God.

These come to the spirit side of life in darkness and gather together, one group here, another there, all in deep gloom. They pray and sing and moan from morning until night, year after year.

It is very difficult to make them understand that they have passed to the spirit side of life; very hard for them to wake up and see the mistake they made in accepting dogmas and creeds. They have clothed themselves with gloom and have shut out the light that should have been shining throughout their lives.

If you love God in the sense I have spoken of, then you will be happy.

This is Dr. Root.

Good Night.

Another extract is taken from a lecture recently given by Dr. Root to a gathering of earth-bound spirits, as well as to our circle.

EXPERIENCE, JANUARY 1, 1924

Spirit: DR. ROOT Psychic: MRS. WICKLAND

Let us concentrate for happiness and contentment, for the betterment of the world. Let us never look backward, but forward. Let us all try to do the best we can and help others.

If little groups such as this one would concentrate in an effort to cheer the world the world would be better. This little light of concentration does not seem much but it will do much good for the ones in darkness and those in trouble.

If all the churches would have concentration circles to help the people and would give them cheer and courage, and try to help them into a brighter condition, instead of condemning them and telling them they are lost forever if they do not believe a certain doctrine, the world would be much happier and better.

THIRTY YEARS AMONG THE DEAD

You must find yourselves within before you can find yourselves without. You must be born again -not in Jesus Christ, no, -you must realize your own self and that you are a part of God.

God gave you light and understanding. Go out and help the people in trouble and those who have not awakened to an understanding of God. Do not merely believe in God but find Him within yourselves, then you will not need belief.

Belief and faith are only the key. If you have the key in your hand and do not know where it belongs, do not know which door it opens, if you have only faith and belief, and nothing more, you only hold the key but do not use it.

Seek for knowledge until you can open the door of Wisdom and Understanding.

Most people have the key but they only hold it in their hands and do not use it. They say: "If I believe in God and Jesus Christ I will be saved."

When the time comes for them to pass to the spirit side of life they merely hold that key, they have only belief and they find themselves in darkness because they have not used the key of understanding that God gave them with which to investigate and find God within themselves.

You do not need to go anywhere; you must open the door of your own heart. Find God and find that you are a part of that wonderful power. When you open the door you have power and strength and health -you have everything and the strength of God's power will flow in and you will do wonderful things.

Christ was a great teacher, but do people carry out His teachings? They believe, but they do not do what he told them.

Each one is a part of God, and when you do what you can for others you love God and worship Him by so doing.

The people and the churches should unite as one power and help each other and try to conquer selfishness.

Spread the truth; find God within yourself and open your heart to Him through understanding. You have power so far as your mind has developed. If you try to develop for more power you will have it. Widen out and try to know God's wonderful mystery in the world.

Let us find God in Nature, everywhere. Look at a snowflake -it is wonderful. It has many beautiful designs. Who made it? It is so natural that people do not realize its beauty. They say: "It is just snow."

When individuals step out of the physical the worst hindrance they have is desire, which must be overcome. Creeds and dogmas hold them down; they are not free. They are, as Jesus said, bond servants, and will be held down.

They think, when they pass to the spirit side of life they will go to Heaven. Stop to think - where is Heaven? Christ said the kingdom of Heaven is within you if God dwells there.

The majority believe that what you call death is a long sleep, and many who have not learned the lesson of life go to sleep. Some will sleep for years because they are self-hypnotized. They think: "I am dying, and I will go to the grave and stay there until the Last Day, and then will be awakened."

Others pass to the spirit side of life believing in certain creeds and dogmas. They go to certain places in the earth sphere where they sing and pray and do not progress any further. They go over and over the same things. It is only mouth prayers they offer. Sometimes they remain in that sphere for years.

Sometimes they go about in the earth sphere and try to convert people. They attach themselves to some mortal and that mortal will be called insane on religion.

What is done then? The victims are sent to the insane asylum and left there for the rest of their lives. They will not be free from the obsessing spirits until the body dies. Then those spirits often attach themselves to other mortals.

Let us understand the truth. Let us do what we can to help ourselves and others to an understanding of God. Worship Him everywhere.

Let us look at the sky and see the beautiful planets and stars. If this earth disappeared tomorrow the suns and stars in the heavens would be just the same. This earth would not be missed. Do you think God sits on this earth and controls nothing more? No, let us think, and understand and study.

Let us all worship God in His whole Universe. There is Life everywhere. The grandeur of the heavens cannot be described -the wonderful stars in the heavens, the planets and all the Universe.

Look through the microscope and you will find you are in another world. You will see germs, one or two of which will kill a big body. They are all under one power -God. Some say, Why did God make all these germs to torment humanity? They must be, in order to have you realize and think and overcome. When you have trouble and try to overcome you become strong.

A child that is protected constantly by its parents and sent into the country grows up in a fine atmosphere. He is good because he has had no temptation. But he has no knowledge that he is good.

A boy from the slums, who has had trouble, will more readily develop into a man who can conquer than the one who has been protected. He will be strong and able to help others.

Let us find ourselves. Let us all concentrate and try to help and give light to every one we find needing help.

Worship God in His true sense and not in a little narrow belief. Let us add knowledge to our faith.

You are the bond servants that Christ speaks of. He was a wonderful teacher, but you believe in His blood and not in his teachings.

Who killed Christ? The very ones that belonged to the church. They did not believe in Him.

Christ is an allegory; He is the Truth. "Christ" is born within you when you have attained understanding. Then you will see, and know, and realize God. When you pass to the spirit side of life you will have knowledge and you will go into a world that is far more beautiful than this. You can then reach the spirit world.

You do not need to call it "spirit world" -some object to that name. Every one is a spiritual being. You may call it the "Higher Sphere"; you may call it "Heaven" -but Heaven is not a place.

THIRTY YEARS AMONG THE DEAD

If you think you are going to Heaven you will have to take it with you, because it is a condition. When you have suffering you are in hell, and many have a hard struggle to get out of that hell. When you are happy you are in Heaven -the Heaven within yourself.

You have trouble and sickness, but everything is to help you learn to find yourself. When you have found yourself, within yourself, you can conquer all conditions from without.

You say: "I am very sick." You attract those forces unto you, and after a while your own mind has created your condition. You are a part of God, the wonderful Creator. What you think, you create. You have power and you can use it for good or evil.

If you have trouble, disease, or suffering, and have not learned to throw it off, you hold it to yourself. Then you become sensitive, and after a time you draw influences around you, and these in turn throw disease and bad thoughts on you, and you are bound.

First, find God within yourself, then you will have power to rise.

Trouble, sorrow, sickness, obsession, everything can be conquered after you find the truth; Christ is born in you and you can conquer.

When you have found Christ within yourself you will still have struggles. Others will say: "Do this, or this, and you will be wise." Some will say: "Overcome the world overcome."

There will be a cross, because there is a tempter. You have found yourself, but the tempter speaks to you: "Do this! Come with me and I will show you the world and happiness."

Here is the cross which shows Christ is born within you. Jesus, the Son of Man, must be crucified on the cross of matter that Christ-enlightenment may live.

When you have reached that stage you see everything as good. You cannot see bad. When you look back you see that what you thought bad only taught you to understand God. Should you condemn it? No. If you had not had that experience you would not be where you are now.

You must teach others and help them to rise with you. If every one would do that the world would be happier.

Let us send out thoughts that all may conquer and that they may understand. You should strive to gain knowledge of God's finer forces. Find yourself and you will find God.

Before I go I want to say that we have a room full of earthbound spirits. I often talk to them to help them. This group we have here tonight are spirits we could not waken because they could not see us. A spirit in ignorance cannot see an intelligent spirit.

So we have to bring them here. I talk through this body and they hear me, but they could not hear me from the spirit side of life because they had no understanding.

Every time you have circles here we have more spirits present than we have mortals. When they see an earthbound spirit control they learn their first lesson, and then we can take them to the spirit side of life and help them find happiness.

We are never idle in the spirit world. Mind cannot stand still. God's wonderful thoughts go on. Planets do not stand still. All is development. Mind is never inactive so long as one tries to develop.

This is Dr. Root. Good Night.

THIRTY YEARS AMONG THE DEAD

For many years, upon various occasions, a symbolical morality play has been given through Mrs. Wickland by a group of spirit actors.

They are twelve in number, eleven actors and a director, all of whom were Russian-Slavonic when in earth life.

Under the direction of the stage manager they successively assume control of Mrs. Wickland with such ease and rapidity that the change is scarcely noticeable.

The play is given in the Russian-Slavonic tongue, a language which Mrs. Wickland herself has never heard, but which is spoken perfectly through her by these actors, as has been stated by different persons, witnessing the play, who are familiar with the language.

The costumes worn by the spirit actors, and unseen by the average mortal audience, have been described by clairvoyants as being authentically Russian-Slavonic and very beautiful.

These actors, with one of Mrs. Wickland's guides as interpreter, have given the following account of "The Morality Play" and its purpose.

"We are twelve actors controlling this psychic sensitive in order to prove spirit return and spirit control, and that we can act as we acted while in the body.

"We come to help people understand that we are still living, that we are not dead but are just as active as we were when in earth life.

"We give this play in the spirit world for the earthbound spirits, many of whom do not realize they are dead to their earth life. We find them in the sphere next to the earth, often in a semi-sleep.

"Preceding the play we have music by excellent musicians; this wakens the earthbound spirits, one after the other. They rise slowly, not realizing where they are, but the music brings them a little understanding of the higher life.

"We then play our drama as a lesson to these spirits. Each character is symbolical, showing that selfish, trivial and debasing attributes must be overcome before spirits can progress."

The leading lady represents Love; the leading man, her lover, personifies Truth. The ruffian typifies Selfishness; the elderly maiden lady depicts Frivolity; the officer represents Justice, and the Judge, Wisdom. The witnesses in the court trial portray Knowledge, Drunkenness, Misery, Sickness, Miserliness and Robbery.

Love, the young maiden, cherishes a true, deep affection for the hero; she dwells in the same abode with Frivolity, who entertains an unrequited love-sentiment for Selfishness. (Here is shown the close association in life of the True and False.)

Truth enters and proposes to Love, who accepts him; he then departs and is followed by Selfishness, who desires Love for himself.

When his advances are rejected, Frivolity, with her most fascinating coquetries, endeavors to charm the Ruffian (Selfishness) from Love to herself. This angers him and he threatens her with death, then leaves in a rage, swearing to kill his rival, Truth.

Love writes a frantic note of warning to her lover and hastily sends her servant to deliver the message, but the servant arrives too late, for Selfishness has attacked Truth by the wayside and fatally wounded him in a sword duel.

Truth dies a lingering death, representing the murder of man's higher nature by selfishness.

The servant hurries back to his mistress with the news of the death of her lover. She rushes to the place of the attack and, finding Truth dead, falls on her knees beside him. With a prayer she draws her dagger and stabbing herself, dies.

When Selfishness sees that Love, as well as Truth, is dead he becomes infuriated, declares there is no God and swears that he will have fullest revenge.

An officer, Justice, arrives, and handcuffing the murderer, takes him into custody, after which follows the funeral of the lovers.

Justice brings selfishness before the Judge, Wisdom, and at the trial the witnesses, Knowledge, Drunkenness, Misery, Sickness, Miserliness and Robbery all testify that had it not been for Selfishness, Love and Truth had not died.

Wisdom then banishes Selfishness from the land.

During a psychic circle held at our Institute, in May, 1923, at which Sir Arthur Conan Doyle and Lady Doyle were present, this play was given, and later, in his book "Our Second American Adventure," Sir Arthur briefly described the play, commenting further:

"It was certainly a most extraordinary performance and left us all in a state of amazed admiration . . .

"I have seen all the greatest actresses of my generation, Modjeska, Bernhardt, Duse, Terry - but I do not think that any one of them could have played these eleven parts without a stage or a costume in so convincing a way.

"The spirits' own account is that they are a band of players on the other side, who represent this play before the undeveloped dead in order to teach them the moral, and that they use the wonderful mediumship of Mrs. Wickland in order to demonstrate their power to us mortals. It was very impressive."

Recently these invisible performers have presented through Mrs. Wickland another drama, "The Soul's Passion Play," symbolical of the development of the soul.

In "The Morality Play," Selfishness kills Truth, and causes the death of Love, while in "The Soul's Passion Play," Truth and Love conquer Selfishness.

"The Soul's Passion Play" represents the contest of the Soul with opposing principles and symbolizes the victory of Truth and Love over Selfishness through Understanding, and the attainment of Bliss.

Dwelling in the Home of Happiness, with Obedience as the servant, are Kindness and Friendship, father and mother of the maiden, Love.

Truth, a young man, admires Love, while Selfishness, another maiden who is found in the same society with Love, but whose father and mother are Hatred and Envy, living in the Home of Unhappiness, boldly attempts to attract the young man to herself.

Truth finally wins Love and they are united in marriage, after having sent Selfishness away from the Home of Happiness.

THIRTY YEARS AMONG THE DEAD

Selfishness, overcome by jealousy and humiliation, goes to seek some means of revenge in the slums, where, in the Home of Misery, lives the villain Revenge with his father and mother, Temptation and Evil.

Together, as time goes on, they plot that Selfishness shall return to the Home of Happiness and, pretending repentance, wait for an opportunity to steal the child Victory, which has been born to Love and Truth.

The child is to be given to Evil, who will bring him up in squalor and sordidness, forcing him to commit crimes and finally become imprisoned.

Selfishness will then go to Love and Truth, tell them of the disgrace of Victory, and, with Revenge, gloat over the ruin of the Home of Happiness.

Selfishness succeeds in stealing Victory, who, for some years, is cruelly mistreated by Evil and Temptation, but is at last discovered by his parents and taken away from the Home of Misery.

Enraged at her defeat, Selfishness becomes insane through anger and dies a violent death.

Truth and Love bring Victory back into the Home of Happiness, and there, with Selfishness vanquished, they dwell together in Bliss.

THIRTY YEARS AMONG THE DEAD

CHAPTER XVII

Conclusion

Demonstrative evidence clearly indicates that much which now seems mysterious can be brought to light by appropriate research. "The supernatural is only the natural not yet understood." Psychical research should he placed on a scientific basis, and made safe and sane by eliminating the dwellers on the threshold of the unseen, who, through deception and falsehood, frequently pervert the truth which the enlightened spirit intelligences are constantly endeavoring to convey to humanity.

Advanced intelligences on the invisible side continually urge that broad minded investigators on the physical plane cooperate with them in establishing research centers in asylums, churches, universities and other institutions.

It is imperative that psychical research should be in the hands of men of science, men who are willing to set aside prejudice and, with unbiased minds, weigh the evidence and classify findings.

In the Chicago Daily Tribune, March 30, 1905, the late Dr. I. K. Funk, of New York, urged that inquiry be made into cases of mental phenomena, and, after reviewing the work which we were carrying on in obsession, concluded with an appeal to the press for further investigation.

"Let us remember," he said, "a single scientifically demonstrated fact of the existence of even an evil discarnate spirit will do more to prove the continuance of life after death than all the sermons on immortality that have been preached in the last ten years.

That single demonstration would be the death knell of materialism. . . .

"Genuine cases, wherever occurring, should be searched for by the press more than if they were lumps of gold and should be verified if possible to the minutest incident, and given, not jocosely, but seriously, to the world.

"Why will not the press soberly take up this matter? Rightly handled, there is sensation in it worthy of the most royal purple journalism.

"Gladstone was right when in his membership letter to the Society for Psychical Research he said that this work of investigation 'is the most important work which is being done in the world by far the most important.'"

Scientific bodies, willing to thoroughly master and observe the governing laws, could readily obtain evidence similar to that presented in this volume. Especially could such evidence be obtained in Institutions for the Insane, as most inmates of the same are potential psychics who could be developed into instruments for psychical research.

After having dislodged the ignorant, obsessing spirits, the psychic faculties of the sensitive could be developed by attracting intelligent spirits, who are always willing to co operate from the invisible side, and who will protect the instrument against untoward results.

Psychic research circles, formed to learn the truth of life and spirit existence should be of inestimable value to churches, for such investigation would prove positively the continued existence of the soul, and convert mere faith and belief in a life hereafter into definite knowledge.

The practice of calling for specific or particular spirits should not be indulged in, as this may lead to deception by mischievous spirits, who may step in and attempt to impersonate the spirit called for.

It should be left to the guiding intelligences to bring whatever spirit is suitable for demonstration, and interesting information will be given from time to time by the advanced spirits, clearly showing the difference between intelligent and ignorant entities.

As a nucleus for more comprehensive investigation the National Psychological Institute was organized and incorporated in Los Angeles, California, for the purpose of placing those problems on a rational, scientific basis. This Institute a "Spiritual Clearing House" has no interest in cult or ism of any kind, but is striving only to obtain data, in the hope of encouraging other institutions to take up similar work, as an enormous field for research has been opened by our experiences.

It is not presumed or held that this avenue of research is a panacea for, or a full explanation of, all mental aberrations or obscure mortal vagaries, but indicative of the need for fuller knowledge of the role which the invisible world plays in human problems.

THIRTY YEARS AMONG THE DEAD

THIRTY YEARS AMONG THE DEAD

www.ingramcontent.com/pod-product-compliance
Lightning Source LLC
Chambersburg PA
CBHW081913170426
43200CB00014B/2719